Eden
in
Egypt

New revised edition

Eden in Egypt

A translation of the Book of Genesis out of the
original Egyptian text.

Adam and Eve were Pharaoh Akhenaton
and Queen Nefertiti.

by
Ralph Ellis

Edfu Books

Adventures Unlimited

Eden in Egypt

First published in 2004 by Edfu Books

Published in the U.K. by:
Edfu Books
PO Box 165
Cheshire
CW8 4WF
info@edfu-books.com
U.K.

Published in the U.S.A. by:
Adventures Unlimited
PO Box 74
Kempton, Illinois
60946
auphq@frontier.net
U.S.A.

First Edition October 2004
revised
Second Edition September 2008

U.K. paperback edition
ISBN 978-0-9531913-9-0

U.S.A. paperback edition
ISBN 978-931882-95-8

Printed in the USA by McNaughton & Gunn.

Religion is regarded by the common people as true,
by the wise as false, and by rulers as useful.

Seneca the Younger

Before the seas and this terrestrial ball,
And heaven's high canopy that covers all,
One was the face of nature, if a face;
Rather, a rude and undigested mass;
A lifeless lump, unfashion'd and unframed,
Of jarring seeds, and justly Chaos named.

Ovid

Acknowledgments

To Copytech of Peterborough, whose inept attempts at printing the book *Solomon* delayed its publication by four months, and whose writ threatened to close Edfu Books down forever. However, no cloud is without a silver lining, and the (reversed) out-of-court settlement from this particular dark and threatening cumulus provided the capital for the publication of this book.

Ralph Ellis
November 2004
Cheshire.

www.edfu-books.com

Contents

River of Eden

It may seem obvious to most readers that the early sections in the Book of Genesis are wholly unreliable as a historical record and therefore must have been based upon some very ancient myths. But even if that were so, where did those myths come from? Were they really based upon the legends that emanated from the banks of the Euphrates in Sumer, or were they instead based upon the myths surrounding the culture that I had already shown to have been the foundation for much of biblical history – Egypt? Having already demonstrated, in the book Solomon, Pharaoh of Egypt, that King Solomon was in reality a pharaoh of Egypt, it seemed highly likely that the Genesis story may actually contain elements of Egyptian mythology.

It was to be the river that flowed through the legendary lands of Eden that began this revision of early biblical history. This river and its branches had long been associated with the rivers Euphrates and Tigris in modern Iraq, and so it has long been assumed that Eden once resided in this region. But these river names, which are used in the English translations of the Bible, are not substantiated in any way by the original Hebrew text. So where was Eden in reality? Well, according to the texts, we are looking for a great river that flows through Eden and then divides off into four branches; and there is only one river in the region that conforms with this description...

Language

This book represents the fourth in my series of revolutionary and revisionary biblical studies, and yet this latest work attempts to tackle the very first chapters of the Bible: those that relate the story of Adam and Eve. In some senses, this subject matter may appear to make this book the ideal introduction to the true history of the Bible, and yet in other respects this may not be the best route to take, as this is perhaps the most in-depth analysis of the Bible that I have so far attempted.

The ideal starting point is still, in my opinion, the book Jesus, Last of the Pharaohs, which gives a good overview of the strong links that exist between biblical and Egyptian history. The books then proceed through Tempest & Exodus, which suggests that Mt Sinai is the Great Pyramid, and on to Solomon, Pharaoh of Egypt, which explains the true historical identity of King Solomon. The latter of these works was relatively easy to research and write because this book dealt with a later era that was better documented both in the historical and biblical records. However, as I found out with some of the material in the book Jesus, the further back into biblical history one probes, the less clear and accurate the story becomes, and it did seem to me that the mysteries of the Garden of Eden may never be solved. Indeed, the Adam and Eve story was so fragmented and the names and family relationships were so confused, it did initially appear that this early material was largely mythical.

However, I then discovered that another key to solving this Eden riddle lay in the language in which it was written, and this is the reason why this particular book took so long to research and write. The original language of the Old Testament (the Torah or Tanakh*) is Hebrew, but the problem with Hebrew is that it was a dead language for many centuries – it may have been a written language for a few Judaic scholars, but it was not a living, spoken language by any community or people. Hebrew has only been revived as a living language in the recent past, with the formation of Israel, but it was revived solely from the language of the Tanakh and Talmud, and this means that the wider knowledge of the language outside the biblical-type texts has largely been lost. While the Septuagint version of the Old Testament was written in Greek, and this gives us some confidence when translating the Hebrew Masoretic version, both of these copies were still written after the Israelite exile in Babylon, which is when I believe that most of the subtle changes were made to the text. It was in Babylon that nearly all the traces of Egypt were erased from the text, and it was in Babylon that any suggestion of a pagan or polytheistic past for the Israelites was masterfully covered up.

There is no doubt in my mind that the Old Testament we read today has been selectively edited and amended, but it is still a fact that these texts were regarded as sacred and inviolable throughout their history. The suspicion is, therefore, that any changes that have been made to the Book of Genesis were relatively subtle rather than wholesale revisions.

---

* The Torah represents the first five books of the entire Tanakh or Old Testament.

Given the fact that we are dealing with a resurrected language and a text that may have been selectively edited, the uncovering of the true story of Adam and Eve might be considered an impossible task. However, it is entirely possible that the Hebrew language was based upon a much earlier language – Egyptian. If this were so, then by making a comparison with equivalent Egyptian words, some glimmers of the original import of the text may still shine through. It is through this painstaking methodology that it may be possible to rewind some of the later revisions that have been made to the Book of Genesis and to rediscover the original import of the Adam and Eve story.

However, no amount of study and resurrection of original texts would help in this research if the story of Adam and Eve were truly mythological or set at the very beginning of Egyptian (Israelite) history, as the Bible suggests. The historical record that exists for the era encompassing the emergence of dynastic Egypt is fragmentary in the extreme and so if early Israelite history were based in Egypt, as the bulk of the remainder of biblical history appears to be, then it is doubtful that any comparisons and conclusions could be made. Luckily, the evidence I began to uncover appeared to show that the Adam and Eve story did not detail the emergence of the Egyptian nation and culture at all; rather, it related the story of the emergence within Egypt of a cult of monotheism – which later metamorphosed into modern-day Judaism, Christianity and Islam. As it happens, the beginnings of monotheism in Egypt are relatively well documented, and so it may be possible to fully decipher and explain the entire legend of Adam and Eve.

Notes to the reader

a.   Because of the radical nature of this book, it has been necessary to highlight the difference between standard orthodox assumptions and those generated by my lateral view of theology. Throughout this book, therefore, I have used curved brackets ( ) to denote orthodox assumptions and square brackets [ ] to denote my radical new assumptions. I hope that this serves to clarify the text.

c.   As readers of the book Jesus, Last of the Pharaohs will have noticed, the history of the biblical exodus is not quite as it seems. Not only were the circumstances and nations involved not quite as advertised in the Bible, but, in fact, there were two exoduses from Egypt. Because there is no longer one definitive Exodus to refer to, the term 'exodus' has been left in lower case.

d.   The references in the text are numerous. To ease the problem of continuously referring to the reference section at the back of the book, some references have been prefixed. Prefixes are as follows:

B = Bible, K = Koran, J = Josephus, T = Talmud, S = Strabo
M = Manetho, N = Nag Hammadi, KN = Kebra Nagast.

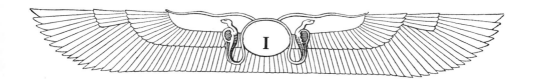

Genesis

בראשית ברא אלהים את ה שמה ואת הארץ
Bereshith bara Elohim eth hash shameh veeth haarets
εν αρχη εποιησεν ο θεος τον ουρανον και την γην
In the beginning, god created the heavens and the Earth.

This has to be one of the most famous quotations of all time, and yet at the same time it is perhaps one of the most misleading and least understood sentences. For it is not simply the standard translation from the Hebrew or Greek that I want to take issue with here, but the very language it was originally written in. It will be my contention throughout this book that our perception of the famous Genesis story of Adam and Eve, from the early verses of the Torah, is based upon a Hebrew translation of a far older text; and so when searching for the fundamental, original meaning of this sentence and this story, we need to look much deeper than the earliest Septuagint or Masoretic copies of the Torah. We need to go back to the Quelle, the theoretical source manuscript for the biblical texts; and while many scholars have attempted to discover such a text, I believe I have stumbled across a method of doing just that.

As I have demonstrated in all my previous works, the true source of the Israelite people and their religion was Egypt; the Israelite people were originally Egyptian and so too was their religion – although the latter was greatly influenced by the monotheistic reforms of the biblical Abraham and Moses, who I have already identified with contemporary Egyptian characters. But if the Israelite religion and many of the associated Israelite customs were based upon Egyptian antecedents, then what of their language? In my previous works I have also laid the foundations for the evidence that shows a considerable similarity between many Hebrew words and their

Egyptian cousins, but this book will take that concept several steps further and demonstrate that, to all intents and purposes, the Hebrew language is a child of the Egyptian language – the one was most definitely derived directly from the other. See Appendix 4 for an extensive dictionary of Hebrew terms and their Egyptian equivalents.

So it should be pointed out from the very start of this exercise that the vast majority of the Hebrew words from the Torah's account of the Old Testament are actually taken directly from Egyptian equivalents and thus they translate directly, and surprisingly precisely, into the Hebrew. This does mean, however, that if the text of the Book of Genesis can be analysed and understood from this original Egyptian perspective, we may still see and read the underlying Egyptian message.

While I have continually stressed the Egyptian content of the Bible in previous works, I was still rather surprised to find that the Old Testament was itself originally written in the ancient Egyptian language. However, while this was a surprise, there was an even greater shock to come, as the context in which the original Egyptian words reside can substantially alter the meanings that have been placed upon the various Hebrew and English translations. So if we are to revive the original and true meaning for the Book of Genesis, we need to investigate the biblical verses in their original language and thus fully understand the context in which they were originally written.

That is essentially the task of the first few chapters of this book: to transliterate the Hebrew words back into the original Egyptian, and then to translate the original context of those Egyptian words directly into the English. One might predict that the result of this arduous manipulation would be exactly the same translation as before; however, the original context can often deliver a radical new insight. For example, a story about a boat journey from west to east in the Hebrew might suggest someone catching a water-taxi across the Nile, but in the original Egyptian it could well refer instead to the journey of Ra's solar boats through the Djuat; Ra's perilous journey through the night hours in the spiritual Underworld. This is perhaps the origin for some of the mythology surrounding the arduous journeys of the Medieval pilgrims, who similarly left the west and travelled to the east in search of the light; a myth that has also become a central feature of masonic lore.

A new day

What enlightenment can this new translation deduce for us? Well, the word used for 'beginning', in the verses from Genesis that have just been quoted, is a good example of this process. This word has been derived from the Hebrew word *rosh (reshiyth)* ראש meaning 'beginning'. But it is highly likely that this has, in its turn, been derived from the Egyptian word *ros* which can also imply a beginning. But the Egyptian word more specifically refers to an astronomer-priest staying awake to view the sunrise, an event which signified the rising of the Sun-god Ra (the Aton); and this function was therefore a prime component in the Egyptian priesthood's daily ritual. So the Hebrew translation is correct, in that this word did signify a beginning, but the context of the Egyptian word is so much more explicit than the generalised Hebrew concept of the word. It is possible, therefore, that the initial verse in Genesis more precisely referred to the beginning of a new day and the rituals that were associated with that event.

If this translation is true, then it is entirely possible that the word *ros* may have originally referred to the dawn or the sunrise. But this small alteration to one insignificant little word represents a major theological stumbling block, as this new interpretation may have a devastatingly profound effect on the entire Book of Genesis. As everybody knows, the Adam and Eve story at the beginning of the Bible (the Torah or Tanakh) was supposed to represent the creation of the entire Solar System (or Universe) by our omnipresent all-powerful local deity; but now the opening verse to Genesis only appears to be speaking about the start of a new day. This is perhaps confirmed by the accounts of the first century historian Josephus, who repeats this Genesis epic in his own words and then notes that:

> ...this was indeed the first day: but Moses said it was one day...[J1]

Remember that the accounts of Josephus are probably more authoritative in this debate than the Bible itself, for Josephus had managed to get his hands on texts that were much older than those used to create our present Tanakh or Old Testament. Josephus was the Jewish quisling who had worked for the Romans during the siege of Jerusalem in AD 70, and his reward for his efforts in defeating his countrymen was several tracts of land in Judaea, an apartment in Rome, a state salary, and the pick of all the Hebrew texts in the now ruined Temple of Jerusalem. Of course, the Romans had plundered all the gold artifacts, coinage and jewellery, but who in the Roman army would be interested in a few battered scrolls in a foreign language? Thus Josephus had the pick of every text available:

> Titus Caesar, when the city (of Jerusalem) was taken by force, persuaded me to take whatever I pleased out of the ruins of my country ... I also had the holy books by his concession.[J2]

William Whiston, the venerable translator of Josephus' works, says of the historian's sources:

> Josephus, when he wrote his Antiquities, seems (to have had the use of) the most authentic copy (of the Torah) in the whole nation; I mean that which had been lain up in the Temple itself: which very book seems to have been given to Josephus ... after the destruction of the Temple.

> That Josephus had a better copy of the historical books, written after the Babylonish captivity ... than either of the present Masoretic copy or even the Septuagint version contains, appears by the particular character of those books.[13]

The alternative version of Genesis according to Josephus, and the new version that is emerging from this new Egyptian translation, are both pointing towards the Book of Genesis discussing a single day in the life of a very ancient solar ritual, presided over and administered by a very ancient solar cult. But, having noticed this simple 'slip' of a translator's pen, a slip that was dutifully confirmed by Josephus, the unimaginable powers of the almighty god are already beginning to fade. In reality, the epic biblical story about the creation of the vastness of the cosmos was perhaps nothing more than an allegorical tale about the mechanics of the diurnal cycle of the Sun.

Remember that Josephus said it was Moses who insisted that this was a single day, not an entire creation, and yet in the book *Jesus* I have already demonstrated that Moses was TuthMoses, the brother of the pharaoh Akhenaton. Since Akhenaton introduced into Egypt a monotheistic solar cult that worshipped the diurnal cycle of the Sun, I think readers can begin to see the direction in which this investigation is turning.

From the Egyptian perspective, this new interpretation of an ancient ritual might appear to be very reasonable. The daily, yearly and millennial movements of the Sun and stars were the prime focus of the Egyptians' religious beliefs, and so the monitoring of the Sun as it broke the new day across the horizon would indeed have been a momentous, if predictable, event. The Egyptian priesthood were more astronomers than theologians, and such events, no matter how humdrum, were central to their philosophy and beliefs. Since the biblical patriarchs were nearly all based in Egypt, as has been explained in great detail in my previous works, they would have been infused with this solar worship – indeed, they probably led the rituals themselves. It was only in the later Judaic phase of this people's history that the solar rituals became an embarrassment and were suitably modified to disguise the true origins of these rituals.

In this case, it is entirely possible that the opening verses in Genesis may have been describing a new day, and this is probably why the historian Josephus placed such a different emphasis on the text. The Torah indicates that god named the aspects of day and night; Josephus agrees with this but then goes on to say that god also named the evening and the morning. This is important, because not only does this reinforce the diurnal aspects of the story, but the evening and morning were the primary ritual periods in the Egyptian priesthood's calendar. Whatever the astronomical observation, the Egyptians invariably made it at dawn or dusk, with reference to the rising and setting Sun. The inference seems to be clear: the first chapters from the Book of Genesis may well have been discussing the daily rituals of the Egyptian priesthood, and so they need further investigation in greater detail than ever before in order to prove or dispel this hypothesis.

One word

Another aspect of this investigation may now become obvious. It has already taken five pages of text in order to investigate the true meaning of just one word in the first verse of Genesis. As may be appreciated, a thorough investigation of Genesis may result in a series of volumes the length of the Encyclopedia Britannica, and so some editing may be necessary.

The first two verses from Genesis are presented again below. Those words marked with the 'number' symbol appear to be derived from Egyptian sources, and so these words have been changed back into their Egyptian equivalents and alternatives. The original Egyptian translation appears in the second block of text, and this version frequently places a slightly different slant on the Genesis story. Since these Egyptian translations represent the original version of Genesis, taken from a period before the Hebrew language had even been invented, these verses probably represent an interpretation that is much closer to the original import of the text. This ancient interpretation of the Old Testament is, as shall be demonstrated, substantially more Egyptian in both content and style and gives a fascinating insight into the true origins of the Torah (Old Testament).

Biblical version:
1:1 In the beginning# god# created# the heaven# and the Earth#.
1:2 And the Earth# was without form#, and void#; and darkness# was upon the face# of the deep#. And the Spirit# of God# moved# upon the face# of the waters#.

Egyptian version:
1:1 At the sunrise the Elohims* illuminated the eastern lands (horizon).
1:2 And the land was an empty wilderness and the last of the night's darkness was upon the face (nose) of the watery abyss of Nu. And the rays of Ra bathed the upturned boat in the waters.

In verse 1:2, the translation of the words for 'Earth' and 'without form' were based upon the Hebrew words *erets* ארץ and *tohuw* תהו; and these were in their turn derived from the ancient Egyptian words *arit* 𓂝𓏤𓈇 meaning 'land', and *ta huhu* 𓏏𓄿 𓎛𓅱𓅱𓈖 meaning 'land of chaos'. In a similar fashion, the words for 'darkness' and 'deep' (or 'abyss') were based upon the Hebrew words *khowshak* חשׁך and *tehom* תהם; and these were in their turn derived from the ancient Egyptian words *khau sek* 𓆎𓎡𓊃 𓈖𓂝 meaning 'darkness ends', and *tehomu* 𓏏𓎛𓐝𓈖 meaning 'watery abyss'.

Notice the precise way in which the Hebrew and Egyptian terms mimic each other: *erets - arit,* which both mean 'land'; *tohuw - ta huhu* which both mean 'chaos'; *khowshak - khau sek* which both mean 'darkness' or the 'end of darkness'; and *tehom - tehomu* , which both mean 'watery abyss'. Each of these word-pairs have the same pronunciation and the same meaning in their two respective languages, and thus the later Hebrew words are likely to have been originally based upon their much older Egyptian equivalents. See the Hebrew-Egyptian dictionary in the Appendix for more details. This epigraphic evidence, plus the contextual environment of the story in which these words were placed, will clearly demonstrate that the biblical texts were based upon an original and much older Egyptian story and mythology.

If this is so, and there is a great deal of evidence to support this hypothesis, then by necessity we have to go back to the root language from which Hebrew was derived to ascertain the true translation of the Torah and Tanakh. Up until now, the root language that has been used for this process has been Arabic; a language which is sometimes considered to be a root language for Hebrew and sometimes a daughter language. At the very least, Arabic is still a living language and has been so for more than one and a half millennia, and so it preserves its original pronunciation, meanings and derivations. The problem with Hebrew, as we have seen, is that it was a dead language for many centuries: it may have been a written language for a few Judaic scholars, but it was not a living, spoken language by any community or people.

Hebrew has only been revived as a living language in the recent past, with the formation of Israel, but it was revived from the language that is contained in the Tanakh and Talmud, and this means that the wider knowledge of the language outside these biblical-type texts has largely been

---

* As a gentle reminder that the term being used for god (Elohim) is actually a plural, I have Anglicised it with the 's' plural. As to whether the name for god should really be read as a plural, the venerable theologian Adam Clarke lists 31 instances of not only the name being in the plural, but the conjoined adjectives and pronouns being plural too. This original plurality, together with the oddity of the later Christian Trinity, shows that the original Israelite ritual did, in some fashion, cater for more than one god.

lost. Because of these deficiencies, Hebrew linguists and theologians must often look towards related languages to assist them in deciphering the true meanings of certain Hebrew words that are not in the Bible, or are not clearly understood in their biblical context, and one of those related languages is Arabic. As Adam Clarke says:

> The deficient roots in the Hebrew Bible are to be sought for in the Arabic language. The reason for this must be obvious, when it is considered that the whole of the Hebrew language is lost except what is in the Bible ... If a man meets with an English word which he cannot find in a concordance to the Bible, he must of course seek that word in a general English dictionary. In like manner, if a particular form of a Hebrew word occurs that cannot be traced to a root in the Hebrew Bible, it is expedient ... and often indispensably necessary, to seek the deficient root in the Arabic.[5]

The reason for Hebrew being related to Arabic has been covered in the book *Solomon*. Although this is not the classical argument for the creation of Arabic, I believe that Arabic is a daughter language of Hebrew, rather than a parent. The reason why Hebrew linguists are sometimes confused as to which of these languages is the older, is that the daughter language (Arabic) survived while the parent (Hebrew) went into cardiac arrest for many centuries.

In short, I believe that the invasion of Judaea [or Egypt] by Nebuchadnezzar in about 590 BC displaced a great multitude of the Israelite population, and a large number of them made their escape firstly into Egypt, where they founded a city at Tel Yehudiyeh in the Delta region; the name of this city still meaning City of the Jews. But after the invasion of Egypt by Cambyses II in about 525 BC, these people migrated once again and this time they sought a safe haven well outside this troublesome region, so they went to Saba in modern Yemen. Having created a great civilisation in that region for over a thousand years, which was known as the Kingdom of Saba and named after the famous Queen of Sheba, who they worshipped as their patron deity, the nation finally went into decline. Their final nemesis was the Persian invasion of the region in AD 570; the fourth bursting of the Marib Dam in about AD 600, which supplied the water for their lucrative cash-crops; and the subsequent conversion of the area to Islam in AD 628.[6] Note that the demise of Saba in AD 600 and the rise of Islam in about AD 610 are significantly coincident.

The most important question in this potted history is from where did Islam receive its greatly abbreviated and yet highly independent and alternative version of the Judaic Torah, from which the Koran was eventually formed? It is unlikely to have been derived from the large Judaic population that lived in Persia at this time, as the details and sources in the Koran are highly original and quite separate from the current Tanakh or Old Testament. Bearing this in mind, it is highly likely that Islam obtained its new Torah-type text from a sect of Judaism that had long been exiled and remote from mainstream Judaism. The ex-Judaic Sabean priests in old Saba not only fit that bill perfectly, but the dates tie in rather well too. Any refugees from the disintegrating kingdom of Saba in AD 600 are likely to have migrated to Persia, and the accompanying priesthood on this exodus would have taken their precious Judaic texts (and their language) with them.

Regarding the language of Saba, Alessandro de Maigret, an archaeologist who has worked in Saba for many years, has said:

> The language used in (Saba) is South Arabian, a Semitic language linked to Arabic and Ethiopian ... Although this language was mostly replaced by Arabic with the advent of Islam. [7]

The inference here is that Arabic influenced the language of Saba. But since the origins of the Arabic language are unknown, this same history does not preclude the possibility that the South Arabian Semitic language of Saba percolated up into Arabia around the turn of the first century and created the Arabic language as we know it. The resulting hybrid language then swept back down through Arabia on a tide of invasion and Islamic conversion, and so the Sabean mother tongue was replaced by its own daughter language. But the religion of Islam could easily have taken the same route and chronology; being taken to Persia on a Sabean exodus around AD 600, growing and multiplying into a state religion, and then returning in its modified form back into South Arabia in AD 628.

Thus, both the Islamic religion and the Arabic language could have been derived from Sabean sources, which themselves originally sprang from ancient Judaic roots that had fled from the burning hulk of Nebuchadnezzar's ransacked city of Jerusalem. That Islam is a Jewish sect is fairly obvious, but the possibility also exists that Arabic culture and language are also Jewish; all of which makes the current Jewish-Arab dispute over Israel a domestic family spat similar in nature to some of the family feuds to be found in the Torah.

Sunrise

Having diverted off the main track for a while, it is time to get back to the first verse in the Book of Genesis. In this new translation of Genesis, the Hebrew word for 'beginning' *rosh (reshiyth)* ראשׁ becomes *ros* , which means 'sunrise'. This suggests, however, that the biblical texts were originally

I Genesis

narrating the Egyptian story of the diurnal circuit of the Sun, rather than an absolute creation of the Universe. If this is so, then according to the original Egyptian version of this story the Sun-god Ra would have been towed across the sky and through the underworld upon the two solar boats of *Mandjet* [hieroglyphs] and *Mesektet* [hieroglyphs], which represented the sacred barques (boats) of the sunrise and sunset respectively.

If the above suggestion is correct, then it is possible that the Hebrew word for 'created', *bara* ברא, was derived from the Egyptian word *barga* [hieroglyphs] meaning 'illuminate'. Since, in Egyptian terms, the rays of the Sun were bringers of life, then in Egyptian terms the concepts of illumination and creation become greatly blurred and virtually merge into a single entity. This is especially true of the theology of the Amarna regime of the revolutionary pharaoh Akhenaton, where one of the central tenets was the praising of the Sun and the sunlight as the bringer of life.

With the Bible having apparently started out on an Egyptian solar journey, the text continues with this theme by using the Hebrew term for 'heaven', which is *shameh (Shamesh)* שמה. This term could well have been derived from the word *shemesh* שמש meaning 'Sun', and this would confirm that Genesis is relating a story about the sunrise rather than the creation of the Solar System. In turn, the word *shemesh* may have been adopted from the Egyptian term for 'summer', *shemm* [hieroglyphs].

Having said all that, this may not be quite the case. In fact, the word *shameh* שמה has most probably been badly copied from an older Hebrew text, and the original was once spelt as *samel* שמאל, which literally means the 'left-hand side', and also has solar connotations. I can assure the reader that this is so because there is an Egyptian copy of this verse on an Egyptian text, as will be shown later. This original Egyptian text, which will be discussed shortly, used the word *semer* [hieroglyphs], which also means 'left-hand side'.

Remember that the Egyptians did not have the 'l' consonant, so the Egyptian 'r' is often translated as a Hebrew 'l', and thus the Egyptian word *semer* would have been translated into the Hebrew as *semel*. So it would appear that these two words are absolutely identical in both pronunciation and meaning. Another good example of this transliteration process between the 'l' and the 'r' is the Egyptian word *qarr* [hieroglyphs], which became the Hebrew word *qall* קלל, with both words meaning 'light' or 'delicate'. In the Hebrew-Egyptian dictionary in the Appendix, a large number of these transpositions will be found.

One reason why the word *semer* fits so well into this biblical verse from Genesis, apart from the Egyptian quote as we shall see later, is that in the Egyptian, the 'left' was also considered to be the east. If the text was speaking about the dawn, then it is to the east that the observer must turn, and that is exactly what is happening here – the Hebrew word for 'heaven' and 'Sun' was based upon the Egyptian for 'east' (the dawn or sunrise).

Now that the initial verses in Genesis can be positively seen to be referring to the sunrise, the celebration of the return of Ra (or Aton), the next clue to the true meaning of verse 1:2 is the translation of the word 'face'. The Hebrew word for this is *paneh* פנה, which can obviously refer on occasions to the 'face' or 'surface' of something. This word can also be pronounced as *phaneh (faneh)* נה and so I would surmise that this was derived from the Egyptian *fenedj* 〜⌂ meaning nose. This translation is quite valid because when the Torah mentions a person's face, it uses *aph* אף, which actually refers to their nose, and so this nose-face allusion is quite valid in both languages.

This derivation would actually explain both occurrences of the word in the Bible, both 'face' and 'surface'; but with it being used in quick succession in this manner (the 'face of the deep' and the 'face of the waters'), it is quite possible that the scribes were making another of their witty rhymes, and the second of these references may have been alluding to the alternative Hebrew meaning of *paneh* פנה meaning 'turning' or 'turning back'. While this translation does not make much sense in the Hebrew, the reason why this alternative could assist us is that the Egyptian original for this word was probably *pana* 〜⌂ , which also means to 'turn' or 'turn over'. But this Egyptian alternative can also, quite graphically, refer to the capsizing of a boat, as can be seen in the glyphs. Now while this explanation might initially sound confusing, with god 'turning back the waters', the original Egyptian context of this verse has to be taken into account.

The biblical verse says that the land was a wilderness and darkness pervaded over the waters. This description concurs with the Egyptian concept of the creation of the world, where the primeval waters of Nu represented the chaotic wilderness of the void, into which the primeval mound of Atum surfaced and represented the first island of sense and order. But the chaos of Nu never really went away from our rational world of sense and order, and the Egyptians always feared its return. Since the primeval mound of Atum that broke through into the chaos of Nu also represented the Benben stone of Heliopolis, and since this was in turn infused with the solar connotations of Ra, it is not so surprising that the Egyptians saw the night-time as a return of the dreaded Nu, the return of the chaos of the primeval waters. Remember that there were precious few lights in those days, as lamps and their oil were an expensive commodity, and so for the common man a moonless night would have resulted in an absolutely pitch-black veil descending over the land. Absolutely nothing constructive could be done without lights or lamps, and the family would simply have to huddle in their home and fearfully await the coming dawn.

Because of this all-pervasive fear of the dark of the night, the Egyptian priesthood saw the return of Ra in the morning sunrise as representing a small-scale rerun of the Egyptian creation epic; a diurnal triumph of the soothing, warming, illuminating rays of Ra over the cold, dark and fearful chaos that was the night. Thus, in the tenth hour of darkness, according to the *Shat am Djuat* – the *Book of what is in the Underworld,* or in more popular parlance, the *Book of the Dead* – a Khepre beetle holds an egg towards the eastern horizon, from which Ra will emerge. The egg is, of course, representative of the original primeval mound upon which Atum-Ra once stood above the chaos of the watery abyss of Nu, and Ra's emergence at the sunrise will banish the fears of the night just as surely as Atum-Ra banished the primeval chaos.

So what does all this have to do with a capsized boat? Well, Ra sailed through the night hours on the barque of *Mesektet* and since the night hours were below the horizon, the solar boat of the night must have been sailing 'upside down' or at the very least it was below the visible waterline of the sea, in other words the solar boat was 'capsized' during the night hours. Again, the imagery of the first dawn light illuminating *Mesektet,* the solar boat of the night, and the rhyme with the previous line is quite compelling.

The confirmation that this was the intended rhyme devised by these long-departed scribes is a further pun that connects the *fentch* and the *pena* words. The *pena* refers to a 'boat', and by inference this was a sacred 'solar boat'; whereas the *fenech* (also *fenedj*) refers to a 'nose', which can be taken to mean a 'face' or, by extrapolation, a 'surface'. The name or phrase that links these two concepts together, and demonstrates exactly what the biblical scribes had in mind when they wrote this tract, is Fenedj-Pet-Per-em-Utu , which was the name of the ground or surface over which the magical Egyptian solar boats sailed. Note that this term uses the word *fenedj,* meaning 'nose', to denote the surface.

The translation of this surface is interesting, as it was the 'Surface of the Sky (over which) travels the Ferryman'. But this was no ordinary ferryman, he was a god who sailed the solar boat across the night skies; and since the Sun was considered to be dead during this time, the name also has deep connotations of death and mummification. This ferryman was the chap that you were advised not to pay – at least not until he gets you to the other side... So it would seem that my secondary translation of this text was correct, and the concept of the upturned boat did refer to *Mesektet,* the solar boat that sailed the night skies.

But then, as the day proceeds, the Sun starts to appear over the horizon and fill the world with its light. The traditional interpretation of the verse from Genesis calls this the 'Spirit of god', but the 'spirit' is actually called *ruwach* רוּח, which was most probably derived from the Egyptian Ruar-ti which refers to the gods Shu and Tefnut, as we shall see. The term 'Spirit of god' is rather confusing, as in modern terms it often gives expectations of a ghostly apparition. In some senses this is true, because both the Hebrew and Greek interpretations can describe this spirit in terms of 'wind' or 'air'. It was for this reason that I have chosen the Egyptian term Ruar-ti 🔲🔲🔲 meaning Shu and Tefnut, because these were the gods of the air and moisture respectively.

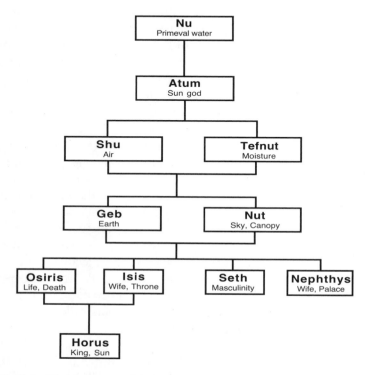

Fig 1.1   The theogony of Heliopolis.

However, the Hebrew term *ruwach* more accurately refers to the 'breath of god' rather than just 'air', but rather than muddying the waters this may actually give us a better understanding of what *ruwach* was supposed to mean. Shu was the son of Atum-Ra, the solitary primeval god Atum who was allied to Ra in some respects. But Shu was the god of air, and since he was the son of the most important god in Egypt, he would undoubtedly have been known as the 'air of god' or the 'breath of god'. But Egyptian theology was ever a practical discipline and so in physical terms that could be perceived by the man in the street, the 'breath' of Ra would have been described in terms of its life-giving rays. In a country like Egypt, where the Sun is quite intense, you can not only feel the radiation on your skin, you can also sense exactly where those rays are coming from, and so this does indeed feel like an emanation or wind coming to you direct from the Sun-god. This is the essence of Shu caressing your skin, the very 'breath of god'.

The verb that describes the action of these rays (or breath) confirms that this suggestion is valid. The English translators have chosen *rachaf* רחף to mean 'hover' or 'flutter', which suits the image of a traditional ghost more than the accurate translation of a 'breath' or 'wind'. A more likely explanation is that this word was originally intended to be *rachat* רחץ, meaning 'wash' or 'bathe', and that this was in turn derived from the Egyptian *rakhet* meaning 'wash'. The imagery of the rays of the dawn Sun bathing the solar boat of Ra with their illumination is surprisingly compelling. The final word in this verse is *mayim* מים meaning 'water' and this was derived from the Egyptian *ma-yim* which simply means 'water water'. Since, in the Egyptian language, a duplication often referred to an exaggeration of a subject, this probably meant that the *ma-yim* was a very large expanse of water – which indeed it was.

The new image that these explanations are beginning to provide means that the fundamental basis of the Genesis story has been radically altered; moreover, it has also been placed back into its original Egyptian context. From this new Egyptian perspective, we can now see the first rays of the sunrise peeping over the horizon, with Ra being pulled across the primeval waters of the abyss in his sacred barque. The Egyptians would have had to have travelled during the summer months to the city that would eventually become known as Alexandria, in order to see Ra rise over the waters of the abyss, but I am sure that some of the elite in the priesthood did just that in order to demonstrate that their theological model was correct.

But this was not the first dawn of the Universe or the creation of the Solar System, as the Judaeo-Christian orthodoxy likes to suggest, it was simply the dawn of a new day. Accordingly, the next thing that we might expect to happen in the Genesis story is the flooding of the world with Ra's life-giving light.

Light

1:3 And god# said, Let# there be light#: and there was light#.
1:4 And god# saw# the light#, that it was good#: and god# divided the light# from the darkness#.

1:3 And Ra-Horus (Elohims) commanded 'the light (of Ra) arises': and so there was light.
1:4 And Ra-Horus (Elohims) saw the sunrise, that it was the first, (the finest): and the Eyes of Horus were divided into light and darkness.

The Hebrew word for 'speak' (or 'said'), *amar* אמר, can also mean 'command'; and my choosing of this translation perhaps gives the scene a little more drama. But the next word, 'let', is more interesting. The translators have chosen *hayah* היה meaning 'let', while elsewhere in Genesis they have chosen 'I am', as in the famous phrase 'I am who I am'. In the circumstances, the translator's choice seems a little confusing as god is now said to be creating light, while the Sun itself is not created until verse 1:16. But this would actually make a lot more sense in the Egyptian context, because the sentence would now read 'And god said, I am the light'. Since the god in question was an aspect of Ra, the sentence is quite logical.

However, there is yet another possible Hebrew translation. Since the original Egyptian text was quite plainly speaking about the sunrise, I would suggest that the true translation of this word, in the Hebrew, is actually *hayah* היה, meaning 'arise'. This is confirmed by the Egyptian original for this word, which was *hai* 𓇌𓏤𓏤, which equally means 'arise' and also means 'rejoice'. This translation would actually be describing the Sun rising over the horizon.

Once more, the original Egyptian translation and setting seems to confirm the true context in which this sentence should be based, and this was again in relation to the ritual celebrations that took place in the Egyptian temples during the all-important sunrise. The return of Ra on the eastern horizon was most certainly a cause for celebration, and the people rejoiced at their god's arrival. It was not so long ago that Christian worship followed this same tradition, with a celebration at dawn in their churches and cathedrals – which were deliberately orientated to face due east to catch the first rays of Ra rising over the horizon. While Christianity has lost its allure and rationale among the people of the West, so that even committed Christians rarely attend mass at six o'clock in the morning, the Muslims of the East still trudge to the mosque at sunrise to celebrate the return of Ra. Muslims might be horrified to discover the 'pagan' traditions that lay behind their religious devotions, but their slavish, servile devotion to their creed annuls any form of reason or rational inquiry. The reason for the continued educational and economic success of the secular and Christian West, in comparison to the Muslim states, is that the former have long been able to ask the simple question 'why?'

Continuing with the Hebrew-Egyptian translations, it is easy to see that the term *uwr* אור for 'light' was derived from the Egyptian *aur* 𓇋𓏤𓂋𓀭 for 'light', while the term *towb* טוב for 'good' was derived from the Egyptian *top* 𓏏𓊪 meaning 'top', 'first' or 'best'.

Elohim

Having begun the process of translating these verses back into the original Egyptian, let's look again at verses 1:3-4 again, for these appear to invoke two versions of god – the Elohim and Ra. Both of these verses appear to separate the Elohim (god) from Ra (the Sun), suggesting that the text is actually talking about two different entities or deities. So if there were two divine beings, then what was this elusive Elohim אלהים, who was strangely spoken of in the plural? Even in the Hebrew language this is a vexed question, as the origins of this word are highly uncertain. The eminent Hebrew theologian, Charles Parkhurst, has suggested the root word for Elohim was *alah* אלה, meaning to 'curse' or 'swear an oath'. But Adam Clarke prefers the Arabic Allah, which is the name of god in Islam, because in the Hebrew this Arabic name for god can be pronounced as either Alah or Elah אלה.

However, in the Torah, or Old Testament, more often than not it is the plural of Elah (or Allah) that is used and this is pronounced as Elahim (Elohim אלהים). This plurality has often been an embarrassment for what is supposed to be a monotheistic religion, but it is a curiosity that may eventually explain the true origins of this name; for I rather think that the root of the name Elah (Elohim) for god is slightly more esoteric and definitely more Egyptian than the authorities would like to admit.

The first thing to note is that the name Elah also has a short form, which is El. Since it has already been demonstrated that the Hebrew god-name Adhon is very similar to the Egyptian god-name Aton (Adon), it is entirely possible that El may likewise have been derived from an Egyptian original. Since Aton was the name for a solar deity, it is likewise possible that El may also refer to a solar deity, and so the task here is to search for a facet of the Egyptian Ra that sounds similar to El. The answer to this is that El may well have been originally derived from the word *Ar* , which refers to the Eye of Horus. Remember that the Egyptian 'r' is often translated into the Hebrew as an 'l', and so the Egyptian Ar or Er would have been translated into the Hebrew as an Al or El, from which the Hebrew and Arabic god-names Elah and Alah were eventually derived.

The right eye of Horus was, in fact, a representation of the Sun, and so this deity called El or Al becomes the equivalent of Ra; and of course it is worth noting that the name 'Ra' is a simple reversal in spelling from Ar or Al. This is why Muslim prayer times are regulated by the apparent motions of the Sun through the sky, because it is likely that Allah was originally a solar deity, and so Muslims are still unwittingly praying to Ra. Interesting as this may well be, it does not fully prove that the Egyptian Er or Ar was the origin of the Hebrew El and Al, and what we really need is a method by which this strange plurality for a solitary god can be explained.

In fact, this task can be rather neatly achieved because the other eye of Horus, his left eye, was known as the 'dark eye' and this represented the Moon. But in the Egyptian, the Moon was known as Ah (Iah or Yah) which, surprising as it may seem, appears to be the second syllable in Elah (Alah). In which case, the two eyes of Horus would have been called Ar or Er (Al or El) representing the Sun, and Ah (Yah) representing the Moon. Of course, when these two terms are combined a small miracle occurs and the resulting name for the two eyes of Horus is El-Ah or Al-Ah (Elah or Alah). So the Hebrew god Elah and the Arabic god Allah are nothing more than an Egyptian reference to the two eyes of Horus or, in other words, the Sun and the Moon combined. This is why the Christian patriarchs and apostles are always depicted with the image of the Sun behind their heads (the halo), and it is also the reason for the predominant image of Islam (the crescent Moon).

Not fully understanding the reasoning behind the god-name Elah or Allah, it would appear that each of these belief systems has picked out and highlighted a portion of this name's true meaning, and still uses it in the modern era as an icon of their deity. Indeed, it is not uncommon to find an image of a star inside the Islamic crescent Moon, and if this star is taken to be a solar icon then the symbology of the god-name Allah would be complete.

While this may seem like an amazing and almost unbelievable discovery, the final piece of evidence in favour of this radical proposal can be derived from the number of eyes that Horus possessed. Arab, Hebrew and Christian scholars have long insisted that there was only one god (Elah or Allah), and since Horus had lost his left eye in his battles with Seth, and since there is only one Sun, then this doctrine might still have been correct even in the Egyptian religion. But, unfortunately for later theologians, the lost or dark eye of Horus was still equated to the darker, silvery disc of the Moon – in fact, the loss and occasional regeneration of this darker, left eye of Horus may have even symbolised the waxing and waning of the Moon. The New Moon was Horus' lost and darkened eye and its periodic regeneration represented the Full Moon.

Although Egyptian theology can be frustratingly obscure at times, it is reasonably well established that Horus was still regarded as having two eyes – one bright and one dark – representing the Sun and the Moon respectively. Because of this, the various scribes through the passing eras have often spelt the word for these eyes in the plural – Aryahuti (Alyahuti) in the Egyptian, or Elahim (Elohim) אלהים in the Hebrew. It was for this reason that the singular god of the Hebrews was inexplicably spelt in the plural. Horus was a singular god, and in many aspects he was also directly linked and equated with the singular all-powerful Ra himself. But his two eyes (sometimes described as the eyes of Ra) represented two separate astronomical bodies and thus two separate deities, and so the singular Horus could also be referred to in the plural.

The all-embracing nature of this explanation – with the Egyptian names for the Sun and Moon (Al and Ah) combining and becoming Elah or Allah, and thus explaining the peculiar plurality of a single god – indicates that it is highly likely that this was the origin of the Hebrew god-name Elah and the Arabic god-name Allah. In which case, the prime god of the Koran and the early parts of the Book of Genesis was none other than Horus, who, as a solar deity, was often regarded as being Ra himself. Again, the Egyptian heritage of the Torah and Koran is being laid bare, and we can clearly see the beginnings of an Egyptian story emerging.

Chapters

Having fully explained the meaning of Elohim, it is also a fact that the Egyptian language invariably had multiple layers of meaning, and so their gods had an equivalent number of identities and roles. Because of this, I think that the god-name Elohim did not always simply refer to the Sun and Moon as such, or even to Horus himself, but instead to an aspect of these gods. It is entirely possible that the god-name El also referred to the chapters of a book, which were called *er (el)* in the Egyptian. But that is not the end of this story, if the pun is to be excused, because since there was more than one chapter to this particular book, the god-name El אל would again have become the plural Elohim אלהים.

Readers might, at this point, be excused a little puzzlement, for this may sound like a very peculiar translation for a god-name. However, it should be pointed out that the chapters (Elohim) being referred to here did not come from any old book, rather these were the sacred Egyptian texts of the *Per m Heru* or the *Shat am Djuat* – the books known as *Flowing by Day* and the *Book of the Underworld;* the latter perhaps being more properly pronounced as *Metcha-t am Djuat* and more popularly known as the *Book of the Dead*. These were sacred texts and what we may be witnessing here is not simply the commands and dictates of god himself, but the word of a sacred book that is being uttered in all solemnity by the high priests. Thus the same Egyptian word that refers to the chapters of these sacred books may also refer to the very mouths that utter them, and again the term would have to be used in the plural – Elohim. So *er (el)* can also mean 'mouth' and 'speech', the solemn utterances and unified chanting of the assembled high priests.

This second translation of the god-name El may seem a little speculative at this stage, but masonic tradition appears to confirm this suggestion. Just as the biblical Trinity and the standard three-lettered

Hebrew word format like to work in threes, masonic tradition also likes to highlight a trinity. In this manner, the three most essential accoutrements of any masonic temple, which must be present before a lodge can be opened, are the Square, the Compass and the Sacred Book (BSL). Each of these three elements represents a concept or an attribute, and so the Square is likened to the psyche, the Compass to the spirit, and this leaves us with the Sacred Book – which can be any of the major religious documents from the Torah, to the Bible, the Koran, the Vedas or the Zend-Avesta – and this is said to be representative of the divine being. So, in masonic tradition, the deity can be represented by a Sacred Book. Thus, even though Elah and Allah are most certainly references to Horus and his solar and lunar eyes, the deity can also be represented by a Sacred Book.

It is for this reason that the Sacred Book is often to be seen in masonic art in conjunction with the image of a circle and two parallel lines. The dot in the center of this circle represents god, while the surrounding circle represents mankind, and so it is said that each individual person is equidistant from god. This is one of the masonic principles that creates such tensions with the Catholic Church, because if we are all equidistant from god then there is no need for a Pope or a Vatican. The republican leanings of Masonry not only undermine monarchies, they similarly undermine the traditional, organised and wealthy Christian Church.

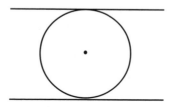

Fig 1.2 Representation of mankind and god.

Since the circle and dot represented the deity and its relationship with mankind, the remarkably similar form of the circular human eye and its associated pinpoint of a pupil was therefore chosen to represent Ra in Egyptian tradition and ritual. In this manner the two hieroglyphs that are used to represent Ra became the eye 👁 and the circle with a dot in the center ☉ . Thus the circle and dot symbolism can be associated with the Sun-god, and since this glyph could also be representative of an eyeball and pupil, the links that the Egyptians made between the Sun and the Eye of Horus are fully understandable.

This masonic link between the Sacred Book, the deity, and the circle of an eye tends to confirm the strong argument I have already made that the biblical Elah or Allah can be a reference to both a Sacred Book and the two Eyes of Horus (the Sun and the Moon). Thus, in masonic ritual, the Book of the Sacred Law and the hieroglyph for Ra (the circle and point) are always placed together on the floor of the ideal lodge, while the Sun and the Moon were prominently drawn above them. This layout is clearly demonstrated in the design of the First Degree tracing board shown in the colour section, where the circle and parallel lines can be seen alongside the BSL at the base of the ladder in the right-hand of the two images.

Logos

Although both of these masonic explanations are reasonably persuasive, they still do not fully explain the confusion that appears to have arisen between a folio of chapters in a book and a symbol for an all-powerful god. So just how did the biblical scribes, and their parallel masonic traditions, link the Sun and Moon gods (or Horus himself) with a book?

As one might expect, this apparent 'confusion' – for it may not have been by design but indeed through confusion – was due in part to the concept of these chapters being the literal 'word of god'. In other words, the written word in the sacred books was considered to be a direct manifestation of that god. The Gnostic writings in the much later New Testament Gospel of John make this fusion between 'god' and 'word' perfectly clear. John says:

> In the beginning was the Word, and the Word was with God, and the Word was God. And the Word was made flesh, and dwelt among us. [B8]

According to the Gospel of John, the Word was both 'with god' and also equivalent to god himself. The Word then came down to Earth and became 'flesh', which is an oblique reference to the birth of Jesus, who was also considered to be a godlet. Here we can clearly see the power and divinity of the written word. Words were considered to be a magical manifestation of the gods, which is why we still *'spell'* them to this day.

The precise term that was being used for 'word' in the Gospel of John was the Greek *logos* or *lego* λογος; but what exactly does this word mean? This is a rather fundamental question, because it is being used to describe the very essence of god; so if we could understand the term *'logos'* we might gain a further insight into who or what this Judaic god really was. But, not surprisingly, the Christian Bible and its many commentators like to leave this word untranslated – for the last thing that they want is for their followers to be able to understand who or what their god really is.

However, although the term *'logos'* is complex and multifaceted, it <u>can</u> be dissected and explained. At the first level of initiation, the term *'logos'* simply means 'word', and it can refer to the spoken word as much as the written. Thus the biblical reference just quoted may be better understood if the term 'Word' *(logos)* were replaced by 'incantation': the reciting of magical words.

However, while a modern magician may get away with a couple of magical words like *ab-ra-ca-dab-re* or *open sesame*** to perform their tricks, a Heliopolian priest might have to remember and recite whole chapters during their rituals. This link between the priesthood and the spoken ritual is one reason why the spoken or written word became so inseparable from the concept of god – the divine being could not act or be brought into the corporeal world without the assistance of the priesthood and their recitation of the magical formulas in the sacred books. The Koran also alludes to this interpretation when it says, in regard to a discussion between Moses and pharaoh:

> Pharaoh said; 'And who is your lord, Moses?'
> 'Our Lord,' he replied, 'is He that gave all the creatures their distinctive forms and then rightly guided them.'
> 'How was it then with the ancients?' asked Pharaoh.
> (Moses) answered: 'My Lord alone has knowledge of that, recorded in a book. He does not err, neither does He forget.' [K9]

Where the Koran says 'Lord' or 'He', it is referring to Allah, the singular Islamic god who we have now identified as being the eyes of Horus and thus a combination of the Sun and the Moon gods. But, knowing that 'He' referred to god, the first time I read this verse I did puzzle over why an all-powerful being would require a book to record things in – for nobody in their right mind would write such nonsense if they truly believed in an all-powerful being. But since the Islamic word for god, Allah, was derived from the Hebrew Elah or Elohim, and since it now seems that Elah may have also referred to a sacred book, the sentence actually makes more sense. If the 'He' in the verse referred to the sacred chapters of the 'Book', the sentence would read as:

> Pharaoh said; 'And who is your lord, Moses?'
> 'Horus,' he replied, 'is the Sun-god that gave all the creatures their distinctive

---

* For a possible explanation of these terms, see Appendix 1.

forms and then rightly guided them.'

'How was it then with the ancients?' asked Pharaoh.

(Moses) answered: 'Horus alone has knowledge of that, recorded in the sacred texts. The Book does not err, and neither does it forget.'

Now this revised rendition of the Koran makes a great deal more sense, even if it is rather less divine and esoteric in its meaning. Indeed, Moses may have been primarily speaking about the Book of the Dead. This is presumably why the Koran refers to Muslims, Jews and Christians alike as the 'People of the Book'. This term is generally thought to refer to the people who revere the Torah (Tanakh) and its subsidiary versions, the Bible and Koran. However, it may well be that the original format stressed the 'People of Horus'; but this was not a term that would have been acceptable to the radical, monotheistic Pharaoh Akhenaton, and so the emphasis would have been, by necessity, changed in favour of the 'Word' or 'Book'. It may have been for this reason that such great stress was subsequently given to the 'Law (or Book) of Moses', and to the 'Logos (the Word or Book) of God'.

But the interpretation of the term *'logos'* does not end there. Taking a step further back into Greek history, it would appear that the term *'logos'* was derived from the concepts of rational thought and argument, and these were, in turn, derived from the concepts of law, order and unity. One can easily rationalise the changes that have taken place here. As the concepts of law and order were debated by the city elders, so they became synonymous with their thoughts and arguments; and then at a later date these concepts became synonymous with the debate itself, and thus with written and spoken words. It is from the central portion of this three-part progression, the 'reasoning' segment, that the word *'logos'* became translated into the English as 'logic'. This logical aspect to the *logos* probably did not refer to the original laws themselves, but instead to man's logical reasoning and interpretation of these 'Laws of the Gods'. In this manifestation, the *logos* was not so much the Torah, but the Talmud.

Maat

But all of this is simply a Greek rendition of a much older concept and, as usual, if we want to get to grips with Greek mythology we need to turn to Egypt and discover what they were doing there. In Egypt, the equivalent concept of 'law and order' was *maat* ⟨hieroglyph⟩, and so it is likely that the Greek *logos* was based on the Egyptian concept of *maat*. But if this were indeed the case, then how did the term *maat* become transformed into a word like *logos*?

The answer is to be found in the writings of Plato, who basically implied that the Greeks borrowed and used foreign words unless they already had an equivalent Greek word that described the same process. In the case of *maat* they did indeed have an equivalent word and that was *logia* λογια or *logios* λογιος, which mean 'collection' and 'wisdom' respectively. Thus the word *logos* was probably derived from a collection of wise sayings, and it was from these assemblages of ancient adages that the subsidiary meanings for *logos*, a 'word' or 'book', were then derived. These sayings represented a portion of the sacred texts that Moses was alluding to when he stated, in the previous quote from the Koran, that 'the Book alone has knowledge of that, recorded in its sacred texts'.

In Egyptian terms, a portion of these wise sayings has been preserved for us in the form of the 'Instructions of Amenemopet', which is a collection of eminently sensible adages that can be used to guide the average citizen through an honest and upright life. Now while these 'Instructions' are not explicitly referring to the concept of *maat*, nor the goddess Maat, in any way, it was conclusively shown in the book *Solomon* that these same 'Instructions of Amenemopet' were the literary foundations upon which the biblical 'Proverbs of Solomon' was written. But it was also demonstrated that the apocryphal biblical book known as the 'Wisdom of Solomon' was manifestly referring to Maat ⤵ 🜊 , the Egyptian goddess who personified the concepts of truth and justice, or *maat* ⤵ .

The biblical evidence demonstrates that both Maat and *maat* were intimately associated with these ancient collections of sayings, or laws; which would make sense as both were intimately associated with the concepts of 'truth and justice'. Thus the Greek *logos* and the Egyptian *maat* were both intimately associated with a body of laws, and it would appear that some of these laws were so fundamental and important that they became, or always were, synonymous with the words, laws or instructions of the gods.

While this may seem a reasonable enough explanation for the similarity between the terms *logos* and *maat*, there is another association that perhaps places their equivalence beyond doubt. There is one final version of *logos* and that is *logizomai* λογιζομαι meaning 'consider', 'take into account', 'weigh up', or 'meditate on'. What we have here, of course, is a reasonably graphic description of Maat's subsidiary role as the arbiter of the souls of the dead through the use of her dreaded scales of justice. As the goddess of truth and justice, and as the owner of the book of the law, it was Maat's duty to sit in judgement on the life of the dead and decide if they had been righteous individuals worthy of passing through into the glorious afterlife, or evil creatures whose hearts would be eaten by a hippopotamus-like monster. It is for this reason that the Old Bailey in London, the central courts of British justice, are surmounted by a blindfolded lady holding up a set of weighing scales. Here, boldly set in the center of the British establishment, is an image of the Egyptian goddess Maat, complete with her weighing scales, dispensing justice to the living in the same manner that the Egyptian Maat once did to the dead.

Fig 1.3   Maat, with eyes closed – because true justice should be blind to the individual being accused.

So how did the Greeks come up with a word like *logi-zomai* to explain the Egyptian concept of *maat*? Well, it is highly likely that they already had the word *logos*, which referred to the 'book of the law', but they wanted to add to this word the concept of weighing the hearts of the deceased by the use of Maat's scales of justice. They did this by adding the Hebrew word *maazen* מאזן or *maaznem* מאזנים, which refers to a set of weighing scales, and this is quite obviously a word that was based upon the Egyptian Maat and her famous weighing scales (*maazen* = <u>Maat</u>sen). The corruption of *maazen* into *zemaa (zomai)* was most probably due to the fact that Hebrew is written 'backwards', or at least the other way around to Greek. In which case, the word *logi-zomai* means 'Law of the Scales' or 'Judgements of Maat' and it refers to Maat in her guise of chief lawyer, or Attorney General. Thus the Judaeo-Greek deity called Logos was indeed a direct successor to the Egyptian Maat.

Now, of course, we can see yet another reason for the Greek concepts of law and order being equated and interchangeable with the actions of writing and speech. In Egyptian mythology Maat was the goddess of law and order, or *maat*; but nearly all the deities of Egypt had partners, and the husband of Maat was Thoth (Djehuti). It so happens that Thoth was the god of writing and language, and so while Maat judged the hearts and souls of the dead, it was Thoth who wrote down the results of those judgements. But in addition to language, Thoth was also the god of mathematics and metrology, and since maths was considered to be the everlasting logical language of the universe, as opposed to the transitory and inconsistent language of mankind, it is only natural that both Thoth and the term *logos* should also be equated with logic. In simplistic terms, Thoth was the Mr Spock of the starship Egypt.

It would seem, therefore, that the Greek word *logos* was based upon a fusion of the attributes of the husband and wife team of Thoth and Maat. These two Egyptian deities between them were responsible for the concepts of 'words', 'logic', 'justice', and 'law and order'; and so all of the attributes that are accorded to the word *logos* were originally the areas of responsibility of Thoth and Maat. Thus the Judaeo-Greek deity called Logos was probably a direct successor to the husband and wife team of Thoth and Maat.

All of this would suggest that the gods of the Torah were originally and firmly based upon Egyptian mythology, and that at least one of the aspects of the Judaic god was based upon Maat and Thoth. This makes the biblical Elohim a rather complex entity, consisting of Ra-Horus and Maat-Thoth combined, or simply Horus on his own with his eyes representing the astronomical bodies of the Sun and Moon. But, in the Egyptian context, all of these gods were normally depicted as being anthropomorphic gods who were supposed to walk, talk, marry and argue like human beings, which does not sound too much like the Judaic and Christian variety of god – or does it? Take this verse from Genesis, for instance:

> And they heard the voice of the Lord God walking in the garden in the cool of the day: and Adam and his wife hid themselves from the presence of the Lord God amongst the trees of the garden. [B10]

Not only do Adam and Eve hear god walking in the garden, later on they actually strike up a conversation with him. This is exactly the sort of interaction that the Egyptians expected from their humanoid gods, and so we see once more that the true foundations of Judaic theology lie in the humanoid polytheism of Egypt.

Here, then, we have a much more comprehensive and rational description of the god(s) that the biblical Gospel of John was trying to describe. The *logos* was not so much the Aten or Ra aspect of god – the all-powerful creator god that oversaw each and every aspect of creation – this was instead a lower order of the divine creation that the Egyptians had quite sensibly delegated to a lower tier of gods. The basis of Egyptian religion was a battle between order and chaos, and on the cosmic level this manifested itself as a battle between the physical world we see and the chaos of the primeval waters of Nu that continually threaten to overwhelm our ordered world. At the social level, however, this same battle was seen as a contest between good and evil; between the righteous and the damned; between the educated and the ignorant; or even between the logical and the irrational. Ra dealt with the cosmos, and it was left to Thoth and Maat – the Logos – to sort out the domestic problems pertaining to mankind.

The Theban Egyptians were able to understand that Maat-Thoth (the Logos) were a fundamental aspect of Ra, but they were also able to rationalise them as separate entities that were best depicted as a separate god and goddess. But the Israelites, for reasons that will be explained more fully later, had dispensed with the polytheistic pantheon of Egyptian gods in favour of a single entity based upon Akhenaton's god called Aton. However, this simplification caused a multiplicity of problems and inconsistencies, as this solitary god picked up all the attributes of the many gods upon which it was fundamentally based. Thus the Hebrew god became:

God-name	Description
Adhon,	the Sun-god who was called Aten, Adjen, or Ra in Egypt.
Shaddai,	the Hebrew devastation god based upon the *shedj* of the ritual slaughter.
Elohim,	the Al and Ah Eyes of Horus, representing the Sun and the Moon, or Ra and Thoth. Because of the latter's well-known attributes, together with his wife Maat, the Elohim also referred to the Sacred Book or Word.
Jehovah,	the god Thoth or Jeheweh (Yaheweh).
Logos,	the New Testament version of Elohim that meant 'Word', and was more firmly based upon the combined attributes of Maat and Thoth.

Trinity

Even from the small beginnings of this investigation, it is again looking likely that the Torah, Bible and Koran were, and are, eminently rational historical books, if only they had been translated correctly. The only thing that has prevented this kind of rationalisation process from taking place in the past is the willingness of the followers of these 'peaceful' religions to burn, torture and murder those individuals who valiantly attempted to shed some historical light onto these otherwise impenetrable texts. But the few hardy individuals who are now attempting to unravel these mysteries cling to the hope that we live in more enlightened times, although my e-mail in-box sometimes tells a different and more depressing story.

But the truth will out in the end, and so having made this new translation for the god-name Elah or Alah (El-Ah or Al-Ah), even the first sentence from the Torah begins to make a little more sense. In fact, it sounds like the scene for the Genesis story was originally set in the predawn glow at a temple somewhere in Egypt. To add drama to the scene, I will assume that the temple in question is Giza – which was the primary Sun-temple in ancient Egypt, as I demonstrated in the book *Tempest* – and in this case the priesthood will have assembled on the eastern side of the Great Pyramid by the 'mortuary' temple. It is exactly one month after the spring equinox, April 22nd, and so the first limb of the rising Sun peeps over the horizon directly along the causeway that stretches out northeastwards from the base of the Great Pyramid – which is why the causeway was designed in this manner. The high priest and priestess, who may even be dressed as Horus, Thoth and Maat, stretch their arms aloft in exaltation to the rising Sun-god and read in unison from the sacred book: 'At the sunrise the two eyes of Horus illuminate the eastern horizon.' The oneness of the two was now complete. The sacred books could not be read without the blessed illumination of Ra, and Ra could not complete its diurnal circuit of the land without the magical incantations of the priesthood – the Word was Ra, and Ra was the Word.

Subsequent verses from the account of Genesis tend to indicate that the Elohim (Horus, Ra or Thoth) spoke or commanded events to happen. While this may simply imply that the Moon-god Thoth was not only an eye of Horus but also the god of language, it may also imply that this is exactly what happened; because when the priesthood commanded an event to proceed through their ritual incantations, it did indeed happen. The power of hoodwinking those with limited celestial knowledge, and thereby achieving great acclaim and status for the priesthood, should not be underestimated.

I have no doubt that the priests at Giza would have invited various high officials from the Egyptian royalty, army and civil service to view these rituals. They may also have assembled them at the foot of the Great Pyramid on August 22nd and said to them something like, 'I will make Ra rise along this pyramid's causeway.' When Ra duly obliged, the priesthood would remind the laity of the power of the Church over the gods and the daily events in the natural world. Even if a curious army general hinted that Ra always rose in this position, the same witnesses could be invited back for another ceremony, on October 22nd perhaps, and Ra could be ordered to rise over the causeway of the Second Pyramid, which is aligned in a completely different direction. With such a demonstration of divine influence, who would then dare to challenge the dominance of the priesthood and to begrudge them the enormous wealth and power that they had at their command?

Herein may also stem one of the roots of the enigmatic Trinity, where the three gods of Christianity are considered to be one. It has already been explained earlier in this chapter that there was an ancient trinity of gods that was formed by Atum, Shu and Tefnut. Atum-Ra was the father, Tefnut was his daughter, and his son Shu – being the god of air – was the Holy Spirit. However, that fundamental trinity was subsequently usurped by the rise to power in Heliopolis of the cult of Osiris. As ever, the old forms and methodologies had to be reworked and adapted to suit the era, and so the new Egyptian trinity became Osiris, Isis and their son Horus.

The Egyptian trinity of deities was then copied in mortal terms by the king, the queen and the elder prince, a scene that Akhenaton tried repeatedly to paint on the walls of his temples and palaces, but failed miserably due to the lack of a male heir. But since the queen was often known as the 'God's Wife', and was therefore 'married' to the god, the king could sometimes be dispensed with. The resulting trinity could then be depicted as the god, the queen and her son, and this is the basis of the Christian Trinity. In its original format, the Christian Trinity would have referred to God, Mary and her son Jesus. However, Mary was the God's Wife, and through a long line of linguistic permutations that will be looked at again in a later chapter, she was also considered to be both Maat and a representation of the air or wind.

This 'wind' aspect to Maat was the same as has been explained for the god Shu 𓇗𓆓𓀭 and so Maat 𓇉𓆄 also became the 'Breath of God', which is why both Shu and Maat used the ostrich feather hieroglyph that signified wind. (With its delicate filaments, the feather may have been used to detect the wind.) Why there has been a change of sex between Shu and Maat I am not so sure. In the Greek language this same 'Breath of God' concept became known as the *pneuma* πνευμα, which means both 'wind' and 'spirit', and it was from this version that the more familiar term 'Spirit of god' was derived. Thus the fundamental Christian Trinity of the New Testament was actually: God, the Son (Jesus) and the Holy Ghost or Spirit, who in this era was represented by Mary.

While this was the royal explanation for the Trinity, it is likely that the scribes deemed that the tools of their trade were every bit as important and divine as the royal family – after all, the Word was an aspect of the god, if not a complete manifestation of Thoth. Thus the ever inventive scribes invented their own semi-divine Trinity. In the Hebrew language, without exception, all nouns are derived from a root verb which describes the actions or properties of the being or thing in question. This root word is known as the *radix*, and the ideal *radix* is always a three-letter word. Thus the whole of the verbal and literary world of Judaism springs from combinations of simple three-letter words. But since the Word is god, and god is the Word, then surely the root or *radix* of god must also be composed of three elements. [11] An eminent Jewish rabbi, Simeon ben Joachi, seems to confirm this when he states:

> Come and see the mystery of the word Elohim; there are three degrees, and each degree by itself alone, and yet notwithstanding they are all one, and

joined together in one, and are not divided from each other. [20]

The word Elohim is the plural for god, based upon the root word Elah or Alah אלה; so would this quote be referring to three degrees of masonic initiation, the three divinities of the Christian Church, or the three consonants of the Hebrew alphabet that form the word for god? The point is open and debatable.

Firmament

> 1:5 And the Elohims# called# the light# Day#, and the darkness# he called# Night#. And the evening and the morning# were the first day#.
> 1:6 And the Elohims said, Let there be a firmament# in the midst of the waters#, and let it divide the waters# from the waters#.

> 1:5 And Ra-Horus called the light Day, and the darkness they called Night. And the evening and the morning were the first day.
> 1:6 And Ra-Horus said, Let there be woman in the middle of the waters, and let her divide the water (*ma-yim*) from the Sun-god Amen (*m-Amen*).

As a reminder, those words marked with 'number symbols' are probably based upon Egyptian originals and have been translated as such in the second version of these verses. These verses demonstrate once more that the original Torah must have been an Egyptian book, by again highlighting the many direct translations from the Egyptian into Hebrew.

The latest of these translatable words is *qara* קרא meaning 'call', which comes from the Egyptian *karuai* meaning 'call'. Another good direct comparison is the word for morning, which is *boqer* בקר in the Hebrew and *baka* in the Egyptian. An interesting but more complicated solution is for *yowm* יום meaning a 'time period' or 'day'. In the Hebrew this word is derived from *kham* חם, which means 'hot'. Not surprisingly, in a country like Egypt, the concept of daytime was determined by the heat of the day. There is, of course, a direct comparison to be made here with the Egyptian word *kham*, which means 'hot', and *kam* meaning 'time period'.

Then we come to the strange term 'firmament', which has always been a bit of a mystery to me. In the Hebrew the word is *raqiya* רקיע, and it sort of describes an extended surface in the heavens, upon which the celestial bodies were attached. The word 'firmament' actually comes from the Latin *firmamentum*, and this describes much the same sort of thing, although the term 'canopy' would be more realistically descriptive in the English. So what does all this really mean? The answer lies in Egyptian mythology once more, where the 'canopy' upon which the stars were affixed was actually the arched body of the goddess Nut. This is the scene that the scribes were trying to describe here, and the original Egyptian word that was used for this was *rekh-t* ⊘⌒𓏏 meaning 'woman'.

Fig 1.4   *The arching body of the goddess Nut forming the surface of the sky, while her partner Geb represents the surface of the Earth below. The solar boat of Ra, also containing Thoth and Maat, can be seen traversing across the body of Nut, or the firmament in biblical terminology.*

The assertion in this verse that Nut was 'dividing the water from the waters' appears to be nonsensical. However, I think that the scribes were playing on words once more and making a little rhyme; which works both in the Hebrew and the original Egyptian. The basis for this verse is explained by the fact that the primeval water of Nu, which has been discussed previously, was only displaced, not eliminated. Beyond the arching canopy of Nut's body, the chaos of the abyss still lurked menacingly and so Nut was dividing this water. But from what was she dividing it?

The answer to this is to be found in the Hebrew word for water, which is *mayim* מים. The Egyptian equivalent of this is *ma-yim* 𓈖𓈗 𓏥 𓈖𓈗 meaning 'sea sea', as has already been discussed. So, the waters of chaos above the skies were being separated from the seas on the Earth below. But this is not the only possible translation, as *mayim* מים is actually a contraction of a word that is supposed to be pronounced as *miyamin* מימין; but if taken more phonetically can be delivered as *m-amen* מימין. This may well give the clue to what is being discussed here, for the Hebrew *m-amen* actually means 'from the right-hand side'. This is actually a direct translation out of the Egyptian, for *m-amen* 𓅯 𓏭 also means 'from the right-hand side'. Now while this may not exactly illuminate the situation greatly, the picture I am trying to describe has to be orientated correctly. In this verse, the observer is facing south, and so the right-hand side becomes the west, the direction of the setting Sun, and so the term *amen* also means 'west'. In addition, by using a different determinative glyph, the phrase *m-Amen* 𓅯 𓏭 can also mean 'from Amen'; that is 'from the Sun-god, Amen'. Since Amen was the god of the setting Sun, he would naturally be associated with the west and the 'right-hand side' (when facing south). As can be seen, the Hebrew word *mi-amen* מימין preserves the exact spelling and meaning of this short Egyptian phrase.

This new translation of verse 1:6 may be illustrating the diurnal journey of Ra through the body of Nut, who gave birth to the Sun each morning – the redness of the sunrise being regarded as the equivalent of the blood associated with birth. In this latter explanation, Nut was again separating Ra from the chaos of the watery abyss that existed outside the protective canopy of her arching body, but more importantly Nut was now also separating the waters of the primeval chaos from Amen (the Sun) and the western side of the sky as Amen sank in the west.

One final thing that should be highlighted in this section is the exit of the Sun, Ra, from the body of Nut. The goddess Nut swallowed Ra each evening and after travelling through her body during the night hours, Ra was born again from the vagina of Nut. However, the crotch of Nut, and of every other female in Egypt, was always depicted as a distinct inverted triangle, which is the ancient symbol of femininity. The symbol for masculinity was a pyramid in its correct orientation, and when these two symbols are superimposed and united during sexual union, the result is a Star of David.

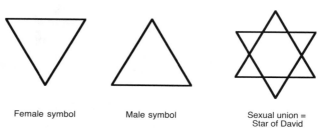

Female symbol   Male symbol   Sexual union =
                                            Star of David

Fig 1.5   The male and female aspects of the Star of David.

But the imagery that this triangle of Nut provides may not have been the exact intended symbolism because Nut is invariably drawn upright, arching her body across the sky, and so the triangle of her crotch is depicted in the usual feminine 'upside-down' fashion. However, if Nut and her crotch were inverted, the image that is so formed is of a large sun-disk sitting on top of a pyramid. This is another reason why I set the scene for the Genesis story at Giza; for the required imagery is of the Sun emerging from the vagina of Nut (over the horizon), while being simultaneously superimposed upon the very apex of a pyramid.

Fig 1.6   The crystal spheres.

In a later era, the more educated and annoying plebeians must have started asking the priesthood the obvious question as to why this great female in the sky called Nut could not be seen. Accordingly, the theological explanations changed to accommodate this new era of enlightenment, and the idea was generated that this canopy formed by Nut's body was actually made of crystal, or glass. This then mutated into the imagery of the seven crystal spheres that composed and supported the sky, planets, stars, and heavens; and I have no doubt that the concept of these layers of concentric spheres was greatly influenced by the multiple nested-door imagery to be found in the Temple of Karnak. The false door is a regular feature in Egyptian tombs;

it usually faced west and signified a link between the living and the dead – or a door into the Djuat (Duat). In several locations, however, the doors are multiple and nested, and a very good example of this is to be found on a chapel on the far side of the temple enclosure at Karnak, where seven nested doors are to be seen. This multiple door imagery has also survived in the design of most medieval cathedrals, where the design of the traditional entrance shows layers of decorated, nested door-frames.

Since the entrance to the Duat was closely linked with an entrance into the heavens, it was probably easy to link these nested doors with the heavens themselves, and so the multiple door imagery became intimately linked with the multiple layers of the cosmic canopy. With the advent of reliable glass-blowing techniques, the multiple layers became the seven crystal spheres, and this view must have been prevalent in the first century AD, as the historian Josephus refers to the biblical firmament as being a 'crystal'.

Second day

> 1:8 And the Elohim# called the firmament# Heaven#. And the evening and the morning# were the second# day#.
> 1:9 And the Elohim# said, Let the waters# under the heaven# be gathered# together unto one place, and let the dry land appear#: and it was so.

> 1:8 And Ra-Horus called the female Shamash (Nut?). And the evening and the morning were the second day.
> 1:9 And Ra-Horus said, Let the waters under the heaven be gathered together unto one place, and let the dry land appear: and it was so.

In actual fact, the original Egyptian sacred books called the female Nut, rather than 'Heaven' – but the word being used for heaven is again Shamash (the Sun), and of course the Sun did travel over and through the body of Nut as it traversed the night sky. The Egyptian terms for 'morning' and 'evening' have already been explained, but since this was the end of a second day in the mythology of Egypt, it is fitting that this was called the *sheniy* שני day, as the Egyptian for the number two was known as *senu* 𓏤𓏤𓏥 .

The term for 'gathering' is fairly certain to have been Egyptian too, as the one is called *qavah* קוה while the other was known as *khef* 𓂧𓂧𓆓 . In fact, this association is doubly secure because it was the waters that were being gathered together, and the Egyptian version of this word has very strong connotations of floods and deluges. The continuing biblical story of dry land appearing in the waters is yet another allusion to the primeval mound of Atum-Ra that appeared in the watery chaos of Nu.

Light

> 1:10 And the Elohim# called the dry land Earth#; and the gathering# together
> of the waters# he called Seas#: and God saw that it was good#.
> 1:14 And the Elohim# said, Let there be lights# in the firmament# of the
> heaven# to divide the day# from the night#; and let them be for signs, and for
> seasons, and for days#, and years#.

> 1:10 And Ra-Horus called the dry land Arets (earth); and the gathering together
> of the waters he called Yam (sea): and the Horus saw that it was good.
> 1:14 And Ra-Horus said, Let there be stars on the female of the Sun (Nut or
> sky) to divide the day from the night; and let there be signs of the zodiac for
> the seasons, and days, and the great circuit of the Sun (a year).

In verse 10 we have the naming of the Earth and the Sea. The translation
of the Earth has already been shown to have been based upon an Egyptian
word, but so too was the sea. This was called the *yam* םי, which was derived
from *iam or yam* 𓇋𓅱𓈖 , and both can refer to either seas or rivers.

Verse 14 is another good example of the original Egyptian origins of
this text. The term being used for lights is *ma-ure* מאור, which was derived
from the Egyptian *maurii* 𓂝𓏤𓀜 meaning 'brilliance'. Since the Egyptian
version of the word clearly refers to the Sun, it would seem likely that the
Hebrew word *maued* מועד for 'seasons' was derived from the movements
of this same Sun. The final word in this verse is *shaneh* שנה meaning 'year',
and the obvious corollary in the Egyptian language for this word is *shenur*
𓈖𓂋 , which refers to the 'great circle' of the Sun. This phrase explains the
mechanics that lie behind the concept of a 'year' very well, although it does
tend to suggest an Earth-centered view of the Solar System.

The story suggests that stars should be placed in the firmament,
which we have already established as being a reference to the goddess Nut.
This statement is perfectly true again, because Nut was a representation
of the heavens and all the images of Nut show her body studded with
stars. Significantly, these stars are said to form 'signs' which just has to be
a reference to the signs of the zodiac and so the zodiac, being mentioned
here at the very beginning of Genesis, must have been one of the original
foundation stones of Judaic theology. Once more, the Genesis story appears
to be describing the Egyptian concept of the heavens, and confirming the
very ancient origins of the zodiac.

Dragons

1:11 And Elohims said, Let the earth bring forth grass#, the herb# yielding seed, and the fruit tree# yielding fruit after his kind, whose seed is in itself, upon the Earth#: and it was so.
1:21 And Elohims created great whales#, and every living creature that moveth, which the waters brought forth abundantly#, after their kind, and every winged# fowl after his kind: and God saw that it was good#.

1:11 And Ra-Horus said, Let the earth bring forth vegetation, the tree yielding seed, and branches of fruit giving fruit after his kind, whose seed is in itself, upon the land: and it was so.
1:21 And Ra-Horus created great 'sea' serpents, and every living creature that moves, which the waters brought forth abundantly, after their kind, and every winged fowl after his kind: and Ra-Horus saw that it was good.

The word being used for 'whale' here is interesting, as even this has a direct equivalent in the original Egyptian. The Hebrew word *tan* or *tanniym* תנים really refers to 'dragons' and 'serpents', although it can also apply to 'sea-serpents', and it was based upon the Egyptian word *djen* or *djannym* 𓂧𓏤𓆙 meaning a serpent or 'worm'. In turn, the word for 'wing', *kanuph* כנף, was taken from *ganush* 𓈖𓏤 meaning 'wing'. While 'grass' or 'vegetation', *deshe* דשא, came from *tchase* 𓂧𓆰𓏥 meaning 'vegetation'. The word *asheb* עשב or *ash* עש, meaning 'herb' or 'vegetation', has been derived from *ashed* 𓆰𓏤 or *ash* 𓆱 meaning 'tree'. Finally the word *ats* עץ for 'tree' or 'branch' came from *at* 𓏏𓏏 meaning 'branch'.

Adam

1:26 And the Elohim# said, Let us make# man# in our image#, after our likeness#: and let them have dominion# over the fish of the sea#, and over the fowl# of the air, and over the cattle, and over all the earth#, and over every creeping# thing that creepeth upon the earth.
1:27 So the Elohim# created# man in his own image, in the image# of the Elohim# created# he him; male and female created# he them.

1:26 And Ra-Horus said, Let us multiply the Edomites in our image, after our manner: and let <u>them</u> hook and snare the fish of the sea, and the fowl of the air, and over the cattle, and over all the land, and over every creeping thing that creepeth upon the earth.
1:27 So Ra-Horus illuminated (breathed life into) the Edomites in his own

image, in the image of the Ra and Horus he illuminated them; male and female created he them.

The first thing to note here is the term *asah* עשׂה for 'make'. The equivalent would be *ashah* ⸺ meaning to 'make abundant', to 'multiply' or even 'a large multitude'. The new wording fits the sentence very well, with one exception. If the gods were simply allowing man to multiply, rather than fabricating him, then a race of men must have pre-existed the manipulations of the gods. Again we see how critical these translations can be; change one simple word ever so slightly, and the entire meaning of the Book of Genesis is altered. The text seems to confirm this argument when it says 'male and female he created <u>them</u>'; so that the new race of 'men' are already being referred to in the plural, even though Adam and Eve have not been formally 'made' as yet.

Some of the other terms being used in these two verses are equally interesting, as they again show the Egyptian heritage of this text. The word for 'likeness' or 'manner', *damuwth* דמות, is taken from *tament* ⸺ meaning 'manner'. 'Dominion', *radah* רדה, was actually derived from *radah* ⸺ and the Egyptian version tends to mean 'hook', 'snare', 'imprison' (corral), which makes more sense than the Hebrew, especially in terms of 'ruling' over fish. The male (*zakar* זכר) and female (*naqebah* נקבה) were derived from *seker-reth* ⸺ meaning 'mankind', and *neqabah* ⸺ meaning 'mother goddess', respectively.

This brings us to the tricky subject of the term being used for 'man', *adam* אדם. Here is a peculiarity for a start, for the Hebrew name Adam, denoting the prime hero of Genesis, was derived from the word *adam* and this word actually refers to mankind rather than a particular individual. Once more, it would seem that the fairytale from the Book of Genesis is being replaced by a more pragmatic history of a particular race of people being allowed to multiply and farm the land. I use the phrase 'a particular race' purposely here, because it is likely that the term *adam* does not apply to all of mankind, nor even to all of the Egyptians; rather it applied solely to the Lower Egyptians of the Nile Delta.

Those readers who have digested the books *Tempest* and *Solomon* will already know that the word *adam* also means 'red', and that this peculiar redness pervaded the Torah's writings; with Adam, Esau and King David all being described as red or ruddy in appearance. According to the Koran's ancient Turkish commentators, even Moses was described as being 'ruddy'.[21]

Some authors have sought to draw parallels between this redness and the traditional Scottish redheaded complexion, suggesting that redheads were common within the Egyptian royalty. Indeed, the recent mummies that have been found in Egypt initially appear to support this idea. Three mummies of the Amarna regime, including Queen Tiye, a young boy and a young lady, were recently rediscovered in a side-chamber of the tomb of Amenhotep II. It has been suggested that the latter of these mummies represents the mortal remains of Queen Nefertiti herself, but this could not have been Nefertiti as the mummy is far too young – but that is another story.

The more important aspect in this regard is that two of these mummies sported rusty, red-brown hair, which again seemed to indicate that the Amarna pharaohs, who were allied to the Lower Egyptian royal line, were redheaded. [22] However, it is a known fact that the mummification and storage process can, over a period of centuries, turn the hair a rusty red; so no particular conclusions can be drawn from this until further analysis is performed on these mummies. However, whatever the hair colour of the Amarna pharaohs may have been, I believe that the redness that was being referred to in the biblical and koranical texts was actually a simple coded allusion to the Red Crown of Lower Egypt; and therefore all of the biblical patriarchs were being associated with that crown and that royal line. It is for this reason that the term *adamah* אדמה means 'Red Lands', the lands of Lower Egypt.

However, in later eras it was becoming unacceptable for the Israelites to be associated with Egypt and the Egyptian royal line, and so the scribes simply used a coded reference to redness to demonstrate, to the highest of cabalistic and masonic initiates, that these people had indeed been pharaohs of Egypt. In this case, the people of *adam* who are being mentioned here in the Book of Genesis would have been a reference to the subjects of Lower Egypt, the people ruled by the Red Crown. More specifically, however, it would have referred to the monarchy itself.

This explanation does have another implication, however, because one of the more famous factions or tribes within the Book of Genesis is the Edomites *Edowm* אדום. This tribe was formed from the descendants of Esau, the son of Isaac, who had fought a military battle with his brother, Jacob. Despite the close blood-ties between them – Esau and Jacob being twins – the Edomites obviously never forgave Jacob for usurping the throne of Lower Egypt and so they were a constant source of revolt and rebellion for the Judaeans of the later United Monarchy. Indeed, it would seem that even some 1600-odd years after the Jacob-Esau dispute, the Edomites were still looking to gain control of the Judaean royal line; and they may have eventually achieved this through the political machinations of King Herod.

It is often stated in reference books that King Herod was a 'commoner' who had no royal connections and who had usurped the throne of Israel with the military backing of Rome. However, Herod was an Idumaean leader, and the Idumaeans were just a Greek rendering for the name of the Hebrew Edomites – thus the Idumaeans were as 'red' as the Edomites. If Herod was an Edomite ruler, from the bloodline of Esau, then his claim to the throne of Judaea-Israel may have been just as strong as King Hyrcanus; who was the priest-king that Herod usurped. Remember that the term Edomite simply means the 'red tribe', and again this is simply a coded reference to the Red Crown of Lower Egypt, which is what the Edomites (Idumaeans) under Herod were trying to reclaim.

Getting back to the main thrust of this investigation, the primary question now has to be: what does the word *adam* really mean, and from where was it derived? The answer in respect of this particular biblical verse is probably that this Adam referred to Edom, meaning 'red people'; in other words, the monarchy of the Red Crown of Lower Egypt. Since the Hyksos Shepherd Kings were in control of Lower Egypt for a large part of its history, and since the patriarchs of the Torah were also said to be both 'red' and 'shepherds', it is abundantly clear that the early Israelites were simply the monarchs of Lower Egypt. See the book *Jesus* for further details.

Finally, it should be pointed out that this verse was the end of the 'sixth day' and so it is appropriate that the word for 'six' is *shash* שׁשׁ or *shishah* שׁשׁה, and the Egyptian number six was called *sas* or *sis* 𓏠 ☰ . Quite plainly, this is another Egyptian word that has found its way not only into the Hebrew but also into the English, where it has formed our number 'six'.

Incidentally, in the book *Solomon* I discussed the origins of the infamous biblical number 666, which was claimed to be the mark of the devil in the Book of Revelations. But these irrational claims are often crying out to be properly interpreted, and the more pragmatic answer to this riddle was the simple explanation that the number 666 referred to money. In fact, it was King Solomon who was being branded as the 'devil', because he received 666 talents of gold each year, no doubt from his famous mines. That much has already been explained in the book *Solomon*. However, through these new translations we now also have a beautiful play on words that confirms the true identity of King Solomon; for the text in Revelations indicates that 666 is also the number, or name, of a man.

> Here is wisdom. Let him that hath understanding count the number of the beast: for it is the number of a man; and his number is Six hundred threescore and six (666). [B23]

The Book of Revelations is interesting, if impenetrable at times, as it is claimed to be the *apokalupsis* αποκαλυψις, which has been interpreted here as a 'revelation': a 'discovery of things that were hidden'. However, this term is also the root of the modern word 'apocalypse', and so this hidden knowledge was laden with a great deal of doom and gloom. So what, if anything, was this 'book of hidden things' revealing to us in this case? Well, clearly the verse is setting us a riddle; and it would seem that those who have sufficient wisdom will be able to see within this verse the name of a particular man, and that name is somehow associated with the number 666. So who in the Bible was called 666?

As was explained in the book *Solomon*, the man I believe that this verse refers to is King Solomon, because of his annual income in gold, but I could not previously see a method by which this number could be more directly linked to this king. Having built up the Hebrew-Egyptian dictionary, however, the situation changed and it became apparent that the ever inventive scribes had not only alluded to the king's wealth but also spelt out the king's name for all to see. In the Hebrew language this number of the 'beast', six-six-six, becomes *shisha-shisha-shisha*, or perhaps that should be *shishak-shishak-shishak* instead. The number 666 was said to be the number or name of a particular man, so which man in the Bible bore the name of Shisha(k)? As it happens, the historical identity I have recently discovered for King Solomon was, of course, the Egyptian pharaoh called Shishak in the Bible.

In the plainest possible terms, the Book of Revelations is telling us that the man or beast was called Shisha(k), while the only man who received money to the value of 666 talents (shisha talents) was King Solomon – *ergo*: King Solomon must have been Pharaoh Shishak. Indeed, the number six is repeated three times in Revelations, which becomes *shishah talath* שׁשׁה תלת in the Hebrew (three sixes). It is not difficult to see a further play on words here, with a Greek rendition of this (in Revelations) giving 'Shisha talanton' Σηισηα ταλαντον, which means Shishak's talents (Shishak's money).

In the reality of history, the biblical pharaoh called Shishak was actually the historical twenty-second dynasty pharaoh called Sheshonq I, and it is this pharaoh who bears such a close historical affinity with King Solomon. Indeed, as the book *Solomon* explains at great length, these two monarchs were most definitely one and the same individual, and thus the Israelites were originally the Hyksos citizens of Lower Egypt.

The reason for King Solomon (Pharaoh Sheshonq) becoming the 'beast' in some people's eyes was that he was too ostentatious in flaunting his great wealth, and that he led Israel (the Hyksos-Israelites) astray by introducing foreign (polytheistic Egyptian) gods and idols. The former transgression was perhaps forgivable, but to the fundamentalist deists of Hyksos-Israel, the latter was most certainly not. Here was the devil, in some people's eyes; King Solomon (Pharaoh Sheshonq), whose annual income was said to be 666 talents of gold.

These explanations are all rather interesting, for this verse directly confirms that John the Divine, the supposed author of Revelations, knew that

I Genesis

King Solomon was Pharaoh Shishak (Sheshonq) and that he wished to secretly encode this information within his prophetic and Gnostic essay. So who was John the Divine? Well, it is clear that his work was composed at about the time of the fall of Jerusalem in AD 70, and he has been strongly linked to the author of the Gospel of John, a document which also shows distinct Gnostic leanings. In the book *Jesus*, I have already shown evidence that the Gospel of John was closely linked with Judas Iscariot, who I have further identified as a brother of Jesus.

Whatever the true identity of John the Divine, and the true origins of Revelations, the presumed date of its composition demonstrates that this highly sensitive knowledge about the Egyptian origins of the Old Testament, the Jewish nation and their principal monarchs and leaders, was still available to a few of the higher degree initiates of the Church of Jesus and James in the first century AD.

Breath of life

> 2:6 But there went up a mist# from the earth, and watered the whole face# of the ground#.
> 2:7 And the Lord# God# formed# man# of the dust# of the ground#, and breathed# into his nostrils# the breath# of life; and man# became a living soul.

> 2:6 There was a dew on the land, and it watered the whole of Edom.
> 2:7 And the Gods pottered (fabricated) the Lower Egyptians from the ashes of the setting Sun, and breathed into his nose the breath of life; and Aton became a living soul.

The term being used for mist, *ad* אד, is taken from *adj* meaning 'dew' or 'mist'. More surprisingly, perhaps, the word being used for 'ground' is *adamah* אדמה, meaning 'land', 'red' or even 'Adam'. Here we see again that the name for Adam actually refers to a people, rather than a person, for here it is also being used to describe a land or region. This dual meaning is also permissible in the Egyptian, as the word *aten* can also mean 'land' or 'estate'; and no doubt this referred to the lands of the Atonists of the pharaoh Akhenaton, who would originally have resided in the Nile Delta before their dramatic move to Amarna. The word for 'breathe' is *naphach (nefach)* נפח, which was derived from the word *nef* meaning 'breath'. And in a similar fashion, the word for nose was *af* אף, which was derived from *anef* אנף, and which was once more taken from *nef* .

There is also a rhyme here, that works in both the Egyptian and

39

the Hebrew, for the phrase being used is the *'adam* is *ad'*, or the 'lands of the Edomites are dewy'. This rhyme is perfectly true, both spiritually and geographically. Firstly, the masonic traditions that have sprung from this region regard this dew as a blessing of god; as it says in the Third Degree ritual, "we ... humbly implore Thee to pour down on this convocation ... the continual dew of thy blessing". Secondly, the lands of the Edomites were in Lower Egypt, and of all the Egyptian lands along the Nile, those of the Delta were the wettest and most fruitful. The biblical dew was a blessing in both a spiritual and physical sense.

In verse 2:7, god then creates man, perhaps having forgotten that he had already created man in verse 1:27, and so it would appear that we have two strands of the same story, each penned by a different scribe. But this does give a second chance at deciphering exactly how man was supposed to have been formed. As might be expected, the answer to this particular verse is to be found once more in the rituals of Egypt.

In my many books, I have consistently linked the Amarna regime of the pharaoh Akhenaton with the Israelite people in general and the second of the two exoduses from Egypt in particular; as indeed have several other authors before me, including Sigmund Freud and Ahmed Osman. The prime deity of the Amarna regime was the Aton (Aten) ⟨𓉻𓏏𓈖 ☉⟩ , and in the contemporary artwork of that era the Aton was depicted as a Sun-disk with extended arms (sunbeams) that held the *ankh* symbol of life. Here again we see the familiar symbology of the 'breath of god' – the Hebrew *ruwach*, the 'spirit of god' extending out from the Sun. In the graphic Amarna symbology of this event, the rays of sunbeams spread out from the Sun and give life not only to all of creation, but to Akhenaton and his family in particular.

In fact, these life-giving rays still provide a 'breath of life' to the sick and infirm in the modern era. The Wellcome Trust has been a well-known medical institution in Britain for many years, where it has researched drugs and vaccines for the prevention of illnesses. Surprisingly enough, the logo for the Wellcome Trust is the Aton Sun-god, complete with arm-like rays. (See the colour section.)

However, although it is not mentioned too often, the god Aton can also be called Adjon ⟨𓉻𓂧𓈖 ☉⟩ , a term that is even closer to the biblical name for god, Adhon אדן, than I at first suspected. The Adjon (Aton) was, of course, a reference to the Sun-god, and since the Sun can become remarkably red during a sunrise or sunset, this was the first clue that the term Adjon (Aton) may be related to both Edom and the colour red. This turned out to be just so, and the words *adjom* ⟨𓉻𓂧𓅓⟩ and *adjom* ⟨𓉻𓂧𓏥 𓏭⟩ do indeed refer to the setting Sun and a red garment respectively. Indeed, the term *adjom* meaning 'red garment' may be the prime basis for the word *adam*, which also means 'red'.

Since this red *adjom* garment was so closely related to the setting Sun and to the god Adjon (Aton, the rising Sun), it may well be that the priests who presided over the ceremony of the setting Sun wore scarlet tunics. To speculate further, since the later Christian traditions were so solidly based upon Egyptian ritual, the scarlet stoles of their bishops may have been derived from this very same ritual. Thus the original Egyptian word *adam (adjom)* may have once referred to the position of a high priest.

Potter

The key phrase in verse 2:7 reads – 'formed (or potter) man (or adam) of the dust (or ashes) of the ground (or Edom), and breathed into his nostrils the breath of life' – with the key words in the Hebrew being:

yatsar adam aphar adamah naphach af nashamah kha

יצר אדם עפר אדמה נפח אף נשמה חי

But this is probably an Egyptian phrase, as the following reconstruction demonstrates:

yatchar adam afu aton nef nef neshu ka

In the Egyptian version we now have the following words:

'forming'	*yatchar,*	the divine potter who made mankind.
'man'	*adam,*	the nation associated with redness.
'dust'	*afu,*	the ashes of the Sun-god who was supposed to die each night and become the ashes of his former self, before being reborn and rejuvenated into the morning sky.
'ground'	*adjon,*	meaning 'land'. Also the Aton, the rising Sun.
'breathe'	*nef,*	a breath or the breath of life.
'nose'	*nef,*	a heavy breath, which was associated with the snorting of the nose. In fact, the reversal of *nef* is *fen*, which does indeed mean 'nose'.
'breath'	*neshu,*	a strong wind.
'life'	*ka,*	the Egyptian soul or life-force.

In the Egyptian original, this sentence would have read as something like 'the divine potter made the Lower Egyptians from the ashes of the setting Sun; and breathed into his nose the breath of life'; and the sentence makes a

41

degree of sense in the context of the rituals and beliefs of Egypt. It has long been understood that in Egyptian mythology man was made from the clay of the earth and formed into shape by the divine potter, but this verse would seem to add that this clay was made from the ashes of Ra; a concept that seems quite appropriate.

This explanation for this particular verse, with its concept of breathing life into the nostrils of mankind, brings us very close to the underlying source of this famous creation epic. In fact, I would say that the original version of the Book of Genesis is reasonably famous too, but the deliberate obfuscation by the biblical scribes has successfully hidden the required connections from view for the last two millennia or more. To find the source manuscript, or Quelle as it is known in theological circles, we only need to summarise the first chapter of Genesis.

The creation myth speaks of the Sun and its illumination of the land; the dawn and dispelling of darkness; the creation of plants, animals, fish and insects; their multiplication and fruitfulness; the first rains; the creation of mankind and their young; and finally it now appears to be mentioning the Aton, the Sun-god of Akhenaton, who is breathing life into the nostrils of man. The reason for the Torah recording this precise sequence of events is that the Genesis creation myth is <u>nothing less than a corrupted copy of Akhenaton's Hymn to the Aton</u>.

Hymn to the Aton

While the Great Hymn to the Aton is one of the most famous pieces of literature from ancient Egypt, it is less well known that this hymn was not solely created by Akhenaton. Like most of the great works of literature, it was based in part on previous works that had already set the scene for the coming literary and cultural revolution that Akhenaton forced upon the people of Egypt with such vigour. The first of these precursors was the Great Hymn to Osiris, which has been preserved on an eighteenth dynasty stele commissioned by Amenemose, an overseer of the cattle. One of the sections in this hymn states:

> Heavens that make wind before his nose,
> That his heart be satisfied,
> Plants sprout by his wish,
> Earth grows food for him,
> Sky and stars obey him.
>
> In its plants and all its cattle,

I Genesis

> All that flies and all that alights,
> its reptiles and its desert game,
> Were given to the son of Nut.
>
> Appearing on his father's throne,
> Like Ra when he rises in the light-land,
> He places light above the darkness,
> He floods the Two Lands like Aton at dawn. [24]

Of his many attributes, Osiris is here being equated with the fertility of the land and the dawn of the coming day. This is presumably why Osiris-beds were left in tombs. These peculiar devices were beds of germinating grain in the shape of Osiris that briefly demonstrated his powers of fertility – until they withered and died in the darkness of the tomb. But Osiris was an anthropomorphic god who was worshipped up and down the Two Lands as a physical being. Whether it was in high or low relief, or whether it was a life-sized statue, Osiris was an idol and the worship of icons was beginning to be outlawed by the Hyksos influences of the Amenhotep kings.

Amenhotep III was the first pharaoh to begin this transitional period and it is clear that his scribes have borrowed this Osiris imagery and donated it to the more impersonal Ra, who is being called the Aton, the Sun-disk. The following is from the Hymn to the Sun-god by Harakhti, an overseer of the works of Amun:

> Hail you Ra, perfect each day,
> Who rises at dawn without failing,
> Khepri who wearies himself with toil.
>
> Sole one, unique one, who traverses eternity,
> With millions under his care,
> Your splendour is like the heaven's splendour,
> Your colour brighter than its hues,
> When you cross the sky all faces see you,
> When you are set you are hidden from their sight.
>
> When you stir to rise at dawn,
> Your brightness opens the eyes of the herds,
> When you set in the western mountain,
> They sleep in a state of death.
>
> Hail to you, Aton of daytime,
> Creator of all, who makes them live,
> Great falcon, brightly plumed,
> Beetle who raised himself,

Self-creator, uncreated,
Eldest Horus in Nut,
Maker of the Earth's yield,
Who seized the Two Lands from great to small. [25]

Note here that Ra (Aton) is being called the 'eldest Horus in the sky'. Horus and Ra were often intertwined and confused, and this is why the term Elohim has been translated in the previous verses as being either Ra or Horus.

Although the hymn above mentions the Aton, which literally means 'Sun-disk', this was probably only meant to be a nickname for Amun or Ra, since this was the god that the overseer of works called Harakhti served. As can be seen, the hymn has now been substantially more de-personalised, by extracting the name of Osiris and giving these powers of fertility and rejuvenation to the Sun-god, Ra or Amun (Amen). But this was not good enough for Pharaoh Akhenaton, because the god Amun also had an anthropomorphic figure and the hymn still contained references to Khepri and Horus. Akhenaton, the greatest of all the iconoclasts until the advent of Muhammad and Martin Luther, sought to expunge all references to gods that had a physical image and so the hymn was once more reworked and stripped of its gods – apart from that of the Sun-disk itself.

This is why many commentators on the Amarna regime speak of the Sun-disk as not being an image of god, but merely a representational token of god. The god of Akhenaton was invisible, all-powerful; it was the power that ruled the cosmos and made the planets and the stars conform to their tidy and predictable orbits. Akhenaton's religion was also designed to be the contemporary explanation for those forces and laws; it was astronomy, physics and mathematics all rolled into one. But therein lies a problem, for how can an artist show the presence of god in a scene if that god has no physical representation? How can you draw physics?

Michelangelo chose a human figure riding on a cloud for his representation of god, which was acceptable to the Catholic world of icons and Madonnas, but Akhenaton was much stricter in his theological interpretations. What Akhenaton chose, therefore, was a wondrous portent from the heavens that everyone could instantly identify with, wherever they were. Akhenaton chose the Sun-disk with its darting rays of sunlight, perhaps modelled on those certain days when the Sun peeps out from behind a cloud and its spreading rays become visible in the moist atmosphere. But he also chose the Sun-disk because everyone, down to the humblest of farmers, knew that the Sun provided the energy for plants, and therefore provided food for the people to live. There was no explanation required, it was obvious that the Sun itself was the most graphic illustration of the powers that existed in the cosmos.

In more recent times, the Protestant revolution of the sixteenth century has aped the iconoclastic reforms of Akhenaton, and so this new faction has again banned the worship of idols. The English Civil Wars were a desperate time of uncertainty and reform, as soldiers entered the sacred precincts of churches and cathedrals and smashed the sacred Madonnas of the Catholic Church. The turmoil of those times must have precisely mimicked the events of the Amarna era; and so it is no great surprise that Akhenaton, like Oliver Cromwell, chose to surround himself with a powerful army. Indeed, some authors have likened the city of Amarna to an armed military camp and have speculated that this show of strength was needed to keep the Amarna population in a very barren and unpopular location. I don't believe that this is so in the slightest. If anything, the reign of Akhenaton should again be likened to that of Oliver Cromwell, who didn't need an army to cajole his supporters as they had quite enough zeal themselves; rather, Cromwell's New Model Army, which was the most efficient and effective army the English nation had ever seen, was there to crush the idolators of the Roman Catholic Church who sought to impose foreign rule on Britain's domestic policy.

But Akhenaton was not entirely a forerunner of Cromwell, as it doesn't appear that he had to take to the battlefields to impose his will on the people of Thebes, and so his religious revolution seems to have been relatively bloodless. Perhaps, therefore, a better analogy for the reforms of Akhenaton might be the similar campaigns of Henry VIII of England, who managed to close all the wealthy Catholic monasteries in England while he himself held court in the sumptuous surroundings of Hampton Court or Nonsuch Palace, which reside to the west and south of London respectively. The religious faction that Henry VIII was opposing had no army of its own to defend itself, and the wealth and isolation of these monastic orders did not exactly make them popular with the common people. Akhenaton may have initially found the same public lethargy towards the rich, isolated compounds that were the great temples of Karnak; until, that is, all the resources of Egypt started to pour into Amarna instead of Thebes and the common people of Thebes began to feel economic hardships.

One of the side effects of these Protestant reforms in Tudor England was that they had again deleted god from religious art, and left both painters and later film producers alike searching for an acceptable representation of god that was not an obvious icon to be worshipped in its own right. Significantly, the modern film producer's choice for a symbol of god was often identical to that of Akhenaton's artists; and so in the majority of classical Hollywood epics the presence of god in a particular scene was represented by the Sun peeping from behind a clouded sky, accompanied by spreading rays of sunlight and an uplifting *crescendo* from an angelic choir. Here is the modern Hollywood version of the Aton, the Sun-disk that supposedly represents a deeper meaning to the concept of god than the physical Sun itself.

Regressing once more to my previous arguments – the comparison that I was about to show was between the Hymn to the Aton and the first chapter of Genesis. There were several versions of the Hymn to the Aton discovered at Amarna, but they all follow the same theme of the Sun-disk representing the all-powerful Osiris-type god, and Akhenaton being god's representative on Earth. The people of Egypt had to use Akhenaton as their conduit to the god, and it was this sole access to the deity, which was emphasised over and over again in Amarna literature, that gave Akhenaton his power and influence over the people. This same rigid hierarchy of a man being god's sole representative was later used by the Catholic Church, which was not slow to recognise the financial and political potential for declaring the Pope as god's sole representative on Earth. It was through this same methodology that the Catholic Church achieved the same level of power and influence as the Pharaohs of Egypt once had.

In what way, then, was the Hymn to the Aton similar to the Book of Genesis? Perhaps the best illustration for this similarity comes from the Hymn itself, but for brevity the following excerpt is taken from the Lesser Hymn to the Aton. [26] The Great Hymn to the Aton can be viewed in Appendix 3.

Splendid you rise, O living Aton (Adjon), eternal Lord,
You are radiant, beautiful, mighty,
Your love is great, immense,
Your rays light up all faces,
Your bright colour gives life to hearts,
When you fill the Two Lands of Egypt with your love.
Great god who fashioned himself,
Who made every land, created what is in it,
All peoples, herds, and flocks,
All trees that grow from soil,
They live when you dawn for them,
You are mother and father of all that you made.

When you dawn their eyes observe you,
As your rays light the whole Earth,
Every heart acclaims your sight,
When you are risen as their Lord,
When you set in the sky's western light-land
They lie down as if to die,
Their heads covered, their noses stopped,
Until you dawn in the sky's eastern light-land.
Their arms adore your ka,

I Genesis

As you nourish the hearts by your beauty,
One lives when you cast your rays,
Every land is in festivity.

Singers, musicians, shout with joy,
In the court of the Benben shrine,
And in all the temples in Akhet-Aten,
The place of truth in which you rejoice.
Foods are offered in their midst,
Your holy son (Akhenaton) performs your praises,
O Aton (Adjon) living in his risings,
And all your creatures leap before you.
Your great son exults in joy,
O Aton loving daily content in the sky,
Your offspring, your great son, Sole one of Ra,
The son of Ra does not cease to extol his beauty.

I am your son who serves you,
Your power, your strength, are firm in my heart,
You are the living Aton whose image endures,
You have made the distant sky to shine in,
To observe all you have made,
You are One, yet a million lives are in you,
To make them live (you give) the Breath of Life to their noses,
By the sight of your rays all flowers exist,
What lives and sprouts from the soil grows when you shine,
Drinking deep of your sight all flocks gambol,
The birds in the nest fly up in joy,
Their folded wings unfold in praise,
Of the living Aton (Adjon), their maker.

Look at the general thrust of these two stories: of Genesis and the Hymn to the Aton. They both speak of light, illumination, the creation of land, plants, animals and people; and they are both creation epics that are nevertheless a celebration of the diurnal circuit of the Sun. Reading the Hymn to the Aton, it can be clearly seen that this is a hymn that must have been sung in a daily ritual, as the Sun appeared over the eastern horizon.

Look also at some of the detail from the two accounts and some closer similarities will be seen. In the following examples, some of the text has been taken from the Great Hymn to the Aton,[27] rather than the Lesser Hymn to the Aton that has just been quoted:

Bible:

In the beginning, god (Aton-Ra) created the heaven and the Earth.

(At the sunrise Aton-Ra illuminated the eastern lands.) [B30]

Hymn to the Aton:

Splendid you rise in the heaven's light-land,

... when you have dawned in the eastern light-land.

Bible:

Aton-Ra ... breathed into his nostrils the Breath of Life; and man became a living soul. [B31]

Hymn to the Aton:

To make them live (Aton-Ra gave) the Breath of Life to their noses.

Bible:

And Aton-Ra separated the light from the darkness. [B32]

Hymn to the Aton:

As you dispel the dark.

Bible:

I have given every green plant for food. [B33]

Hymn to the Aton:

Everyone has his food.

Bible:

And Aton-Ra said, Let the waters bring forth abundantly the moving creature that has life, and fowl that may fly above the earth. [B34]

Hymn to the Aton:

You (Aton) made ... all peoples, herds and flocks.

All upon Earth that walk on legs,

All on high that fly on wings.

Bible:

Everything on the dry land in whose nostrils was the breath of life died. [B35]

Hymn to the Aton:

They lay down to die ... their noses stopped.

Bible:

And confuse their language, that they may not understand one another's speech. [B36]

Hymn to the Aton:

Their tongues differ in speech.

Bible:
So Aton-Ra scattered them abroad from there over the face of all the earth. [B37]
Hymn to the Aton:
For you (Aton) distinguished the peoples.

Bible:
And rain fell upon the earth forty days and forty nights. And the waters prevailed so mightily upon the Earth that all the high mountains under the whole heaven were covered. [B38]
Hymn to the Aton:
You (Aton) made a heavenly Hapy (rain) descend for them,
He (Aton) makes waves on the mountains like the sea.

Bible:
Let there be lights (the Sun and Moon) in the canopy of the heavens to divide the day from the night; and let them be for signs, and for seasons, and for days, and years. [B39]
Hymn to the Aton (of Amenhotep III):
Rising in heaven formed as Ra (the Sun),
He makes the seasons and the months.

Bible:
And the spirit of god (Ra) moved upon the face of the waters.
(And the rays of Ra bathed the boat in the waters.) [B40]
Hymn to the Aton:
The Aten's rays are in the midst of the sea.

The first of these many quotations contains the translation from the Egyptian that was made at the beginning of this chapter. The standard biblical translation indicated it was the 'Heaven and Earth' that was being illuminated (or created). However, it is likely that the intended word for 'heaven' was not shameh שמה, but shamel (shemer) שמאל, which literally means the 'left-hand side' in the Hebrew. The reason for thinking this, is the fact that the Egyptian version from the Hymn to the Aton used the word semer (semel) 𓇋𓃀𓎬𓄿 , which also means 'left-hand side'. But since in Egyptian terms the 'left side' was always the east, it must have been the 'eastern lands' that were being illuminated, or in other words this was the dawn, with Aton rising in the east.

The result from this particular piece of the investigation is that the opening passage from the Torah or Old Testament is almost exactly the same as the opening passage from the Great Hymn to the Aton. Given these strong similarities between these two works, it is extremely likely that the Book of

I Genesis

Genesis was actually based upon the Hymn to the Aton.

Bible:
In the beginning, god created the heaven *(shemer)* and the Earth.
(At the sunrise Aton-Ra illuminated the eastern lands.)

Hymn to the Aton:
Splendid you rise in the heaven's light-land,
... when you have dawned in the eastern *(semer)* light-land.

That the biblical scribes who created the Torah were familiar with the Hymn to the Aten is absolutely certain, as the later scribes who devised Psalm 104 chose to incorporate nearly all the elements from the Hymn to the Aten into their material. At the end of Appendix 3, I have made a comparison between these two works, and the degree of correspondence is staggering. Quite plainly, the Hymn to the Aten was well known to the Israelites, and it appears to have influenced two important sections within the Old Testament.

But if the Book of Genesis and a section in Psalms were both based upon a text from Akhenaton's Amarna regime, then this rather suggests that the rest of the story in Genesis may be connected with Amarna too. It means that Eden may be connected with Amarna; that Adam and Eve might be connected to an Amarna story; and that Moses may also be connected to Amarna in some manner. I have already spent a great deal of effort in the books *Jesus* and *Tempest*, demonstrating that Moses was indeed connected to Amarna – he being Akhenaton's brother TuthMoses – but what of the other two possibilities, what of Eden and what of Adam and Eve?

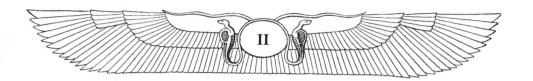

Garden of Eden

From the initial explorations of Chapter I, it would seem that the early sections of the account of Genesis are nothing more nor less than a corrupted account of the Hymn to the Aton, one of the few great epics that have survived the subsequent predations of Akhenaton's great capital city at Amarna. Having reached the creation of man in our investigations into Genesis, the biblical story then changes its tone at this point in the story, and there is good evidence to demonstrate that two separate stories have been sewn together, and the end of the Hymn to the Aton (the end of chapter one in Genesis) represents that union.

The evidence that demonstrates this is as follows. Firstly, there is the strange duplication of the creation of mankind. Man and woman are created in the image of god in chapter one of Genesis, but then we come to chapter two and god is again busy making man from the dust of the earth. The reason for this is that two documents detailing the creation of the Earth's fauna have been dovetailed together, and because there was some overlap within the two stories, a certain amount of the material was thus duplicated, including the formation of mankind. Secondly, it is recognised that the name of god changes at this exact same point in the text, from Elohim to Jehovah-Elohim, which would indicate a different scribe was in charge of this new section at the very least. William Whiston says of this change in the god-name:

> The change in the name of god at this place ... also favours some such change in the narration or construction.[1]

Thirdly, the text of the historian Josephus, which Whiston was translating, similarly supports this argument for a change in the storyline. After the seventh day of the biblical 'creation' had finished, Josephus adds that:

Moreover, Moses, after the seventh day was over, begins to talk philosophically.[J2]

This small detail gives us some vital clues in this investigation. It indicates that the source of the Genesis story was Moses himself, and yet Moses has already been linked to the pharaoh Akhenaton and the Amarna regime by a steady trickle of authors, including myself. Furthermore, since Josephus mentions in his introduction to his version of Genesis that Moses sometimes spoke wisely, enigmatically and allegorically and at other times in plain words, the clear inference is that the Genesis story up to the seventh day of creation was pure allegory, and that is exactly what I believe it was. The Biblical seven days of creation were actually a heavily disguised rendition of the Hymn to the Aton, an allegorical description of the movements of the astronomical bodies and their effects on the Earth. Beyond that section, where Moses begins to speak philosophically, we begin to enter the more rational historical story – the story of Akhenaton's Amarna and its people.

The continuation of the Genesis story in chapter two now begins to describe the location and setting within which the seven days of creation story was being narrated. Now if this story really was the Hymn to the Aton from Amarna, then it is likely that we should begin to uncover not only an Egyptian setting, but perhaps also a peculiarly Hyksos or Amarna location. The traditional translation of these particular verses say:

Tree of knowledge

> 2:8 And the Lord# God# planted a garden# eastward# in Eden#; and there he put the man# whom he had formed#.
> 2:9 And out of the ground# made the Lord# God# to grow every tree that is pleasant to the sight, and good for food#; the tree# of life# also in the midst of the garden#, and the tree of knowledge of good and evil.

> 2:8 And Ra-Horus planted an enclosed grove in the eastern part of Eden; and there he put the man whom the potter had made.
> 2:9 And out of the red lands (Lower Egypt) Ra-Horus made to grow every tree that is pleasant to the sight, and good for food; the backbone (djed pillar or river Nile) of life also in the midst of the garden, and the tree of knowledge of good and evil.

Note how the garden is being described as being <u>in</u> Eden, rather than being Eden itself. This is an important point, as it may imply that the garden was a smaller entity within the greater area known as Eden. It is likely that the term being used for the 'garden', which was *gan* גַן, was based upon the Egyptian word *kan* 𓈎𓈖𓈗𓊪, meaning 'garden' or 'vineyard' and which was itself derived from *kam* 𓈎𓈖𓈖𓏏𓏤, which also means 'garden'. So is this consonant change, from a 'g' to a 'k', a reasonable alteration, or am I guilty of manipulating the spellings to make things fit? Well, I think that this alteration is fully justified, and I say this with some confidence because the word *gamel* גמל, meaning 'camel', has almost the same spelling and yet this word was derived from the Egyptian *kamal* 𓂝𓈖𓃀𓈖𓏏𓅱 . This demonstrates that the Hebrew 'g' and the Egyptian 'k' were sometimes equivalents. For further confirmation of this equivalence, see also the translation for the word 'complete' in the dictionary in Appendix 4.

The Garden of Eden was said to be located 'eastward' in Eden, and this can be confirmed even in the original Egyptian because the Hebrew word for 'east', *qedem* קדם, was directly translated from *qedjem* 𓂝𓈖𓈖𓈖 , meaning 'land of the east'. But how far to the east? As I have already indicated several times, I don't think that we need to travel to the Euphrates and the Tigris to discover Eden, as the biblical text seems to be fully compatible with both the Egyptian language and mythology. What we are actually looking for here is a garden, or large fertile area of land, that was watered by four rivers. This phrase invariably has researchers off on a grand tour of the Middle East looking for four rivers that lie in close proximity, which is a pretty futile quest. But if the truth were known, there *are* four rivers that match this exact description, and they lie a great deal closer to Egypt than those of the Euphrates and Tigris.

Fig 2.1 The arboreal garden and sacred pool was a key element in Egyptian garden design.

II Garden of Eden

Delta

The location and the extent of the land of Eden was defined in the Bible by the four great rivers that ran through the area. David Rohl has identified these rivers as those that flow out from the catchment area around Lake Urmia near the Caspian Sea, and these include the tributaries that eventually form the Tigris and Euphrates. However, although this region is reasonably fertile and does grow many kinds of vegetation, it is difficult to say that it is close to four <u>great</u> rivers. While the rivers associated with this region do eventually become great, they are not much more than a collection of small streams at their source.

In trying to decipher the enduring mystery of the location of the biblical Eden, what we are really looking for are four <u>great</u> rivers that flow in close proximity to each other, and that is a near impossible request. Great rivers do not flow parallel to each other without joining up into one even larger river, and so this kind of topography simply does not exist – except, perhaps, in the great delta lands of the world, including the example to be found in Egypt. It is entirely possible that the rivers of Eden were not rivers, as such, and neither were they tributaries; instead, they may have been branches. As a possible confirmation of this suggestion, the Bible does not talk about four rivers, but one river and four 'heads':

> 2:10 And a river# went out of Eden# to water# the garden#; and from thence it was parted#, and became into four heads#.

> 2:10 And a river went out of Eden to irrigate the garden; and from there it was flowed out, and became four heads (branches).

The Nile is the greatest of rivers in this region, but where it hits the Delta lands it slows its pace and branches off into two great rivers, the Rosetta and the Damietta branches. But in antiquity there was at least two extra branches that have now largely silted up, and these were the eastern Pelusiac branch which served Avaris and the western Canopic branch that terminated near modern Alexandria, making four branches in all.

In fact, this continued reduction in the number of branches can also give us a rough estimate for the date of the Genesis story. It is known that during the Old Kingdom there were up to six Nile branches within the Delta, and these included (from east to west) the Pelusiac, Saitic, Mendesian, Sebennytic, Rosetta and Canopic. These six branches had been reduced to four by the New Kingdom era, and then the Pelusiac branch silted up just after the reign of Ramesses II. Thus the biblical account of there being four branches on the Nile conforms to a New Kingdom era prior to Ramesses II, an era which comfortably straddles the Amarna episode.

Look at Genesis 2:10 again. This is exactly what the text is trying to explain – there was a river (the Nile) that runs through a garden (the fertile banks of Middle Egypt) and then parts into four branches (from east to west the Pelusiac, Damietta, Rosetta, and Canopic branches in the Delta). It is also significant that the Hebrew term for 'head' is *rosh* ראש meaning 'head' or 'top', which was taken from the Egyptian *roshau* 𓂋𓄿𓄓𓏤𓇋𓇋𓆓 which has exactly the same meanings. Now this word would suggest that the four branches lie at the extremity (the top) of the river, and in the guise of the Nile Delta branches, this is exactly what they do. This argument is further reinforced by the accounts of Josephus, who was using an older version of the Torah than the version currently in use, and who mentioned that:

> Now the garden was watered by one river, which ran around the entire Earth, and was parted into four parts.[13]

Again we can see a succinct and accurate description of the river Nile, one long river – and the Nile is, of course, the longest river in the world – that eventually splits into four branches. Facts need to be faced. Once more, we are plainly dealing with an Egyptian story and therefore a description of Egypt, and so if we are to decipher the true meaning of Genesis' Garden of Eden, we should once more look towards Egypt and its language.

In the biblical texts, the term being used for 'river' *nahar* נהר was taken from the word *nekhir* 𓈖𓐍𓂋 , meaning 'river'; which also has connotations of *nekhat* 𓈖𓐍𓄿𓏏 , meaning large breasts. The text then says that the river watered (*shaqah* שקה) the garden, and this was taken from *Sekh-t* 𓋴𓐍𓏏𓏤 , a word which means 'water meadow' and often implied the Nile Delta region. The breast connotations bring us back, once more, to the mythical source of the Nile, which was supposed to flow from between the Twin Peaks that Herodotus called Crophi and Mophi. But, as was discussed at length in the book *Tempest*, the Twin Peaks, which were euphemistically referred to as breasts, were actually coded references to the two largest pyramids at Giza. The reason for the breast euphemism is twofold. Firstly the pyramids are indeed very breast-like in their appearance. Secondly, the Nile was symbolically said to gush from between these two 'breasts', and then the Nile nourished the land of Egypt in the same way that a pair of breasts nourished a newborn child. This reasoning explains why, in the Hymn to the Aton, the Sun-god nurtures and cares for each element in his creation as a mother would her child. The Aton (Aten), having become a single entity, was forced to become both mother and father to the nation and world, as we shall see shortly.

The description in verse 2:10 therefore conforms to standard Egyptian theology, but only if the term Eden also refers in some way to Giza. One further piece of evidence in favour of this suggestion is the term *eden* אֶדֶן, which in this alternative pronunciation refers to a pedestal that holds up a pillar or even a pedestal that holds up the Earth. The allusion here is again similar to the arguments I aired in *Tempest*, where I suggested that the four main pyramids at Giza and Dahshur represented the four pillars that held the Egyptian heavens aloft. If Eden was supposed to be the pedestal upon which the pillars (pyramids) rested, then Eden sounds like a good description of the sharply elevated Western and Giza plateau, upon which the pyramids still stand. Since Giza was the prime ritual site in Egypt, with the pyramids representing the two great gnomons that tracked the annual path of the Aton through the daytime sky, it was the Giza site that was regarded as the regulator of the Nile floods.

Having made these various assertions, it has to be reiterated that the description in verse 2:10 is very clear. The river went out of Eden (Giza) and from thence it was parted into four heads (branches), and a better description of the beginning of the Nile Delta would be hard to find. In the Egyptian translation, the river did not 'part' as such, for the word here is *parad* פָּרַד, which was taken from *perat* 🔲𓆑 , referring to a river 'flowing out', which is a good description of the beginning of the Delta.

Within this larger area known as Eden, there was probably also a smaller garden, as the term being used for garden here can imply a walled enclosure. If the suspicion is that Eden was Egypt, then where in Egypt might one find a walled garden? There are two possible answers to this question and both of these utilise some of the explanations that have already been given in the previous chapter – with the suggestion of there being a symbolic red colour, and that colour's direct association with both the Red Crown of the Lower Egyptian monarchy and the Hyksos people in general.

This gives us two possible locations to look at in greater detail, and the first of these lies in the Delta. Excavations have been conducted at a location near modern Zagazig in the Nile Delta since 1966, and one of the prime discoveries that was made at this site was of a large enclosed garden, or more specifically an enclosed orchard or grove.

> The site commanded the river ... (and) was fortified with a buttressed wall (originally 6.2 m wide at the base, later enlarged to nearly 8.5 m), which enclosed a garden of trees ... We have evidence of two strata of gardens in the form of a series of tree pits, set in a regular grid system of 5.5 cubits. The system runs parallel to the buttressed enclosure wall.[4]

Manfred Bietak presumed that there must have been a palace within such a massive fortification wall, as nobody would build such a fortress just to contain an orchard – or would they? Actually, they might go to all this trouble and expense if this orchard were somehow central to the nation's religious beliefs, just as the Upper Egyptians built massive mud-brick walls around their many temples.

Sacred grove

So who did this massive defensive wall and enclosed orchard belong to? The answer to this question adds weight to the suggestions that these biblical accounts were describing events and rituals from the Delta lands, because this orchard or grove has been positively identified from the site stratigraphy as being from the Hyksos period, and the location of this grove lies within the boundaries of the ancient Hyksos capital of Avaris. Apart from the associations that have already been made between the biblical 'redness' and the Hyksos people, in the book *Jesus* I have also linked the Hyksos exodus from Avaris with the first biblical exodus from Pi-Ramesse. Of the many similarities between these two events, perhaps the most compelling link is that Pi-Ramesse and Avaris are the same city: the one was built upon the other.

In which case, we now seem to have a biblical story about the Hyksos nation who were eventually expelled from Egypt to Jerusalem [or Tanis] after a battle with the Upper Egyptian pharaoh Ahmose I, and yet this same story also includes a pointed reference to a special garden – the Garden in Eden. This garden was said to have been located towards the eastern side of Eden, and if this garden was anything to do with the one discovered at Avaris, and if Eden does refer in some manner to the Nile Delta, then it is worth noting that Avaris is indeed in the eastern side of the Delta.

In the parallel historical record of the Hyksos people, we now see that this nation did indeed possess sacred gardens, and this particular orchard was so important to these people that they surrounded it with a massive fortified wall. This massive wall was later extended and the site made even more secure, and it seems likely that this was in response to threats that had been issued by the Theban pharaoh Kamose, the elder brother of the victorious pharaoh Ahmose I who finally threw the Hyksos out of Egypt. Kamose wrote to the Hyksos people saying:

> The vile Asiatic ... I shall drink of your vineyard, which the Asiatics whom I captured press for me. I will lay waste your dwelling place, I will cut down your trees. [5]

This demonstrates the importance of this fortified orchard and these trees.

The enemy pharaoh Kamose was not interested in rape or pillage, nor even the mutilation of the Hyksos soldiers; no, of all the despicable acts that Kamose wished to inflict upon his northern enemy, the most heinous was to 'cut down his trees'. Clearly, these were very special trees to the Hyksos; sacred trees that formed a sacred grove.

Fig 2.2   Enclosure and tree pits for the Hyksos sacred grove at Avaris.

But if such a place was so sacred, and if the biblical story arose from the Hyksos people and these events, then why are sacred groves not a central part of biblical mythology? Well, if it were not for the inventive Judaic scribes who have done their best to cover up many of the more 'pagan' or embarrassing Judaic rituals, the sacred grove would have been very much a central tenet of Judaism. The books of Exodus and Deuteronomy state that:

> But you shall destroy their altars, break their images, and cut down their groves:

> But thus shall you deal with them; ye shall destroy their altars, and break down their images, and cut down their groves, and burn their graven images with fire.

And you shall overthrow their altars, and break their pillars, and burn their groves with fire; and you shall hew down the graven images of their gods, and destroy the names of them out of that place.

You shalt not plant a grove of any trees near unto the altar of the lord your god, which you shalt make. [B6]

Quite obviously, sacred groves were originally a central part of Judaic life, but the new priestly regime were doing their level best to expunge this 'heresy' from their new form of Judaism. Thus it is recorded that Gideon, Maakhah, Ahab, Jeroboam, Ahaz, Manasseh and Hilkiah were all chastised for making sacred groves. The fact that so many of the kings and priests of Judaea and Israel were making sacred groves demonstrates that they were once a central part of Judaic theology, and the final proof of this assertion is to be found in the account that says that Abraham, the father of the Israelite nation, also planted a sacred grove. But, perhaps, because he was such an important figure within Judaism, the scribes chose not to find fault with his actions:

And Abraham planted a grove in Beersheba, and called there on the name of the lord, the everlasting god. [B7]

But what exactly was this 'sacred grove' and what rituals were performed within it? From the little evidence that is available, it is possible that there were two types of grove. The first of these was a proper walled orchard that resembled a kitchen garden from an English country house. The trees in this type of orchard were decked with cloth hangings, and so the scene would have been quite decorative. A reference from the book of Kings gives a description of this type of grove:

And he broke down the houses of the Sodomites, that were by the house of the lord, where the women wove hangings for the grove. [B8]

It would appear that this type of ritual is still practised in parts of Ethiopia, and the author Graham Hancock gives a good, first-hand description of this kind of event in his book *Sign and the Seal*. But what kind of trees were these, and where did such a ritual originate? As with most things in the Bible, the answer is to be found in Egypt where rather similar sacred trees and groves are to be found. The Hebrew word being translated as 'grove' is *asherah* אשרה, and this just has to have been derived from the Egyptian *aser* or *ashej* which both refer to sacred trees. The exact type of tree that was grown in these groves is not precisely known, and Sir Flinders Petrie suggests either the tamarisk or the sycamore fig (not to be confused with the North American sycamore). This interpretation may be supported by depictions like the one to be found at the ancient Jewish cemetery at Lido near Venice, which shows a succulent plant not unlike a fig. This particular image was supposed to be a representation of the Judaic 'Tree of Life' and it shows how tenacious these beliefs were, despite the disapproval of the Judaic hierarchy.

On the other hand, the Egyptian *ash* ⚒〇 apparently refers to the cedar, which would at least be a suitably valuable piece of timber to grow. The cedar is also known to have been used in the construction of the sacred solar barques of Ra, and so its wood may therefore have been regarded as sacred. But since we have descriptions of cedar for such boats being purchased in Lebanon, it is unlikely that the Egyptians went to the bother of making huge fortified groves in which this timber could be grown.

Although these may be sensible explanations, the layout of the garden at Avaris would tend to make all these options unlikely. The tree pits at Avaris are 1.5 meters in diameter, and although such a dimension does suggest a substantial tree rather than a shrub, the pits are also situated in close proximity to each other. The pit centers are only 5.5 cubits* or a shade under 3 meters apart, with the space between the pits being only 2.75 cubits or under 1.5 m wide.

This pattern of closely spaced holes would suggest that a tall, thin tree was grown in this orchard, and I would suggest that it may have been something like the *Cypress Sempervirens*, which is still grown today in cemeteries all across the Mediterranean. These are tall, thin trees that could have easily been grown together in closely spaced ranks, and since they are slightly pyramidal in shape they may also have reflected an image of the Hyksos' primary religious site at Giza.

However, an interesting alternative to this might be the *Taxus Baccata*, or European yew tree. While the yew is not traditionally known for being tall and slender, the *Fastigiata* variety is exactly this, and it closely mimics the tall, slender form of the *Cypress*. This particular variety also has an interesting history, as every specimen now living is ultimately descended from two trees that were discovered in 1780 in Co Fermanagh, Ireland. The Egyptian links with Ireland have already been made in the book *Jesus* and will be reinforced in the book *Scota*, and since the more traditional species of yew are native to Africa and Egypt, it is entirely possible that these two lonely specimens originated in more southerly regions and were deliberately brought to Ireland many centuries ago.

The yew tree is also interesting in the context of a sacred grove, as

* In the book *K2*, I argue strongly for a unit of length measuring 5.5 cubits, and here appears to be yet more evidence pointing towards this being a known unit of measure.

it has long been a sacred tree to 'Pagan' Ireland and Britain. The frequency of its presence in the former of these countries is attested to by the common Irish name 'Mayo', which means 'yew forest', and so County Mayo on the west coast of Ireland must have once been covered in yew trees. The yew was also said to have been the sacred tree of queen Banbha, the last great warrior queen of the Tuath de Danaan, the mythical progenitors of the Irish people.

Likewise, the yew was also considered to be sacred in Britain, where it still grows in nearly every churchyard in the country to this day. It has been claimed that the reason for the yew's prominent position in Christian graveyards is that it is a poisonous tree, with the potency of the yew being explicit in its name – *Taxus*, from which we derive the word 'toxic'. Yet the yew was still a very useful resource, as its timber is eminently suitable for the making of longbows. Since graveyards were traditionally one of the few areas that have always been fully enclosed, even during Medieval times, it has been suggested that the trees were grown in churchyards to prevent the trees poisoning the local free-roaming herds. While there may be an element of truth in this, I rather think that the yew's position in churchyards was more influenced by early Irish history, where the yew was claimed to represent eternal life. Such a symbol would have been perfect for a graveyard, especially during eras when people believed that the soul could live for eternity. It hardly needs emphasising that this kind of symbolism, together with these trees' strategic position in walled Christian graveyards, places the yew in exactly the same type of context that I have already suggested for the Avaris sacred groves. But what was it about the yew tree that made it so special?

It is entirely possible that the yew was considered sacred, associated with eternal life, and positioned in graveyards to represent the everlasting souls of the deceased, simply because it is so incredibly long-lived. The reason for this longevity is that new sections of trunk spring up alongside the old, and so the entire tree constantly regrows and renews itself. The Tandridge yew in Surrey, for instance, grows some 8 meters away from the Saxon church there; yet the original architects of this Saxon church built a small vault over the tree's spreading roots, so that they would not be disturbed. The distance of the tree from the church demonstrates that the tree was already quite mature when the church was built, more than a thousand years ago, which is why some of the larger specimens of yew are considered to be up to 3,000 years old. Indeed, the claim for the oldest living thing in Europe goes to the Fortingall yew, which is situated in the churchyard of the village of Fortingall, Perthshire. This tree once measured 16m around its trunk, and has been estimated to be between three and five thousand years old. There is also an element of longevity in the wood itself, which can be fashioned and highly polished, and yet resists decay and lasts for millennia. If a high priest of Egypt or Great Britain were looking for a tall, slim tree to represent the everlasting soul and the longevity of the Church itself, they would be hard-pressed to find anything more appropriate than the *Fastigiata* yew.

So, was the yew tree available in ancient Egypt, and was it associated with the afterlife in any way? Such evidence is hard to find in the literature, as it is often impossible to trace which type of tree was being referred to; but of the artifacts discovered over the years, the majority of yew examples occur in the sixth to twelfth dynasties. However, there is at least one small piece of evidence that comes from the eighteenth dynasty, and that is a wooden head of Queen Tiy, the wife of Amenhotep III, which was discovered at Amarna.

Some enterprising individuals from the politically-correct sector have argued that this bust demonstrates that Tiy was Negroid, because the head is black and shows a few vague Negroid features. But such arguments are merely a sad reflection of our culturally correct times; the true fact of the matter is that in Egypt the colour black more often than not implied death, and the unusual features on the bust show that Tiy was quite old at the time of its manufacture. What we probably have here, therefore, is a death-mask; and in wishing to portray the late Queen Tiy in the traditional dark colour of the dead, the sculptor chose the dark wood of a yew tree. Considering this tree's association with eternal life, such a choice would have been eminently sensible for the recently deceased, and it demonstrates a possibility that this association between the yew and eternal life was an Egyptian as well as an Irish tradition.

Maypole

As with many languages, it is quite noticeable that in the Egyptian language, words of the same pronunciation tend to be associated with the same events. As a simple example, in English a book is a collection of pages, but the noun has also become a verb because this same 'collection of pages' is used to take down your details when purchasing a ticket. Thus, when comparing languages, it is often profitable to look at some of the associated words or homophones, to see what kind of context we are dealing with. So, in regard to the sacred *aser* tree, what can this technique provide?

In this particular example we can find *ash*, to 'cry out' or 'lament'; *ash*, a 'multitude' or 'crowd'; *asher*, a 'fire'; *asher*, to 'roast meat'; or even *Asar* (Osiris), the god of the dead. I think that the general thrust of these similar-sounding words is giving a picture of a religious festival, perhaps associated with death, and so it may well be that if these sacred groves were planted with the *aser* tree, then they may well have formed a central component in some kind of national cemetery or a monument to the dead. Note here how the pronunciation of the name for Osiris, Asar, and the name for a sacred tree, *asar*, are nearly identical. This is probably the result of Osiris being associated so closely with vegetation, and the veneration of Osiris as a god of the dead has similarly endowed these sacred trees with connotations of death. This link between Osiris and trees has lasted to this day, with his depiction in Christian churches as the pagan Green Man.

The connection between trees and death has also endured the millennia and, even today, in locations as diverse as Jerusalem and Perth in Australia, trees have been planted to mark the graves or lives of each soldier and hero of the two recent World Wars. Thus the threat by Pharaoh Kamose to cut down the Hyksos' trees may well have been a threat to cut down a monument to the nation's war heroes – to sever the glorious dead's arboreal souls – and this would indeed have been a despicable act.

In much later Judaic traditions, however, it is apparent that the sacred grove has changed in character. No longer was there a real grove of trees; instead, the trunk of a stout tree was brought into the local town, to be decked out in various items of finery and used in the local rituals. This vestigial form of the sacred grove may have been a reaction to the harsher climate of Judaea, which was not always conducive to the growing of verdant enclosed groves. A tree trunk, on the other hand, could be reused annually for decades. A very good description of this new form of 'tree' veneration is to be found in the book of Jeremiah:

> For the customs of the people are vain: for one cutteth a tree out of the forest, the work of the hands of the workman, with the axe. They deck it with silver and with gold; they fasten it with nails and with hammers, that it move not. They are upright as the palm tree, but speak not ... Silver spread into plates is brought from Tarshish, and gold from Uphaz, the work of the workman, and of the hands of the founder: blue and purple is their clothing: they are all the work of cunning men. [B9]

This 'abomination' that Jeremiah was describing was a simple vertical tree trunk, with gold and silver decorations and cloths of blue and purple. I have no doubt that these brightly coloured cloths were formed into long ribbons, which were held by the town's children and were woven into pretty patterns around the tree trunk as the children danced around the pole. Quite obviously, Jeremiah is describing a traditional 'English' maypole here. At the tender age of seven I was the leader of the school maypole dance, together with a young girl called Sarah. By skillfully ducking and weaving around the other ribbons held by the other children in the circle, we danced around the maypole and plaited the entire top of the pole in a web of vibrant colours. Different dances resulted in different patterns, and so the show could go on and on. I thoroughly enjoyed the whole performance, which was attended by all the parents, and it is a shame that this tradition is no longer maintained in this politically-correct world. Who really cares if the pole is a 'pagan' phallic symbol? After all, sex and procreation are the way of the world, and the children themselves had no idea of the underlying symbolism.

It would seem that the people of Judaea during Jeremiah's era were living in the same kind of politically-correct, or at least religiously intolerant world as ourselves. The ancient traditions of the region were being changed, and those who still clung to their ancient ways and rituals were suffering a degree of religious persecution. The Torah makes it obvious that the sacred groves were no longer acceptable to the priesthood. Any sacred grove in the region was going to be a sitting target for the iconoclasts and, as the previous biblical quotes indicate, the groves were being cut down and the graven images were being burned. A maypole, on the other hand, was both transient and mobile, and so we have another compelling reason for the switch from sacred groves to maypoles. While the maypole certainly came out at the appropriate festival, perhaps it pretended to support a roof for the rest of the year. The temple clergy would have to be fleet-footed to catch the local population in the act, or positively identify an offending pole.

Eden

Now we arrive at a central component of this entire Genesis mystery, the true location of Eden. Did it reside in the Nile Delta, or might there be a subtle twist to this story?

The first thing to note is that the words Eden עדן and Adam אדם may have been linked, and they were originally conjoined through their meanings of 'plenty' and 'redness' respectively. The meaning of 'plenty' has been arrived at because the name 'Eden' was probably derived from the name of the Sun-god Aten (Aton) �always depicted in Amarna rituals as being surrounded by vast offering tables laden with every fruit, grain and meat that could possibly be imagined, and so the link between the Sun-god Aton (Adjon - Adon) and 'plenty' was quite natural. Life at Amarna, according to the ancient media experts, appears to have been one long Harvest Festival. The Aton was depicted as being truly bountiful to the people of Amarna, even if this was only true in the propaganda illustrations of the monarchy's artists.

In like manner, the redness that is associated with the name Adam was also due to the Aton, who demonstrated a distinct redness as he dawned over the eastern horizon. So how, in this case, has there been such a change in pronunciation from Adam to Eden, if both words mean the same thing and were both based upon the Aten (Aton)? The solution to this conundrum is that these two words do not quite refer to the same event or god; they are, in fact, two diametrically opposed aspects of the same symbolism.

The origin of the name for the Aton (Aten) was probably the much earlier name for the god of the evening and morning Sun, who was called Atem. But this is not the usual pronunciation of this name, as this god was previously known as Tem. But I believe that at some point in the past, there were actually two aspects to the name of this god, Tem and Ten, and their meanings were as follows:

Name	Tem	Ten
meaning	To finish	To rise
implying	sunset	sunrise
Which became	**Atem (Adjem)**	**Aten (Adjen)**
meaning	red, sunset	sun, horizon
Hebrew name	Adam (Edam)	Eden (Aden)
meaning	red, man	plentiful

This is why the Hymn to the Aton (Adon) was primarily a hymn to the sunrise, rather than the sunset. I have a feeling that the original celebration was of Tem, the setting Sun, and I imagine that a great celebration of this diurnal event would be held at both Heliopolis and Giza, with a multitude of priests and officials partaking in incantations and prayers as the Sun set behind the pyramids. No doubt the ceremony ended with a ritual roasting of beef, duck and fish, which appeased the gods and coincidentally sated the appetites of the priests – especially if they had been keeping to a Ramadan-style fast. The Theban priesthood of the New Kingdom concentrated their ritual on this evening ceremony of the Sun setting in the west, and since the Egyptian for 'west' is amen-t their prime deity became known as Amen . Since the god Amen was only an aspect of the setting Sun, it naturally became infused with solar connotations and eventually merged with the Sun-god Ra to become Amen-Ra.

Once more we can get a feel for what went on during these evening ceremonies by simply looking at the similar words, or phonemes, to Amen. These include words that mean 'burn', 'blaze', 'light rays', 'boat', 'cry out', 'exclaim', 'worship' and 'hidden'. From this scattering of words it is not difficult to imagine a scene consisting of an assembled crowd lamenting the last rays of the dying Sun as it coursed across the sky in its solar boat and eventually concealed itself over the horizon, in the Djuat or the spiritual underworld. But although this was a ritual celebration of the end of a day, this ceremony was still, in essence, all about death and dying; which is why the word *ament-t* not only means 'west' but also the 'Land of the Dead'.

This concentration on the negative aspects of god's creation obviously did not impress the revolutionary pharaoh Akhenaton, who wanted something more uplifting for his creed. His salvation would come in the form of another, smaller celebration that marked the sunrise; and so Pharaoh Akhenaton chose to concentrate his belief system on this event because it celebrated new life, rather than the dying Sun. Thus the Great Hymn to the Aton subtly changed the traditional worship, and this was one of Akhenaton's major breaks with the Theban traditions of the New Kingdom. This is why the Hymn to the Aton deliberately contrasts the lament towards the dying Sun of the evening (Atem, Adem) with the joy at the Sun's rebirth the next morning (Aten, Aden): concentrating the bulk of its text on the latter aspects of the Sun's diurnal cycle. Akhenaton's ritual was all about hope for a joyous new day, and hope for a fruitful future, and no doubt this was part of the attraction for this new creed.

It is worth noting that Akhenaton was not the eventual winner in this theological trial of strength, as both he and his creed were to be ejected from Egypt within a few short years. It was the victorious Amenites from Thebes who would now write the history of this era and they took the opportunity to denigrate each and every facet of the former Amarna regime – from the bricks of the city to the artwork of its scribes and the meaning of their faith, each and every component of the regime was to be systematically dismantled and destroyed. So how does one achieve this aim with something as tenuous as a faith? The answer is to twist the meaning of the old liturgy into forms of abuse or ridicule and teach this to the next generation as a matter of normality and fact, without ever mentioning the previous regime. The detail of this verbal destruction of the Amarna regime is interesting, as we still use the same terminology today.

The Aton god of Akhenaton was primarily focused upon the rising Sun, and so its veneration was closely allied to the eastern horizon. But the Egyptian term for east was also identified with the notion of 'left', and so the word *aabti* ⌾ for 'east' was the same as *aabti* ⌾ meaning 'left side'. Conversely, the Theban Amen deity was firmly identified with the setting Sun and the west, and so the word for 'west' was *amen-t* ⌾ and the word for 'right' was also *amen-t* ⌾ . This is how the name for the god called Amen was derived: it simply described the evening ritual of the Sun setting in the west. But since the victorious Theban veneration of Amen oppressed the defeated Atonites of Akhenaton and suppressed their religion, it would seem that the latter faction kept their traditions alive by forming the later word *ab* ⌾ meaning 'wisdom' and 'understanding'. No doubt this word was derived from *aabti* ⌾ , and it subtly referred to the 'left side' – the eastern horizon where the Aton resided – and so the wise venerated the east.

Both of these words were later transcribed into the Hebrew language; and thus the word for 'right' in Hebrew became *amen* אמן, which is still exactly the same as the Egyptian *amen*. The term for 'left' is slightly more problematical, as there is no such equivalent word to the Egyptian *aabti* in the Hebrew language. But it is demonstrable that the early Jews did once know of the Egyptian word *aabti* for 'left', and we know this because of a biblical quote from the life of the patriarch Joseph. In the propaganda of the era, the biblical Joseph is said to have risen from the position of slave into the highest rank within the Egyptian civil service; he became the vizier, or prime minister of Egypt, and this is a story that has been fully explained in the books *Tempest* and *Jesus*.

When Joseph was sworn into this high-ranking office, the ceremony that was used must have been very similar to a modern knighthood or a first-degree masonic initiation, where the candidate has to kneel down on their left knee and supplicate themselves before the monarch or worshipful master. When Joseph did this, the command to go down onto the left knee was *abrek!* אברך!, which was derived from the original Egyptian word *aabrek*

𓏺𓂝𓏤𓎡, meaning 'left side' or 'left leg'. This was also taken to be a command, in the Egyptian, and no doubt this command was derived from the military tradition of starting to march by the left leg. The modern sergeant major will command 'by the left, quick march', whereas his Egyptian forebear would have barked '*aabrek, khek mesu*' or ' 𓏺𓂝𓏤𓎡 , 𓂝𓂝 𓀀𓂋𓏤 '. Thus it is axiomatic that the Hebrews did know of the word *aabrek* because it has been used in the correct context in the Book of Genesis, but its true meaning has been lost to modern Hebrew as it is not used anywhere else in the Torah and only the Hebrew from the Torah has survived into the modern era.

The technique used by the Theban Amen supporters, to outlaw the Amarna regime of Akhenaton, was simply to use these words of east and west as templates for right and wrong. Since east and west also referred to the left and right, it was these everyday terms that were subtly altered. These new meanings have somehow survived the millennia and have been transferred to the Latin and thence eventually into the English language; and so the word 'right' can also mean 'correct' and the word 'left' can also mean 'sinister'. So if any youth from Egypt to Europe was to point to the rising Sun in the east (left) and indicate that it was good, the answer would be 'no that is sinister – the right side is correct'. Since those words were ingrained into the psychology of the youth of the nation, it would be obvious to most of the future population that right was right (correct), just as their language indicated.

This notion was also transmitted into the Hebrew and through into first century Jerusalem, and this small snippet of information gives us an interesting clue as to what the Jewish Civil War of AD 67 - 70 was all about. It is beyond doubt, from everything that I have gleaned over the previous three books on this subject and the revelations in this chapter, that the Israelites once worshipped in the original Egyptian fashion and, furthermore, that this religion had a definite Hyksos-Amarna bias. It is also obvious that the original Israelite liturgy was radically altered by later scribes and priests, who considered the overtly idolistic and sexual Egyptian ritual to be unacceptable, and even immoral.

In effect, this was just a logical extension of the reforms that had been initiated by Akhenaton himself. The 'heretic' pharaoh had noted that the veneration of an icon, in this case a living Apis-bull, had corrupted the original Egyptian belief system and the people had begun to venerate the physical bull itself, rather than its cosmological counterpart of Taurus. The short, sharp answer to this problem was the banishing of icons, a policy that had been initiated by Abraham [Pharaoh Mam-Aybre] in the proceeding centuries. But to complete these reforms, Akhenaton also banned the other traditional icons of Osiris, Isis, Thoth and Horus. It was these additional reforms that went a step too far for the Egyptian people and prompted the counter-revolution that led to the downfall of the Amarna regime.

It is likely, however, that a number of Akhenaton's followers believed that his reforms had not gone far enough. Akhenaton had retained the worship of the Sun as a disk, if not a complete deity, and this had the potential to lead down the road to yet more idolatry. Thus a team of later Judaic scribes and priests went through the original texts, ensuring that the god became an indefinable, unimaginable being that had no particular form or physical location. It may also be that these reforms were targeted at renegade elements within the Israelite nation that still preferred the idolatrous worship of the Theban regime. The whole of the Book of Exodus is peppered with references to the people opposing these iconoclastic reforms and making their own idols, including one of the Apis-bull, and so it appears to be clear that not all of the Hyksos-Israelite people supported Akhenaton's or Moses' reforms. These disputes probably included the heated debate between the westerly (right, correct) Amen supporters and the easterly (left, sinister) Aton supporters, with both factions claiming primacy.

But the question remains as to when these reforms actually took place, and when the east (left) became 'sinister' or 'wrong'. I initially surmised that the original Amarna-style worship of the Israelites was lost shortly after the rule of King Solomon. Certainly the Aton or left side (east) was still in favour just before the reign of King David, because the name of a very famous judge and priest was Samuel שׁמוּאל. It is sometimes suggested that Samuel was a composite figure, rather than one individual, and that may well be true, for this is a title rather than a name. It is my belief that the name Samuel was derived from the Egyptian *semur* 𓇌𓃀𓂧 meaning 'left side'. Remember the standard 'e' to 'l' transliteration, which would result in the Egyptian *samur* becoming a Hebrew *samul* שמואל (Samuel).

But the similar word *semur* 𓇌𓏏𓏏𓏏𓏏 was also the title of a very important part of the Egyptian priesthood and nobility, and the fact that these priests presided over the ceremonies that took place on the Giza plateau is implicit in the similar word *mer* 𓇌𓃀𓂧𓉴 meaning 'pyramid'. So, from all the previous discussions aired in this chapter, it is highly likely that these priests presided over the eastern (left) side of the Giza plateau and observed the sunrise. In other words, they venerated Akhenaton's Aton rather than the Theban Amen. Thus it is possible that Samuel, the high priest who crowned Saul as king of Israel, was a Semur priest (Samul priest) who would have officiated at the left-hand (eastern) side of the Giza temple (pyramid) complex, had it been available in his lifetime. However, it is likely that in Samuel's day the Giza site was in the hands of the Theban priesthood, and Samuel was forced to venerate the Aton at a temple in the Delta instead.

As might be expected, this entire explanation for the role of the Semur priesthood can also be translated into the Hebrew, and so we find that the name Samuel was similarly derived from the word *samal* שמאל meaning 'left side'. Since Samuel was a priest, this Hebrew word has exactly the same meanings of 'priest' and 'left side' as does the Egyptian. Indeed, since the word *semur (samul)* also refers to an ornamental garment, it is likely that Joseph was also a Semur priest.

So, if left-sided priests (Aton-venerating priests) were still working up to the eve of the United Monarchy of Israel [in Lower Egypt], then perhaps this demonisation of the left side (the eastern horizon of the Aton) occurred during the Israelite exile in Babylon. The Babylon episode would have been a classic opportunity for a small group of priests to get together and alter the texts, especially as they now blamed all of Egypt for their very public downfall. It was in Babylon that all traces of the Sun-god were excised from the Torah, and it was there that some of the 'westerly' Amen supporters claimed a minor victory by making the Hebrew word *amen* אמן refer not only to the right side, but also to the words 'confirm' and 'verily'. In other words, 'right' (the right side) in the Hebrew means 'correct', just the same as it does in the English. In a similar fashion, the Hebrew for 'left-handed' can also be given as *atter-yagor* אטר יגר, which can be literally translated as 'shut up and be afraid'.

While I still think that this hypothesis is probably true, it is also likely that some small elements of the easterly, left-side Amarna worship remained within Judaism all the way through to the first century reforms of Jesus, and this 'heresy' formed one element of the greater dispute that fomented the

Jewish civil war of AD 67 to 70. The evidence for this is to be found in the New Testament, where the priesthood were goading and mocking Jesus. They said to him:

> The Pharisees also with the Sadducees came, and tempting desired him that he would show them a sign from heaven. He answered and said unto them, When it is evening, ye say, It will be fair weather: for the sky is red. And in the morning, It will be foul weather today: for the sky is red and lowering. O ye hypocrites, ye can discern the face of the sky; but can ye not discern the signs of the times? [B10]

Here, the Pharisees and Sadducee priests were saying that a setting Sun in the evening is good (fair weather), while a rising Sun in the morning is bad (foul weather). While meteorologists have tried to devise a physical logic from this verse – with the red sky of the morning indicating an approaching warm frontal weather system, and the red sky of the evening perhaps representing a passing cold frontal system – this is a rather contrived explanation that is over-dependent on northern European frontal weather systems, instead of the prevailing conditions that are to be found in the Levant.

In truth, this statement by Jesus has nothing to do with the weather; instead it is a commentary on the most important thing in Jerusalem – religion. This comment is actually a continuation of the traditional battles between the Amonite (west) supporters and the Atonist (east) supporters. The Sadducee priests were saying that west is good and east is bad, which positively identifies them as being a continuation of the Theban Amonite supporters. Jesus, on the other hand, was probably an Atonist eastern supporter, and was countering this argument by declaring that these priests were hypocrites who could not 'discern the sign of the times'.

These statements are interesting as they demonstrate that some elements of the New Testament were originally heavily influenced by the Hebrew-Aramaic languages, and later translated into the more familiar Greek by Saul and his supporters. In the first sentence, the text includes the phrase 'sign from heaven'. In the Greek the two nouns appear as *semeion ouranos* ημειον ουρανος, which does not have much of a ring to it. But in the original Hebrew we see that this was actually one of the Bible's traditional rhymes as it was based upon the nouns *shem shameh* שם שמה, which literally means the 'name of heaven', just as it does in the Greek. Perhaps more importantly, it could also be interpreted as *shem shamesh* שמש שמה which preserves the same rhyme but now means 'name of the Sun'.

The Sadducees were not asking Jesus for a commentary on the weather, they were asking him if he could name the Sun-god. In Judaic terms this naming of the deity was not allowed, but in masonic terms Jesus could have said to the priests, 'I will halve it with you': meaning that he will give half the word and they will have to complete it. However, this was not a test of passwords, grips and tokens; this was instead a test as to which side of the theological debate Jesus was really on. Did he support Amen or Aton? Jesus, ever the polished diplomat, sidestepped the question completely by throwing the question back in their faces, as we shall see. But just to let us know which side of the fence some of the New Testament scribes were on, let us remind ourselves that the word *shemol (shemer)* שׂמאל means 'left' (east), and so the *shamesh* (Sun) was on the *shemol* (left).

In order to deflect the Sadducees' question, Jesus' reply contains a counterbalancing rhyme that mimics the first, and so it ends the paragraph very nicely both in tone and meaning, which was and is the primary goal of every scribe and poet. In the Greek, the two nouns appear as *semeion kairos* ημειον καιρος, which again does not exactly please the ear. But in the original Hebrew-Aramaic it would have been based upon the nouns *shem zeman* זמן שׁ, which rhymes nicely with *shem shameh* and literally means the 'sign of times' or 'name of the seasons', just as it does in the Greek. But the inference may not have been simply to the seasons, as in the Egyptian a specific season was implied. The term *shem* ⏦ refers to the summer season, and so the true meaning of the term *zeman*, meaning 'season', may well be yet another allusion to the Sun.

But what did Jesus mean by this cryptic reply? Well, the underlying meaning of this entire paragraph is perhaps contained within the sentence that follows it. This sentence reads:

> A wicked and adulterous generation seeks for a sign; and there shall no sign be given unto it, but the sign of the prophet Jonas. [B11]

So, a sign would be given after all, and it was the sign of Jonah; so what did this mean? Well, the Greek name Jonas Ιωνας has been taken from the Hebrew Jonah (Yonah) יונה, with both of these words meaning 'dove'. Jonah was the unfortunate prophet who was thrown out of a boat to calm the raging seas and was swallowed by a 'whale' (a large fish), only to be spat out onto dry land again three days later. Now that is a baffling tale to appear in the Bible, but it is not quite so silly if one looks at the underlying Egyptian ritual. In the original version of this tale it was the Sun-god Ra that descended into the waters of the abyss and was swallowed by Nut, the goddess of the skies.

How the goddess of the skies managed to swallow something that was descending into the seas is a bit of a mystery, but the dichotomy has probably arisen because the 'underworld' or Djuat, the land of the dead, was closely allied to the 'overworld', the celestial sphere in the skies above. Much of the underworld (Djuat) and its characters were elements contained in the skies above, and the newly deceased individual was promised the immortality of being a star and joining the twinkling firmament above. Since the night sky was the 'underworld' it is likely that the Egyptians knew there were stars underneath them as well as above them; that is, they knew that the Earth was a 'floating' sphere. Since the representations of the earthly and celestial spheres were supposed to have graced the pillars outside the Temple of Solomon [Temple of Sheshonq], this is highly likely, and so the Djuat, the 'underworld', may have been the region of space on the opposite side of the Earth from Egypt.

It has also been suggested that there was a dual symbolism to the goddess Nut. She was not only the vault of the heavens above, but also a representation of the Milky Way: the sinuous cluster of stars that marks the plane of our galaxy and meanders across the sky in a similar fashion to a human figure. The myth of the Sun being swallowed represented the Sun setting at the 'head' of the Milky Way, which in turn is represented by the region around Sagittarius at the winter solstice. Whereas the myth of the Sun being born again was marked by the Sun rising between the legs of the Milky Way, represented by the region around Sirius at the turn of the summer solstice. This fortuitous link with the solstices, however, is only a feature of our modern era. In about 3000 BC, due to the precession of the equinoxes, the swallowing would have occurred at around October and the birth in May. This earlier cycle now represents nearly nine months of the year, and so the links with the oral conception (swallowing) and a later birth of the Sun are doubly reinforced.

Personally, I see no paradox between these two different explanations. Egyptian religion was initiatory, and it is therefore entirely possible that the different levels of the priestly hierarchy were given ever more sophisticated explanations for their religious symbolism. This increasing complexity is rather like the astrological explanation I gave in the book *Jesus*. At the simplest level, astrology is said to be the position of the stars affecting our daily lives: the standard tabloid newspaper form of astrology. Conversely, at the deeper precessional level, astrology is actually about the millennial eras (the precessional constellations) under which each king was born. The Nut explanation is rather similar. At the one level it was a description of the daily cycle of the Sun in the sky, but for those of a higher calling, the same myth could also predict the seasons.

Anyway, having descended into the waters, been eaten by Nut and traversed through her body, Ra was then reborn through her vagina into the dawn of the next day. The Judaic scribes obviously knew this story and wanted to preserve it, but they must have blanched at the thought of writing about a woman eating the Sun with her red lips and then giving birth to it the next morning in the bloody redness of a menstrual vagina, as it all sounded a bit Pagan and perhaps even daft. The solution was to alter Ra's and Nut's identities, but what should they be changed into?

The solution for Nut was to combine her imagery and folklore with the equivalent mythology from the Book of the Dead, where the Sun courses through the Djuat or underworld (instead of through Nut) during the hours of night, encountering all manner of problems and foes. In the seventh hour of the night the Sun encounters the great serpent called Aapop (Apophis) ☐ ☐ *uuu* who tries to swallow the Sun, just as the 'whale' swallowed Jonah. The Tanakh (Old Testament) calls this creature a large fish, while the New Testament calls it a whale or a sea serpent instead. We can clearly see that this is the intended imagery from the Hebrew word that is being used here, which is *dag* דג or *dagon* דגון meaning 'fish', from which the Latin '*draco*' and the English 'dragon' are derived. This was not simply a sea serpent, but a great dragon of the oceans.

This is the creature that, in biblical traditions, is said to have swallowed Jonah. Aapop was the great serpent of the underworld, so it is not surprising that later traditions would eventually confuse him with a sea monster or whale called Dagon (dragon), that lived in the depths of the great oceans.

But what of the role of Ra in this modified biblical story? The answer to this was equally simple: the scribes just used the ubiquitous flying Sun motif, which everyone knew represented Ra, and called it a 'dove' or, in the Hebrew, a Jonah יונה. So the story of Jonah was not a story about a man in a whale at all, it was actually a story of the diurnal circuit of the Sun [Jonah], and its travels through the stomach of the underworld monster, Aapop. The Bible actually says of this event that:

> And the Lord appointed a great fish to swallow up Jonah; and Jonah was in the belly of the fish three days and three nights. Then Jonah prayed to the Lord his God from the belly of the fish ... And the Lord spoke to the fish, and it vomited out Jonah upon the dry land. [B12]

When this is translated back into the original, it becomes:

> And the gods appointed Aapop, the serpent-dragon, to swallow up the Sun; and the Sun was in the belly of the serpent-dragon three days and three nights. Then the Sun prayed to the gods from the belly of Aapop ... And the gods spoke to the serpent-dragon, and he spat out the Sun upon the horizon. [B13]

The word being used for 'vomit' was *qoa* קוא and this has been taken from the Egyptian *qaa* meaning 'vomit'. But since this same term can also mean 'high', 'mountain' or 'horizon', we can perhaps deduce that the vomiting can also refer to the rising of the Sun over the distant hills (or pyramids) on the horizon. Apart from the length of time being increased to three days, the biblical story of Jonah can be clearly seen to have once represented the travels of the Sun through the body of Aapop (through the Djuat or underworld), and rising again behind the hills of the eastern horizon. Once more we see that the more peculiar aspects of the biblical story were originally based upon Egyptian mythology and have been rather comprehensively and clumsily altered so that they no longer show any solar or Egyptian influences.

It was for this reason that the dove motif became so central to the Christian religion, which perhaps demonstrates that someone still knew the true imagery of these stories and promoted their most favorite solar icon. Everywhere one looks in Christian iconography there is the image of a dove, which is supposed to represent the concept of 'peace', but in reality it is just another symbol for the winged Sun-disk of the Sun-god Ra. Its presence in nearly every New Testament image must have brought a wry smile to the deeper initiations within the Catholic Church.

Coming back once more to the verse about the weather previously quoted, I think that the Hebrew word *jonah (younah)* יונה may well have been derived from the word *uenemi* 𓏏𓃀𓏤 , meaning 'right side' or 'west'. This word not only implied the setting of the Sun, it was also a direct reference to the Sun, and while this explanation may not look entirely convincing at this stage, there will be evidence in a later chapter that positively confirms this association. Interestingly, the Egyptian word *unemi* can also be pronounced as *qaqami*, and so in the original script this would have produced a very good rhyme with the term being used for 'vomit'.

If the sign of Jonah, the dove, was nothing less than the winged Sun-disk of Ra, as I suspect, then the true meaning of the New Testament paragraph about the weather we have been discussing was most certainly designed to compare the relative merits of Amen, who set in the west, and Aton, who rose in the east. The original passage must have read something like:

> The Pharisees also with the Sadducees came, and teased (Jesus) that he would tell them <u>the name of the Sun</u>. He answered them and said, 'When it is evening and the sky is red you say **Amen**-Ra is good. And in the morning when the sky is red you say that **Aton**-Ra is bad'. O you hypocrites, you can observe the appearance of the Sun, but you cannot see <u>the name of the summer season</u> (the Sun). A wicked and adulterous generation seeketh after a name; yet there shall be no name given to it, but <u>the sign of the winged Sun-disk</u> (the dove).

In other words, Jesus understood the distinction between Amen and Aton and also understood the conflict that these terms generated. His answer to this was worthy of any politician – if the names generated discord, then the names should be banned. Thus the Judaic principle of not uttering the name of god was being reinforced by Jesus, and the names <u>Amen</u> and <u>Aton</u> were not to be mentioned as they promoted civil unrest. The only allowable exception to this was to be an oblique and covert reference to the image of the flying Sun-disk – the dove (Jonah).

Crusaders

This New Testament conflict is rather interesting, as it would appear that significant elements within the Judaic priesthood were sufficiently acquainted with the old religion to be debating the merits of Amen versus Aton, and wondering which name to use. This would suggest that despite the outer appearance of Judaism at this time as being a fully monotheistic religion, the inner workings of the priesthood were still remarkably Egyptian and the various factions were still at odds with each other. Thus it is possible that the upper echelons of the Jewish religion had become so divorced from the perceptions and beliefs of the common people, that it was as if they were involved in two entirely different religions. Now if this was the case, then this would have been a highly unstable situation that was just begging for a revolution, and it came in AD 67 at the outbreak of the Jewish Civil War.

Furthermore, it can be speculated that the two enforced exiles of the people from Jerusalem produced the new Judaic religion as we know it. In the first instance, the hierarchy from Jerusalem were all taken to Babylon in about 587 BC, leaving the proletariat in Judaea to create and promote their own version of Judaism. But the priesthood in Babylon were still faithful to their old Egyptian belief system and when they returned to Judaea two generations later, they created a two-tier religion with two entirely different outlooks and beliefs. This dichotomy festered and perpetuated itself into the first century AD, when the divide between the two factions had become so pronounced that it could no longer be plastered over, and so Judaea erupted into anarchy. This turmoil precipitated the fall of Jerusalem to the Romans in AD 70 and this produced a second opportunity for Judaism to evolve. Since the Judaean hierarchy were once more either killed or transported away to far-flung locations in the Roman Empire, it was again to be the religion of the common people that remained in Israel and developed into the religion that we observe today. However, the religion of the aristocracy and priesthood also had the means to escape Judaea, either before the final tragedy or after their eventual release from bondage, and it was from the former of these routes that the traditions of Mary sailing to France were derived. There, in Europe, the old religion from Judaea would have mingled with the established refugees from Egypt's previous exoduses, and the resulting flux of ideas and traditions became the foundations of modern Masonry.

The Egyptian religion had now permanently migrated from Egypto-Judaea and had sunk its roots firmly into European culture. But it was forced to keep its belief system secret because of continuing Roman opposition and also because of the new Christo-Judaic influences that were invading Europe at the time. Despite the freedom of being in new lands, it was the all-pervasive and aggressive nature of Christianity that kept the Egyptian religion from showing its true colours. This explains why the later Crusaders, who were often Masons as much as they were Christians, were not exactly great friends of the Jews. The new Judaism of the Jewish proletariat was indeed a brother faith of these masonic Christians, but they had altered the original Egyptian belief system almost out of all recognition and had precipitated a civil war that had ended in the Judaic hierarchy's exile from Israel, and this was hard to forgive.

However, this lack of forgiveness may well have been the Crusaders' undoing, because they were never able to stabilise the conquered Holy Lands as a new Christian nation. Despite trying to attract Christians into the region from all over Europe, to create a new pro-Christian population, very few Christians were persuaded to live in this rather inhospitable and dangerous region. Saladin was only able to eject the Crusaders from Judaeo-Israel because the local population were supportive to Arab aspirations and were fighting for their 'homeland'; and warriors who are fighting for their home and family are far more motivated even than those fighting for religious ideals. This strategic error was recognised long ago, but it was not until 1917 that it was rectified. Britain had taken Palestine from the Turkish Ottoman Empire during the First World War, but this victory had been in part assisted by Arab fighters under the nominal command of Lawrence of Arabia. But the last thing that the British wanted was another Saladin coming out of the newly unified Arab East and retaking Jerusalem and Judaea in the name of Islam.

What the twentieth century British 'Crusaders' desperately needed was a sympathetic local population who could assist them in keeping this region Western, democratic and friendly. This goal was achieved by the 1917 Balfour Declaration, which semi-officially paved the way for the establishment of a Jewish homeland in Israel, and so the error made by the earlier twelfth century Crusaders was at last reversed and rectified. Indeed, there may have been a political link between these events, as it would appear that the Balfour Declaration was a thank-you present to the Jews in return for their considerable influence in getting the Americans to enter the First World War. Thus Britain and its allies won the war, the Jews got their homeland, and everyone was happy except for a few Palestinians.

Whatever the case, the world had polarised during the centuries since the first crusades of the Middle Ages; Europe had moved on into a modern technical revolution, while the Arab lands of the victorious Saladin had stagnated into a Medieval time-warp. The Jews, who were predominantly settled in Europe, had moved on in step with European aspirations, and many of their hierarchy had also been infiltrated with masonic influences. Thus it was considered desirable within the British administration of the early twentieth century that the Jewish people, who were desperate for a Jewish homeland, could be used as a bulwark in Israel against Arab aspirations in the region.

Thus, some of the promises that had underpinned Lawrence of Arabia's recently successful campaigns in the region were sidelined, and instead a co-operative and fully Westernised Jewish democracy was established in the Holy Land. Jerusalem was firmly in the Crusaders' hands once more, complete with a supportive local population; and best of all, the external maintenance of the state of Israel cost a fraction of the enormous sums of money that would be needed to keep a standing army in the region. Bearing all this in mind, it is of no surprise, therefore, that the former nationalist Jewish Likud Party used to use a masonic eye and pyramid as their logo.

However, as a *quid pro quo*, the Arab states saw the Palestinians in much the same light, and so they have been maintained and financed in much the same manner as a mercenary army for the adjacent Arab states. In fact, the dispute in the region has become so entrenched that the Palestinians seem to serve no other purpose. The entire Palestinian economy and social structures are geared solely towards fanatical terrorism on behalf of their absentee Arab sponsors, and so their entire education system is geared towards fostering a hatred of both the West in general and Israel in particular. This system results in students emerging with a fanatical hatred of their Jewish cousins and, just in case they forgot these lessons in later years, the Palestinian media keeps up the propaganda of hatred; even using violent subliminal clips during television programmes to produce a deep-seated animosity.

The fact that the Jews have been performing such a valuable military role for Western political and theological aspirations for the last sixty or so years also demonstrates how out of step Hitler was with the global politics of this era. Had he been a more sensible and pragmatic individual he could have exiled all the German (Khazar) Jews into Israel, for which he may have even achieved a degree of approval – albeit a highly veiled approval – from the international community for his actions. That he chose to exterminate the Jews instead was a tragic and pointless exercise that brought nothing but condemnation and contempt for his regime, and turned many a potential nationalist supporter against his fledgling empire.

Hitler was also out of step with his condemnation of Masonry. A little publicised fact about the Third Reich is that Hitler actively suppressed Masonry, with the Craft being outlawed in Germany in August 1935. Masonry was seen to be a central component in an international Jewish conspiracy, and it was also a democratic institution while Hitler was becoming decidedly fascist. The same was also true of General Franco's military uprising in Spain in July 1936. Since Franco's policies were similar to German aspirations, it is not surprising that Hitler had supported Franco militarily during the Spanish Civil War; and so as soon as Franco had consolidated his grip on the country, he banned both Freemasonry and Communism in March 1940. ¹⁴

As Hitler's campaign for European domination continued, so did his suppression of Masonry. The Craft was banned in Austria and Czechoslovakia in 1938, in Poland in 1939, in Belgium in 1940 and even in the Island of Jersey in 1941, and there were sporadic deportations and executions in each country. For example, after the fall of France in 1940 all masonic records from that country were taken to Paris, and from these records some 5,000 French Masons were identified and deported to concentration camps. Masons fared little better in Italy, where El Duce, the fascist dictator Mussolini, also rounded up and disposed of hundreds of Masons. This pogrom started in 1926, with the appropriation of the Grand Orient building, the execution of scores of Masons and the deportation of hundreds more to the Lipari Islands. ¹⁵

In one sense this demonstrates how powerless Masonry can be in the face of a determined enemy, but it may also demonstrate how the Craft can rally the troops and use their influence to oppose their enemies. In short, rather than setting out to save Poland, it is entirely possible that Britain went to war with Germany to save Masonry. Informed readers may counter this suggestion by indicating that George, the Duke of Kent, was not only Grand Master of English Freemasonry, but he was also involved with the peace overtures that were delivered to the Duke of Hamilton by the Nazi deputy leader, Rudolph Hess. That may well be so, but those peace overtures towards and from Germany did not necessarily involve Hitler remaining in power. For all his supposed great strategic abilities, it is perhaps lucky for us that Hitler was so out of the international political loop and so politically inept on occasions – as a more sensible and rational German dictator could well have been successful in their European imperialist goals.

If Britain's wartime goal had been the liberation of Poland, then we failed miserably. However, had the primary objective been the saving of Masonry, then the Second World War was an outstanding success story. This alternative perspective to the Second World War may also explain why the Vatican stood to one side and said very little about the activities of the Third Reich. Such was the indifference of the Vatican that Pope Pius XII became widely known as 'Hitler's Pope'. Indeed, some elements of the Catholic Church were complicit in their active support, with characters like Father Krujoslav Dragonovic setting up and running the Rat-line for former German S.S. officers escaping to Argentina, from his office in the Vatican. Among the many criminals that the Catholic Church spirited away from justice in 1945 were Klaus Barbie, Adolf Eichmann and Josef Mengele; and for this service they charged $6,000 in 1945 values, a sum that was well known to the Americans as they used the same Rat-line for some of their spies.

But why was the Catholic Church so supportive of German fascism and these assorted butchers who had committed crimes against humanity? Some have argued that the Vatican supported Germany because of their systematic destruction of the Jews, the traditional enemy of Christianity, due to their perceived role in the execution of the Christian's second god, Jesus. Alternatively, it has been argued that the Catholics supported Hitler in his uncompromising war against Communism, an ideology that had closed down churches all across the east and tutored its citizens in the 'wicked' doctrine of Atheism. However, the Vatican may equally have supported Hitler because of his pogrom against Masonry, which the Church saw as a dangerously subversive society that could bring Catholicism to its knees, because it harboured secrets and doctrines that seriously undermined the traditional Catholic creed.

Thus the Vatican probably saw the Third Reich as a highly convenient ally that would destroy its three primary enemies in one uncompromising strategic blow – and restore the Catholic Church to its traditional role as the most powerful governing body within all Europe. Unfortunately for the Vatican, they not only backed the most ruthless horse they could find, they also backed the wrong one.

Life

The continuation of verse 2:9 in Genesis, as quoted at the beginning of this chapter, presents us with another interesting conundrum, for the revised translation is again precise, but the new meaning is deeply enigmatic. The troubling phrase here is the well-worn 'tree of life', which has already been discussed to a degree. The Hebrew wording for this is *etsah kha* עצה חי, meaning literally the 'tree of life'; and the word *etsa* may have been derived from *at* עץ meaning 'tree'. But this does not really give a logical meaning for the phrase, and so I think that the original Hebrew text may have actually spoken of an *etsah kha (atsah kha)* עצה חי, which has exactly the same spelling and pronunciation but it means instead the 'backbone of life'. Now this phrase is much more meaningful in an Egyptian context, and the original version of this was the *aat ka* 〈glyphs〉 〈glyphs〉, also meaning the 'backbone of life'.

This new context may also give us a deeper insight into the enigmatic Egyptian word *ka*. The *ka* was supposed to be the life-force that inhabited each human or god. It came into being when we were born and it continued to live after we died, and so it represented one aspect of the Egyptian belief in an afterlife. But the life-force required sustenance, which is why offerings were made to the gods and why food, whether real or representational, was provided for the deceased in the afterlife. Feeding the *ka* was so essential that it became a favourite festive toast – instead of saying 'cheers' or 'good health', the guests were told 'to your Ka'.

But the *ka* did not have a backbone, and so the task is now to discover a reason for this 'backbone' imagery. I suppose the first thing to note is that the backbone plus a set of ribs can look a little like a tree, and if one superimposes the two arms of the *ka* hieroglyph onto that backbone, the resulting image is of a substantially complete skeleton. Thus the *aat ka*, the 'tree of life', may have been an image of the skeleton that comprises and supports the body. But somehow I don't think that this is the full explanation. There are two other options for this imagery, and they are as follows:

a.   The 'backbone' element could have been based upon the *pesdj, djedj* or *tchedj*, which described the 'backbone of Osiris' and was represented by the *djed* pillar 〈glyph〉. This pillar was supposed to represent and provide permanence and stability to the Egyptian nation, and so it became a popular amulet that provided the individual wearer with the same 'permanence and stability'. No doubt the 'permanence and stability' in question was largely concerned with the individual's life, and so the *djed* pillar – Osiris' backbone – became the most popular lucky charm in the country. Look at the amulet collection in any Egyptian museum and a vast array of *djed* pillars will be found; I would recommend the collections in the Petrie Museum in London and the Turin Museum in Italy.

The only link that has still to be made here is the connection between the *djed* pillar and a tree. The full explanation for this will be given in the next chapter, but for now it may be worth looking at the pronunciation of the name Osiris. The widespread modern name for Osiris is a Hellenised version of the name, and the most likely original pronunciation was Asar 〈glyphs〉 . But, of course, the word *asar* is very similar to the sacred tree that we have already discussed, which was known as the *aser*. Thus Osiris (Asar) and his backbone could have easily been mistaken for a sacred tree.

b.   The second rationale, which is in many respects complementary to that already given, can be derived from the Osiris myth. After Set had tricked his brother Osiris into climbing into a coffin, the coffin was cast into the Nile in the hope that Osiris would die. The coffin finally lodged in the roots of a tree, which happened to be the *aser* tree. The tree grew up and completely surrounded the coffin, with Osiris inside, and there he would have remained had his wife Isis not discovered him and released him from his wooden tomb. [20]

The story went on to tell of Osiris being chopped up into pieces, but here in the initial details we appear to have a myth that connects many of the aspects of the 'tree of life' conundrum. The *aser* tree not only sounds like Osiris (Asar), it also surrounded him, becoming his tomb. Not surprisingly, another meaning for the word *aat* [glyph], meaning 'backbone', was *aat* [glyph] meaning 'tomb'. In this tomb, Osiris had effectively become a wooden pillar, an integral component of the tree in which the coffin had lodged, which links this myth with the *djed* pillar which was supposed to be the 'backbone of Osiris'.

It is for this reason that I believe the garden in Avaris was most probably created as a necropolis, a 'city' of the dead. Each tree would have been planted over the body of the deceased, and it would have become the living *ka* of the dearly departed – thus the deceased were absorbed into the tree in the same way that Osiris was. Rather than the family coming to see an inanimate piece of stone with an inscription upon it, they could instead press their hands and heads against a living entity that had inherited the life-force (not the soul) of their dearly beloved. This tradition, if that is what it was, has survived to this day, and the relatives of the dead from the First and Second World Wars can mourn their dead in exactly the same way, in Perth (Australia) and Jerusalem, where 'sacred' groves have been established and individual trees are ascribed to the memory of individual fallen soldiers.

This explanation would also shed a little further light on the maypole imagery. It has long been understood that the maypole was a phallic symbol, but the precise reasoning behind this ritual has always been a little obscure. One possibility is that it was simply a representation of the phallus of Atum, which had created the world and thus became a potent symbol of fertility.

Here, though, we have another compelling possibility. In both of the explanations just given, it is Osiris (Asar) who was being associated with the *aser* tree and the sacred grove. Thus the *aser* tree was being associated with both the physical body and the *ka* life-force of Osiris – as it was his *djed* pillar and his backbone. However, after Osiris had been cut up by his brother Set, there was one part of his body that was never found – his penis. Therefore, it seems to make sense that if one has to perform a ritual outside the precincts of the grove, the improvised ritual should celebrate the only part of Osiris that was not discovered and would not have been associated with the trees in the grove – his penis. If this is a true explanation, then the fertility maypoles of the Vernal (spring) equinox may be representations of the phallus of Osiris, rather than Atum – especially since one of Osiris' primary attributes was as the bringer of the Nile floods and the germinator of the corn in the fields.

In conclusion, it may also be that Osiris and his missing penis, which was eventually recreated by Isis, was simply taking on the traditional role of Atum. As Atum's popularity waned, the rising star of Osiris was required to fill all the roles that had been vacated. Atum's penis created Shu and Tefnut and fathered all of creation, whereas the new penis of Osiris created his son, Horus and brought fertility to the land.

This is a reasonably all-embracing explanation for the presence and importance of these sacred groves. But as far as the Garden of Eden (the sacred grove in Avaris) is concerned, these must have been very special burials. The actual enclosure of this garden was quite large, measuring some 75 x 50 cubits (40 x 26 meters), but with the 5.5 cubit grid system that was employed for the trees, only 140 or so burials could have been made at this site. Considering the scale of the walls surrounding the grove, and considering the reinforcements that were subsequently made when the site was threatened by the Theban pharaoh Kamose, these must have been very important burials indeed.

Rivers

The evidence is continually pointing towards Eden being located in the Nile Delta, but what of the four rivers that the Torah describes? According to the traditional interpretation these must refer to the Middle East, as the text even names the Euphrates and sometimes the Tigris too – so how can I assert that these were Egyptian rivers instead? Well, the English translators have done us a disservice here, for this is not quite what the Hebrew text says. The Torah actually names the river Parath פרת, which is not quite the same thing as the Euphrates, as we shall see. The four rivers that are named are as follows:

> 2:11 The name of the first is Pison: that is it which compasseth# the whole land# of Havilah#, where there is gold#;
> 2:13 And the name of the second river is Gihon#: the same is it that compasseth# the whole land of Ethiopia#.
> 2:14 And the name of the third river is (Tigris) Hiddekel#: that is it which goes toward the east# of Assyria#. And the fourth river is (Perath) Euphrates#.

2:11 The name of the first is Spreading: which circles and snakes though the land, and where there are floods.

2:13 And the name of the second river is called Spreading: the same is it that snakes through the land of Kam.

2:14 And the name of the third river is the river of the Twin-Caverns: that is it which goes toward the sacred grove. And the fourth river is Divide or Fruitful.

1. Piyshon פישׁון

The name of this river is based upon the word *puwsh* פוּשׁ which means to 'spread'. This gives an instant image of a river that spreads out into a delta as it approaches a lake or sea, and this is exactly what it does mean. It was derived from the Egyptian *pesesh* meaning 'divide'. The pronunciation and imagery that this provides are identical, with the river dividing and spreading as it flows through the Delta.

But the text gives further information, and so we see the description of the river 'compassing the land of Havilah', *cabab erets Chaviylah* חוילה סבב ארץ. But this is a slight mistranslation, as *cabab* means to 'circle' and the location of Havilah was derived from a root meaning to 'wind' or 'writhe'. So even in the Hebrew, the phrase could mean to 'circle and snake through the land', which would be a good description of a branch of the Nile in the Delta region, especially as this particular branch was known for spreading and dividing. Not surprisingly, the words *cabab* and *haviylah* are both Egyptian, with the originals being *qeb* and *hefau* , meaning 'circle' and 'snake' respectively. Once more, the Egyptian translations are identical to the later Hebrew descriptions.

The Torah then goes on to say that there is gold, *zahb* זהב, in this region, but there is not much evidence of gold in the Delta. In the circumstances, since the text is already describing a winding, sinuous river, it is more than likely that the original text read as *tsaba* צבע, meaning to 'wet' or 'immerse' (the land) and it was therefore describing a flooded area. The Egyptian equivalent for this would be *tsabagi* , which also describes a 'flood' or 'immersion'.

2. Gihon גיחון

While the Pishown was sluggish, the Gihon (Geehon) instead refers to a river that bursts forth. But somehow, I think that this name does not refer to the speed of the river, but more to its tendency to burst its banks, and a possible Egyptian version of this name is *qehait* meaning 'spread'. That the initial 'q' in this word may be the equivalent of a 'g' is suggested by the words *qehes* and *gehes* , which both mean 'gazelle', and perhaps these two words again point towards a river that regularly 'jumps' over its banks. That a river in the Nile Delta had a tendency to burst its banks is entirely understandable.

However, rather than flowing through the Delta region, this river is said to circle Ethiopia, and although the Nile rises out of Ethiopia, this is not what the scribes were trying to describe. In the book *Solomon* I discussed the apparent confusion, in the various biblical-type texts, between the names for Ethiopia and Egypt. It was obvious to me that the Kebra Nagast especially was really referring to Egypt when it said 'Ethiopia', not least because the boundaries of 'Ethiopia' apparently ended on the shores of the Dead Sea. Clearly, this description of 'Ethiopia' must have encompassed all of Egypt.

The true source of this confusion is actually to be found in the Egyptian original of these texts. The Hebrew name that is being translated as 'Ethiopia' is actually Kuwsh כוש, and rather than describing a land it simply means 'black'. Now some may argue that this term refers to the black people of Ethiopia, and that is probably the train of thought that was used by the later English translators. This reasoning was perhaps further reinforced by the similar recent usage of the word *niger*. This term may have had a great deal of bad press at the hands of the politically-correct brigade recently, but it is simply the Latin for 'black' and is the basis for the name of the river Niger and the country of Nigeria. The implication would seem to be inescapable, the 'black land' must have referred to the black people who inhabited the land of Ethiopia.

But that logic is not necessarily correct, and in the original text, I am certain that the word used here was actually *kam* 𓆎𓅓𓏏𓏤 , meaning 'black'. However, there is a big difference between this blackness and the traditional reasoning. The word *kam* not only means 'black', as does *kush*, but it is also one of the primary names for the land of Egypt – Kam 𓆎𓅓𓊖 . Instead of referring to the pigmentation of the people, the term *kam* is supposed to refer to the rich, black soil of the fertile Nile valley, as opposed to the dusty-red sands of the desert. The bottom line here is that the river Gihon did not encircle Ethiopia, rather it encompassed the black lands of Egypt, and so it is in Egypt that we may find its true identity. As the historian Josephus said:

> And Gihon runs through Egypt, and denotes what arises from the east, which the Greeks call the Nile. [J21]

Thus, according to Josephus, who had access to the original biblical texts from the Temple of Jerusalem, the river Gihon did indeed flow through Egypt. Just as interesting, however, is the fact that the word *kam*

⌂⌂⌂⌂⌂ can also refer to a garden. The inference here is that all of Egypt can be thought of as a garden, and so Egypt itself may be Eden. However, I still think that there is a particular walled garden within the greater garden that is somehow special and has become the true Garden in Eden.

3. Khideqel חדקל

The RSV and NIV versions of the Bible manage to translate this river as the Tigris, but there is no evidence in favour of this identification whatsoever in the original Hebrew. No doubt these translators saw that the fourth river was often called the Euphrates and so they simply made a huge assumption, bordering on deliberate deceit, that this river must therefore be the Tigris.

In fact, the direct translation of the Khideqel from the Hebrew simply describes a rapidly flowing river, once more. But it is entirely possible that the Khideqel חדקל was actually founded upon the words *khedj qel* ⌂⌂⌂⌂⌂ , meaning 'river of the twin caverns'. The twin caverns were the mythological twin sources of the Nile that sprang between the Twin Peaks, the two pyramidal breasts that surmounted the Giza plateau. This translation is perhaps confirmed by the meaning for *khedeq* חדק, which is 'thorn' or 'prickle', two terms that have already been strongly linked to both Mt Sinai and the Great Pyramid.

The verse then goes on to describe a different location altogether – Assyria, or Ashur אשר. That this word refers to Assyria is a highly debatable assumption, as I would have rather chosen *ashurah* אשרה, which refers to a 'sacred grove'. Many of the Genesis texts refer to trees, maypoles, enclosed gardens and sacred groves, so the possibility exists that this was the intended description and not Assyria. It is likely that this river was really flowing eastwards towards the 'sacred grove', the enclosed garden that resided in Avaris, which is indeed in the eastern portion of the Nile Delta.

4. Parath פרת

The name being used for the river 'Euphrates' is actually the Parath פרת and, as has already been mentioned, this simply means 'fruitful'. There is no direct indication that this term has any connection whatsoever to the famous river in Iraq; but unfortunately, since there is no accompanying description for this river in the Torah, it is more difficult to get a considered translation. There are several possibilities for this name, and the first of these is simply another version of the Hebrew. If the name in question were actually Parad פרד, then the name of this river would simply mean 'divide', which is rather similar to the meanings for all the other rivers and is also the translation that Josephus gives. This would probably have, in turn, been derived from the word *paratcha* ⊔ ⌐ ⌐ (since the 'd' and the 'tch' are often confused), a word which also means 'divide'.

The bottom line in this new evaluation is that all of the rivers that flowed through Eden can be associated with the concepts of spreading, dividing and snaking; all of which are perfectly acceptable adjectives for describing the lazy, meandering rivers that flow through the Nile Delta.

More importantly, all of these names for the rivers that ran through Eden can be connected both to the Egyptian language and to the land of the Nile Delta itself. It is abundantly clear that the long solitary river that grew four 'heads' as it flowed through Eden was actually the long solitary river Nile and the four major branches of this river that once divided off from the primary stream. Therefore, Eden must have resided in Egypt, and more importantly its sacred garden may well have been constructed at Avaris in the east of the Nile Delta, the primary capital of the Hyksos nation. But in the books *Jesus*, *Tempest* and *Solomon*, the Hyksos nation have already been indisputably linked with the Israelites, and many of the rulers of these 'two' peoples have been shown to be the same individuals.

Thus the Genesis story was not simply Egyptian, it was more precisely a Hyksos-Israelite tradition that was renewed and updated by Pharaoh Akhenaton and transported to Judaea along with the second of the two exoduses from Egypt. But if the Genesis story can be linked to Pharaoh Akhenaton and his regime at Amarna, then what of the famous individuals in that same story? Could Adam and Eve be linked to Akhenaton and Nefertiti in some manner?

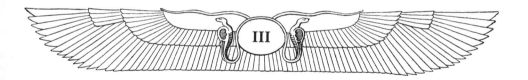

Eve

2:21 And the Lord God caused a deep sleep to fall upon Adam#, and he slept: and he took one of his ribs#, and closed up the flesh# instead thereof.
3:20 And Adam called his wife's name Eve; because she was the mother of all living.

2:21 And the two eyes of Horus caused a deep sleep to fall upon Adam, and he slept: and he took one of his ribs, and closed up the flesh instead thereof;
3:20 And Adam called his wife's name Khavah; because she gave Kha (life).

I had hoped that the story of the creation of Eve and her temptation might have led to something interesting. But beyond the words for 'rib' and 'flesh' (body) being direct transliterations from the Egyptian, the story did not seem to change at all. But it was interesting to note that Adam took a whole chapter before getting around to giving his wife a name. Eve was called חוה, and the consensus of opinion is that this name should be pronounced as Khavah (sounding somewhat like Havah). This name was eventually translated into the Greek Ευα (Eua) and thence into the English Eve. Khavah can mean either 'breath' as in the 'Breath of Life', or even 'life', and so the sentence from verse 3:20 is supposed to be read as:

And Adam called his wife's name Life; because she was the mother of Life.

As Eve was a female, who would give birth to the next generation, the sentence seems logical and sensible. It also makes sense in the Egyptian, as the word being used for 'life' is *kha* רח, and this was derived from the Egyptian *ka* ⊔⸾, which refers to the body's life-force. The scribes were simply making a rhyme here between Khavah and *kha* – between the name for Eve and the word for life – and again this rhyme seems to work in both languages.

III Eve

The word for mother was *am* אם, which may have been taken from the Egyptian *amaa* 𓈖𓏤𓆷𓀀 meaning 'mother'. However, there was an alternative, and this word could easily have been derived from the word *ama* 𓂝𓈖𓄿 meaning 'give'. With this alteration, the verse would then become:

And Adam called his wife's name Life; because she gave life.

Again, change a single word and the meaning of the verse becomes subtly altered. However, it is entirely possible that the name of Eve was also based upon an alternative translation; instead of Khavah חוה meaning 'life', it could equally have been intended as Khavah חוה meaning 'speak' or 'explain'. Both of these meanings are direct equivalents of the name of the real Eve (Khavah), who will be shown to have been a real and famous character in the Egyptian historical record – although her biblical name is likely to have been a nickname.

The primary reasoning for Eve's name appears to have been the concept of 'life'. However, the name the scribes chose did not simply mean 'life', as that would be far too simple for them, and so they chose instead a name for Khavah (Eve) that would rhyme with her primary biblical adversary, the snake. Thus the Egyptian name that was chosen for Eve (Khavah) was *hafa* 𓄿𓆑𓄿𓆙 meaning 'snake', and the link with the concept of 'life' is drawn from the Caduceus, the intertwined snakes of medicine. Although these snakes are sometimes confused with the rod of Asclepius, they were actually taken from the rod of Hermes, who was in turn a Greek version of the Egyptian Thoth. So although the Caduceus is said to have been a Greek symbol of medicine, and therefore life, it is more than likely that the original imagery came from Egypt, as most Greek theology and science appears to have done.

A piece of modern evidence in favour of this suggestion comes from the medical library of the Wellcome Trust in London. The exterior of this building is adorned with both the Caduceus snake-rod of Thoth and also the Aton Sun-god of Akhenaton. The use of the Caduceus on a medical library would be an obvious choice, but to use the Aton symbol as well is unusual, as the Aton is not normally regarded as being medicinal. However, a close reading of the Hymn to the Aton, which we shall look at again later, does invoke the Aton as the bringer of life.

Fig 3.1   The double snakes of the Caduceus.

88

III Eve

But the fact that these two images should be placed in such close proximity to each other, on the same building, would suggest that the designers considered there to be a link between the two, and I myself think that opinion is justified.

The scribes have therefore arranged the biblical text to indicate that the *hafa* would have been tempting Khavah: the snake would be tempting Eve, and so the sentence previously quoted may well have originally been written as:

Hebrew: And Adam called his wife's name Khavah; because she gave *kha*.

Egyptian: And Adam called his wife's name Hafa; because she gave *ka*.

Translation: And Adam called his wife's name life; because she gave life.

Now the critical reader might exclaim that I am being very selective in my translations and that *hava* is not necessarily a good phoneme for Khavah (Eve). But, as ever, the scribes had a trick or two up their cassocks, and there are a couple of alternative versions of the Khavah name that will eventually prove exactly who this character was in the historical record. So who was Eve?

The first thing to note is that Josephus calls womankind *issa*, and the first woman to be created, Eve. It is fairly obvious that this title for women in general, *issa*, was based upon the name of the Egyptian goddess, Isis. Although the pronunciation may look a little different, there is an explanation for this. In the original Egyptian, the name of Isis was actually pronounced Ast 𓊨𓏏𓆇 , which was the female form of Osiris, who was called Asar 𓊨𓁹𓀭 . From the many translations in the Egyptian Hebrew dictionary in the appendix, it will be noted that it is not unusual for the Egyptian female 't' suffix to become the Hebrew 'ah' ה. If this had happened to the Egyptian Ast (Isis), her name would have been rendered as Asah in the Hebrew and Issa in Josephus' Greek. It was in this fashion that womankind became known as *issa*.

As an aside, the original Egyptian pronunciation for Isis (Ast) must have been known and understood in more recent eras, for her name was taken and used for the Christian celebration of Easter (Aster). The evidence for this assertion can be seen in the modern ritual use of the egg at Easter. The Easter-egg was not derived as a symbol of springtime simply because birds tend to lay eggs in this season, rather it was based upon the ritual fertility of Isis (Ast) 𓊨𓏏𓆇 and the fact that her name included the egg glyph ○ . Thus the Easter-egg is simply a coded reference to the name of Isis; but since the role of the New Testament Mary was similarly modeled upon the fertility attributes of Isis, this should not be so surprising.

There are two possibilities as to why Josephus should have mentioned

89

the name *issa* in relation to the creation of womankind. In the first of these, it is possible that Eve had a second title which identified her with women in general. The initial thought, therefore, was that Adam and Eve were actually representations of Osiris and Isis, and therefore the taking of a rib from Adam to form Eve was a corruption of the Osiris story. In Egyptian mythology it was Osiris who was dismembered and cast upon the Nile, and it was Isis who managed to use her magical powers to find the pieces and reassemble her beloved husband Osiris – minus his penis, of course. Rather than taking a rib from man, the original symbolism probably invoked the taking of a penis. Also note that Eve was said to be the giver of life and Isis was also venerated as the goddess of fertility, which is why her name includes the egg glyph. But if this was the original source of the Adam and Eve story then the biblical version represents a rather radical alteration of the original, and so I reconsidered the situation once more.

The more likely answer, I believe, is that the gods Osiris and Isis were often intimately associated with the royal couple throughout Egyptian history, and on occasions the latter were also seen to be physical manifestations of Osiris and Isis. This is certainly true of the queens of Egypt, as has already been explained, and many of the more influential queens held the title of 'God's Wife' and were therefore directly associated with the goddess Isis. The first of the more famous 'God's Wives' was Nefertari, the wife of Ahmose I; the second was Hatshepsut, the dominant mother of Tuthmoses III, who became pharaoh during her stepson's minority; and the third was perhaps the most famous queen of all Egyptian history – Nefertiti, the wife of Akhenaton. Like Nefertari, Nefertiti was a forceful personality, charismatic enough to complement her husband's position on the throne and influential enough to engage in political decision-making. Although Akhenaton and Nefertiti would not have identified themselves with Osiris and Isis, as Akhenaton had banned such idolatry, it would not have been out of character for this royal couple to have usurped the religious aura that surrounded Osiris and Isis. Thus if the population wanted to invoke Osiris and Isis in their prayers, who no longer existed, they would have to praise Akhenaton and Nefertiti instead.

We have already seen a reasonably positive link between the rivers of Eden and Egypt, and a clear link between the Genesis story and the Hymn to the Aton, but now we can also see the tentative beginnings of a link between Eve herself and Nefertiti. While more evidence needs to be uncovered before this idea can be taken as a definite possibility, under the circumstances, the single reference to Isis that Josephus mentions in relation to Eve is distinctly suggestive.

So, the name Issa may have appeared in the works of Josephus because a queen like Nefertiti was assuming the role of Isis. However, there is always the possibility that we should actually be looking for a queen named Isis. So was there ever such an individual? Well, like her husband Akhenaton, it is likely that Nefertiti underwent a change of name when she married and moved to Amarna. As it happens, the family history of Nefertiti is confused; there is no mention of her parents and, with one exception, no individual claims to be related to her. Traditionally, historians have either seen the translation of her name as indicating that she had come from abroad, or they have instead sought to link her with the family of Yuya and Tuyu, who were the parents of Akhenaton's mother, Tiye. The links never go any closer to the royal family than this because Nefertiti herself never claims to be 'king's daughter', a common royal title that would have positively declared her direct affiliation to the royal family. But if Nefertiti had undergone a name change when she became queen, then perhaps, like her husband, the references to her being the king's child were all made under her previous name.

The reason for all this speculation is that Amenhotep III had a number of children. His two sons were called Tuthmoses and Amenhotep (Akhenaton), while his five daughters were named Beketaton, Sitamun, Henut-Taneb, Nebetah and finally Isis. It may well be, therefore, that in the works of Josephus, and through this newly discovered link between Amarna and the Genesis story, we at last have a reference that gives the true family history of one of the most famous and celebrated queens from ancient history. The traditional marriage for any pharaoh was to a member of his immediate family, and this normally meant a union with a sister or perhaps a daughter. The evidence in Josephus' *Antiquities* is indicating that Akhenaton followed in this tradition and married his sister Isis (Issa), a lady who subsequently changed her name to Nefertiti and was known in the later biblical traditions as Khavah, or Eve.

This growing association between Eve and Nefertiti can be further reinforced through an epigraphic trail, which takes us on a rather circuitous journey through Egyptian mythology and history. Just to quickly recap the situation, Khavah (Eve) was supposed to have received her title because she was the 'image or mother of all living things'. In other words Khavah was a symbol of fertility, and mother of creation. Since the god Atum was male and solitary, he required a female counterpart to assist in the conception of all this natural creation, and that was the function of God's Wife. This is a topic that will be discussed later in this chapter, but the thing to note here is Khavah's central role in the fertility of the world. But in the parallel world of Amarna, Nefertiti was also closely identified with fertility:

> She is the mother figure in the lesser triad of king, queen and their children. Her sexuality, emphasized by her exaggerated body shape and revealing

III Eve

garments, and her fecundity, stressed by the constant appearance of the royal princesses, indicates that she is to be regarded as a living fertility symbol.[1]

So both Nefertiti and Khavah (Eve) were seen to be potent fertility symbols. In addition to this, the Hebrew name for Khavah (Eve) can also mean either 'breath' or 'talkative'. So what I next set out to look for was a queen from the New Kingdom dynasties, and preferably one connected with the Amarna regime of Akhenaton, who could also be connected with both winds and speech. Strangely enough, the first individual that seemed to fit the required criteria was again Nefertiti. But the traditional translation of this queen's name is actually 'Beautiful Woman Comes'.

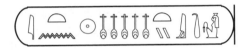

Fig 3.2   Cartouche of Nefertiti.

With reference to the glyphs in figure 32, the translators have assumed that the first *nefer* and *t* glyphs were forming the feminine form of the word 'beauty' , which they can indeed do. In this case, perhaps the dual sign *ti* and the multiple *nefer* glyphs implied great beauty. This would result in a translation of 'Female Beauty' or perhaps 'Very Beautiful Woman', as has been suggested. The final elements in this name are the *ii* and *ti* , which adds the word 'comes' or possibly 'comes together' to Nefertiti's name. Thus the final pronunciation should really be something like Neferet-iiti or Neferut-iiti, meaning 'Very Beautiful Woman Comes' or even 'Very Beautiful Women Come Together'.

However, there can always be an alternative translation to the orthodox version, and this new translation for Nefertiti presents us with some rather intriguing possibilities. The first element in the name is the *nefer* glyph once more, and this glyph is supposed to be representative of a 'heart and windpipe' , which would indicate a degree of confusion between the functions of the heart and the lungs by the Egyptian medical experts. In truth, this glyph does not have any meanings that convey the imagery of a heart, and plenty of *nefer*-type words that relate to breathing and winds, and I couldn't help noticing that these 'wind' and 'windpipe' references for the *nefer* glyph point towards one central concept – 'breathing'. This does, of course, potentially identify the name for Nefertiti with exactly the same attributes as Eve. The classical Hebrew version of Eve's name refers to 'breath', and more specifically to the 'Breath of Life', which is why Eve was synonymous with life. But so too was Nefertiti, as the word *nefu* 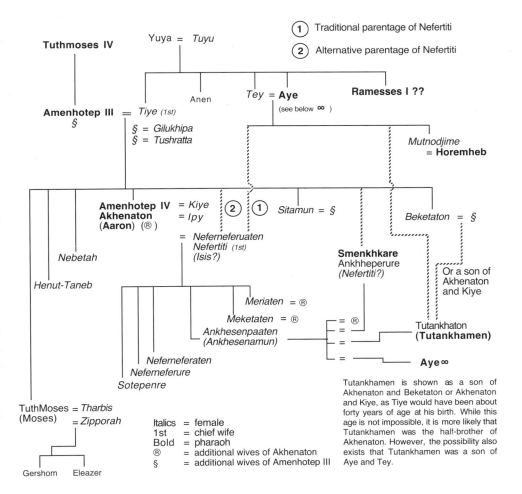 can also be used to mean 'Breath of Life'. This alternative interpretation would result in a name for Nefertiti that means 'Breath of Life Comes Together', a title that is again synonymous with the biblical myth of the creation of Eve. Both Eve and Nefertiti were seen to be and venerated as the givers of life, because both were associated with the goddess Isis.

Fig 3.3 Genealogy of Akhenaton and Nefertiti.

This similarity between Nefertiti and the biblical text of Genesis can be taken one step further, for the alternative Hebrew translation for Eve can also mean 'talkative'. Rather surprisingly, the alternative translation for the 'titi' portion of Nefertiti's name is *titi* 𓇌𓊃 means 'chatter' or 'babble'. Therefore, a secondary title for Nefertiti may well be something like 'Beautiful Voice', or perhaps 'Breath of Speech'.

But what about this meaning of 'talkative'? Does it have any relevance to this investigation? Now while this meaning may have been a simple wisecrack at the perceived talkativeness often associated with women, or a more serious observation about the trilling ululations performed by the women of this region, the title may have had yet another meaning. The link between 'breath' and 'life' was well established in Egypt, and this was especially so within the Amarna rituals. The Hymn to the Aton confirms this, when it says that the Aton is the:

> Giver of breath
> To nourish all that he made
> When he comes from the womb to breathe
> On the day of his birth
> You open wide his mouth
> You supply his needs [2]

So the god gives life by the opening of the mouth and the giving of breath. This is no doubt why the 'opening of the mouth' ceremony for the deceased was so important. The *ka*, the life-force of the living person, was said to continue to exist after death; but in order to do so it required the same sustenance as the original physical body did in life. Thus the *ka* was provided with food and drink in the afterlife to sustain it, even if this sustenance was only representational. But one of the prime needs of the *ka* was the 'Breath of Life', and no doubt the 'opening of the mouth' ceremony provided this divine breath so that the *ka* could be revived and eventually be able to leave the body. The original magical formula for this action was stipulated in the Book of the Dead, and chapter 23 said of this custom:

> My mouth is given to me,
> My mouth is opened by Ptah,
> With that chisel of metal,
> With which he opened the mouth of the gods. [3]

Surprisingly enough, this tradition survived the passing of the centuries and eventually it found its way to first century Jerusalem, where a famous prince of the Egyptian bloodline by the name of Jesus used this very same ritual.

> And when he had said this, he breathed on them, and saith unto them, Receive
> ye the Holy Ghost (Holy Wind). [B4]

The main difference here is that Jesus was performing this ritual on the
disciples, the living priesthood of the Church of Jesus and James, rather than
a mummy of the recently deceased. But nevertheless, the text is still explicit
in its meaning. Firstly it is confirming to us that the Holy Ghost was a wind,
as its spelling suggests; secondly it is confirming that wind can be associated
with breath from the lungs; and thirdly it is confirming that this divine
breath conferred something spiritual upon the recipient. I would suggest
that the original ritual involved an invigoration of the *ka*, in preparation for
its journey through the *Djuat*.

So was Jesus' interpretation of the Breath of Life so very different
to the Egyptian, in its application to living priests? Unfortunately, the vast
majority of Egypt's ancient liturgy has been lost to history, and we now view
Egyptian ritual almost solely through the highly restrictive prism of their
funerary rituals. It may well be that the Egyptian priesthood once used this
ritual on fellow priests in exactly the same way that Jesus was recorded as
doing, and the evidence for this suggestion lies in the Vatican. Like so many
of these ancient customs, it is a fact that this same ritual eventually found its
way into the Christian Catholic Church, where it became a part of the liturgy
associated with the rites involved in the creation of new cardinals. After the
death of Pope Leo XIII, back in 1903, new cardinals were installed *en masse*,
as is the custom. But the Daily Mail of London reported that:

> ... a Consistory (meeting) would be held to close and open the lips of the
> cardinals (who had been) newly created. [5]

Notice here that we have a curious reference to the 'opening of the lips' –
there could not be a closer description of the original 'opening of the mouth'
ceremony from Egypt, and so the new cardinals were effectively entering
the Egyptian priesthood. The newly installed cardinals may have wondered
what this strange, arcane ritual was supposed to mean, and they may have
been reassured that it was based upon a ritual that had been performed by
the resurrected Jesus upon his disciples. But they would have been rather
astounded, or even horrified, to discover that this was formerly an ancient
ritual that was once used to ensure everlasting life for the *ka* of a pharaoh.

But none of this really explains the true symbolism that lay behind
the Breath of Life. As is usual with Egyptian theology, I think that these
explanations were both complex and dualist. The first of these explanations

comes from the fact that the Breath of Life was often associated with the north wind:

> I breathe the sweet breath which comes forth from your mouth and shall behold your beauty daily. My prayer is that I may hear your <u>sweet voices of the north wind</u>, that my flesh may grow young with life through your love, that you may give me your hands bearing your spirit and I receive it and live by it...[6]

The explanation for this symbology is probably quite straightforward. The prayer is from an Amarna coffin and so it is referring to the Aton, the Sun-disk. It must have been obvious to the watchers – the Giza astronomer-priests or guardians who studied the night sky and observed the movement of the constellations through the seasons and the millennia – that the diurnal and seasonal movement of the Sun caused winds to occur.

In the desert, the wind will often drop to a complete calm overnight, as a temperature inversion separates the upper winds from the lower atmosphere. While watching the morning sunrise, which was the most important event in the daily ritual of Atonist Egypt, even the most unobservant of priests must have felt the rays of the morning Sun stir the atmosphere and puff small gusts of wind around the Giza plateau. As the morning progressed and the temperature increased, this mixing of the atmosphere tends to rejoin the upper and lower atmospheres (at a level between 1000 and 2000 feet), and so the lower winds will begin to follow the upper winds once more. Since the upper winds are predominantly northern in Egypt, because of the enormous heating effect of the Sahara desert in comparison to the cool of the Mediterranean, the predominant surface wind in Egypt is a strong northerly. It would not have taken a great deal of common sense to link these northerly winds with the Sun, and thus with the god Aton.

Axe

Another possible effect of this wind is to be found in the generic Egyptian name for god, which was *neter*. Now the glyph that was used as the determinative for 'god' has often been referred to as an axe, and this is certainly the representation that was used to denote a god in the Minoan empire. But this Minoan interpretation may have been simply a pun on the Egyptian word *neter*, which referred to an axe. The Minoans, if they had copied this emblem, may have been duped into thinking it was an axe when in actual fact it was not. But if the god glyph was not an axe then what could it be?

III Eve

The other usual alternative, which is still given in some reference books, is that this glyph was either a roll of cloth with a loose end, or perhaps a flag. Since this glyph would be a poor representation of a roll of cloth, I personally think that the flag concept is the more likely. But how, then, did a flag come to represent a god?

Some time ago, when I was writing the book *Tempest*, I did wonder whether these flags had anything to do with the flagpoles that lined the front of every temple. The logo for Edfu Books is not entirely correct, because on the face of the entrance pylon to the temples there are actually recesses to take a number of very large flagpoles. The precise number of poles varies, with Karnak having eight on the outer pylon, plus six and four on the inner pylons. In contrast, Luxor has four and Philae only two. The precise number of flagpoles is variable, but the important point to note is that all the temples seem to sport this feature, and since these were the entrances to god's temples they may be linked to the god-flag glyph.

My original thoughts on these flags were that they may have sported an image of the god to whom the temple was dedicated. Thus each temple advertised its god, and perhaps the flag went up and down depending on whether the god was in residence or not. But this new research into the Divine Breath gives an alternative line of thought. Instead of the image of the flag being the primary function, perhaps, instead, it was the sound of the flag.

As we have seen, the predominant winds in Egypt are from the Mediterranean southwards into the desert interior, which is rather fortuitous really, as it means the sailors can sail with the wind, upstream against the fast-running current of the Nile, but when they want to sail north they can furl their sails and let the current take them along. The small *feluccas* on the Nile today can tack across the breadth of the river and utilise reasonable head-wind components, but I am sure that the larger barges from the quarries at Aswan would have needed the assistance of the river currents to make any kind of progress. These same winds will, however, give a constant breeze across the temple entrances and make their flags flutter continuously.

This is perhaps why the generic name for god, *neter* ⌐, is so similar to the name for the wind, *nefi* ～⊤, and the name for the Breath of God, *nefer neter* ～⊤⌐. The fluttering of the flags would have made the temples resonate with a constant, background low-frequency hum, like the sound of a modern yachting marina, and I have no doubt that this sound was regarded as a component of the Breath of God in the same way that the sound of a song was. Just as the gods breathed life into each animal through its nostrils, so they also breathed a matrix of sound across the temple enclosure; a gentle, fluttering lullaby that permanently reminded the priests of the presence of god.

But, as ever, that is not the full story, for all of creation was able to receive the Breath of Life. The symbology for this is given by the tool that was used to open the mouth, which is traditionally identified as the *pesesh-kef* or *peshen-kef* ⌐◻▭◦Υ . While this may look like a surveying tool, and exactly like the tool that was discovered in one of the small shafts in the Great Pyramid, contemporary pictures tend to show the priesthood holding an adze to the mouth of the deceased. This would tend to show that the 'opening of the mouth' tool was the *nut* ◦○◦ , and this would make more sense as the phonemes for the *nut* (adze) are 'see', 'observe', 'guardian' and 'to operate the mouth'. In fact, the word *nut* seems to encompass all the traits of the Breath of Life that have just been discussed.

The reason for the adze being associated with the Breath of Life is due to its close association with the sculptors' craft. Rather than using a chisel to carve a statue, contemporary drawings show sculptors using the adze to carve its form. Presumably this technique was used just on wood and limestone, as an adze would not have much of an impact on granite. The importance of the statue should not be underestimated in Egyptian life and theology; the statue was a complete replica of the individual and it was probably thought that if this inanimate form could be infused with the deceased's *ba* and *ka*, it would function as a living being. Indeed, some funerary statues were carved in the form of the *ka*, the body's 'life-force', and were specifically designed to represent the deceased's *ka*. I have no doubt that the 'opening of the mouth' ceremony was connected in some way with this transfer of the *ba* and *ka* to the statue, and since the adze was the tool that had created this statuesque copy of the deceased, it was the adze that facilitated this transfer during the 'opening of the mouth' ceremony.

Music

While the divine breath – which was no doubt envisaged as being a physical manifestation of the *ka* – provided god's creation with life, the exhaling of that divine breath was equally important. By modulating and oscillating that divine breath, mankind, and apparently mankind alone, could transmit thoughts and concepts in the form of words; and some of these ritual, sacred words may have been powerful enough to invoke their own creation and life. As has already been demonstrated, from the biblical point of view the Word was a powerful tool that focused god's powers into a beneficial creative force that could be controlled and manipulated by the priesthood.

This may have been the true reason for Nefertiti's strange title. It may rather have implied 'Breath of the Word Comes', with the 'Word' probably referring to a divine incantation, and this interpretation would mean that

III Eve

Nefertiti would have held a rather senior position within the priesthood. These incantations may again have included the trilling ululation that is traditionally made by Arabic women to this day, but since this invocation is invariably called the 'Word', I would imagine myself that it was actually a solemn, spoken incantation.

This would also explain the reason why the word *nefer* was primarily taken to mean 'good', 'virtuous' or 'beautiful', and was represented by a lung (heart) and windpipe glyph. This curious windpipe symbology has long been a mystery, but if the air being expelled through this trachea was semi-divine, and if the two lines at the top of the trachea were representative of vocal chords that modulated that sacred wind and formed it into the Word, then this would explain everything.

This form and arrangement of lung (heart) and windpipe was subsequently manufactured in wood and turned into a musical instrument, and the early Israelites called this device a *nebel (neber)* נבל, which was eventually refined and became the modern guitar. I think that Wallis Budge was influenced by this Hebrew instrument and so he indicated that the similar-sounding Egyptian instrument, called a *nefer-t* , was also a guitar. In fact, from the design of the *nefer* glyph, one cannot but wonder if the inspiration for this glyph is not a heart and windpipe at all, but a guitar instead. Indeed, the modern guitar still echoes the feminine form in the shape of its soundbox.

However, there is an alternative explanation here, for the Hebrew term *nebel (neber)* נבל can also refer to a 'skin bag', meaning a water-carrying skin. Since the Egyptian glyph *nefer* refers to a 'lung (or heart) and trachea', it is quite possible that the instrument that looked like the heart and trachea was actually a set of bagpipes. Thus the tradition of the bagpipe may have stemmed from Egyptian origins, as some researchers have suggested previously. This is also why I think that the *nefer* glyph refers more to the pumping action of the heart, with the ancient physicians perhaps falsely thinking that this pumping acted upon the trachea during breathing.

In terms of Egyptian mythology and ritual, it may well be that god himself was mute and had to present his commands (Words) through the intermediary of a priest. But the priest now had two methods of demonstrating the Words of God: they could perform that role vocally, with the lungs, or perhaps musically, with the guitar or bagpipes. It gives a different perspective to the traditional imagery we have of these great Egyptian temples, to imagine that they may once have resonated to the tuneful strumming of a guitar or the mournful drone of the bagpipes, plus the lyrics of god's Word being sung or chanted by the priests. Gone is the imagery of an austere Anglican Church service and in comes the all-singing, all-dancing ritual of the Pentecostal Church. That this musical gaiety is a distinct possibility is hinted at by the events that were recorded in the court of King David:

> And David spake to the chief of the Levites to appoint their brethren to be the singers with instruments of music, bagpipes and harps and cymbals, sounding, by lifting up the voice with joy. So the singers ... were appointed to sound with cymbals of brass. And (others) with bagpipes and young women (soprano?). And (others) with harps on the guitar to excel. And Chenaniah, chief of the Levites, was for song: he instructed about the song, because he was skilful. [B7]

I have already taken the liberty of changing the term *'psaltery'*, an ancient stringed instrument, into 'bagpipes', as this instrument was actually translated from the Hebrew *nebel (neber)* נבל meaning 'skin bag'. Likewise, I have changed the *'sheminith'*, an eight-stringed instrument, into 'guitar'. But the most important thing to note here is the scale of the orchestra. During King David's ceremony to move the Ark of the Covenant, all of the leading dignitaries and relatives of King David were involved in playing instruments, to the delight of the great deity. But the similarity with the court of Akhenaton goes much deeper than this, for it is highly likely that the court of King David was actually based in Lower Egypt, as I explain in great detail in the book *Solomon*.

While this has been a long diversion from the story of Eve, this all suggests that the sacred Words from the lungs (or bagpipes) of the high priestess (Nefertiti) were not simply there to please the deity, they may well have become the actual Word of God, sung *fortissimo*. Since Nefertiti's title suggested 'beauty', breath', 'voice', 'speech' and 'coming together', perhaps all of these concepts can now be combined, resulting in a name that may once have implied 'Beautiful Woman's Breath of Life Comes Together like Singing'.

Since Nefertiti's mother, Tiye, was a musician for Amen and pioneered the royal association with the sistrum, it is likely that Nefertiti followed the family tradition. Indeed, the Hymn to the Aton makes this point very clear when it states that:

> And of the Great Queen (Nefertiti), his beloved, rich in beauty,
> Who contents the Aton with a sweet voice,
> With her beautiful hands on the sistra,
> The Lady of the Two Lands, Nefer-neferu-Aton Nefertiti, everliving
> Who is at the side of the Sole One of Ra (Akhenaton) for all time. [8]

The text here appears to be confirming that the claims I have made for the true meaning of Nefertiti's name are correct. The words *nefer-titi* can have the dual meaning of 'beauty' and 'voice' and here we can clearly see the Hymn to the Aton making that very same comparison and thus reinforcing the dual nature of her title. In the first line, Nefertiti is praised for her great beauty, which is hardly in doubt considering the exquisite form of her image in the Berlin bust; but the second line immediately counterpoints this evident beauty with her sweet voice that so charmed the Aton. What the revised and expanded title for Nefertiti suggests to me, with its reference to voices 'coming together', is something like a *soprano* choir, with Nefertiti as its *prima donna*, whose sweet, trilling voice sang the sacred words of the Hymn to the Aton. The voice of the god often spoke through the priests and priestesses, and it is entirely possible that these divine incantations were sometimes performed with all the harmony of a *soprano* version of a Gregorian chant or a Welsh male-voice choir.

Even the Koran indicates that this third-party vocal communication was a traditional method for the gods to converse with mankind, when is says:

(Abraham) replied ... 'Ask them if (the idols of their gods) can speak' ... Confounded as they were, they said to Abraham: 'You know they cannot speak'. Abraham answered: 'Would you then worship that, instead of God, which can neither help nor harm you? Shame on you and your idols! Have you no sense?' [K9]

The problem that Abraham was having with the idol worshipers mirrors the problems that Akhenaton and Nefertiti were having with the Theban regime in Upper Egypt. Like Abraham, Akhenaton was an iconoclast, and passionately against the worship of the pantheon of gods from old Egypt. This is why I argued, in the book *Jesus*, that Abraham was an ancestor of Akhenaton and the struggle of the Amarna regime against icons was an old dispute that had started some 500 years previously with the rise of the Hyksos Shepherd Kings in Lower Egypt.

Note, however, that Abraham is preventing idols from becoming the mouthpiece of god, and not explicitly preventing a priest from taking on that role. Since his later *protégé*, Akhenaton, styled himself as the Only Son of God, it is likely that he used this position to present himself as the spokesperson for god, as do most modern high priests and popes. This would mean that the word of Akhenaton was the Word of God, except that Akhenaton appears to have given an element of this privilege to his second in command, Nefertiti.

It was perhaps from this arrangement that we derive yet another forerunner of the Christian Trinity. Within the Trinity there is supposed to be the three deities, which during the Amarna era consisted of the Aton, Akhenaton and Nefertiti:

God (Aton).

The Aton was not simply the Sun-disk but rather the 'power that lay behind the Sun'. The prime deity was more a description of the great forces and mechanics that regulate the Universe, and that was one of the reasons why astronomy was so important to the Egyptian priesthood. The Aton was unusual in having a cartouche that also made him a king. This was probably a clever device by Akhenaton, as this subtly reduced the seniority and authority of the Aton and boosted Akhenaton onto a level that was nearly equal to the god-figure. The titles given to the Aton were:

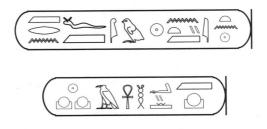

From the upper cartouche:

Iim ren f	Praise his name
Iim shu netii	Praise the Light exists
Iim Aton	Praise the Sun-disk

Fig 3.4   Cartouches and names of the god Aton.

The Son (Akhenaton).

The son of the Aton was Akhenaton himself, for he was the Son of God. His titles also included the names Neferkhepure Ua-enre, which mean 'Beautiful like the Forms of Ra' and 'Only one of Ra'. So Akhenaton styled himself as the 'Only Son of Ra' and this title was deliberately mimicked by Jesus, who similarly styled himself as the 'Only Begotten Son':

> For God so loved the world, that he gave his only begotten Son, that whosoever believes in him should not perish, but have everlasting life. [B10]

Thus it would appear that Jesus had inherited at least two of the traditional titles of the pharaohs. He was known as Ua-enra, the 'Only Begotten Son', and he was also called Setepenra, or 'God's Carpenter'.

Akhenaton Neferkhepure Ua-enre

Fig 3.5 Cartouches and names of Akhenaton.

The Holy Spirit (Nefertiti).

As we have already seen, the terms 'Holy Spirit' and 'Holy Ghost' were both derived from the Hebrew *elohiym ruwach* רוח אלהים or the Greek *hagios pneuma* αγιος πνευμα. These can both mean 'Divine Spirit' but since the words *ruwach* and *pneuma* can both mean 'breath', these terms can be more rationally translatable as the 'Divine Breath'. In terms of the Sun-god Ra, this divine breath has already been equated with the air-god Shu, and through this to the rays or emanations that can be felt coming from the Sun, or perhaps to the atmospheric winds that are stirred up by the Sun.

But, as with most things in Egyptian religion, the divine events that occur in heaven invariably had an equivalent within the mundane world of priests and men; and this was certainly true of the concept of the 'Divine Breath'. As has already been demonstrated, the name for Nefertiti was primarily based upon the *nefer* glyph ⌽, which represents a heart and a windpipe; the primary emphasis here being on the concept of 'breath'. Thus, her full title referred to the 'Breath of the Word Comes'. Since this 'Word' that the breath was creating was representative of the divine word of god, Nefertiti herself could also have been known as the 'Divine Breath'; or if we are to translate this phrase into New Testament terminology, she was called the 'Holy Spirit'. Thus the name for Nefertiti conforms precisely to the title given to this peculiar entity called the Holy Spirit or Holy Ghost.

While the new translation above may initially sound peculiar, the traditional concept of what the Holy Ghost actually represents is also shrouded in mystery. The venerable theologian Adam Clarke firstly gives us a list of rational answers to this question, but then settles on a divine interpretation. He says of the Holy Ghost (Holy Spirit):

Others understand by it an elementary fire. Others, the sun, penetrating and drying up the earth with his rays. Others, the angels, who were supposed to have been employed as agents in creation. Others, a certain occult principle, termed the *anima mundi* or 'soul of the world'. Others, a magnetic attraction, by which all things were caused to gravitate to a common center. But it is sufficiently evident from the use of the word in other places, that the Holy Spirit of God is intended, which our blessed Lord represents under the notion of wind.[20]

Unfortunately for the rational inquirer, this final and divine explanation for the Holy Spirit of God was never clarified by Clarke, and the concept was left in a blur of suggestive possibilities that this may have been an 'energy' or 'emanation' of god that formed some component within the tortuous communications that exist between god and man. As is usual with theologians, their understanding of the subject is poor because quite often the answers are simply not known; so to cover their ignorance they clothe themselves in a cloak of meaningless metaphysical jargon and hope the inquirer will be satisfied and go away. The cardinal or pope will not permit himself to say 'I haven't got a clue', as this would rock the foundations of the organisation.

However, through the process of dogged rational enquiry, we now have a much clearer vision of what this Word or Holy Spirit actually represented. It was indeed a communication device, but it was more often than not a reference to a priestly incantation, led in this case by the strikingly beautiful Queen Nefertiti. This is confirmed by the Prayer to the King and Queen, which again came from Amarna:

...and for the Great King's Wife, his beloved, abounding in her beauty, her who sends the Aton to rest with a sweet voice and her two beautiful hands bearing two sistrums, the mistress of the Two Lands Neferuaton Nefertiti, living for ever.[21]

Here, the image of the Word is less of a resounding Gregorian chant and more of a sweet lullaby, accompanied by the mesmerising jingle of two sistrums, as the Sun-god majestically sets in the west (or rises in the east).

Akhenaton and Nefertiti, Adam and Eve

This small investigation has now come a long way from its humble beginnings in the depths of the Genesis story. Amazing as it may seem, it is evident that the titles for the Amarna trinity of Aton, Akhenaton and Nefertiti have precisely the same attributes and meanings as the New Testament Trinity of God, Jesus and the Holy Spirit. Thus the Amarna worship and ritual is highly likely to have been a forerunner of the Christian creed.

In order for this to have happened in this manner, it is certain that the later cult of Christianity was firmly based upon the traditions that emanated from the remains of the Amarna regime. As I speculated in the book *Jesus*, the cult of the Aton was not completely extinguished by the predations of the Theban priesthood; instead, it uprooted itself and embarked on a smaller exodus to Avaris, Tanis and thence at a later date to Jerusalem. It was this event, intermingled and entwined with the legends of the earlier and greater Hyksos exodus out of Avaris, that became the Torah's Exodus story.

Having taken these myths, legends and traditions to Jerusalem, and beyond to the extremities of the Mediterranean, the Amarna scribes in exile set about compiling their great scroll. This was going to be a compendium of ancient traditions intermixed with genealogies, court gossip and the actual events and tragedies that the royal family had suffered at the hands of the evil (Theban) Egyptians. Thus the scribes started their great scroll with a version of the Hymn to the Aton, and the two main characters who were to grace this diurnal celebration of the dawn were the king and the queen of Amarna. But the Torah (Bible) has quite obviously undergone a transition period of obfuscation, whereby the original Egyptian ancestry and history of the early Israelites became an embarrassment or a political hot potato. It is quite apparent that all of the heroes in these texts underwent a process of cloaking, whereby they were assigned nicknames that concealed but nevertheless alluded to their real identity, and accordingly we are unlikely to find the names 'Akhenaton' and 'Nefertiti' within the Torah. This concealment is particularly visible within the United Monarchy who, despite their much more recent appearance in the history-book of the Israelites, all picked up concealing nicknames, as I explain in the book *Solomon*.

Akhenaton

The name for Akhenaton is a bit of a muddle in the first place, because there is no consensus on what this title actually means. Akhenaton was born as Amenhotep IV, but changed his name to Akhenaton in deference to his new deity: the Aton. Peter Clayton indicates that the name means 'Servant of the Aton', which would be fine except that *akhen* is not readily translatable as 'servant'. James Breasted styles him the 'Heat which is in the Aton', which seems a bit peculiar. Cyril Aldred gives 'Great Bull of Aton', which does translate, but since Akhenaton was of the Hyksos Shepherd lineage his being identified with a bull is unlikely. In the circumstances, perhaps the terms *aakhu* 🐦𓏛 meaning 'words', and *aakhu* 🐦𓏛 meaning 'light' would be more appropriate. Thus Akhenaton was regarded as the Word of

III Eve

God or the Light of God, all of which are terms that have percolated through into the New Testament. Since Akhenaton promoted himself as being god's spokesman on Earth, the first of these appellations would have been eminently suitable: Akhenaton means 'Word of the Aton'.

But in what manner can Akhenaton be associated with the Genesis story of Adam and Eve? Well, despite the unusual nature of his administration, Akhenaton was still related to the Hyksos pharaohs of Lower Egypt and thus when his regime failed, these refugees from Amarna initially fled to Avaris in the Nile Delta, the original capital city of the Hyksos dynasties. As a descendant of the Hyksos pharaohs, Akhenaton would naturally have been associated with redness, as was the Aton itself with its strong association with the sunrise. Thus the nickname ascribed to Akhenaton in the revised Judaic Hymn to the Aton (Genesis) may well have been Adam, meaning 'red'.

Nefertiti

The scribes appear to have similarly changed Nefertiti's name. That the Israelites knew of the name Nefertiti is confirmed by the fact that they had picked up the words *nefesh* נפש and *nafach* נפח – which mean 'life' and 'breath' respectively – from Egypt; and so these words remain very close to the Egyptian concepts of *nefer*. But a name sounding like *nefer* was too obvious for the devious biblical scribes, who wanted to conceal forever the identity of Eve, and so another name had to be chosen to hide the identity of the queen. The association with the *hafa* snake has already been covered in some detail at the beginning of this chapter, but there were two other witty puns that could be derived from Khavah's (Eve's) new nickname, and so the word that they eventually chose as a pseudonym for Nefertiti also managed to reflect some of her rather obvious physical attributes. The conveniently similar words the scribes had in mind were *khefa* and *kefa* .

Early on in the reign of Akhenaton, the style of Amarna art began to exaggerate the hips and thighs and also to elongate the skull, and so the first of these nicknames, *khafa*, referred to Nefertiti's swollen imagery. The reason for these strange depictions of the royal family at Amarna was that this body-form was thought to have been the precise physical image of the gods, as Akhenaton understood them to be; an argument that will be debated at length in Appendix 1. However, I would doubt that the artists and sculptors were all privy to this secret theological information, and I would expect that some kind of cover story was given to them instead. Not understanding the full reasoning for these distorted and swollen depictions of the royal family, the artists and scribes may have thought them to be rather comical, and so

III Eve

they secretly called Nefertiti *khefa* ⊘⚊🖿📿 , meaning 'swollen', or 'puffed up'. A better description of Nefertiti's image at Amarna would be difficult to find, and so this has to be a part of the reasoning that lies behind Khavah's (Eve's) biblical name. But the full explanation for the term *kefa*, and thus the confirmation of this explanation, will have to wait until Chapter IV.

It is sometimes implied that the Greeks destroyed the entire original pronunciation of Eve's Hebrew name, Khavah, when they altered the pronunciation to Eua Ευα. Actually, the Greek 'Eve' is a truncated transliteration from the Hebrew, with the initial 'kh' – which should be rendered like the 'ch' in a Scottish 'loch' – being all but deleted. Thus, the Greeks pronounced the name as Heua, or Eua, with a 'u' vowel, whereas the English version utilised the Hebrew 'v' consonant and derived Eve. Another derivative for this Greek interpretation of Khavah is *euaggelizo* ευαγγελιζω, which normally results in the English word 'evangelise' and implies 'proclamation' or 'preaching'. The term 'proclaim' can be directly associated with the concept of the 'Word' that has already been discussed, which is based upon speech and breathing. Thus, this Greek rendition of Khavah's (Eve's) name seems to be as close to the original Egyptian meaning for Nefertiti – that of the 'Breath of the Word' or the 'Word of God' – as is the Hebrew version.

We are now faced with a rather intriguing result to this investigation. In the last chapter, I have already shown the direct similarities between the biblical creation myth and the Hymn to the Aton. The Hymn was created by the heretic pharaoh Akhenaton, but now it can be clearly seen that the hero and heroine of this biblical story, Adam and Eve, have strikingly similar attributes to those of Akhenaton and his wife Nefertiti. Never being one to shy away from making bold suggestions, it would appear to be entirely possible to me that Adam and Eve were actually pseudonyms for Akhenaton and Nefertiti.

This famous name for the first woman of Amarna, Nefertiti, or at least the particular attributes of 'winds' and 'spirits' that we have already identified, were handed down through the ages and they surfaced again within the New Testament. There we find two more princesses, Mary the Virgin and Mary of the Tower (Mary Magdalene), who were also associated with winds:

> And certain women, which had been healed of evil spirits and infirmities, Mary called Magdalene, out of whom went seven devils. [B22]

As was discussed in the book *Solomon*, the spirits being mentioned here were called *pneuma* πνευμα, which can mean 'spirit' as in 'ghost', or it can refer to a 'wind' as in the *hagios pneuma,* the 'Divine Wind' or the 'Divine Breath'. So, like Nefertiti herself, Mary Magdalene was also associated with the 'Word' or 'Voice', the divine exhalations and incantations of the gods or the high priestesses. But the comparison goes even deeper than this, for at least one, if not both, of these Marys were known as Virgins, and yet so too was Nefertiti. One of the possible translations for *nefer*  is not simply 'beautiful' or 'breath', but 'virgin'. Despite the long span of time between these two events, it would appear that the traditions had been maintained and the concepts of 'Virgin' and 'Breath' were still associated with the royal princesses.

These titles were, of course, a part of the traditions associated with the position of God's Wife, a subject that was covered in some detail in the book *Solomon*. But from the point of view of this new investigation, it is worth noting that Mutnodjime, a daughter of Nefertiti, held the title of God's Wife. This would tend to suggest that the Amarna wives were related in some way to one of the earliest and most famous of the God's Wives, a lady who had a rather familiar title as she was called Nefertari, the chief wife of Ahmose I.

Fig 3.6   Cartouche of Nefertari

There are a number of other similarities between Nefertiti and Nefertari, as both appear in the same diaphanous robes, both use the Nubian wig, both used the royal cartouche for their names, and both are shown in the daily worship of the gods, a role which is quite unlike that given to other royal queens. The only point of contention in this ancestry, however, is that Ahmose I was the pharaoh who expelled the Hyksos from Egypt, and yet my previous assertions indicated that Akhenaton was descended from the Hyksos regime; his father and grandfather having used the Hyksos' shepherd's crook in their titles. But this problem is easily overcome if it is assumed that these influential wives were from another branch of the royal family, who were using the age-old technique of the royal marriage alliance to win control over Thebes and Upper Egypt. It is thought that Nefertari was the cousin of Ahmose I, not his sister, and so this possibility does exist.

The next of the influential God's Wives was Queen Maakhare Hatshepsut, who was another influential woman who managed to elevate herself onto the throne while her stepson, the future Tuthmoses III, was only a child. This was in the post Hyksos era, and so Pharaoh Ahmose I would have already destroyed the gardens of the Hyksos pharaohs in Avaris, and yet the mortuary temple that Hatshepsut built for herself was known as the 'Garden for Amun', and was depicted as containing a veritable jungle of rare plant species. The queen also sent a very famous expedition down the coast of Africa, which brought back a number of animals, plants, treasures and novelties from the southern half of the continent, for the delight and wonder of the royal court. This expedition could easily have been associated with and woven into the even more ancient flood myth to produce the Torah's story of Noah and the Ark – but more of that later.

Fig 3.7   The arboreal garden and sacred pool of Nebamun.

The palaces of Amenhotep III and his son Akhenaton likewise used to portray glorious scenes of wildfowl in amongst dense vegetation, which is reminiscent of the Delta lands. Amenhotep's palace at Malkata in Thebes contained some stunning decorated plasterwork portraying the marshlands, as did Akhenaton's palace at Amarna. This naturalistic decoration from Hatshepsut onwards through to the Amarna family was a dramatic departure from Egyptian tradition, and once again it strongly links the Amarna family with the concept of a sacred garden.

Under the influence of these pharaohs, these gardens and their depiction became a common feature of Egyptian life. The Theban tomb of a nobleman called Nebamun, who lived during the reign of Amenhotep III, contains a fresco of what was presumed to have been his back garden: complete with pool, fish, ducks, trees and various lush plant life. However, bearing in mind that this was a tomb and the scene includes a number of offerings, these lush domestic gardens may have also represented an image of the imagined afterlife and so even the domestic garden may have held sacred overtones. It may well be from this emphasis on the lush, idyllic garden that the concept of a special Garden of Eden was derived; and we shall discuss this in more detail later.

III   Eve

Yahweh

In addition to encountering the name Eve, we now – for the first time in the Torah – have another name for god, that of Yahovah (Yahweh) יהוה. I have already taken a look at this name in the book *Tempest*, but there are some further aspects of this name that may be worthy of further investigation.

The method of discovering the true meaning of this name is again through that enigmatic phrase, 'I am that I am' (*hayah asher hayah* היה אשר היה), which was supposed to describe the name of god. But with all this additional information from the last two chapters, we are now in a much better position to further explain this phrase. The word being used for 'I am' is *hayah* היה which means something like 'to be' or 'to exist'. But, as was shown back in the early verses of Genesis, the term *hayah (ha-yaw)* היה can also mean 'arise', and it may well have been derived from the Egyptian word *hi-ia* 𓎛𓏤𓇋𓄿𓏛, meaning 'rise'. But Hebrew scholars indicate the root word for *hayah* is actually *havah (ha-vaw)* הוה, which paradoxically means 'to fall', and which may have been derived from the Egyptian *ha-aa* 𓉐𓄿𓄿𓂝, which again means 'fall'. The middle word in this phrase is *asher* אשר meaning 'that', 'which' or 'until'.

Using these two new Hebrew words for 'I am', we would now derive something like 'I rise until I fall'. The phrase is beginning to make sense, but it can be refined further because the word *asher* אשר can also mean 'advance' or 'travel', and this could easily have been derived from *asa (ashem)* 𓇋𓏤𓂻𓏤, meaning 'travel'. This new interpretation is doubly reinforced because the Egyptian words for rising and falling both imply motion or travel. If this were the case, then the enigmatic biblical phrase would now become 'I rise, travel, and fall', or in a more expanded format it could also be read as 'the celestial body rises in the east, travels across the skies and descends towards the western horizon'.

Thus it is likely that the phrase 'I am that I am' היה אשר היה was simply a graphic description of the physical attributes and actions of a celestial body. This would actually make sense, because Moses was asking for a description of god (his name) and that is more or less what he got. Fitting these new translations into the biblical verse, it should now read as:

> And Moses said unto God, Behold, when I come unto the children of Israel, and shall say unto them, The God of your fathers hath sent me unto you; and they shall say to me, What is his name? What shall I say unto them? And God said unto Moses, '<u>I am he that rises in the east, crosses the sky, and sets in the west</u>': Thus shalt thou say unto the children of Israel, '<u>he that rises hath sent me unto you</u>'. [B23]

III Eve

As we saw in the last chapter, the primary meaning for the god-name Elah or Allah was El-Ah or Al-Ah meaning the Sun and the Moon, or the Two Eyes of Horus. So both of these elements of the god-name were referring to a celestial body. But the Hebrew god had two other names. Sometimes he was called Adhon אדנ, and it is highly likely that this name was derived from the name of Akhenaton's Sun-god Adjon (Aton) 〰⊙ . While this name for the god matched the El or Al in Elah or Alah, traditional Egypto-Judaic dualism would dictate that there should be another god-name to equate with the Ah portion of the name and counterbalance the text. This would seem to be exactly what has happened and, as I discussed in the book *Tempest*, the Egyptian name for the Moon-god is *Aah (Yah)* 𓇹 , while the short form for Yehova is Yah יה, and is almost identical in pronunciation.* Thus Yehova represents the Ah in Elah or Allah.

It would seem that the god's answer to Moses was (deliberately) ambiguous. There was obviously a lot of competition between the various gods at this time, because the Moses era is the era of Akhenaton and his monotheistic revolution. Moses was probably the brother of Akhenaton and he is asking the god (the pharaoh?) what name he should use for god in front of the people. Knowing Akhenaton's views, he can hardly stand up and introduce Thoth (the Moon-god) to the people, because Akhenaton's guards would lynch him (similarly, the Koran says that Moses dragged Aaron around by the hair because of the golden calf incident). The exquisitely diplomatic reply to overcome this situation is remarkably similar to the reply made by Jesus regarding predictions of the weather, as we have already seen. Thus Moses chose the complicated title of 'I rise in the east and set in the west'. The beauty of this phrase is that everyone can see in this title what they want to see. The pure Atonists would see the Aton (Sun) dawning in the east; the supporters of Thoth could quite happily venerate the same title while imagining the Moon-god; while the Amen supporters might equally imagine Amen-Ra setting in the west.

A much later example of this same kind of diplomatic expediency was created during the Jacobean rebellion in eighteenth century Scotland. Charles Edward Stuart, who was better known as Bonnie Prince Charlie, was in exile from his native Scotland. In 1745 he went to Scotland to rally the troops against England, but was comprehensively defeated at Culloden Moor in 1746 and he was forced into exile again. In defeat, the Scottish nobles

---

* Since the verb *hava* הוה (to fall) is likely to have been derived directly from the god-name Yahweh יהוה, this would imply that the original Victorian pronunciation of this title may have been actually closer to the original. The term *havah* would have been derived from a word that sounded like Yehava or Yehova, rather than the modern version of Yahweh.

were forced to drink toasts to the English king, which they proceeded to do with some gusto, much to the surprise of the English. However, what the nobles were doing was toasting 'To the King!' over a bowl of water. Unaware of the symbolism, the English saw this as a toast to their English king, but to the Scots it was a toast to the 'king over the water' – Bonnie Prince Charlie.

Eye

The Sun and Moon were not simply linked together through being the two eyes of Horus, they were also regarded on occasions as being two forms of the same deity. The Moon not only happens to have the same apparent diameter as the Sun, it also appears to the layman that the Moon follows the Sun around in the night sky. It was because of these similarities that the Moon became the Silver Aton (Adon): the ghostly night-time counterpart of the blazing daytime Aton, which completed the duality of the heavenly bodies. This is hinted at in verse 1:16 of the biblical creation epic, where the two predominant celestial bodies are being fashioned:

> 1:16 And God made# the two great# lights#, the greater light# to rule the day, and the lesser# light# to rule the night.

> 1:16 And the Ra-Horus multiplied (made) the two great eyes, the Sun to rule the day, and the Moon to rule the night.

The creation of the two 'lights' quite obviously refers to the Sun and the Moon. The fact that a Sun-god is said here to be creating the Sun may seem a paradox; but in the guise of Atum, Ra was the primeval creator god, the god that fashioned himself from the watery chaos of Nu. Atum-Ra was the only god capable of self-creation, and this is why the name being used for Ra in this particular case, Ar ⲟ̄ , can also mean 'create' or 'fashion'.

The term being used for these celestial bodies in this biblical quote is also interesting, as they are called 'lights', or *mer* מאֹר in the Hebrew. The word *mer* is supposed to mean 'light', but unfortunately there is no equivalent of this in the Egyptian. This had me puzzled for a while until I saw that *mer* ⲟ̄ referred to an 'eye', or, more importantly, the divine eyes of the Sun and the Moon. It would seem that the text from the Torah is not only telling the same story as Egyptian mythology, it is also using the exact same terminology. The Sun and the Moon were indeed the two great eyes, just as the Bible describes, and in the original liturgy of Heliopolis these eyes belonged to Horus - the Hebrew Elah or Allah.

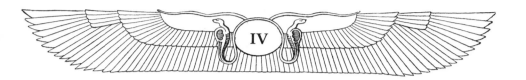

Forbidden Fruits

Having introduced the first heroine, Khavah (or Eve), the story of Genesis then goes on to explain a little more about the life and times of this legendary couple. It is from these new legends that we can glean more details that demonstrate that Akhenaton and Nefertiti were actually known in the Bible as Adam and Eve.

> 2:25 And they were both naked, the man and his wife, and were not ashamed.
> 3:1 Now the serpent# was more subtle# than any other wild# creature# that the Lord# God# had made. He said to the woman, "Did God# say, 'You shall not eat# of any tree# of the garden#'?"
> 3:2 And the woman said to the serpent#, "We may eat# of the fruit# of the trees# of the garden#;
> 3:3 but God said, "You shall not eat# of the fruit# of the tree# which is in the midst of the garden#, neither shall you touch# it, lest you die#."
> 3:4 But the serpent# said to the woman, "You will not die#."

> 2:25 And they were both naked, the man and his wife, and were not ashamed.
> 3:1 Now the *uraeus* was more naked than any living woman that Ra-Horus had made. He said to the woman, "Did the gods say, 'You shall not eat of any branches on the estate'?"
> 3:2 And the woman said to the *uraeus*, "We may eat of the fruit of the trees of the garden;"
> 3:3 but Horus said, "You shall not eat of the fruit of the tree which is in the middle of the garden, neither shall you strike it, lest you die."
> 3:4 But the *uraeus* said to the woman, "You will not die."

The first question to answer, I suppose, is the identity of this 'snake' that outwitted Adam and Eve in this battle of temptation. The Hebrew here is *nachash* נחש and this is a word that has been taken from the Egyptian once more. The literal meaning is not simply a 'serpent', rather it is a combination of two meanings – 'serpent' and 'brass' – which, when combined, result in a more fundamental meaning of 'divination' or 'enchantment'. This combination of meanings may have been derived from the scene where Moses confronted the Pharaoh's magicians with his brass rod, which became a serpent, but it may also have an Egyptian explanation. The word *nachash* may have originally been taken from the Egyptian *nehes* , which also means 'incantations', and so the initial imagery may be one of a high priest muttering his incantations and performing some kind of ritual.

The words being used for the phrase 'wild creature' are interesting too. The Hebrew *sahdeh kha* שדה חי can indeed mean 'wild creature', but again there may be a masculine bias to the translation because the alternative is 'living woman'. The word being used for 'creature' was a *ka*, a 'life-force' or 'soul', and this is a term that has already been explained in both languages. The combination of these words would point towards this being a female individual rather than a wild creature, and the new translation does appear to be more suitable in the context of the story. But this new interpretation would have been instantly rejected, as it again undermines the traditional Genesis setting of the first man and woman – because here we see that Eve (Khavah) was being compared to other females.

The more important question of what this particular paragraph is trying to say is not easy to answer, but we can make some educated assumptions. The first thing to note is that there appear to be two gardens once more. Khavah is allowed to eat of the trees of the garden, but not those in the middle of the garden. This would equate to the arguments already made, whereby Eden is Egypt and within Egypt there was a special sacred garden inside which the fruits were forbidden. But since we have already firmly associated this entire Genesis story with the Hyksos nation in general and perhaps with the Amarna regime in particular, this new perspective may now assist us with an entirely new interpretation of this particular story.

Although Pharaoh Akhenaton built his new city of Amarna prominently and symbolically in the center of Egypt, he was not a king of Upper and Lower Egypt in the true sense of the word. His titles may have included the designation 'Lord of the two Lands', but Akhenaton was only ever depicted with the *uraeus* cobra symbol of Lower Egypt – which was called the *arat* in the Egyptian – and never with the *nekhbet* vulture symbol of the south. Furthermore, his father, Amenhotep III, and both his queens, Nefertiti and Kiya, also sported the *uraeus*. Nefertiti did sometimes wear the double *uraeus*, which is said to somehow represent the joint *nebty* (the cobra and vulture symbols of Lower and Upper Egypt respectively); but the display of a double cobra instead of a cobra and vulture would seem to me to be a double sleight on the traditional symbology of the south. It could well have implied that not only was the queen going to ignore the vulture symbology, but she was going to replace it with a cobra too! Note also that Tutankhamen – the boy-king who effectively followed Akhenaton onto the throne and was being manipulated by the Upper Egyptian priesthood – was most pointedly depicted with the *uraeus* and *nekhbet* symbols. This sudden reversion to the traditional symbols of the Two Lands indicates to me that Akhenaton's refusal to wear them rankled somewhat.

As I have argued previously, it would seem that the foundations of the Amarna regime were firmly centered in the lands of Lower Egypt, the traditional homeland of the Hyksos kings. Since the story of Khavah (Eve) seems to have been based upon the life of Nefertiti, who always wore the *uraeus*, the sudden appearance of a snake in the biblical story would tend to suggest that this event was also something to do with the *uraeus*, the traditional symbol of Lower Egypt. Note that the name used for serpent in the biblical text was *nachash* נחש, which can mean either 'serpent' or 'bronze'. Traditionally, of course, the *uraeus* was a bronze insert that was added to the icons and statues of the pharaohs. The serpent that tempted Nefertiti (Eve) may well have been the traditional symbol for Lower Egypt, and so the solution to this textual enigma is likely to be Egypto-political.

In the Hebrew, the term being used for 'nakedness' (*arum* ערום) can also mean 'shrewdness' (*arum* ערום), so it would seem likely that the scribe was making another rhyme here, as both the snake and the primeval couple were said to be *arum*. This would imply that the chapter has been divided in the wrong position and verse 2:25 should have been placed in the Bible at the beginning of chapter 3. The linking of the craftiness of the snake with the nakedness of Adam and Eve might indicate that the attributes of a crafty snake could also be applied to Adam and Eve (they use exactly the same word but assume a different meaning). Alternatively, it could also imply that the incorrect meaning for *arum* has been chosen for the snake, and the text was trying to say that both the snake and Eve were naked. What we may be looking for, therefore, is a word that means both 'naked' and 'snake', and is somehow related to Eve (Khavah).

There is such a word and we have seen examples of it previously. The word in question is actually Khavah, and in the Egyptian we can derive *hafa* 〔glyphs〕 meaning 'snake', *khafa* 〔glyphs〕 meaning 'swollen', and now there is also *kafa* 〔glyphs〕 meaning 'naked'. So in what way does this 'crafty naked snake' imagery apply to our historical equivalent for Eve?

Again, for an answer to this we need look no further than the Amarna royalty and to Akhenaton and Nefertiti in particular. Not only were the Amarna couple very shrewd and cunning in their steady persecution of the old religions of Egypt, but nearly all of the Amarna depictions show the royal couple in diaphanous robes that render the king and queen virtually naked, and dramatically display their distended waistlines and thighs. Thus, when wearing their prominent *uraeus* cobra symbols, both Akhenaton and Nefertiti could have been derogatorily referred to as the 'swollen naked snakes'. So the Egyptian equivalents for the name Khavah (Eve) all match the attributes of Nefertiti. She was nearly always *kafa* (naked), invariably *khafa* (swollen), and always wearing the *hafa* (snake) emblem; so her logical nickname was Khavah, or Eve. Here, then, are the primeval couple from the Torah, the naked Adam and Khavah (Eve), who in reality ruled over Upper and Lower Egypt during the latter part of the eighteenth dynasty.

Fig 4.1   Akhenaton and Nefertiti (Adam and Eve) portrayed as being naked and swollen.

Of course, Adam and Khavah lived in the Garden of Eden, and while I have been previously pointing towards the Nile Delta for the location of this most famous of pleasure parks, this identification of Adam and Khavah (Eve) with Akhenaton and Nefertiti does mean that the Garden of Eden should be more closely associated with their new capital city at Amarna (Akhetaton). This is entirely possible, because although the concept of the sacred grove or garden started with the Hyksos pharaohs of the Delta region, it is more than likely that their descendants would have carried this tradition to the many other locations in which they were to be exiled. This would also make sense of the description of Eden that was discussed earlier. Chapter two of Genesis says:

> And a river went out of Eden to water the garden; and from thence it was parted, and became into four heads. [B1]

Thus far, I have taken the term Eden to refer to all of Egypt, or perhaps a part of the Nile Delta. But the verse says that the river ran out of 'Eden' before parting and becoming the Delta region, and so the sacred Garden in Eden must have been south of the Delta. There are two suggestions that would fit this report. Firstly, the location may have been Amarna, and the Nile symbolically ran from Akhenaton's new city to the Delta region. Secondly, the suggestion has already been made in the book *Tempest*, that the Nile symbolically flowed from between the two great pyramids that stood on the Giza plateau, because these pyramids were known as the breasts that nourished the land of Egypt with their milk.

The latter concept was probably taken up by the biblical chroniclers when they described the Israelites as travelling to a 'land flowing with milk and honey'. As will be explained in a later chapter, the initial destination for the second exodus of Aaron and Moses was Avaris in the Nile Delta, and so the symbolic 'milk' that flowed through these 'new' promised lands was the waters of the Nile, and this milk was originally sourced from between the symbolic 'breasts' on the Giza plateau. As usual, the scribes were wading deeply into their reservoir of allegory with these descriptions.

This suggestion can be supported by the epigraphic evidence, as the Hebrew for milk, *khelub (kherub)* חלב, is rather similar to the Hebrew for lion, *kerub* כרוב; while the Egyptian for milk, *aar-t* 𓃭𓋴𓏏, is rather similar to the Egyptian for lion, *aar* 𓃭𓎼. I believe that these two terms had the same root source, and that root was actually the great Sphinx that stands between the two pyramidal breasts on the Giza plateau, from where the Nile was symbolically supposed to originate. The link between honey and lions is also given in the book of Judges, where Samson puts a riddle before the people of Timnath:

> And (Samson) said unto them, Out of the eater came forth meat, and out of the strong came forth sweetness. [B2]

IV Forbidden Fruits

The answer to the riddle was that the eater that gave meat was a lion, and out of this strong animal's carcass came honey. This can be seen in a description of the events that caused Samson to devise the riddle:

> And ... (Samson) turned aside to see the carcass of the lion: and, behold, there was a swarm of bees and honey in the carcass of the lion. [B3]

Now this phrase has often caused bewilderment among scholars, and they have sometimes resorted to saying that the scribe had confused the flies around a dead carcass with the bees around a hive. But even the densest of Egyptian yokels would have known the difference between a swarm of flies and a swarm of bees, so how did this myth ever come into being? How did the carcass of a lion produce honey?

The answer lies once more in the description of a land 'flowing with milk and honey', which was actually a reference to a land flowing with the nourishing waters of the Nile. Once again, that milk and honey was derived from a location between the two great breasts (pyramids) that stood near the Sphinx on the Giza plateau, and so the milk and honey was sometimes said to be derived from a lion (the Sphinx). This explanation also forms a bit of a rhyme in the Egyptian, because another name for a lion is *rabai (rabu)* ░░░ and so the original phrase once read as 'out of the *aar* ░░░ and *ra-bai* ░░░ (two lions) came forth *aar-t* ░░░ (milk) and *bi-t* ░░░ (honey)'. Incidentally, the English word 'bee' was probably derived from the Egyptian *bi-t (bee-t)* ░░░ meaning 'bee'.

This link between a lion and bees may have been reinforced by another epigraphic quip. Transferring this argument into terms from the theology of this era, the lion was most easily identifiable as Sekhmet, the lioness goddess. Sekhmet was the wife of Ptah and a favourite deity of the Memphite clans in Lower Egypt, including Amenhotep III, the father of Akhenaton. It was Amenhotep III who oversaw an orgy of Sekhmet statuary creation during his reign. But the biblical quote is implying that the bees came forth from the lion, or perhaps in this case they came forth from Sekhmet.

As it happens, the bee is quite a symbolic insect in Egypt and this special manifestation is called the *bi-t* ░░░ meaning 'king'. Since Amenhotep III was so closely associated with Sekhmet, it could be said that a number of bees (royal princes) had come forth from the lion (Amenhotep III); and their names were Tuthmoses, Akhenaton, and possibly Smenkhkare and Tutankhamen too. In which case, Samson was proposing a riddle that was based upon a deep understanding of the Egyptian language and its royal history.

This dual imagery for the lion-bee-milk-honey associations may well have been borrowed by Akhenaton when he built his new city at Amarna.

Since he was the bee, born of the lion-sphinx-Sekhmet (Amenhotep III), his city may have been referred to as the new Eden, the new source of the river Nile that flowed like milk and honey.

While some of this argument may be a little speculative, the Hebrew aspects of this symbolism were used by the Tate & Lyle sugar company in Britain, and so this famous lion-bee imagery has been displayed upon each and every tin of their golden syrup since.

New Eden

Akhenaton, whether by choice or by force, was thrown into a kind of internal exile in middle Egypt, where he and his band of some 80,000 followers began to carve out a new capital city for themselves at a location that he called Akhetaton, which is now called Amarna. In fact, this modern name may well have been based upon an original name for this location, which was in turn based upon the cartouche of the god Aton. The cartouches for the Aton were as follows:

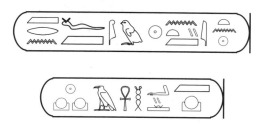

Fig 4.2   Cartouches of Aton.

Translations of these cartouches are hard to find, but as was mentioned in the last chapter it is likely that the upper of these titles was based upon the following sentiments:

im	cry out (praise)
ren	sacred name
f	his
im	praise
shu	Sun
neti	exists
im	praise
aten	the god Aton

IV Forbidden Fruits

A likely translation for the name of the Aton was therefore 'Praise his Sacred Name, Praise the Sun exists, Praise to the Aton'. Later forms of this cartouche changed the word *shu*, as it contained an oblique reference to Shu, the air-god and the husband of Tefnut. Since all gods other than the Aton had been banned, the offending name *shu* was deleted along with the *nti*, and these were replaced with *it* 𓇋𓏏 meaning 'father', and *aii* 𓏭𓏭 meaning 'comes'. The name of the Aton was now 'Praise his Sacred Name, Praise the Father who Comes, Praise to the Aton'. This is perhaps a good demonstration of how the term 'father' may have become synonymous with god in the later Christian tradition.

Going back to the modern name of Amarna, however, it can be seen that from the first two words in the upper cartouche we can derive the words *im-ren*, meaning 'praise (his) sacred name'. But these words may well have been pronounced as *amarena*, and it may have been from this initial portion of the Aton's title that the modern name 'Amarna' may well have been derived. But it is from this same cartouche that another famous name was also derived.

It has already been argued that Adhon (Adon) אדן, one of the many names for the Israelite god, was derived from the name of Akhenaton's god: the Aton 𓇋𓏲𓏏𓇳 . This is especially possible since some of the spellings of this god's name use the form Adjon 𓇋𓆓𓇳 instead of Aton 𓇋𓏏𓇳 . But, as I have already suggested, it is just as likely that the name for Eden was derived from the same source. In the Hebrew, Eden is spelt as עדן, whereas Adon is spelt אדן. All that has happened here is that an *ayin* has been swapped for an *aleph*, and while a few pedants will still argue that these are entirely different consonants, I have already demonstrated in the book *Solomon* that there are a number of words that interchange these consonants with apparent ease. Indeed, the English translations of the *aleph* and *ayin* out of the Hebrew also show a remarkable fluidity between pronunciations using the 'i', 'e' and 'a' vowels (the consonants being changed into vowels in the English translations). In short, Eden (Edon) may be the equivalent of the Hebrew deity Adon (Adhon), which may have been in turn derived from Akhenaton's deity Aton (Aten, Aden, Adon).

In the Hebrew, the name given to this sacred enclosure was the Garden of Eden, or Gen Eden גן עדן. In the dictionary in the appendix, I have argued that the term *gen* came from the Egyptian *ken* or *kam* which both mean 'garden'. However, the word *kam* is more specific than this as it is also the root word for Kam 𓂓𓈖𓏤 , which, as we have already seen, is probably *the* primary name for Egypt. Thus it would seem that the 'garden' that had been created for the god Aten (Eden) was sometimes considered to be the whole of Egypt, and so the Garden of Eden (Gen Eden גן עדן) may sometimes have been a reference to the entire land of Egypt.

But it is entirely probable that during the reign of Akhenaton, the term 'Garden in Eden' became slightly more focused and referred specifically to the city of Akhetaton at Amarna. I believe that Akhenaton had been forcibly exiled to Amarna due to political and theological considerations, as none of the established temple complexes wanted to deal with his new monotheistic ideas. Since Akhenaton had imprisoned himself in this barren strip of land in Middle Egypt, he decided to set up not only a new capital city but also something akin to a closed community, within which he declared that he would never leave. The implication seems to be clear: Akhenaton took the Hyksos traditions of the sacred grove along with his Arian followers to his new capital city at Amarna, where they declared this new metropolis as being the new city and Garden of the Aton. I believe that for a short time during the eighteenth dynasty, the Garden of Eden [Garden of Aten] was the newly irrigated plain at Amarna itself, and its two most prominent citizens were Akhenaton and Nefertiti, who were also known as Adam and Khavah (Eve).

The fall

But there was to be a crisis in the lives of these two Amarna lovebirds, for the *uraeus* was about to tempt them into eating of the fruits of special tree. There were two trees of note in the Garden of Aten [Garden of Eden] at Amarna, the Tree of Life and the Tree of Knowledge of Good and Evil. The Tree of Life was the tree of *Kha* חי, which was derived from the Egyptian *Ka* 𓂓𓀭, which refers to the essence of life. But it was from the latter tree that Khavah (Eve) stole a fruit:

> And when the woman saw that the Tree (of Knowledge) was good for food, and that it was pleasant to the eyes, and a tree to be desired to make one wise#, she took of the fruit thereof, and did eat, and gave also unto her husband with her; and he did eat. And the eyes of them both were opened#, and they knew that they were naked; and they sewed# fig# leaves together, and made themselves aprons. [B4]

It is difficult to be certain about the true meaning of this tree, but I think that the following represents a good insight into the problem. The definition of the Tree of Knowledge was derived from *ets daath* עץ דעת. Now while the *ets* did mean 'tree', it is entirely possible that the 'knowledge' portion of this phrase was not quite what the reader may have envisaged. The Hebrew *daath* does indeed mean 'to know', but it also means 'to be known' or 'to make known', and it is the latter versions that are most probably correct here.

From the Egyptian perspective, the Tree of Knowledge bore fruits, upon which the god Thoth (Djehuti) would inscribe the name of the pharaoh as a memorial to the pharaoh's name. The Temple of Luxor has a good representation of this event, and Thoth can be seen to be inscribing the fruits with the name of the pharaoh Seti I, whose throne name was Menmaatre (see the colour section). The name of the pharaoh was all-important, as the survival of his or her name would ensure the survival of the deceased's soul, and so great expense was devoted to inscribing the name of each pharaoh in every location throughout the land. So it was not just mankind that needed to know the name of the pharaoh, it would seem that the gods required the same information, and this is perhaps where the tree came into play. Thus the tree in question was not so much the Tree of Knowledge, it was more a Tree of Identity, or even a Tree of Remembrance. It was a tree that recorded the successive names of the royal dynasties – it was a family tree.

In this outer layer of reasoning, it was the overriding imperative for the preservation of the history of the royal bloodline that made these enclosed gardens so sacred and important. The trees in these royal gardens at Avaris and elsewhere held the symbolic history, spirit and memory of the royal dynasty, and so anyone caught stealing from its 'fruits' was desecrating the memory and history of the monarchy. These same sacred trees may also have been regarded as Trees of Praises, as the name of the pharaohs may have been read out by the priesthood in memorial to the departed kings. Just like Henry VIII, who left a small legacy to ensure that Mass was said for his soul for years to come, undoubtedly the Egyptian monarchy also ensured that their names would be invoked and praises sung in their honour for millennia. In which case, the Hebrew word *daath*, for 'knowledge', may well have been derived from the Egyptian *Duat* ⌐𓂋𓈖✳𓏌 , meaning 'praises' or to 'cry out'.

So the Tree of Knowledge may have been a metaphor for a written or spoken memorial to the royal family of Egypt, and this argument is confirmed by another verse that states that Khavah (Eve) saw that the tree 'desired to make one wise'. The word being used for 'wise' here was *sakal* or *saker* שכל, which can mean 'wisdom', but it also means 'understanding' or 'consideration'. The Egyptian equivalent was *sakha* 𓏏𓈖𓏏𓏌𓄿 , meaning 'remember' or 'think'; but more importantly, perhaps, this same word also refers to a 'remembrance' or 'memorial'. In which case, the verse should actually have been translated as the tree 'desired to make a memorial', and this is exactly what it once did. The Tree of Remembrance served to keep the name of the pharaoh spoken by both mortal and divine beings alike.

A further clue to the role of the Tree of Remembrance may be found in the word that was used for the fruit of this tree, a *periy* פרי, which was derived from *peree-t* 𓏏𓆰𓏥 . In the Egyptian, the word goes beyond the normal meanings of 'seeds' and 'fruits', and the term can also refer to a person's 'seed' or 'descendants'. Once again we can see evidence that the tree may have represented a Tree of Remembrance, a family tree, and the fruits recorded upon it may therefore have been the descendants of Akhenaton and Nefertiti.

But this is not the full story, for the fruit from the Tree of Remembrance was obviously sacred, and both Adam and Eve and also the snake were all punished for taking this particular fruit. The snake was supposedly deprived of its legs and forced to wriggle on its belly, while the primeval couple were forced to work unproductive lands, and make bread by the sweat of their brow. Clearly, the Book of Genesis is indicating that Adam and Eve were once a pampered couple who had now fallen from grace and were forced to work the land for a living; and the references to sweat and dust graphically demonstrate that this was a life that they were totally unaccustomed to. In addition, Adam and Eve were apparently sent into exile, where they became ashamed and were forced to clothe themselves for the first time.

> And when god had appointed these penalties for them, he removed Adam and Eve out of the Garden into another place. J5

If the Genesis story does refer to Akhenaton and Nefertiti, what we are looking for, therefore, is a hiatus in the lives of the Amarna couple that may have altered their fortunes, perceptions and attitudes. Not only that, we are also looking for a possible eviction from the Garden of Aton [Garden of Eden] at Amarna; an event that caused them to fall from grace in the eyes of the people and become ashamed or embarrassed.

The origins of this event can actually be traced to a rather precise moment in history, for it is to be found in the 12th year, 6th month, and 8th day of Akhenaton's reign. In that year, a great *Heb-Sed* (Jubilee) festival was organised, and foreign dignitaries from all over the known world came and paid homage to Akhenaton. But what was the purpose of this festival? It did not seem accord to the usual 30-year jubilee interval and it didn't seem to concentrate on the usual agricultural, fertility of the land and demarcation of the borders of Egypt imagery. Instead, this particular *Heb-Sed* festival seemed to highlight tribute and foreign relations, so what was its real purpose?

There is a body of information and a number of classical commentators who believe that this event actually marked Akhenaton's formal coronation. Up until this time, Akhenaton had been ruling under a co-regency with his father, Amenhotep III; it was only now, in the 12th year of the co-regency, that Amenhotep III died and Akhenaton acquired the full kingship of Upper and Lower Egypt. This, I believe, is what the Torah was alluding to when it

IV Forbidden Fruits

said that a serpent invited Adam and Eve to eat of the Tree of Knowledge. The serpent was an allusion to the *uraeus*, the kingship of Lower Egypt, and the Tree of Remembrance referred not only to the genealogy of Akhenaton's family, but perhaps also to the genealogies of the gods of the Theban theogony.

The accession of Akhenaton to the throne, in the 12th year of his co-regency, heralded a turbulent time of change. Akhenaton, given the full authority as sole pharaoh, started a new purge against idolatry in Egypt. Symbols and names of the old gods were hacked out across the land, and even the hieroglyphs that represented the old gods were expunged from the spelling of the names of the Aton. It is highly likely that it was these names which were the 'forbidden fruits' that Akhenaton and Nefertiti were plucking from the Tree of Remembrance, and deleting from history. The imagery of Thoth and the Tree of Remembrance in the colour section of this book clearly demonstrates that the fruits contained names, and it was names – including those of the gods – that Akhenaton was destroying.

Guided by the serpent, the symbol of the Lower Egyptian regime based in Avaris, the soldiers of the king were busy deleting the gods' names from history, even those that were inscribed in the very heart of the Temple of Karnak. This was similar to Henry VIII's purge against the Catholic monasteries in England in the sixteenth century and the purges of Oliver Cromwell in the seventeenth century, whose soldiers entered monasteries and cathedrals up and down England and smashed the statues of Mary and Jesus in the name of Protestant iconoclasm. Leviticus 19:4 and 26:1 specifically forbade the manufacture of idols, and yet there they were, brazenly displayed in every Catholic cathedral in the land, in direct contravention of 'god's law'. It was enough to make a Leveller's blood boil, and so Cromwell's New Model Army smashed these imitation gods just as Moses had smashed the golden calf at the foot of Mt Sinai [the Great Pyramid].

While Oliver Cromwell's reformation of English Christianity had a broad base of support among the common people and was enduringly successful, the equivalent reforms by Akhenaton were anything but enduring. Akhenaton went too far too quickly, and the backlash against his suppression and destruction of the old gods was swift. By year 14 (the second year of Akhenaton's full reign) his regime was in dire trouble. It is said that shortly after this time Tiye, Akhenaton's mother, had died; his wives Nefertiti and Kiya had also passed away; plus his daughters Meketaten, Neferneferure and Meritaten. A calamity had struck Amarna from which it would never recover.

It is rumoured that a plague, which was ravaging much of the Near East at the time, had struck the royal court, but I am not so sure that this is true. Akhenaton also disappears from the records of Amarna shortly after this time, and yet it is known that he lived for another three years, until year 17, when Tutankhaton (Tutankhamen) took the throne. While classical history will say that Akhenaton and Nefertiti died at this time, there is absolutely no evidence to support this – absence of evidence is not evidence of absence, as they say. Although Akhenaton's tomb at Amarna has been discovered, no trace of his mummy was ever found. The only evidence in favour of his burial there being the presence of 'magic bricks', which were thought to be placed in the tomb only at the time of burial. However, since our knowledge of Egyptian funerary ritual is far from complete, this is hardly conclusive evidence. The same is true for Nefertiti. The only evidence for her death is a *shabti*, a figurine that is produced for the remembrance of the dead. But Nefertiti's *shabti* was purchased on the antiquities market, and so even if it is genuine, its origins are completely unknown. Anyway, the death of Nefertiti is not in question here, as we know that she died at some point in time; what we don't know is where and when she died.

Recent evidence that purported to demonstrate the fate of Nefertiti came from the investigation of a side-chamber within the tomb of Amenhotep II. It has long been known that this chamber contained the naked mummies of two women and a young boy, but their identities have always been a mystery. The older woman has since been fairly certainly identified as Queen Tiye, the wife of Amenhotep III and the mother of Akhenaton. But what of the other two? As they are both younger than Queen Tiye, it has been suggested by Dr Joann Fletcher that the boy was Tuthmoses, the elder brother of Akhenaton, while the young woman was Nefertiti herself. While Dr Fletcher has gathered a body of information that points towards this identification, the fact of the matter is that the female mummy in question appears to be far too young. Nefertiti had six children, had ruled alongside Akhenaton for at least 14 years, and had a statue that showed her in middle age. In contrast, the mummy appears to be in the age range of 20 to 25 years. Even if the mummy does bear physical similarities to Nefertiti, these are easily explained by her being a close relative, which is more than likely.

Since the names of Nefertiti and Akhenaton disappear from Amarna between the years 14 and 17, we know that at the very least they were deposed as rulers and left Middle Egypt, but that is not in itself evidence of their deaths. However, if we are to equate the Amarna and Moses episodes – the second exodus of 'lepers and maimed priests', according to Manetho – then an alternative scenario is given by both Manetho and the biblical account. Both of these records indicate that there was an exodus, and Manetho indicates that the refugees initially went to Avaris in the Nile Delta.

In the book *Jesus*, I have already associated Manetho's exodus of the [theological] 'lepers' with the Amarna incident. Manetho indicates that a pharaoh called Amenhotep had banished these 80,000 'lepers' to the stone quarries on the east-bank of the Nile. [M6] This story was clearly referring to the 'banishment' of Akhenaton and his followers to Amarna – which was a 'quarry' on the east bank of the Nile – by his father Amenhotep III, for the period of his co-regency. While the historical record does not record this move to Amarna as a banishment, it does record that Nefertiti was not exactly impressed by the move, and so the term 'banishment' may be quite accurate.

Manetho then goes on to say that the priesthood could do nothing against these people for 13 years, for fear of divine wrath and unnamed allies who might join in with the 'lepers' [theological lepers, the people of Amarna]. This is almost precisely correct, for it is now thought that the real problems at Amarna started after the death of Amenhotep III in year 12 of Akhenaton's co-regency. After the sole coronation of Akhenaton there was no longer a father-figure in the form of Amenhotep III to protect the new king, and there was a decreasing amount of support from allies in Syria, as the Mitannite and Naharin had already been conquered by the Hittites. Akhenaton's position in Amarna was looking dangerously exposed, and so he sought to retreat to the friendlier territories of the Hyksos heartlands in the north. Manetho says of this:

> When the men of the stone-quarries [Amarna] had suffered hardships for a considerable time, they begged the king to assign them a dwelling place and refuge in the deserted city of the (Hyksos) Shepherds, Avaris. [M7]

The king being referred to must be Akhenaton, and it is the leading dignitaries of Amarna who are begging the king to leave the city as it is becoming a dangerous place to live. The location they eventually went to was Avaris, which was highly suitable considering the Hyksos sympathies of Akhenaton that I have already mentioned.

> They appointed as their leader one of the priests of Heliopolis called Osarseph [Son of Osiris] ... but when he joined the people he changed his name and was called Moses. [M8]

Ahmed Osman indicates that Moses was Akhenaton himself, whereas I suspect that Moses was actually the brother of Akhenaton who was called TuthMoses. (For the true reasoning behind Moses' name, see the heading 'water' in the dictionary in the appendix.) TuthMoses was the elder brother of Akhenaton, but he did not become king either because of a speech impediment, hinted at in the biblical texts, or because of a law of inheritance that we are unaware of. Repeatedly within the biblical accounts, it is the younger son that becomes the leader or king, and this happens so regularly that I suspect it was normal practice in this era.

The Egyptian record shows the same trends, with the younger sons of Tuthmoses I, Amenhotep II and Amenhotep III all becoming pharaoh. Some of this may be due to infant mortality or sibling infighting, which resulted in the older siblings dying. Alternatively, it may well be that with royal marriages occurring at such a young age, the firstborn of the royal couple was not much younger than the king himself. To create stability in the nation it would be useful to reduce the number of changes in administration, and the choosing of a younger son for the succession would achieve just that. One final option may be that the most important position within the land was actually the lower-profile position of high priest, rather than the high-profile position of pharaoh, and so the elder son may always have been sent into the priesthood. In modern Masonry, the Grand Master of England (the high priest) is not allowed to be the monarch, which is why this post is currently held by a cousin of the Queen. In a similar fashion, Manetho is indicating here that TuthMoses (Akhenaton's brother) became the high priest of Heliopolis, and this is possibly why he disappears from the historical record so early in his life, and was superseded by his brother, Akhenaton (the records of Heliopolis having all been destroyed). Manetho then goes on to describe Moses' new constitution:

> First of all he framed a law that they should neither worship the (old) gods nor refrain from (eating) any of the animals prescribed as sacred in Egypt (the Apis-bull), and that they should have (social and sexual) intercourse with none save those of their own confederacy. After framing a number of laws like these, completely opposed to Egyptian custom, he ordered them to repair the walls and make ready for war... [M9]

The actions of this historical Moses concur precisely with those of both the biblical Moses and also of Akhenaton. Both of these historical characters were iconoclasts set on destroying the polytheism of the old gods and installing in the temples of Egypt a single, enigmatic god who bore no physical image. Both of these characters were also having problems with bull-worshippers in Egypt, and so demanding that their followers eat beef would have been a logical method of sorting out the true followers from the hangers-on and spies.

The reference to the framing of many new laws at this point in time is also undoubtedly biblical. This was the second of the two Hyksos exoduses from Egypt, and in the biblical accounts it was Moses who then wrote down the ten famous commandments, plus the hundreds of others that litter the book of Leviticus. According to Manetho, the framing of these laws took place at Avaris in the Nile Delta, whereas my identification of Mt Sinai as the Great Pyramid at Giza demonstrates that the first ten of these new laws were actually devised en-route to Avaris as the Amarna refugees passed Memphis and Giza.

> Manetho adds that, at a later date, Amenophis advanced from Ethiopia [Thebes] with a large army, with his son Rampses (Ramesses) also leading a force, and that the two together joined battle with the Shepherds (the Hyksos) and their polluted allies and defeated them. [M10]

This is nearly correct, as far as we understand the chronology of this era, but Manetho's chronology is slightly different to the orthodox version. This battle occurred in the years and generations after the exodus of Moses [TuthMoses plus Akhenaton and Nefertiti], and so the biblical text makes no mention of them. The battle was being waged against the next generation of Hyksos Shepherds from Amarna, who were living in Avaris, and their Hyksos allies who had come from Syria (Israel) to assist them; although this influx of people from Syria (Israel) was perhaps due in part to Hittite predations in their homelands.

      The question is, does this account of Manetho square with the known facts of this era? Well, the two primary chronologies of the pharaohs of this era are as follows:

Manetho's chronology	Classical chronology
Ahmos (Ahmoses) (Tethmoses) - 25, 25, 25	Ahmose I - 24
Chebron - 13, 13, 13, 13	
Amenophis - 20, 24, 21, 21	Amenhotep I - 27
	Tuthmoses I - 6
	Tuthmoses II - 14
Amesse (f) - 21, 22	Hatshepsut (f) - 15
Mephres (Misaphris) - 12, 13, 12, 12	
Mephrammuthosis - 20, 26, 26, 26	Tuthmoses III - 54
	Amenhotep II - 34
Tuthmoses - 9, 9, 9, 9	Tuthmoses IV - 33
Amenophis - 30, 31, 31, 31	Amenhotep III - 37
Orus - 36, 37, 38, 28	(See Horemheb)
Achencheres (f?) - 12, 32, 12, 16	Akhenaton - 17 (12 as co-regent)
or Rathos (Moses' brother)	
Acherres (f) - 12, 12, 8	Nefertiti (f)?- 14?? (all co-regent?)
	or possibly Smenkhkare - 3
Chebres (Cherres) - 12, 12, 15	Tutankhamen - 9
Armesis (Harmais) (Dannus) - 4, 5, 5, 5	Aye (Armait) - 4

IV Forbidden Fruits

Ramesses - 1, 1, (Aegyptus)

Horemheb - 28 (see Orus)
Ramesses I - 2
Seti I - 13

Ramesses - 66, 68

Ramesses II - 67

Amenophath (Ammenophis) - 19, 19, 40

Sethos (Ramesses) - 10

(see Seti I, above)

Numbers after the pharaoh's name are reign lengths.   (f) = female.

The accounts of Manetho have arrived via a number of ancient historians: Josephus, Theophilus, Syncellus, Eusebius, and the Armenian version of Eusebius. It is the variations between these different versions that give the differing titles and reign lengths in the above list.

This list demonstrates the problems involved in equating the known archaeology of the region with the historical accounts of Manetho. Some of the names are obvious equivalents, like Tuthmoses being Tuthmoses IV, and Amenophis being Amenhotep III, although the reign lengths differ significantly. Other names are not so obvious, but many of them can nevertheless be resurrected from Manetho's distorted renderings by using a little common sense. Central to the present discussion is Pharaoh Akhenaton, and he can just about be made out in the name Achencheres (also called Rathos in another account).

The first syllables are the same, 'Akhen' versus 'Achen'; the former being a syllable that has been taken from the ibis glyph 𓅞 which is pronounced as 'aakh'. The Greek version of 'Achen' uses either a hard 'k' or a soft 'kh' ('ch') in the different accounts and so there is a direct correspondence between these two words or syllables.

The second syllables to these names are merely two variants of the Sun-god, with one version using 'Aton' and the other using the Hebrew 'Cheres' חרם meaning 'Sun'. Several Egyptologists have challenged my interpretation of Cheres, indicating that the Hebrew for 'Sun' is actually Shemesh שמש. This may be so, but the biblical Mt Heres (Cheres - Kheres) חרם was known as the 'Mountain of the Sun', and so Heres (Cheres - Kheres) חרם does indeed mean 'Sun' in Hebrew. (Bearing in mind the general thrust of my investigations, the true location of Mt Heres is not difficult to fathom.) Another challenge that has been made is that the Egypto-Greek world of Manetho would not have been influenced by a Hebrew word like Cheres. However, it is a fact that Manetho uses the term Cheres in many of the pharaonic names that include a reference to the Sun-god (be it Aton, Amun or Ra). Thus it is abundantly clear that Manetho was using the term Cheres for the Sun-god, and during the Amarna era this would have denoted the Aton.

In addition to all this, Manetho also asserts that Achencheres was female. While this may seem a major stumbling block in my interpretation, it is a fact that early Egyptologists were also under the impression that Akhenaton was female. The majority of Akhenaton's images display an overtly androgenous, if not totally female physique, and so the confusion of both Manetho and later historians is understandable. Indeed, this gender-confusion is likely to have been fostered and encouraged by the victorious Theban priesthood, who sought to denigrate each and every aspect of the 'heretic pharaoh'.

While orthodox intransigence has become an everyday aspect of my work, this new interpretation for Achencheres nevertheless represents a very important point in these investigations, for Manetho says that the Moses exodus from Egypt occurred during the reign of Achencheres. If, therefore, Pharaoh Achencheres was Pharaoh Akhenaton, then the (second) biblical exodus must have occurred during the Amarna era. Since the brother of Akhenaton was called Moses; the mortal remains of both Akhenaton and his brother (Tuth)Moses have never been found; the city of Amarna was destroyed after Akhenaton's death; and the people of Amarna were therefore dispersed, it would seem highly likely to me that the biblical and Manethoan history can take over from classical history at this point in the story. In other words, we can safely assume that just prior to the destruction of Amarna, Akhenaton, (Tuth)Moses and their weary but faithful followers embarked upon an exodus to Avaris.

Likewise, the pharaoh known as Aye has already been identified in the book *Solomon* as being Manetho's Harmais (Armesis), as one of Aye's many titles was Armait. Aye was closely identified with the symbol of the red glove, which he proudly displayed to the crowds in scenes from his tomb; the red glove symbology has, of course, been retained in Northern Ireland as a symbol of the Protestant faction, and the links between Aye and Ireland will be discussed in a later work. In between Akhenaton and Aye, the classical chronology gives two pharaohs, Smenkhkare and Tutankhamen, while Manetho gives Acherres and Chebres. This would imply that the female pharaoh called Acherres was Smenkhkare and Chebres was Tutankhamen. This would add weight to the idea that has been floated some time ago that Smenkhkare was an alternative name for Nefertiti, who is said to have taken the throne upon the death of Akhenaton while Tutankhamen was too young to rule. Although there are many pieces of evidence in favour of this scenario, and despite its simplistic appeal, there are also many problems to this identification. However, this is not the place to fully debate these issues and I would point interested readers towards Joyce Tyldesley's book *Nefertiti* for further information.

The archaeological record has, over the years, thrown up numerous texts and accounts that both support and contradict Manetho's account, in titles, reign length and order of succession. But where the archaeological record is missing, like in the history of the twenty-first and twenty-second dynasties covered in the book *Solomon,* it is the records of Manetho that are used to fill in the gaps. It is this process that has led the chronology astray and resulted in the apparent 50-year gap between the Thera eruption and the Hyksos Exodus during the reign of Ahmose I.

Take the case of Manetho's pharaoh called Orus, for instance. Earlier in his text Manetho makes clear that this form of name relates to the god Horus, and the only pharaoh in this era who invoked Horus in his title was Horemheb. Manetho then places Orus (Horemheb) before Achencheres (Akhenaton), rather than after. The most logical reason for this error is that the Amarna pharaohs had all been deleted from Egyptian history and so all of the king-lists in Egypt ran from Amenhotep III to Horemheb and thence to Ramesses I. This gave Manetho, who obviously knew of the history of the Amarna royalty, a problem: for where was he to place the Amarna family in the king-list? Manetho chose a location after Horemheb, which is close, but not quite correct. Despite this minor error, and other major disagreements, it is upon the chronological skeleton of Manetho's history that the entire Egyptian royal chronology hangs.

In regard to Manetho's account of the war against the 'lepers' from Amarna, who now resided in Avaris, it is the last few pharaohs in the list who are implicated. The story has moved on a generation, and so the Amenophis and Ramesses involved are of the era of Ramesses II. In the historical record, the name Amenhotep does not seem to appear at this time, so the identity of this pharaoh is uncertain. But the pharaoh who did eventually send his armies up through the Delta and into Syria (Israel) was known to be Ramesses II and so it must have been this pharaoh who Manetho was referring to here. But, as I point out in *Solomon,* the biblical accounts indicate that this campaign by Ramesses II only held the Hyksos-held lands for 18 years. In contrast to the Egyptian propaganda, the Torah indicates that there was always an opposing Hyksos-Israelite presence in the northeastern Delta region, and that they were only completely subdued for a short period of eighteen years during the reign of Ramesses II.

Apron

This move from Amarna to Avaris would have been a sensible tactical retreat for Akhenaton, as he saw the wolves surrounding his small empire at Amarna, baying for his blood. Avaris was at the center of the ex-Hyksos lands, and no doubt if there was any support left for him and his family it would have been in the marshlands of the Delta. Unfortunately, the climate and history of the Delta has not been kind to the historical record, and none of the few remains that have been unearthed in this region refer to a deposed and forlorn Akhenaton.

Thus it would seem likely that Akhenaton and Nefertiti left Amarna and journeyed to Avaris in about year 15 of his reign, and it was for this reason that the unknown boy-king Smenkhkare took the throne of Amarna in a co-regency with the absent Akhenaton. Like Akhenaton before him, Smenkhkare was now the puppet king of Amarna while the elder royal, Akhenaton, controlled state affairs from another location in the north. It is thought by some Egyptologists that Smenkhkare was Nefertiti herself, as his parentage is unknown and he used the same royal title as the famous queen; but Smenkhkare was recorded as marrying Meritaten, Nefertiti's daughter, and so this does seem unlikely.

So what does all this have to do with the story of Adam and Eve? I believe that the eating of the fruits of the Tree of Life episode represented the destruction of the god-names following the coronation of Akhenaton in his 12th year of co-regency. Apparently, it was Khavah or Eve (Nefertiti?) who deleted the fruits (god-names) from the Tree of Knowledge, and the result was a condemnation by the Theban priesthood. Thus the biblical condemnation of Adam and Eve was a dimly remembered record of the chaos that struck Amarna in the short years after Akhenaton's coronation; while the realisation of the biblical couple's nakedness was probably caused by the exodus of the royal family out of Amarna.

Akhenaton and Nefertiti had existed in their never-never-land of Amarna for about 14 years, totally isolated from the concerns of the outside world and floating in the midst of luxury in a state of perpetual physical near-nakedness. In scene after scene from Amarna, the complete outline of the bodies of the royal couple can be clearly seen. Joyce Tyldesley, in her book on Nefertiti, says of the queen's attire:

> However, representations of Nefertiti did not necessarily conform to modern ideas of feminine modesty, and her garments are occasionally so clinging that they can only be detected by the presence of the thin line denoting the neckline. [15]

In fact, on some of the Amarna images, like the boundary stele 'S', the queen's gossamer-like robe is also split open from the bust downwards, and the queen is, to all intents and purposes, naked. In the Egyptian she would have been described as being *kafa* (naked), from which the Israelites derived the nickname of Khavah, which the Greeks pronounced as Eua and the English as Eve.

Like Adam and Eve, it would seem that Akhenaton and Nefertiti spent a great deal of their public life physically naked and completely unashamed; roaming around their magnificent palaces in a state of pampered idyll. However, when the Amarna family were forced to flee their increasingly unsafe haven at Amarna and move up to Avaris in the Nile Delta for their safety, they were forced out into the big wide world of workers, farmers and sailors. The royal family, who had previously been so isolated in the secluded cloisters of the royal palaces, must have been like fish out of water. As the Torah's account suggests, 'the eyes of them both were opened, and they knew that they were naked'. Here among the gawping throngs of the common people, the diaphanous robes that had seemed so befitting in the royal palaces looked positively indecent. There was only one thing the royal couple could do – cover up!

The Torah informs us that the couple were forced to 'sew fig leaves together, and make themselves aprons'. While the fig-leaf story may sound suitably rustic, this was probably another literary device to cover up the truth. The fig in question was called a *tan* תאָן, but it is likely that the original spelling was *tsan* צן, meaning 'thorn'. Although sewing thorns together to form a loincloth does not sound very productive, nor very comfortable, the derivation of the *tsan* צן was *sin* סיִן or Sinai סיִנַי, which also means 'thorn'. Now, while sewing two Mount Sinais together may appear to be equally improbable, the Egyptian counterpart of this story was not so strange. Mt Sinai was simply the Hebrew rendering for the name of the Great Pyramid of Giza and, surprising as it may seem, the royal kilts that were worn in Egypt were all derived from the sewing together of the sides of a pyramid. The shape and design of the 'aprons' that graced the front of the royal kilt was most definitely a pyramid, and the use of such aprons survives today in some masonic lodges.

This explanation does, however, give a slightly different slant to the crucifixion of Jesus. He is said to have worn a crown of *akanthinos* ακανθινος or thorns, and bearing in mind the Egyptian and masonic claims I have already made in regard to Jesus, this crown was most unlikely to have been made of thorns, and much more likely to have comprised a crown of small pyramid shapes. This is, after all, the shape of the traditional royal crown – a horizontal ring of gold affixed with a series of small, vertical golden triangles, or pyramids.

Cherubim

The epilogue to chapter three of Genesis is certainly worthy of further investigation, as this section certainly ties the Tree of Knowledge episode into Egyptian culture. The verse in question is suggesting that although the Tree

IV   Forbidden Fruits

of Knowledge had been 'violated' in some manner, the other tree, the Tree of Life, was untouched and in need of protection. The verse reads as:

> 3:24 So he (god) drove out the man; and he placed at the east# of the garden# of Eden# Cherubim#, and a flaming# sword# which turned# every way, to keep# the way# of the tree# of life#.

> 3:24 So he (Horus, Ra) drove out the man; and he placed at the east of the Garden of Eden a Great Sphinx which observed the firery dawn of the solstice travelling over the Nile Valley.

The question is, therefore, what were these cherubim (plural) that were placed in the Garden of Eden as protection for the Tree of Life. The simplistic theological answer tends to suggest that they were winged angelic beings, but the standard Christian ideal of an angelic being is not really an entity that could protect something of value. However, the more complex theological investigation into the form of the cherubim suggests something altogether more fearsome. Adam Clarke says of the cherubim:

> From the descriptions in Ex 26:1 & 31; 1Ki 6:29 & 32; 2Ch 3:14, it appears that the cherubim were sometimes represented with two faces, namely, those of a lion and of a man. But from Eze 1:10 we find that they had four faces and four wings; the faces were those of a man, a lion, an ox, and an eagle ... It is probable that the term often means a figure of any kind, such as was ordinarily sculptured on stone, engraved on metal, carved on wood, or embroidered on cloth. [16]

That the cherubim also had wings and were said to have been able to fly is well known, but now it would appear that they also had the face of a lion and a man – or should that be a lion or a man – plus imagery of an ox and eagle. This description, plus Adam Clarke's more rational explanation, should already have given the game away, but perhaps the Egyptian name for this same beast will help in the identification. The Hebrew name is taken from the root word *cherub (karub)* כרב, but the origins of this word are apparently completely unknown. One suggestion is that:

> Parkhurst thinks the כ to be here a note of similitude; and (so) translates *ke* כ as 'like' and *rab* רב as 'the mighty one', and in consequence, makes the cherubim an emblem of the Holy Trinity. [17]

Some of these venerable theologians write with forked quills; but, simply stated, Parkhurst is separating the word cherub כרב into two syllables, *ke* כ meaning 'like' and *rub* רב meaning 'mighty one'. Surprisingly, given the fact

134

that Parkhurst was operating in the wrong language, his suggestion of a split in this word is precisely correct, and so the Egyptian translation is almost identical to this.

Note that the original Hebrew gives the word a hard 'k', giving the pronunciation of *ke-rub* or *ka-rub*, rather than the English cherub. This is important, as the Egyptian original also had a hard 'k'. The word in question was *ka* 𓂓 , and like the Hebrew this means 'image' or 'likeness'. The second element to *ka-rub* is the Egyptian *rub* 𓃭𓏤𓃥 meaning 'lion'. Thus instead of Parkhurst's translation of 'like the mighty one', the original Egyptian translation was 'like a lion'; and since the *cherubim (ka-rubim)* were supposed to have sported the face of a lion, the Egyptian version makes perfect sense. In fact, the biblical *keru* (cherubs) were possibly magical lions, because the original Hebrew transcripts invariably record them as being *hakarubim* הכרבים. It has been assumed that this should really be read as *ha-karubim* ה-כרבים meaning *'the karubim'*, but if the word-break were to be placed back into the position where it just was, we would derive *haka-rubim* instead. In the Egyptian, the term *hakar* 𓎗𓂓 is spelt in a similar way to *ka*, but it means 'magic' instead. Thus the term *haka-rubim* would actually refer to 'magical lions'.

Perhaps the full meaning for the *karubim (cherubim)* is now fully explained. They were magical lion-like beasts with wings, which were used for protection, and in one particular case they were used to protect the 'mercy seat' on the Ark of the Covenant. In addition, they sometimes had the head of a lion and sometimes the head of a man, plus some imagery of a bull and eagle too. In Egyptian terms the implication is obvious, the *karubim* were simply sphinxes. Remember that by the time the Israelite Torah had been rewritten and re-recorded to prevent the ancient, original texts from falling apart, the Israelite heirarchy had spent several generations in Babylon. It is not so surprising, therefore, that by the time the Book of Ezekiel had been written, the traditional Egyptian imagery of the sphinx had also taken on the winged and bovine format of the Babylonian sphinx.

This explanation may explain two other Egyptian words. Firstly, it may explain why a lion became known as a *rabu* 𓃭𓏤𓃥 . The word *bai* or *baba* 𓃭𓏤𓏥𓏛 refers to a 'hole', 'den' or 'lair', while the word *ra* 𓇳𓏤 may refer to Ra. The spelling of Ra's name with a lion would represent the not uncommon link between Ra and a lion, which would also explain why the name for a lion was sometimes shortened to *ra* 𓂋𓏭𓃭 . So one possible source for the name *rabai* 𓇳𓏤 𓃭𓏤𓏥𓏛 for a lion is a combination of Ra and *bai*, which would mean the 'Ra's lair'. But when taking into account the fact that Ra is being spelt with a lion glyph, this was probably a reference to a real lion as much as the god Ra, and so a better translation might be the 'lion's den'. Thus, this particular name for a lion could have been an oblique reference to the Giza plateau, or rather it would be a very apt name for the great recess on the eastern edge of the plateau in which the Great Sphinx still resides.

This name would also explain some more details about another biblical conundrum that I touched upon in the book *Solomon*, and that is the peculiar story of Daniel. I demonstrated in that book that Daniel's Babylonian nickname may have been divided into the syllables Bata-sar; a name that uses the words *bat (bit)* which refers to the King of Lower Egypt, and *sar* which means 'prince'. Daniel (Batasar) became a provincial governor for the Persian King Darius, presumably with responsibilities for Lower Egypt; but he temporarily fell foul of the regime for praying to his god during a prohibited period and was thrown into the 'lion's den'. Now this phrase did not mean too much to me the last time I came across it, but since it occurs in the context of an Israelite leader who could have been intimately connected with the monarchy of Lower Egypt – a leader whose name can be readily translated as 'Prince of Lower Egypt' – this 'lion's den' may well be connected with the Sphinx enclosure.

According to the biblical story, the lions in the den did not attack Daniel, and so he was pardoned. In more rational terms, it is not entirely clear what Daniel would have been doing in the Sphinx enclosure at Giza, but it is known that princes of Egypt did sometimes come and consult the Sphinx and pay homage to it. The Dream Stele of Tuthmoses IV, which is still in the Sphinx enclosure, informs us of a very similar story to that of Daniel. Tuthmoses was a prince of Egypt, but it would appear that he was not the first in line for the throne. While sleeping in the Sphinx enclosure – the 'lion's den' – the god Ra in the form of the Sphinx made a bargain that if Tuthmoses cleared the Sphinx enclosure of sand, Ra would ensure that he became pharaoh of Egypt. The sphinx was therefore an oracle, to be consulted by royalty in the same manner as the later Greek oracles, and this was why Daniel was in the 'lion's den'.

One possible confirmation of this link between the *karub* (cherub) and the Sphinx comes from the masonic lecture that accompanies the Holy Royal Arch initiation, which is a separate initiation for Master Masons that almost represents a fourth degree (or perhaps the $3^1/_2$ degree). The lecture talks about the masonic candidate being lowered into a crypt and finding a block of marble in the shape of a double cube. However, in the American version of this ritual, this block of stone is said to be the Ark of the Covenant instead – although it has to be said that the Ark was not quite a double cube. (According to the Bible, the Ark measured 2.5 x 1.5 x 1.5 royal cubits (tc) and so its major length was 0.5 cubits short of a double cube.) There are said to have been various initials on the Ark, or stone, which the modern masonic candidate has to decipher. Since the candidate is supposed to be in a crypt, it is from this task that we get the word 'cryptic'. In addition, in the American version there is said to be a simple triangle on the Ark, instead of the normal triangle within a circle. But the Bible insists that there were also two cherubs on the lid of the Ark, which presumably sat either side of the triangle. Thus the Ark of the Covenant was originally surmounted by a triangle and two cherubs, which we now know to be sphinxes.

This suggestion is confirmed by the 'Hand of Fatima', which was used as a Dervish standard during the eighteenth century AD. The hand clearly shows an image of the Ark flanked by two sphinxes. On top of the Ark is a piece of text that happens to be bordered by a triangular design. Here, then, is a graphic rendition of the masonic Holy Royal Arch degree, and it demonstrates that this same symbolism was once widespread across the Middle East – indeed, the hand itself appears to be a faithful rendition of the hands that were printed on Judaic *mizrah*, or prayer mats, from Iran. These were designed as an aid to finding the direction of Jerusalem to pray, as Muslims do for Mecca today, and the presence of two hands on the mats indicates that these eastern Jews once bowed down and touched the mats with their two hands during prayer; again as Muslims do to this day.

This similarity between Judaism and Islam should hardly be surprising; after all, Muhammad was a Jew and the religion he created was just another Jewish sect. That the daughter religion became so opposed to its parent is an all too common event with these new radical sects, but the fact that this opposition and aggression can continue into the enlightened twenty-first century is an indictment of both the Medieval attitude of Islam and the negative effects that traditional religion in general has on our society.

So what did this Ark of the Covenant symbolism actually mean? Well, the triangle on top of the Ark was a representation of a pyramid,

Fig 4.3   The Hand of Fatima.

as will be shown in a later chapter, and the two cherubs either side were representations of sphinxes, as has just been discussed. The symbolism that this presents is now obvious – it is simply a representation of the Giza plateau, where the Sphinx guards the causeway that leads to the Great Pyramid. The dualist masonic and Islamic symbolism of this scene might suggest that there is another Sphinx on the western side of the Great Pyramid which would complete this symmetry, and I did once sit through a lecture by an Egyptian researcher who argued this very point. However, although the western side of the plateau is covered in dunes and has had very little in the way of excavations, there is no real evidence to suggest that a second sphinx may have ever existed.

The other word that these various explanations may assist us with is the curious term Kheper (Khepri), which was often used in connection with the Great Sphinx. The *kheper* 𓆣 was the dung beetle, which is thought to have become synonymous with the Sun-god Ra because of its habit of rolling balls of dung across the desert sands. The *kheper* could therefore be envisioned as the motive force behind the movement of the ball of the Sun, as it courses along its set path in the sky. In pure theological terms, therefore, the Sphinx was linked to the Sun-god Ra because of its prominent position as the watcher of the eastern skies at Giza, and the Kheper was linked to the Sun-god through its ball of dung. Presumably it was through these two solar associations that the term Kheper also rubbed off onto the Great Sphinx.

But the Sphinx is decidedly un-beetle-like in its form, and I rather think that the true reason for this strange appellation is the enduring and frustrating fascination that the Egyptian scribes had with creating puns and phonemes. Solid evidence has already been provided to demonstrate that the Sphinx was known as a *ka-rub* (cherub), meaning the 'image of a lion'. But the ever inventive scribes were not slow in realising that if they swapped the 'rub' portion of this word around they could derive *ka-bur* or *ke-bur*, and since the 'b' and 'p' are often interchangeable in the Egyptian, this could easily be read as *khepur*. Thus the lion that watched the Sun could become the beetle who propelled the Sun; all very witty, and tiresome!

While these many epigraphic explanations can sometimes look contrived, the confirmation of this explanation is to be found in the English. In Britain we call this same beetle a scarab, a word that was derived from the Latin *scarabaeus*, which was in turn derived from the Greek word *karabos*. I think that the Hebrew word for a cherub, a *karub* כרב, is clearly visible within the Greek *karabos* καραβοσ. This confirms that the scarab beetle was indeed a *karub* (a biblical cherub), and since the Egyptian scarab beetle is known to have been a representation of the Great Sphinx, then the biblical cherub must also have been the Great Sphinx.

Script	Angelic being	Beetle
English	Cherub	Scarab
Heb/Grk	Karab	Karabus

Here, then, is the true tradition of the biblical cherubs that were placed in the east of the Garden of Eden in order to protect the Tree of Life; they were simply a 'pair' of Great Sphinxes, perhaps designed to ward off the 'evil' of the Akhenatons of this world who had dared to erase the names of the gods.

Flaming sword

Continuing with this same verse about the cherubs, it would seem that the flaming sword phrase is also Egyptian. In the Hebrew the words read as *lahat khereb haphak shamar derek* להט חרב הפך שמר דרך, which can indeed mean 'flaming sword turned, to protect the road'. This translation may sound rather peculiar, but in the equivalent Egyptian translation the same phrase can have more logical, celestial connotations.

Firstly, we should take a look at these translations. The word *lahat* (*rahat*) להט means 'flame' and was based upon the word *rahat* which refers to fires and the evening. The word *khereb* חרב * means 'sword' or 'destruction', and was based upon *kheryba (kherybesh)* meaning 'sword' or 'destruction'. The word *haphak* הפך means to 'turn', and was based upon *haphap* , meaning 'turn' or 'retrace a path'. The word *shamar* שמר means to 'keep' or 'watch', and was based upon *semer* ( ) meaning 'to watch'. The word *derek* דרך means 'tread', 'march' or 'road', and was based upon *djeg* meaning 'tread' or 'march'. Thus it is possible that the Egyptian version could have had exactly the same meaning as the Hebrew.

But the Hebrew translation of 'flaming sword turned, to protect the road' appears to be somewhat contrived, with the reader having to imagine some kind of gleaming, swordlike magical apparition appearing over a road to protect the Tree of Life. Either there is something adrift in this translation, or the Torah is really the mystical nonsense that some people claim it to be. However, it is the Egyptian version that can ride to the rescue here, because this new interpretation can be seen to be consistently referring to one subject

---

* The word *khereb (kheleb)* חרב is also the foundation for 'Excalibur', the name of the magical sword of King Arthur. This demonstrates the Egypto-Judaic origins of this Celtic mythology, which will be explored in more detail in the book *King Jesus*.

– the movement of the Sun. The direct translations of each of the Egyptian words have already been given; however, the alternative contexts of each of these words are as follows.

Rahat refers to the sunset or sunrise. *Haphap* means to 'turn', but more specifically refers to the turning of the Sun at the solstice. *Semer* means 'watch' but more specifically refers to the 'east' and also to the *Semer* priests or the astronomer priests who watched the movement of the stars from the Giza observatory. Finally, *djeg* refers to a 'journey' and, by inference, the journey of an astronomical body. The only odd one out here is the Egyptian *kherru*, meaning 'sword', which has no stellar context whatsoever. However, since the equivalent Hebrew word *khareb* חרב,* meaning 'sword', has been placed in this verse almost adjacent to the word *karub* כרב, which refers to the Sphinx, it is likely that there is a deliberate pun being made here. Either the Sphinx and the sword were related in some manner, or perhaps there was no sword at all and the Sphinx was the intended item.

If this was the case, and having gone through these arduous permutations, a number of keywords can be identified in the original Egyptian version of the sentence that was quoted earlier. These are: eastern side; Sphinx; flaming sunrise; turned at the solstice; east or priestly observer; journey; and tree of life. In which case, the original combined sentence might have once read as something like: 'he placed at the east of the Garden of the Aten a Great Sphinx which observed the turn of the solstice travelling over the Tree of Life'. Now while this revised sentence may seem like a radical departure from the current biblical translation, it makes every sense in terms of astronomy, Giza topography and Egyptian mythology.

Bearing in mind the fact that the original purpose of the Giza plateau was as a solar and stellar observatory, as was discussed in the book *Tempest*, there would seem to be only one conclusion that can be drawn from this sentence. The *khereb* that 'guarded the road' did not refer to a flaming sword; instead, it was a reference to the *karab*, the Great Sphinx that sits on the eastern edge of the Giza plateau and watches the Sun rising each morning at dawn. The causeway from the Second Pyramid points towards the cross-

---

* It is worth noting that *khereb* חרב is also an alternative name for the biblical Mt Sinai, and it is referred to in the English translations as Horeb. Since I have previously identified Mt Sinai as being the Great Pyramid, it is highly likely that the word *khereb* also refers in some manner to one of the Giza pyramids.

Note that the pyramid of Horeb now has a very similar title to the angelic cherubs and the scarab beetles that were being discussed earlier. One reason for this may be the fact that the Sphinx is connected via a causeway to the Second Pyramid at Giza. Since the Sphinx was known as the *karub*, it is likely that the Second Pyramid became known as the Karub (or Khereb) Pyramid.

quarter sunrise, an angular midpoint between the equinox sunrise and the winter solstice sunrise. The Sphinx itself looks due east towards the equinox, and if the rumours about its antiquity are true then it has already observed over four million sunrises. Of all the stellar observers, the Sphinx is certainly the most dedicated and patient.

Tree of Life

While this translation for the flaming sword is relatively revolutionary in itself, this sentence may also give another clue to the real meaning for the esoteric Tree of Life. The term being used for 'sword' has been reinterpreted in this new Egyptianised version as referring to the Great Sphinx. But it has already been demonstrated that the two greatest Giza pyramids, being the mythical Twin Peaks, were intimately associated with the seasonal flooding of the Nile. Since the entire biblical sentence appears to be discussing the turning of the seasons at the solstice, and since the first season in Egypt was *akhet*, when the Nile began its flood, it is likely that this reference to Giza was again associated with the rising of the Nile in some manner.

Akhet is said to have started on July 20th, with the heliacal rising of the star Sirius (Sothis), but if this season and the flooding of the Nile are to be related to the solstice, an event that the layout of the Giza plateau was designed to track, it would have been associated with the summer solstice on June 21st. As summer moved back towards autumn, and so as the dawn sunrise began to move southwards along the horizon, the sunrise angle would have approached the line of the Great Pyramid causeway; reaching it on August 22nd, just a month after the beginning of the season of the flood. The sunrise, continuing its journey southwards, would then reach the line of the Second Pyramid causeway at the end of October, just as the season of *peret* started and the crops had to be sown. So the Second Pyramid causeway and the Sphinx, which looked due eastwards towards the rising Sun, were used to mark the months and the agricultural seasons.

Bearing this in mind, the complete sentence in verse 3:24 now appears to be equating the Tree of Life with the Nile and its annual flood, and the reason for this was again pictorial. The Tree of Life has already been explained as being a representation of the backbone and the ribs of Osiris, and the image of these bones do indeed look a little like a tree trunk and its spreading branches. But it is also a fact that the long serpentine course of the Nile and its spreading branches in the Delta also look like a backbone with ribs, or even a tree and its branches – indeed we still call the spreading rivers in the Delta region 'branches' of the Nile (not tributaries), and so the tree analogy still holds good even today.

IV Forbidden Fruits

The true reason for the Tree of Life imagery is now obvious. It was the Nile that provided Egypt with its life-sustaining waters, and the physical shape of the Nile also resembled a tree, and so it was, therefore, the Egyptian people's Tree of Life. The Nile was also the backbone of the nation, supplying the Egyptians with a fast, reliable transport network that sustained trade and agriculture throughout the land. It may be a coincidence, but the Ford motor company used this exact same imagery to promote is small truck design in Britain, which was called the 'Transit'. It was marketed as being the 'Backbone of Britain', and the graphics displayed a backbone of these light trucks superimposed upon a map of Britain. Since the Ford company in Britain had already marketed a small car called the Ka, and prominently highlighted the Egyptian origins of the word and its association with 'life', the link between the Transit van and Osiris' backbone may not be so fanciful.

Here again, as with the Sphinx arguments, we can perhaps see a re-focussing of the term 'Eden'. The references to the Sphinx and the Giza pyramids seem to once more place Eden specifically at Giza, as did the translation that indicated Eden was a 'pedestal'. So sometimes the Kam, the term for the Garden of Eden (or the Garden of Aton), was a reference to all of Egypt and sometimes it seems to narrow itself down to a specific location like Giza or Amarna. But this equates quite well to the biblical description of there being a wider Eden, and also a specific garden within Eden. Just as a reminder, the Bible says of this:

> And a river went out of Eden to water the garden; and from thence it was parted, and became into four heads. [B18]

So the river went out of Eden, it then watered the Garden, and only after all that did it split into four heads. In geographical terms, the wider Eden may have been the long, winding oasis of the River Nile, while the specific Garden of Aton (Eden) could well have been at Giza, which would have been especially fitting since the Aton was the Sun-god of the dawn and Giza was a solar observatory that was orientated towards the sunrise. Only after this point on its journey does the Nile then split into the four branches that flow into the Mediterranean. But Pharaoh Akhenaton, having been relegated into (self-imposed?) exile at Amarna, would not have had any access to the Giza plateau, and so during his reign the Garden of the Aton (Eden) would, by necessity, have to have been changed to an Amarna location.

Perhaps the most subtle and interesting piece of evidence that demonstrates that Giza was originally the prime location for the Kam (the Garden) is the name that was given to the humble camel. In the Hebrew this animal was known as a *gamel* גמל, and in the Egyptian it was known as a *kamar*, or *kamel* ⌣𓅓𓈖𓇌𓏏𓃲 . I initially thought that this name may have been devised through the camel being named after the word Kam, which can also mean 'Egypt'. Since the camel eventually became the most prominent animal species in Egypt, an animal that defined the very character of the nation, it would be quite understandable for it to inherit the same name. However, there is a problem with this argument, and that is the fact that the camel is not native to Egypt. The single humped *dromedary* is actually native to Arabia, while the two humped *bactrian* is to be found primarily in Asia. So why, in this case, was the camel so closely identified with Egypt as to have the same name?

The answer lies in the association between Kam and Giza. While Kam was a name that was supposed to refer to the black lands of Egypt, the nation itself was more popularly represented by the two great pyramids that sat upon the Giza plateau. But the pyramids themselves were made of stone and so the ever-inventive scribes were able to link the words Kam, which was an oblique reference to the pyramids, and *aar* , which refers to a block of stone. Thus the camel was called the *kam-aar (kam-aal)*, because it was an animal with one or even two (stone) pyramids on its back and therefore it was a potent symbol of Egypt even if it was not a native species.

As an aside, I am not so sure the name Kam, for Egypt, was solely based upon the colour of the rich, black soil of the irrigated lands. The word *kam* has very few meanings and these are 'black', 'garden', and 'finish'. Since the primary interest of Egypt was its religion, it is equally likely that *kam* was derived from the end of the Amen-Aton ritual, when the Sun had set in the west and everything went extremely black. Since lamps were costly and not of any great intensity, the assembled priesthood who had just watched Amen-Ra disappear over the western horizon would have had to find their way back down from the Giza plateau in virtual pitch darkness. The same would have been true for the priesthood who were assembling in the morning to watch the rise of Aton-Ra. This stumbling around in the darkness would have been a significant and memorable part of the daily rituals, and it may have been through this route that the link between 'black' and a title for Egypt was derived. More pragmatic nations ensured that every citizen was safely in their home during the perilous hours of night, but the Egyptian priesthood spurned such logic and ensured that the required rituals to their gods were performed on a daily basis.

Sphinx and Akhenaton

What, then, are we to make of the Sphinx being invoked to watch the sunrise in this manner? What was the reason for writing this biblical verse, and what did it signify in terms of the banishment of Adam (Akhenaton) from the Garden of Eden? It is not as if Akhenaton was associated with Giza or the Sphinx in any way; indeed, as an icon of the polytheistic beliefs of old Egypt, the Sphinx would have been a bit of anathema to Akhenaton. But rather than destroy the Sphinx's potent imagery, Akhenaton appears to have simply ignored it, much as the Communists in Russia ignored St Basil's cathedral. Both of these structures overtly represented the old religion, but both were too closely identified as icons of the nation to be defaced or destroyed, and the best strategy in each case was simply to ignore them.

Besides, it was the new post-Akhenaton regime who were deliberately using the Sphinx imagery to demonise someone who they saw as the 'heretic pharaoh'. So, in terms of the Akhenaton-equals-Adam argument, the significance of this verse using the Sphinx to mark the seasons once more probably marks a return to the old ways. It was a return to the old rituals, the old beliefs, the old ways that Akhenaton had banned. In post-communist Russia, the first thing the people did was to restore their dilapidated cathedrals and their ancient rituals; in post-Akhenaton Egypt, they refurbished the temples and restored the astronomical observations of the priesthood and Sphinx on the Giza plateau.

Significantly, however, this biblical account only appears to be referring to Giza. This same text does not mention the temple at On (Heliopolis), nor does it mention Zoan (Tanis), despite the fact that the Bible knew these cities well. While this absence does not necessarily prove anything, it does still allow for Akhenaton to have been exiled to, and to be ruling from, these great cities in the Nile Delta. Classical history will indicate that Akhenaton and Nefertiti died at Amarna but, as we have already seen, the parallel history of Manetho indicates that Akhenaton fled to Avaris in the Delta:

> When the men in the stone quarries (on the east bank) [Amarna] had suffered hardships for some considerable time, they begged the king [Akhenaton] to assign them as a dwelling place and a refuge the deserted city of the Shepherds, Avaris, and he consented. According to tradition this city was from the earliest times dedicated to Typhon (Seth). Occupying this city and using the region as a base for revolt, they appointed as their leader one of the priests of Heliopolis called Osarseph (Son of Osiris), and took an oath of obedience to him in everything.
>
> First of all, he made it a law that they should neither worship the [traditional] gods nor refrain from (eating) any of the (sacred) animals ... and that they should have (sexual and social) intercourse with none save those of their own confederacy ... After framing a great number of laws like these, completely opposed to Egyptian custom, he ordered them with their multitude of hands,

to repair the walls of the city and make ready for war ... the priest who framed their constitution was a priest of Heliopolis called Osarseph, after the god Osiris, but when he joined his people, he changed his name and was called Moses. [M19]

So is Manetho to be trusted in his history, or are his works simply the assemblage of mythology that they are so often portrayed as being? Certainly he has the terminology and geography correct. It is known as a historical fact that the Hyksos were called Shepherds and that they were based in Avaris. The association between Typhon and Avaris is also correct, as Avaris was a center for the worship of Seth, who was identified with the Greek god Typhon. The link between Osiris and Moses would likewise be a confirmation of Manetho's authority, as it would explain the biblical narration of Moses' birth. Being the 'Son of Osiris' (Osarseph) it would have been natural for Moses to have had a childhood that mimicked the Osirian myth of being cast adrift on the Nile in a coffin (basket). So Manetho's account is historically correct in many respects, but what of the rest of this passage?

As I relate more fully in the book *Jesus*, this passage actually refers to Akhenaton and his brother TuthMoses, who the Bible calls Aaron and his brother Moses, and it encompasses many elements that are entirely faithful to the biblical account. This does, of course, mean that Akhenaton gets three walk-on parts in the biblical saga. His first mention is in regard to his Great Hymn and his belief system, which resulted in the first few garbled chapters of Genesis; his second mention is as Adam and his wife Eve; while the third is a part of the long history of the Hyksos people, which is represented by the rest of the biblical story from Abraham onwards.

While readers may have noticed that there is a direct comparison to be made between the names Moses and Tuth<u>Moses</u>, the names Aaron and Akhenaton may not initially look very similar. However, the Hebrew version of this name is actually Aharown אהרון, and if the name Akhenaton is said quickly enough it compares reasonably well with Aharown (Ah<n>ar<t>own). Furthermore, the biblical explanation of this name is 'bringer of light', which would be an entirely suitable name for the pharaoh who so closely linked himself with the Aton Sun-god. As confirmation of this, it is also worth noting that the Egyptian syllable *akh (akhu)* 𓄿𓇌𓏤𓈖𓏏𓎛 at the beginning of Akhenaton can indeed mean 'light'.

Unlike the classical history of the Amarna era, this passage from Manetho's history indicates that Akhenaton and his brother TuthMoses fled from the city of Amarna (Akhetaton) in middle Egypt and staged a last stand at Avaris in the Delta. There, he asked for help from the Hyksos-Israelites who were already in Jerusalem following the earlier great exodus of the Hyksos nation some 250-odd years earlier. These blood-brothers in Jerusalem rallied around and managed to raise some 200,000 fresh soldiers to fight for Akhenaton's cause (undoubtedly an exaggeration, as is usual).

According to Manetho, the Theban king who was threatening Akhenaton in Avaris was called Amenhotep, who is said to have been the son of a Ramesses and the father of a Seti. History has not shown any evidence for a pharaoh of this name in this era as yet, but Manetho does include him in his king-list. This Amenhotep then gathered together a force of some 300,000 men to destroy Osarseph (Moses), but decided not engage with the exiles in Avaris, and returned instead back to Memphis, which lies next to Giza. It was this stalemate between the forces of Akhenaton and TuthMoses [Aaron and Moses] and those of this unknown Amenhotep, which was probably the source of the Bible's story of the Sphinx and Great Pyramid being rededicated. This unidentified pharaoh called Amenhotep was now definitely in control of the Giza area, and so the old rituals could be restored.

According to Manetho, it was only in the next generation following the unknown Amenhotep, under the reign of another pharaoh called Ramesses, that the exiles from Amarna and the Hyksos-Israelites from Israel were eventually driven out of Avaris and the Delta region. This again has a ring of historical truth about it, as we know that Ramesses II did indeed push out the borders of Egypt, and defeated all of the lands up to and including Syria. But if the plan was to permanently banish the Hyksos-Israelites from Egypt then the plan failed. As I relate in the book *Solomon*, according to the biblical version, Ramesses II's conquest of the Delta and Israel only completely subdued the people there for eighteen years. Following Ramesses' death, the Hyksos nation regrouped and they were firmly back in the Delta region again in just over 100 years – a feat they organised and executed with the help of the Sea People mercenary soldiers. Eventually, the Judaeo-Hyksos pharaohs that the Bible calls King David and King Solomon spread this fledgling empire far and wide, and the Hyksos-Israelites ruled all of Egypt once more.

Addendum to Chapter IV

Having just put forward this comprehensive argument, which demonstrates that Khavah (Eve) was actually a pseudonym for Queen Nefertiti, there is another intriguing possibility that is equally compelling but does not nullify the arguments already put forward. Unfortunately, this new possibility was only noticed as the book was going to press, and so this alternative scenario will be offered to the reader as an addendum to this chapter.

The Old Testament name for Khavah (Eve) was derived from Khavah חוה meaning 'life'. However, this word was, in turn, derived from Khiyah חיה which again refers to 'life' but also has connotations of a lively animal.

One could easily speculate how the variation in the Hebrew spelling, and thus the pronunciation, has been derived from the simple slip of a scribe's quill making the second alphabetic character slightly longer than it should have been.

But this alternative spelling is interesting, because it so happens that the second wife of Akhenaton was called Kiyah (Kiya) 𓏏𓃀𓄿𓏥 , a name that is almost the exact equivalent of Khyiah (Eve). The Egyptian name, Kiyah, is said to have been derived from *kia* 𓂝𓏤𓏤𓃻 meaning 'monkey'. Thus the Bible's 'lively animal' who was called Khiyah (Eve), may well have been the pet-name for Akhenaton's second wife, Kiyah. It has long been suspected that this pet-name portrayed Kiya's lively temperament, rather than her looks, and the Hebrew translation would seem to confirm this. In fact, the few images we do have of Kiyah show that she looked rather similar to Nefertiti. This is not too surprising, since to become Akhenaton's 'favourite wife' she would have to have been a close bloodline relative of the Amarna dynasty. Since the accounts of Josephus link Eve with Isis [the daughter of Amenhotep III], it is possible that Kiyah was the sister of Akhenaton, which is a slight variation on the arguments previously made. In this case, Nefertiti could still have been the daughter of Aye and Tey, as previously suspected.

So if, as appears likely, Khiyah (Eve) was actually Kiyah (the second wife of Akhenaton), then how would this identification affect the overall biblical story-line? Well, the threads of this new history can be difficult to follow, because nearly all the references to Kiyah were excised from Amarna during the Amarna era. The reason for Kiyah's dramatic fall in status from 'favourite' to pariah is not known, but the fact that she was the 'other woman' (Kiyah can also mean 'other woman') and the possibility of jealousy by Nefertiti, may well provide all the answers we need.

The general chronology for the last years of the Amarna regime is as follows. Nefertiti seems to disappear from the records in year 14 of Akhenaton's reign; some historians presume her to be dead while some presume she

Fig 4.4   Kiyah, the biblical Eve?

147

affected a change of name and role, to become the ephemeral Pharaoh Smenkhkare. Kiyah appears on a late carving at Hermopolis and she continued to have consignments of wine delivered until year 16, and so her fall from grace may have been after year 14; which might initially seem to exclude any jealousy by Nefertiti. Akhenaton is said to have died in year 17. The shadowy character called Smenkhkare seems to have had a co-regency with Akhenaton from year 14, and then briefly took the throne upon Akhenaton's disappearance in year 17. Smenkhkare died within a year or two of taking the throne, to be succeeded by Tutankhaton (Tutankhamen). So, by mixing this sketchy chronology with the accounts from Genesis, and assuming that Khiyah (Eve) is Akhenaton's second wife Kiyah, can we derive some sort of coherent history from these ragged snippets of information?

One possibility is that the rivalry between Nefertiti and Kiyah split the Amarna family asunder. Nefertiti was undoubtedly the Chief Wife and held a considerable amount of political and religious power within the Amarna regime; however, it was Kiyah who was always called Akhenaton's favourite and bore the rather illustrious title of Great Beloved Wife. Like many a powerful career woman, Nefertiti may have assumed too much of the aggressive, masculine royal role; and perhaps Akhenaton preferred the lively femininity of his 'little monkey', Kiyah.. In year 14 of Akhenaton's rule, this domestic rivalry may have caused a permanent rift. In this scenario, Neferneferuaton Nefertiti increased her royal status by becoming Neferneferuaton Ankhkheperure Smenkhkare, the shadowy co-regent of Akhenaton and future pharaoh of Egypt. The only problem with this theory is the fact that Smenkhkare appears to have married Meritaten, the daughter of Nefertiti. But perhaps this anomaly can be negated if one presumes that Nefertiti, as a female pharaoh, needed a ritual consort, and so she took her daughter as a 'wife' simply to fulfil the requisite royal roles; as the female pharaoh Hatchepsut appears to have done.

Kiya and Akhenaton both disappear from the records in year 16 or 17, and are normally presumed dead. However, if Akhenaton and Kiyah were the biblical Adam and Khiyah (Eve), then the accounts of Genesis and Manetho would suggest that Akhenaton left the Garden of Eden (the Garden of Adon or Aton) at Amarna, and eloped with his 'little monkey', Kiyah, to Avaris in the Nile Delta. Left to rule Amarna and Upper Egypt on her own, it was then Nefertiti, in the guise of Pharaoh Smenkhkare, who defaced all the images of Kiyah. Tellingly, many of these images had their eyes gouged out, which is still a typically female form of retribution, and this might again suggest that Nefertiti was responsible.

Smenkhkare (Nefertiti) 'died' very shortly after year 17, to be replaced by Pharaoh Tutankhaton (Tutankhamen). Tutankhamen's precise parentage is unknown, but he does claim to be the 'fruit of the King's loins'

– but which king was his father? Although Amenhotep III was capable of being Tutankhamen's father, he was effectively in retirement; Smenkhkare is an unlikely candidate as 'he' may well have been female; and so the king in question is likely to have been Akhenaton. But what of Tutankhamen's mother? A son is never shown in the many portraits of the Amarna family, and so Nefertiti cannot have been his mother; and although Akhenaton subsequently married his elder daughters, they would have been too young. This leaves Kiyah as being the most likely mother of Tutankhamen.

This new theory represents an original but highly plausible solution to the identity of Khavah or Khiyah (Eve). However, this new scenario does <u>not</u> invalidate very much of what has already been written in the preceding two chapters. Like Nefertiti, Kiyah would have adopted the typical Amarna imagery of nakedness and swollen limbs, and so Kiyah would also have been equally *kafa* 𓈎𓄿𓆑𓏏 and *khafa* 𓐍𓆑𓄿𓀀 (naked and swollen).

The addition of an 'f' in this alternative nickname for Kiyah, to produce the biblical Khavah, is also explainable – because the *kyia* 𓎡𓇌𓄿 'ape' can also be spelt as a *kefia* 𓎡𓆑𓇌𓄿 'ape', and so Kiyah can also be Kafah (Khavah). This also translates to a degree into the Hebrew, where the word *kavfe* קוף similarly means 'ape'. No doubt Akhenaton continued to use the ape symbology for his favourite wife with great affection, while Nefertiti increasingly used it as an image of ridicule. In summary, the permutations of this name are:

Origin	Name		Meaning	Name		Meaning
Egyptian	*kefia*		ape	*kiya*		ape
Hebrew	*kavfe*	קוף	ape	*khiya*	חיה	animal
Hebrew	*khavah*	חוה	life	*khiya*	חיה	life
Hebrew	Khavah	חוה	Eve	Khiyah	חיה	Eve

In biblical terms, this new scenario means that the fall from grace of Adam and Khiyah (Eve), as previously explained, would only need to be amended slightly. The tasting of the fruits from the Tree of Knowledge (Tree of Remembrance) may now become a reference to Kiyah trying to usurp the authority of Nefertiti and become Akhenaton's Chief Wife; while the role of the snake may well refer to Nefertiti's jealous rage that (may have) banished Akhenaton and Kiyah from Amarna. Nefertiti wore the double uraeus, the double snake symbol of Lower Egypt, while Kiyah never did; and it was also Nefertiti, in the guise of Smenkhkare, who (may have) subtly manipulated her way onto the throne of Egypt.

Here, then, is the alternative version of Adam and Khiyah (Eve). The famous biblical couple were most probably Akhenaton and Kiyah, the true lovebirds from the Garden of Adon-Aton (Amarna); while the previously saintly Nefertiti becomes the snake. Kiyah's reputation has always suffered because of her role as the mistress or second wife, a position which the early Victorian historians probably despised, but in reality perhaps Kiyah (Eve) was Akhenaton's greatest love and thus his principal guiding influence. Like Anne Boleyn, who effectively coerced King Henry VIII into destroying the power and influence of the Catholic Church in England, perhaps it was Kiyah who coerced Akhenaton into destroying the power and influence of the Amen priesthood in Thebes. Since Kiyah is first mentioned just before Amenhotep IV changed his name to Akhenaton, this suggestion is not quite so fanciful.

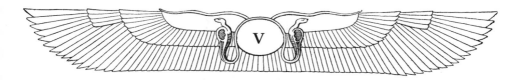

Noah and the Ark

There are several clearly defined breaks in the construction of the Book of Genesis, which are denoted by the way in which the name of god was written. From the beginning of Genesis up to the finishing of god's work on the seventh day, god is called Elohim אלהים, the plural of Elah or Alah אלה. This takes us up to Genesis 2:3. In fact, the first chapter of Genesis should have ended at this point, as the next verse starts with "These are the generations of the heavens", which is a turn of phrase that is often used to open a new chapter. From this point to the end of chapter three, which describes the eviction from Eden, god is called Jehovah Elohim יהוה אלהים. From chapter four through to chapter nine god is described singly as either Elohim אלהים or Jehovah יהוה; and thereafter we find the first introduction of the term Adhonai אדני (Adon).

Thus the start of the generations of Adam and Eve represents a different history from a different scribal source, and so the list of generations of Adam and Eve do not come from the same source or tradition as their life-history. There are several possibilities that may apply here and may affect our view of the material that is given. As already related, it is possible that Akhenaton and Nefertiti (or Kiya) had successfully fled to Avaris, and so it is entirely feasible that they could have had further children and created the new dynasty that was detailed in chapter four of Genesis; but if that is true then we have no historical information from the Delta region that can confirm this. Indeed, there is little or no material from the Delta to confirm the majority of events that occurred in this region.

The alternative possibility is that this jump in the style of the text represents material from another era that has been tacked onto the Akhenaton and Nefertiti (or Kiya) story. This may well be so, because Josephus indicates that Seth, who was a son of Adam and Eve, was the pharaoh Sesostris. In the chronology provided by Manetho, this Sethos is said to have been the pharaoh now known as Senusret I, who reigned for some 45 years during the twelfth dynasty. Of his many achievements there was the construction of a temple at Heliopolis, which was graced by two large granite obelisks. But if Seth was Senusret I, it is difficult to see who Cain and Abel were supposed to be and how this genealogy fits into the rest of the story. Note, however, that it is widely accepted that Josephus, in the first century AD, was writing about biblical characters who were related to Adam and who were possibly pharaohs of Egypt.

However, if this interpretation of Josephus' text causes too many problems, then how about the suggestion that the descendants of Adam were substantially the descendants of Akhenaton? If this were the case, then Seth could well have been Seti I, who was indeed hailed as the new seed of a new dynasty (disregarding the one-year reign of Ramesses I). Apart from the names Seti and Seth being rather similar, is there any evidence that could support such a possibility?

Well, perhaps the first thing to note is that although Seti I continued with the programme of destroying every trace of the memory of the Amarna dynasty, he was essentially a Lower Egyptian ruler himself, with his family originating from the previous Hyksos stronghold of Avaris. So Seti sprang from the same influential circle of Lower Egyptian leaders and rulers as did Amenhotep III and Akhenaton himself. As his name might suggest, Seti's patron god was Set (Typhon) and he built several temples to this god including one in Avaris, and yet the god Set was predominantly a Hyksos deity rather than a Theban one.

Likewise, it is more than likely that the name for the biblical Seth was derived from the Egyptian Set, as the name has similar meanings:

Hebrew	meaning	Egyptian	meaning
Sethah שׁתה	seat	Set	throne
Sethah שׁתה	foundation	Set	stone
Sethan שׁתן	urinate	Set	animal with tail up

The table above would indicate that the names for the biblical Seth and the historical Seti were based upon the same god-name. There is another snippet of evidence in favour of this comparison, which is to be found in inscriptions at the temple of Redesiyeh to the north of Edfu. Here, Seti styled himself as being 'the good shepherd' and again this declaration may well align Seti with the Hyksos nation, who had been known as the Shepherd Kings. A further pointer is that Seti I's chief wife was called Tiye; a name that was descended from the names of the wives of Yuya and Amenhotep III. This would imply that Seti I married into the influential family of Yuya, who was a central component within the Amarna dynasty. Somehow, it would appear that the influential dynasty of Yuya and Tuyu, who always seemed to lie in the royal shadows, managed to realign themselves with the royalty of the victorious post civil-war era, with their daughters becoming the chief wives of Horemheb (Mutnodjime) and Seti I (Tiye).

This would suggest that the nineteenth dynasty was not a completely new dynasty at all, at least not through the maternal line. Instead it was substantially descended from the same influential families from Avaris in the Nile Delta, and following the demise of Akhenaton they had simply reincarnated themselves in a new image. This could mean that the Amarna era truly was an aberration, and the embarrassed families involved simply tried to pretend that their black sheep (Akhenaton) never existed and that everything was back to normal. Alternatively, it could mean that these families secretly endorsed Akhenaton's views; but clearly saw that the world was not ready for them, and if they were to keep control of the country they had better tow the proletariat line a bit more.

Between these two monarchs we have the intermediate rule of the military commander Horemheb, an era that was perhaps similar to the military rule of Oliver Cromwell; it was possibly a necessary stabilising influence on the nation after an era of turmoil. But after both of these dictatorships, it would appear that the royalty were invited back to rule their respective nations. In England, the restoration of the monarchy involved Charles II, but in Egypt the new monarchs were Ramesses I and Seti I.

Giants

While most of the continuing Genesis story was probably based upon distorted historical facts, some of this material is not history at all, it is simply snippets of Egyptian religion, ritual and mythology that have been rewritten and inserted as if they represented historical events. One of these small snippets, which is just crying out to be retranslated and reinterpreted, is the strange tale of the biblical giants. The text here insists that there were giants on the Earth, who are perhaps more widely known as the other-worldly Nephil (Nepher) נפיל, a race of super-beings that have taken on mythological proportions in some modern books. The verse that mentions these beings is as follows:

> 6:2 That the sons of God saw the daughters of men that they were fair; and they took them wives of all which they chose ... There were giants# on the earth in those days; and also after that, when the sons of God came in unto the daughters of men, and they bore children to them. B1

V Noah and the Ark

6:2 That the sons of God saw the daughters of men that they were fair; and they took them wives of all which they chose ... There were virgins (young maidens) in the land in those days; and when the sons of God came in unto the daughters of men, and they bore children to them.

The Nephilim (plural) are translated as being 'giants', but the context of their appearance looks highly contrived. The general thrust of the passage, and all those that lie around it, is of young maidens and their procreation with the gods, so why do we suddenly see 'giants' roaming the Earth? The 'giants' don't appear to be references to the gods themselves, so where do they fit into this story?

The answer, I believe, lies in a gross mistranslation of the word Nephil (Nepher). The word is supposed to have been derived from *nefel* (*nefer*) נפל, meaning 'lie down', 'prostrate' or even 'miscarriage' and 'abortion'. With the first of these meanings, we are presumably supposed to imagine these 'giants' knocking down their opponents, an image that is not all that convincing. But what of the other derivations? What of 'abortion', for instance, where does this meaning fit into the imagery of a fierce giant? Frankly, this all seems highly unsatisfactory and, after a long examination of the alternatives, the most likely derivation of this word seems to be from the Egyptian *nefer-t* meaning 'young maiden', 'youth', or even 'virgin'. While this translation may seem like a wild guess at this point in time, take a look at the revised verse that has just been given, and notice how it makes a great deal more sense when the word 'virgin' is used instead of 'giant'.

This alternative meaning would certainly make more sense of the various meanings of the word *nefel* (*nefer*) נפל – especially if it could also be linked with (ritual) prostitution. The link between the action of lying down and the term 'virgin' is not too hard to make, and a link to the meaning of 'abortion' is fairly obvious too, as the profession of prostitution would have been the first to have realised the benefits of aborting an unwanted pregnancy. But it would appear that this subject is more confusing than it seems, and this confusion is perfectly demonstrated by the original meaning of the term 'prostitute'. The role of the Virgins who were wives of the gods has already been fully explored in the book *Solomon*, and it was explained there that these 'virgin' priestesses were more than likely the forerunners of the ritual prostitutes from the New Testament era. But what was the role of these virgins and prostitutes? Were they serving the ritual needs of the gods or the physical desires of the priesthood?

The answer to this may lie in the epigraphic evidence, and the first of many clues lies in the fact that the term 'prostitute' is said in the various dictionaries to have been derived from the Latin *pro* meaning 'before' and *statuere* meaning 'stand'. Now I did have to scratch my head over this one for a few days, as I could not understand why the prostitute was standing up. While the Kama Sutra may illustrate a number of permutations on a similar theme, one would have thought that the overriding position for a prostitute is prostrate: ie, lying down. But then I remembered that the original role of the ritual prostitute was to serve the gods, not men, and the particular god in question was Atum.

Atum did not have intercourse with the priestess, he merely had his phallus caressed, which is probably why these priestesses were known as Virgins despite the overtly sexual nature of their duties. No doubt this ritual sexual activity was performed within the depths of the Temple of Karnak, with a priestess caressing the phallus of a statue of Atum in remembrance of the mythology that described the creation of the world. This was the solution to the entire problem, if you excuse the pun, because the Latin word *statuere* not only means 'stand', it also means 'statue'. However improbable it may seem, the Latin term for 'prostitute' is graphically precise in its description of this ancient ritual – the Virgin priestess, or ritual prostitute, was indeed *pro-statuere*, or 'before the statue'. Thus, the word prostitute graphically describes the actions of the temple virgins, or the temple 'prostitutes'; so it can now be fully explained that the *statuere* in question was a representation of the god Atum, and the 'prostitute' who was *pro*, or in front of it, was actually caressing its penis.

But it is likely that this ritual became debased and confused in later generations. The Israelites, in their overwhelming desire for a monotheistic religion, destroyed all the idols of old Egypt and eventually destroyed the entire pantheon of Egyptian gods. Atum was gone and the role of the Virgin, the Wife of God, would have been largely redundant if it were not for the carnal desires of the priesthood. It would seem that in place of this Atum ritual, the Virgin had become the sacred prostitute, and she now served the desires of men rather than the ritual needs of god. See Michael Jordan's *Mary, the Unauthorised Biography* for an in-depth discussion on the rise of the ritual prostitute during the New Testament era. The point being made here is that the Virgin no longer stood before the statue, rather she lay down before her customers, and in the Latin this was termed *prosternere*, or prostrate. The prostitute was now prostrate, or perhaps that should be read as the *nefer-t* 𓏏𓊪𓏥 being *nefer* נכל.

The final pieces of the jigsaw, which demonstrate that the Nephil (Nepher) were actually young maidens, is to be found in verses from Deuteronomy, which state that:

> That also was accounted a land of giants: giants dwelt therein in old time; and the Ammonites call them Zamzummims. [B2]

Here we can actually see two more versions of the names used for these 'giants'. The final sentence in the verse above informs us that the Ammonites [the worshippers of Amun in Thebes] called the giants Zamzum זמזם, and as it happens, this word is also derived from the Egyptian. The biblical 'z' ז is often translated from an Egyptian 'tch', and so the translation has been taken this time from *tcham (tsam)* ⌇⌇, meaning 'young maiden', 'young soldier' or even 'copulate' – words that have much the same meaning as *nefer*.

The final version of the name is the alternative term being used for 'giant', which comes this time from *rapha* רפא, meaning 'all' or 'giant'. This word was derived from the Egyptian *rapia* or *rapia-t* ⌇⌇, meaning 'young person', 'young maiden' or 'princess'; and here at last we see why these young maidens, or prostitutes, were translated as being 'giants'. As was explained in the book *Solomon*, the role of God's Wife, or Virgin, was extremely prestigious, and so the lady in question was often one of the highest ranking women in Egypt. More often than not she was the pharaoh's eldest daughter, and she would eventually, according to the ancient tradition, become his chief wife. Thus the term *rapia-t* ⌇⌇ does not necessarily refer to any young maiden, it more often than not refers to a lady of very high rank or a princess.

This explains the context of these biblical references to 'giants', most of which merely explain that a particular character was 'the son of a giant'. What the text is trying to impart is that this particular character was 'born of a Virgin', the temple priestess, or more often than not 'born of the elder daughter of the pharaoh'. Perhaps, understandably under the circumstances, the English translators felt unable to explain this correctly and chose the word 'giant' instead. Indeed, it is possible that the daughters of Akhenaton were born of just such a 'giant', for the term *nefer* ⌇⌇ may also have been a subsidiary meaning for the name of Nefertiti. It is known that Nefertiti was a priestess and that she embodied the concept of national fertility, and so it is likely that she too was a God's Wife. Although the god Atum would not have been revered in this era, Nefertiti could have played her role with god's representative on Earth – her husband, Akhenaton. An alternative meaning for Nefertiti's name might therefore be 'Sacred Prostitute Comes'.

But since the words *tit* ⌇⌇ and *tiyt* טיט can both also refer to a sticky emission, we could also derive 'Sacred Prostitute makes Ejaculation'. Such overt sexual imagery should not come as such a surprise to readers, as the Egyptians openly appreciated the fact that male semen and pollen fertilised the animal and plant kingdoms upon which civilisation depended, and so the wonder of this creation mechanism was to be celebrated rather than shunned and denigrated. This was, after all, the central theme of the Atum ritual; the celebration of the semen of Atum as a creative force.

V Noah and the Ark

While the thought of biblical scribes writing about the masturbation of Atum was out of the question, these same scribes and translators probably felt that the term 'virgin' was also too controversial; and this would have been especially so during the post-New Testament era. In Christian terms the only Virgin was Mary, and to have had similar virgins peppered all over the Old Testament story, filling the same role as mothers of great men, would have debased the myths that were being created about the events in Galilee. By necessity, these great women from ancient history had to have their identity and roles covered up, and so they became known instead as Nephilim or 'giants' – a term that eventually fostered its own brand of mythology.

Flood

The subject of Noah and the flood is a complicated issue that is difficult to fully solve, but I am relatively certain that the story is based upon Egyptian mythology rather than an actual flood – although it is entirely possible that the Mediterranean, Black Sea and coastal-fringe flooding that occurred after the last ice age may have greatly influenced this enduring Egyptian mythology.

Firstly, it should be pointed out that Noah נוח himself is unlikely to have been a historical character; instead his name was most certainly based upon the term *nu* meaning 'flood', and *nuia (nuaa)* which means 'lake' or 'sea'. Clearly, the biblical character was named after the event for which he was famous and so there is no point looking for a character called Noah in the historical record. This explanation is similar to the land of Nod (Noud) נוד that Cain is supposed to have emigrated to. The historian Josephus amends this story slightly and says that Nod was actually a city rather than a land, and the reason for this assertion just has to be due to the fact that the name Nod (Noud) was based upon the Egyptian word *nout*, meaning 'city'.

Secondly, Josephus also has a slightly different perspective on the flood event, and he says of this that:

> This calamity (the flood) happened in the six hundreth year of Noah's government, in the second month called by the Macedonians Dius ... for so did they order their year in Egypt.[J3]

Now this short extract lets an interesting point out of the bag. It begins by informing us that Noah presided over a government, and by implication a whole nation; a notion that contradicts the usual inference of Noah being the village idiot from a small farming community with an unhealthy obsession with catastrophes and boats. The verse then goes on to mention that the calendrical system that was being used to determine this event was Egyptian, which gives us a good idea of the location for Noah's government. It is likely that the 'year' being referred to is the lunar year, which would place the flood in the 48th solar year of Noah's 'reign'.

The details of the flood event also have to throw doubts upon any notion of this being an account of a true historical flood; for as soon as a story starts describing a mass of water in an Egyptian context, and then provides us with a character called <u>Nuah</u>, rational thoughts are inevitably turned towards the primeval waters of Nu (Nun) and the Egyptian creation myth. The version of the flood that was recorded by Josephus simply adds to this explanation, by describing the Ark coming to rest on a mountain called Ararat אררט, which Josephus describes as being in 'Armenia'. Josephus calls this mountain Baris, but since the word *bari* means 'boat', the origin of this term is not hard to fathom.

The imagery this 'boat and mountain' scene provides is inescapable. In the biblical accounts we have a boat on a mountain top, surrounded by water – while in the mythological equivalent we have the god Atum standing on the primeval mound surrounded by the chaotic waters of Nu. This similarity is then heightened when one realises that in Egypt the images of the gods were often placed in boats. Indeed, if the top of the Great Pyramid were available for these rituals (a topic that will be discussed later), one could imagine Atum being placed on his barque and being hauled up to the platform at the top of this 'unfinished' pyramid. If this ritual were then to be organised during the season of the flood, the pyramid (mountain) would have been substantially surrounded by water.

Further support for this imagery is provided by the term 'Armenia'. This term has proved to be the ultimate in diversionary tactics, sending dozens of researchers off into the wilds of northern Turkey looking for the Ark of Noah, when in fact this (or these) boat(s) are probably situated in a rather more accessible location. It is likely that the 'Armenia' in question was actually the Egyptian *Amen-t* , which referred not to a location in Turkey but rather to the spiritual western region ruled by the god Amen – Amen-t or Amenia was the land of the dead; the underworld; the Egyptian Duat. While the Duat was not quite the same as the chaos of Nu, the image of the Ark on a mound of earth, surrounded by water, somewhere in the depths of the Duat (Amen-t or Amenia), is unmistakably taken from the Heliopolian creation myth. This tallies nicely with the previous explanation in the book *Tempest*, which claimed that the location of Mount Ararat was at Giza, and that the Ark of Noah was one of the two great wooden Arks that were discovered at the foot of the Great Pyramid of Giza. Note that the Ark of the Covenant and the Ark of Noah can now be seen to be based upon the same symbology – the layout of the Giza plateau.

Fig 5.1 Construction of Noah's Ark.

Incidentally, the phrase 'gone west' is still used in England to describe a death (the land of the dead). This phrase is often said to have been derived from criminals being taken to the gallows at Tyburn in the west of London, but if the truth were known, the dead have being 'going west' to Amen-t for thousands of years before the gallows at Tyburn were invented.

So is the story of Noah really a simple retelling of the Heliopolian creation myth – the first mound that rose out of the primeval waters of Nu, upon which plants, animals and mankind were eventually created? One reason for believing that this may well be so, is the subsequent story of Noah sending out a raven and a dove, so that they could search for dry land. The verses that describe this are as follows:

> 8:7 And he sent forth a raven#, which went forth# to and fro, until the waters were dried up from off the earth#.
> 8:8 Also he sent forth a dove# from him, to see if the waters were abated# from off the face of the ground#;

> 8:7 And he sent forth a Moon, which sailed along until the waters were dried up from off the earth.
> 8:8 Also he sent forth a Sun, to see if the waters were slight (delicate) on the face of the ground.

The first rendition in the verses above may sound like a reasonable, natural scene, with two birds flying off from Noah's Ark to find evidence of dry land. But this is not the original import of these particular verses. The initial reason for saying so is the obvious duality that is deliberately being created between these two verses – for the raven was black, and the dove was white. However, to discover the underlying reasoning behind this duality we must, as ever, travel back into Egypt.

The raven was said to be an *arab* ערב, and this is a word that can also mean 'dark'. But this is not simply a reference to the darkness of a raven's plumage, because the word can also mean 'evening'; and so we are already heading towards the familiar Egyptian duality of day and night. As expected, this is exactly where the word has come from, because the original term was aab(ti) 𓈖𓃀𓏏, meaning 'east' or 'left'. But this was not any old left-hand side, this was more specifically a reference to the left eye of Ra-Horakhty, or the Aa-aab (Araab) 𓂝𓃀𓏏 . Ra-Horakhty was a combined image of Ra and Horus, and during Horus' supernatural battle with Seth he lost an eye, which was fortuitous because it allowed the dark eye of Horus to represent the Moon and the brilliant eye to represent the Sun. So, the left eye of Horus was a coded reference to the Moon and, as has been explained previously, the colour of this Moon-eye has caused some confusion over the centuries. While the Moon may look white to us, the required duality was actually a comparison between the Sun and the Moon. Since the Sun was the brighter of the two solar disks it was said to be white, while the duller Moon was said to be black. Here, then, was the original meaning for the raven imagery – its blackness was simply a reference to the Moon and the blackness of the night over which it ruled.

What, then, of the other partner in this Genesis duality, the dove? As has been explained previously, the dove was called *jounah* יונה, which is also the name of the prophet called Jonah. Now while this word may mean 'dove', it is based upon the word *youmem (jounem)* יומם meaning 'daytime', and so we have a possible reference to the midday Sun. The Egyptian derivation shows this to be so, as the word comes from *uenemi (younemi)* 𓏺𓈖𓅓 , which refers to the right eye of Ra-Horakhty. So the Hebrew name Jonah *(jounem)* is an almost direct translation of *younemi*, the name of Horus' right eye; and being the alternative partner in this optical duality, the right eye of Horus represents the Sun.

So the duality is complete – the raven is the Moon and the dove is the Sun. But what are the chances that two Hebrew words that refer to light and dark, as well as birds that fly, can be precisely matched with the two Egyptian words that refer to the left and right eyes of Horus? Indeed, the whole of the imagery between these two versions of the story is just perfect. In the Egyptian imagination, the Sun and the Moon were coloured white and black respectively and were represented as being borne aloft on a bird's outstretched wings – the winged Sun-disk. In the Hebrew version of this cosmic tale, the dove and the raven were similarly white and black and both flew across the sky on their outstretched wings.

In fact, the resulting biblical story-line is very familiar. It details the two cosmic aspects of Ra-Horakhty, the Sun and the Moon, flying across the chaotic waters of the flood while looking for signs of dry land – a story-line that dovetails precisely with the mythology of the Egyptian creation. While it was often written that it was the god Atum who stood upon the primeval mound as it first surfaced above the primeval waters of Nu, it is also true that Atum was eventually conjoined with Ra to become Atum-Ra. Thus it was sometimes reported that it was Ra who rose upon the primeval mound surrounded by the waters of the chaos, just as the biblical version of this event indicates.

Clearly, the Noah story is nothing less than a very detailed and reasonably accurate version of the Heliopolean creation myth, and doubtless some of the other elements in the Noah story were also derived from the same Egyptian sources.

Ramesses I and Sethos

Again we must travel back to the main topic of this chapter, which was the possible links between Seth and Seti. Since the parentage of the pharaoh Seti I is unknown, does this link between the biblical Seth [Seti] and Adam [Akhenaton] provide us with any further clues to this new dynasty's history? It is pointedly said in the biblical account that Seth was conceived while Adam was in his dotage, the last years of his life. Adam is said to have been 930 years old at his death, and if we assume these to be lunar years then he would have been nearly 72 years old at his death. Transferring this same history onto the life of Akhenaton, we find that he was born in about 1370 BC, and reigned from 1350 to 1334 BC. This takes Akhenaton to the age of 36, but if he had survived the overthrow of Amarna and lived to the age of 72, as the Bible suggests, then he would have died in Avaris in 1298 BC.

On the other hand, Seti I came to the throne early on the unexpected death of Ramesses I. Since Seti's reign started in about 1291 BC, he must have been born in or around 1306 BC. This would have meant that Akhenaton would have been 64 years old at the time of Seti's birth, which means that a blood relationship between the two is entirely possible. So was Seti I a son of Akhenaton? Unfortunately, as far as this argument goes, there is an inscription in Thebes which says:

Seti (I); he made it as his monument for his father, the good god, Menphtyre. [4]

161

Menphtyre is, of course, the throne name of Ramesses I, and so this inscription positively identifies Seti I as being the son of Ramesses I. Thus, it would seem that there is no way in which Seti could have been related to Akhenaton, apart from the influences from the maternal line that have already been discussed.

That may well be so, but I have also become convinced that the biblical record is reasonably reliable, and so if it mentions a name like Seth being the youngest son of Adam [Akhenaton], I think it is worth throwing caution to the wind and trying to imagine the impossible. So, by utilising the most lateral of assumptions, how could Seti I be related to both Ramesses I and Akhenaton?

Actually, there is a method of pursuing this conundrum further, and the answer may lie in the fact that we don't know who Ramesses I was. What we do know is that Ramesses I was not related to the previous pharaoh, Horemheb, and that he became king at a very old age and only ruled for a year or two before his death. Ramesses' proper name from before he became king was Paramessu [5], but since this was derived from ☐ 𓀭𓏤, which could be taken to mean 'born of the royal house' or even 'born of the king', this doesn't really tell us who he was. Or does it? For this is an interesting question. From what part of the royal family was Ramesses I born? It is thought that Horemheb didn't have any male children, and neither did Smenkhkare, Tutankhamen or Akhenaton (not while he was at Amarna, at any rate). In fact, if Ramesses I was about 75 years old when he died in about 1290 BC, then he must have been conceived in about 1365 BC, and this is a date that lies squarely within the long reign of Amenhotep III, the father of Akhenaton (Amenhotep's reign would have been between about 1386 and 1338 BC, including the co-regency with Akhenaton).

In which case, there are only two candidates who were so closely linked to the royal line as to warrant donating the title Paramessu upon a royal son. The first of these was the king himself, Pharaoh Amenhotep III, the father of Akhenaton; and the second has to be Yuya, the father of Aye and also of Tiye, who became Amenhotep's chief wife. The latter parentage would mean that Ramesses I was the brother of Aye, a relationship which is not attested to in the historical record but closely follows Manetho's reasoning instead (Aegyptus being the brother of Dannus). If this were so then Seti would not have been the son of Akhenaton, but simply a close relation. However, this would still mean that the 'new' nineteenth dynasty was simply a continuation of the eighteenth, through a very closely related strand of the same Amarna family.

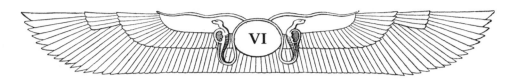

Tower of Babel

Black and White

We now enter the post-diluvium era – the events that occurred after the Great Flood. Noah has three sons and these sons set out for a new homeland and proceed to build a tower 'whose top may reach unto heaven'. So what can these new translations tell us about this famous tower – the Tower of Babel?

11:1 And the whole earth# was of one language#, and of one speech#.

11:2 And it came to pass, as they journeyed from the east#, that they found a plain# in the land of Shinar#; and they dwelt there.

11:3 And they said one to another, Go to, let us make brick#, and burn# them thoroughly. And they had brick# for stone#, and slime# had they for mortar#.

11:4 And they said, Go to, let us build us a city and a tower#, whose top# may reach unto heaven#; and let us make us a name#, lest we be scattered abroad upon the face of the whole earth.

11:5 And the Lord came down to see# the city# and the tower#, which the children# of men# builded#.

11:6 And the Lord said, Behold, the people# is one, and they have all one language#; and this they begin to do: and now nothing will be restrained from them, which they have imagined to do.

11:7 Go to, let us go down, and there confound# their language#, that they may not understand# one another's speech#.

11:8 So the Lord scattered# them abroad from thence upon the face of all the earth: and they left off# to build the city#.

11:9 Therefore is the name of it called Babel#; because the Lord did there confound# the language# of all the earth#: and from thence did the Lord scatter# them abroad upon the face of all the earth#.

11:1 And the whole land was of one pair of lips (speech), and of one religion.

11:2 And it came to pass, as they journeyed from the east, that they found a valley near the Giza plateau; and they dwelt there.

11:3 And they said one to another, let us make Tura limestone bricks, and burn them thoroughly. And they had Tura limestone for stone, and bitumen had they for mortar.

11:4 And they said, Go to, let us build us a watchtower and a pyramid, whose top may reach unto the Sun; and let us make us a monument, lest we be scattered abroad upon the face of the whole earth.

11:5 And Jehava (Thoth) came down to see the watchtower and the pyramid, which the men of Adam (Hyksos) had created.

11:6 And Jehava said, Behold, the Hyksos is one, and they have all one language; and this they begin to do: and now nothing will be restrained from them, which they have imagined to do.

11:7 Go to, let us go down, and there wreck their lips, that they may not hear one another's lips.

11:8 So Jehava (Thoth) scattered them abroad from thence upon the face of all the earth: and they sealed up the watchtower.

11:9 Therefore is the name of it called 'Pyramid' (Belbel); because Jehava (Thoth) did there cast out (wreck) the language of all the earth: and from thence did Thoth scatter them abroad upon the face of all the earth.

Verse 11:1 indicates that the world was of one language and speech, a sentence that is almost right but the repetition gives away the error. The word for 'language' was derived from *sepheth* שׂפת, which in both Hebrew and Egyptian more literally means 'lips'. The Egyptian original of this is *sepet* . Meanwhile the term for 'speech' was taken from *dabar* דבר, and the Egyptian version of *dabhu* demonstrates that it was the meaning of 'utterance' or 'prayer' that was intended here. It is worth noting that the 'people' are defined as being the *am* עם, and yet the Hyksos nation that are so closely associated with this whole story were also called the Aamu . Through this term, the Torah is positively indicating that this entire Genesis story was the history and events that were associated with the Hyksos nation, which again supports my previous arguments that the Hyksos were the Israelites.

The direct translations from the Egyptian continue, and the word for 'plain' *beqa* בקעא was based upon *baqa* בקע, meaning 'cleft' or 'gorge'. This was, in turn, taken from *baka* which again means 'cleft' or 'gorge'. But this gorge or valley was found in the land of Shinar שנער, a name which supposedly has no direct Hebrew translation. That assertion, however, is simply too convenient. In fact, the name Shinar (Mt Shinar) was based upon an alternative name for Mt Hermon חרמון, which was *shinar* שניר.

Quite obviously, what we have here is another rendering for the name of Mt Sinai, but Mt Hermon (Mt Shinar) couldn't be called Sinai as the Israelites were supposed to be in another location entirely by this time in the account of the exodus (Deuteronomy). But the fact that Mt Shinar was Mt Sinai can be seen by the similar descriptions being used; *sinai* means 'thorn' or 'prickle', while *shiniynah* שנינה means 'sharp'.

However, in the book *Tempest*, I gave a very plausible explanation that showed Mt Sinai to be the Great Pyramid of Egypt. Surprising as this radical identification may seem, the physical form and location of the Great Pyramid conforms to each and every one of the descriptions that apply to Mt Sinai. Furthermore, as has been demonstrated, the history and culture of the Israelites were positively linked to the Hyksos regime, who were Egyptians. The association of these people with Giza, rather than a barren mountain somewhere in the Sinai peninsular, would therefore make a great deal more sense.

In the book *Tempest*, the original Egyptian name for Mt Sinai (the Great Pyramid) was explored, and although some familiar terminology was discovered, the actual meaning of the name remained elusive. But this new name for Mt Sinai, that of Mt Shinar, gives us some interesting new meanings for this word that can possibly help in this investigation. The most interesting of these alternatives is the fact that Mt Shinar was turned into an Amorite term meaning 'snow mountain'. Now when the Great Pyramid was originally built, it was covered in pure white Tura limestone, and it must have looked exactly like a snow-covered mountain peak – indeed, in the book *K2* I have already stated that this was the prime intention of the Giza architect. Mt Shinar, or Snow Mountain, couldn't be a better description of the original form of the Great Pyramid. But *shinar* was not an Egyptian term, and so the search continued for an equivalent term that could be the original description for this Giza monument.

The search for this was a little tortuous, but eventually the picture seemed to gel into something more tangible. The route to this discovery lay in the Hebrew root word upon which the name for Mt Shinar was based, and this is *shenyi* שני meaning 'sharp'. The equivalent Egyptian word would be pronounced as *shennu*, and as it happens, the various phonemes of *shennu* mean 'tempest', 'hairy', 'cavern' and 'breast', which are all euphemisms that seem to have been applied to Mt Sinai. More importantly, perhaps, is the fact that the word *shennu* refers to a granary and this was, of course, the favourite (possibly tongue-in-cheek) Greek explanation for the function of the Great Pyramid.

But the proper Hebrew translation of *shenyi* שני is the number 'two'. Now this word has already been tackled, and it means the number 'two' in both Hebrew and Egyptian. The Egyptian version is spelt *seni* or *senu*.

Initially I wondered if this may have been based upon a similar conception to the modern designation for one of these Giza monuments – the Second Pyramid. However, on ruminating further I do not think that this was the precise translation that the Egyptians had in mind when they named this location; instead they were thinking of the word *senui* or *sinyi* 𓂋𓏤𓏏𓏥 , meaning the Two Brothers. As I mentioned in the book *Tempest*, the two largest pyramids at Giza were often associated with pairs, and so they became known as the Two Sandals, the Twin Peaks, the Twin Breasts, and the Twin Brothers. But this was not supposed to be any old brothers, these were the Two Brothers of Horus and Seth (although to be precise they were not really brothers, but uncle and nephew).

The king was supposed to have been the 'heir to the Two Brothers', and this was a symbolic position inferring the ruler of the Two Lands. This symbology came about because the surviving 'brothers', Seth and Horus, became linked to the duality of the Egyptian nation and culture. Seth became identified with the north or Lower Egypt, while Horus became the patron of the south or Upper Egypt. Because Seth was the god of the north he was depicted as the red god of Egypt, and he naturally became associated with and revered by the Lower Egyptian Hyksos regime. He was also said to be the most warlike of the two gods, the guardian of chaos, the bringer of storms. Indeed, he was probably the god that should be most closely identified with Shadday שׁדי, the Hebrew Bible's god of storms and destruction, who is identified in the English translations of the Bible by the term 'Almighty'.

The close association between Seth and all things evil was probably not a part of the ancient creed, as Ra himself chose Seth to rule the Earth; although Seth was later deposed by Horus, who then became the ruler of all Egypt. Rather, I think this association between Seth and evil was promoted by the Upper Egyptians after the Hyksos exodus from Egypt, and since the Theban regime considered the Hyksos to be the embodiment of all evil, no doubt this animosity was transferred onto Seth at the same time. But Seth was, nevertheless, the most warlike of the two gods, and so his association with Lower Egypt is interesting, as I will argue later for ancient rituals that were masculine in the north and more feminine in the south. For further information on Seth see Appendix 2, where he is closely linked with St George.

If the original Egyptian name for Mt Sinai (Mt Shinar) was actually Sinyi, referring to the 'Two Brothers', then it is likely that the biblical term being used in the previous verses, the land of Shinar, was actually a veiled reference to the Giza plateau. While this may seem to be a leap of faith, the evidence in favour of this suggestion lies in what the family of Noah did when they got to this location. What did they do? Well, in verse 11:3 it can be seen that they decided to make a 'tower'; but this was not any old tower, rather it was said to be a 'tower made of brick'. Now that description is a little misleading because even in the English translation, the phrase 'and they had brick for stone' is a bit clumsy. Bricks are man-made, stone is natural, so there is no equivalence to be made between the two.

Actually, the original Hebrew text sorts out this muddle because it says that they made a tower of *lebanah* לבנה, and while *lebanah* can mean 'brick' it can also mean 'white', which is why it is also the name of the region called Lebanon לבנון (the land of snow-capped mountains). So the original text was not referring to a 'brick of stone', it was describing a 'white stone'. There is only one source of truly white stone in Egypt and that is the limestone quarry at Tura, from which the casing stones for the Great and Second pyramids were taken. So the text is blatantly saying that the sons of Noah went to Giza and built a 'tower' (a pyramid) that was clad in white Tura limestone, which looked like the mountains of Lebanon. It is entirely possible, therefore, that this is actually a garbled but original text, describing the construction of the pyramids on the Giza plateau.

The sons of Noah were Shem, Ham and Japheth and, as we shall see, just as this tower was being finished these three sons (tribes) were scattered by the gods into three different countries. But this is not all, for the scribe is also having a little fun here with this text, and making a rhyme or two. Significantly, however, the rhyme works better in the Egyptian than the Hebrew, as it gives further information about the true meaning of this verse. The pertinent words here are:

Lebenah לבנה meaning 'brick' or white'; from the Egyptian *repenon (lepenon)* , meaning 'white(?)'. *

Oben אבן meaning 'stone' or a 'circle'; from the Egyptian *uten* , meaning 'heavy stone'.

Khemar חמר meaning 'pitch' or 'bitumen'; from the Egyptian *kam* , meaning 'black' or 'end of day'.

---

* In actual fact, *lepanon* means 'bitumen' in Egyptian, and *lebanon* means 'white' in Hebrew. I can't help thinking that there has been a mistranslation along the way somewhere, for these two very similar words to end up with totally opposite meanings. This must be quite an ancient muddle, as the Coptic word for bitumen is *erponon*, which follows the Egyptian meaning.

I imagine that this mistranslation must have something to do with the terminology being used to describe Egypt. Egypt was known as the Kam , the 'Black Land', which is thought to have been a reference to the black soils of Egypt, in contrast with the red sands of the desert. However, the biblical account seems to have mis-identified King Hiram as coming from Lebanon, when he may well have been a prince or king of Lower Egypt, based in Tanis. If this theory is correct then, historically, Hiram would have been a king of the Kam, the Black Lands, and so the term 'King of Lebanon' should also refer to Black Lands. But the Bible has identified...

Continued...

VI Tower of Babel

Khemar חמר   meaning 'mortar' or 'clay'; from the Egyptian *kam* 🕊🦅⊗,
meaning 'black earth, or mud' or 'Egypt'.

In the Hebrew, the rhyme becomes:
> And they had *lebanah* for *oben*, and *chemar* for *chemar*.

In the Egyptian, the rhyme becomes:
> And they had *lebanon* for *uben*, and *kam* for *kam*.

In the English, the rhyme becomes:
> And they had white limestone for stone, and black mud for mortar.

As can be seen, the rhyme works in both Hebrew and Egyptian, and the typical dualist contrast between black and white also works in both languages. Traditional interpretations of this sentence note the mention of bricks and bitumen and predictably point towards a ziggurat in Sumer being the Tower of Babel. However, this new interpretation invokes Tura limestone and the black muds of Egypt as mortar, which is exactly how the pyramids at Giza and Dahshur were constructed.

It is this conjunction of black-and-white and night-and-day that gives the clue to what kind of tower the sons of Noah were going to build – if any further clues are required, of course. As I pointed out in the book *Tempest*, the two great pyramids on the Giza plateau appear to have been identified with the Sun and the Moon, and thus, by inference, with day and night or with white and black. Note again how the Moon is being identified with the blackness of the night, over which it ruled, in contrast with the lightness of the daytime Sun. It is this duality of the pyramids that has generated the similar duality of their construction materials.

Cont...

Hiram most closely with the House of Lebanon, which was a reference either to the royal treasury or the king's palace, as this was always known as the White House in Egypt. With the White House being the primary governmental building in the Black Land, there is a great deal of room for confusion between these two terms.

Another potential source of confusion is that the term *lebanah* לבנה happens to mean 'Moon' as well. Common sense would dictate that the Moon is actually white, but in terms of Egyptian dualism it was actually regarded as the dark eye of Horus, in contrast to his bright solar eye. Again, it would be easy to confuse the original meanings of these two terms. The Egyptian term for 'black' was *lebanon*, and since this could refer to the dark eye of the Moon, later scribes could easily presume that it actually meant 'white' in reference to the silvery Moon. In the rhyme just quoted, it is quite obvious that the scribe was intending the term to mean 'white'. All of which adds a new dimension to the well-worn phrase, 'arguing that black was white'. Strangely enough, the same kind of confusion seems to have occurred between the French and English terms for 'black' and 'white'.

VI Tower of Babel

The 'tower' of Babel is actually a *migdal* מגדל, which, as has been demonstrated in my previous books, is the Egyptian *maktar (maktal)* 🦅⛏️◌〰️ or *magadjar (magdjal)* 〰️△🦅🐦🔘 meaning 'tower'. In addition, this *magdjal* tower has already been linked to the Great Pyramid in those works. The biblical text is therefore indicating that the sons of Noah are setting out to construct the Great and Second Pyramids. It then says that they made a 'name' for themselves, which just has to be a Hebrew mistranslation. The word here is *shem* שם, which can mean 'name', but it can also mean 'monument'. Since the text is detailing the construction of a pyramid, I think that 'monument' is the better option, and it also translates nicely into the Egyptian as *semen-t* 𓈖〰️𓏥 , meaning 'statue' or 'monument'.

As an aside, the Tower of Babel may well get its final biblical mention in the Book of Revelations. There, it is said that the final battle between good and evil will be fought at the famous location called Armageddon Αρμαγεδδων, which is derived from the Hebrew Har Megido הר מגדו. While many interpretations have been placed upon this location, including an ancient *tel* or raised town in the valley of Megiddo in Israel, it is far more likely that the term 'Armageddon' was actually derived from the Egyptian Har Magdjal 🔲🐦 〰️△🦅🐦🔘 meaning 'Mountain Tower'. Since the original scattering of the Judaic people occurred at the Tower of Babel (the Tower of Magdal) then surely the final battle will eventually take place in the same location. This is doubly likely, as this location has already been identified as being both Mt Sinai and the Great Pyramid of Egypt, the most sacred site of Egypto-Judaism (in reality, Mt Sinai and the Great Pyramid are the same location).

Semai Taui

The reason for constructing this great pyramidal 'monument', the Tower of Babel, was to prevent the people being 'scattered abroad', and the Egyptians feared nothing more than the perceived chaos that existed beyond their borders. The word for 'scattered' here is *puts* פוץ, which is another Egyptian term derived from *putput* 🏠🏠✖️ , a term that implies a forced dispersal through its subsidiary meanings of 'pursue' or 'trample' or 'crush to pieces'. So in what way could this 'monument' prevent this forced dispersal of the people? The answer lies in an alternative meaning to *sem*, the word being used for 'monument', as it is entirely possible that the word *sem* was also taken to imply *semai*, as in the Semai Taui knot, the uniter of the Two Lands.

Before investigating the uniting of Egypt, perhaps it would help if we looked firstly at why Egypt needed uniting in the first place. To the casual observer it may initially appear that Egypt had always been a single entity;

one pharaoh, one religion, and one nation. However, that image is incorrect, for Egypt had long been a union between the two nations that resided at either end of the country. The Theban priesthood resided in the south of the country, with their concealed cave-like temples, while the Heliopolian priesthood with their open Sun-temples and Sun-pyramids inhabited the north, in or near the Delta. What we have within this religious divide, of course, is the standard gender-based theological duality that is to be found in much of the megalithic world. The southern cave-like temples at Thebes are the equivalent of the Irish henges at Newgrange, and at one time they, or their earlier equivalents, must have represented the female component of the deity. So the rays of the solstice Sun were allowed to penetrate the long, dark birth canal of the temple once each year and to illuminate the Holy of Holies, which represented the womb of Mother Earth. Conversely, to the north of Egypt, the open Sun-temples of Heliopolis and Giza were quite plainly and openly phallic in their design, and so the Sun was allowed to cast a shadow over the phallus of Atum, and the position of that shadow could be measured to derive the solstice. Both of these types of temple were, therefore, Sun-temples that tracked the position of the Earth relative to the Sun, but they achieved this by different methods and represented opposite genders.

In fact, the differences between the north and south of Egypt are so marked and so obvious that it is as if the two ends of the country were deliberately set up in this fashion to represent the different sexes. It is as though someone set up alternative governmental systems – one based on a female theology and one based on a male theology – in order let them compete against each other and to see which of these systems would triumph. Although this suggestion may seem a trifle speculative and bizarre, I believe that this is exactly what was done, but the reasoning behind this supposition is perhaps too esoteric for this chapter. Interested readers should read the masonic explanations in Appendix 1, and then take a look at the book *Thoth* for a more detailed examination of the esoteric nature of the world's megalithic societies.

However, I can hear the complaints already about this suggestion, with the loudest of these pointing out that Ramesses II built most of the great temples of Karnak and Luxor, and it was unlikely that he would have built edifices that are representative of the female aspect. While it is true that the New Kingdom pharaohs from Horemheb to Ramesses IV built the great central colonnade within the Temple of Karnak, they probably did so with or over the remains of older temples. There is also the possibility that these ancient temples were originally plain and uninscribed, as are the pyramids at Giza and Dahshur, and the evidence for this comes from the Temple of Luxor.

The evidence that Ramesses II adopted and usurped many of

his great monuments is widespread across Egypt, which is why he was sometimes known as the 'great chiseler'. A good example of this is to be seen upon the colossal statues that line the eastern colonnade at the Temple of Luxor. The statues and the colonnade itself are supposed to have been made for Ramesses II, as that is what the cartouches indicate. However, while the statues are exquisitely carved in granite, it is a fact that the majority of the finer granite statues and carvings in Egypt tend to come from the earlier dynasties. In this respect, Egypt is highly unusual, in that the early craftsmanship and constructions from the Old Kingdom are the finest, and the quality and dimensions of each monument reduces from then on throughout the following millennia. The evidence that these statues at Luxor were not made during Ramesses II's reign, is that the cartouches of Ramesses cut across all of the statue's daggers. The dagger is a key feature of the statue, and obliterating parts of it with a cartouche is clumsy in the extreme, which would indicate that these cartouches were probably not an original feature of these monuments. As these statues only have a single identifying cartouche on the torso, and since that cartouche is quite plainly a later addition, these statues may have stood for some considerable time as completely uninscribed and anonymous monuments.

If there was one set of monuments in Thebes that was uninscribed, I am certain that there were more; a tally that would have included all the blank stelae that were eventually taken to Rome. What I think has happened here is that there were a number of magnificent monuments that were made during mankind's early megalithic era. These include monuments as diverse as Stonehenge and Avebury in England, Teotihuacan in Mexico, Chou-Chou in Manchuria, Hagar Qim in Malta, Baalbek in Lebanon, Ephyra in Greece, Cuzco in Peru, Giza in Egypt, and the Osireion at Abydos. Despite the geographic diversity of these monuments, they all share some common features – they were all built in the prehistoric era; they were all associated with religious centers; they were all made from megalithic architecture; they were mostly exquisitely carved and manufactured (often bafflingly so); and last but certainly not least, all of these monuments were utterly devoid of inscriptions. Archaeologists will say that the lack of inscriptions simply demonstrates that these constructions date from a pre-literate era, but why then should they also be so completely devoid of art or imagery? This was hardly due to a lack of stoneworking technology, as many of these monuments would be either difficult or impossible to produce even with today's technology. The granite megaliths carved into a giant jigsaw puzzle at Cuzco, and the 1,000 tonne bricks that were being used at Baalbek, would stretch any modern stone mason's imagination and skills to their limits. So why, then, the lack of inscriptions?

The answer is that when they were constructed, these temples were not dedicated to any one particular monarch, nor to any one particular god. They were, instead, dedicated to the observation and the study of the Universe. The original theology and ritual of the megalithic priesthood demanded that there were no idols, no imagery and no inscriptions, as the design of these monuments was not supposed to give away the identity of the architects or builders. This is why Abraham, Moses and Akhenaton led such uncompromising crusades against idolatry, although it has to be admitted that Akhenaton still allowed inscriptions and imagery to be made as long as they did not explicitly identify the true nature of his god. But perhaps the ultimate crusade to return to the original plain, unadorned architectural format of the original megalith builders, has been waged by Islam; where any form of idolatry and imagery has been banned from mosques. Thus Islamic religious art has always comprised complex decorative patterns and motifs, as was Celtic artistry on Europe's northwestern megalithic monuments.

What we have in Egypt are two entirely different types of temple, which appear to be devoted to opposite genders. In the north (Lower Egypt) they are overtly masculine, while in the south (Upper Egypt) they are clearly feminine. While the evidence for uninscribed temples in the south is debatable, at the very least it can be demonstrated that the northern temples were originally uninscribed. Conversely, while the northern pharaohs were demonstrably male, the evidence for an alternative line of female monarchs that once ruled the south of Egypt is less visible, as the New Kingdom pharaohs that took over Thebes and rebuilt it most probably destroyed much of the evidence. But, as Cyril Aldred says about the line of God's Wives who once governed the south:

> As a celibate, (the God's Wife) adopted her successor from the daughters of the pharaoh, and governed the whole of the Thebaid (the area around Thebes) and Upper Egypt with the aid of a Steward or Major Domo.[1]

Aldred is actually talking about the Third Intermediate Period princesses or queens who were known as God's Wives, but he speculates that since this governmental structure was already well formed during the reign of Nefertari, the wife of Ahmose I of the eighteenth dynasty, it is likely that the custom preceded the New Kingdom era. If this is true, then this female 'monarchy' would have been the female counterbalance to the male pharaohs in the north. Thus the phallic temples of the north maintained a male-dominated monarchy and society, while the uterine temples of the south were presided over by a female-dominated leadership and society. A central component of Egyptian theology was dualism, and so it should not be a surprise if this rule also extended to the makeup of the governmental structures.

This explanation may also shed some further light on the curious reign of Akhenaton. It is a fact that Akhenaton set up his new capital city of Amarna (Akhetaton) in the very center of Egypt, and it is also a fact that Akhenaton portrayed himself as being androgynous. One possible reason that would explain both of these observations is that Akhenaton was declaring to the population that he was neuter(al) – favouring neither of the dualist components of north and south, nor male and female. But if that was the intent, the policy clearly failed.

This dual gender imagery of the temples of Egypt is also mirrored in the modern masonic world. Although Masonry is predominantly a male institution, with only one or two female or co-gender lodges being established, the masonic hierarchy have nevertheless chosen to represent their temples with the symbology of both genders. In London we have Cleopatra's needle and in America there is the Washington Monument, both of which are masonic-inspired phallic symbols. But when it came to the new masonic Grand Lodge in Great Queen St, London, this same masonic hierarchy decided to build a symbolic womb. This 'shaft' and chamber design at Grand Lodge is exactly the same as is to be found in Egypt, and is not dissimilar to the great henge at Newgrange in Ireland or even Stonehenge in England. The only real differences between these monuments is that the light from the dormer window above the entrance door at Grand Lodge cannot reach the chamber. This upper window design is important in both megalithic and masonic architecture, and it is through this same feature that the light reaches the inner chamber in the Newgrange henge.

Other differences between these monuments include the fact that Newgrange is aligned to the midwinter solstice sunrise, whereas Stonehenge is aligned to the midsummer solstice sunrise. In contrast, although Grand Lodge is a covered uterine-style monument in a similar fashion to Newgrange, its alignment is not focused upon the winter solstice. Grand Lodge is actually aligned on a sunset that is 22 days displaced towards the winter solstice. In other words, it appears to be aligned with the sunset on March 1st and October 13th.[2] Since modern masonry is descended in part from the rituals of the Knights Templar, the date of the demise of the Templars forms a central component in the masonic calendar, and that date is Friday 13th October 1307.

Prior to this diversion from the primary topic, we were discussing the union between these two diverse nations that were situated at either end of the Nile. The United Egypt was known as the 'Two Lands' and the unity of these two nations was celebrated by the joining of the Red Crown of Lower Egypt and the White Crown of Upper Egypt into the United Crown of the Two Lands. It is perhaps worth noting that these two crowns conveniently fit together, physically, almost as if they were specifically designed to do so.

It would have been a bit of a shame if the king of the United Two Lands of Egypt had to wear two crowns that had to be stacked one upon the other, because they did not fit together properly. So, like the very convenient dualism of the monarchy and constitution of Egypt, the regalia of the Two Lands also looks as though it were pre-designed, rather than being a chance event.

But, in addition to the two crowns, there was another image of the union between the two lands of Egypt and that was the Semai Taui 𓊽, the tying of the official knot that bound the Two Lands together. The unifying qualities of the *semai taui* are further reinforced by the alternative meanings to this word, which are 'gang', 'troop', 'allies', 'confederation'. Clearly, this was a powerful force that united the people of Egypt, but what kind of force was it? What would have that kind of influence over these two lands?

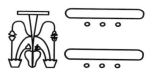

Fig 6.1   *The Semai Taui.*

As it happens, the Semai Taui returns us all the way back to the discussions that surrounded Nefertiti in a previous chapter, and the precise role of the Holy Spirit – for the knot that was supposed to bind Upper and Lower Egypt together was actually tied around a trachea extending from a pair of lungs, as can be seen in the glyphs above. At first, this might seem to be an unusual symbol for a bond or union between two nations, as it would appear that the knot is actually strangling someone. So what was this symbolism supposed to represent, and what was the true union between these two nations?

Although there is not much evidence to back up this suggestion, the answer may lie in a variation on the theme of the 'Word' that has already been discussed. It is possible that the lung and trachea symbology represented 'language'; the word as spoken by the common people, rather than the divine Word of the priesthood. Note that the knot is placed halfway up the trachea, and in the human equivalent this position would represent the larynx, the prime location of speech. This may be the primary symbology involved in the imagery associated with the Semai Taui, but a complementary possibility is discussed in Appendix 1.

VI   Tower of Babel

The biblical verses that we have just been looking at from the beginning of this chapter were detailing the possible scattering of the people and the confounding of their language, and the device that was going to prevent all this tragedy and chaos was the Semai Taui – the lung and trachea or the language of the nation. Language has always been a unifying force, which is why the United States of America works well but the United States of Europe struggles miserably to unify itself. People cannot unite in religion, politics or culture unless they have the common bond of a common language and a common nationality – in other words, multiculturalism simply does not work, as the histories of the ancient cities of Alexandria and Jerusalem have amply demonstrated. It would appear that the Egyptians understood this basic requirement of the human existence, and they turned it into a central component of their history, mythology and ritual.

Gordian

This is also probably the basis of the strange tale of the Gordian Knot, reputedly tied by Gordius, the king of Phrygia. The knot, which was supposed to be incredibly intricate, was tied to the shaft of a cart in a not too dissimilar fashion to the knot on the trachea of the Semai Taui; indeed, if the lungs and trachea of the Semai Taui were drawn horizontally, the resulting image would produce a passable imitation of a cart and its shaft. But the knot of Gordia was reputed to be magical, and the person who managed to loosen this knot was supposed to become the ruler of all Asia. Alexander the Great, having been manoeuvred by his entourage into looking into this knotty problem, was not in a position to say that he could not solve the problem without losing a great deal of credibility. With defeat of any nature being anathema to Alexander, he reputedly solved the problem by cutting the knot in two with his sword.

So much for the Greek myth, but the reality is that the biblical equivalent of this story was more likely to have been a scribal device to describe the results of untying the knot of Egypt. According to the Torah, the scattering of the people across the Mediterranean was prompted by god seeing that the people were doing well and were united. Being a mischievous and sometimes malevolent deity, god therefore decided to throw a spanner in the works. Thus, at a few junctures in Egyptian history, the knot was untied, the people were scattered, and their language was confounded and changed. But it is likely that their descendants did eventually rebuild their power bases in new lands, and became rulers of all the lands that border the Mediterranean.

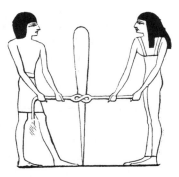

Fig 6.2 Egyptian version of the Gordian knot?

Finally, perhaps it is worth noting that the tradition of the Semai Taui has survived within the Christian tradition as a component of the marriage ceremony. During the service, the priest will wrap the hands of the couple together with piece of decorative ribbon. It is from this component of the ritual that the institution of marriage is known as 'tying the knot', but it is more than likely that this phraseology was originally derived from the formal union of the Two Lands.

Tower of Babel

The final sentence from the verses quoted at the beginning of this chapter is equally interesting, as this mentions the famous Tower of Babel. The tower was given this famous name because god disapproved of its construction by mankind, and so it was the presence of the tower that caused god to scatter the people. The name Babel בבל was supposed to have been derived from *balal* בלל, meaning to 'confuse' (the language), and it was from this name that the English word 'babble' was derived.

Alternatively, some hint that Babel was derived from the name 'Babylon', and thus the 'tower' was actually a ziggurat situated somewhere in Sumer. However, the theologian's and historian's analyses are both incorrect. In truth, the word Babel was derived from the Egyptian *berber* ⏗⏛⏗⏛△ , meaning 'pyramid'; a word which would, of course, have been translated into the Hebrew as *balbel*. So the Bible's 'Tower of Babel' was actually the 'Maktal of Balbel' ⏚⏛⏗⏚ ⏗⏛⏗⏛△ , or the Great Pyramid of Egypt. The Egyptian word *belbel* was being used to describe the pyramid, because in the original biblical verses it rhymed perfectly with *balbel* ⏗⏛⏗⏛⏚ meaning 'scatter'.

Plate 1. Satellite image of the River Nile flowing into the fertile Delta region. Note that there are only two main branches of the Nile within the Delta, but in ancient times there used to be four; and so the Nile Valley conforms precisely to the description of the biblical Eden.

Plate 2. The main door for the Wellcome Trust medical library near Euston, London. The image is an exact copy of the Aton Sun-god of Akhenaton, and the lower of the hands even carries the symbol of the Ankh.

Plate 3. Examples of Cypress Sempervirens, which are often associated with cemeteries.

Plate 4. The Abu Dulaf minaret in Samara; a Persian spiral pyramid.

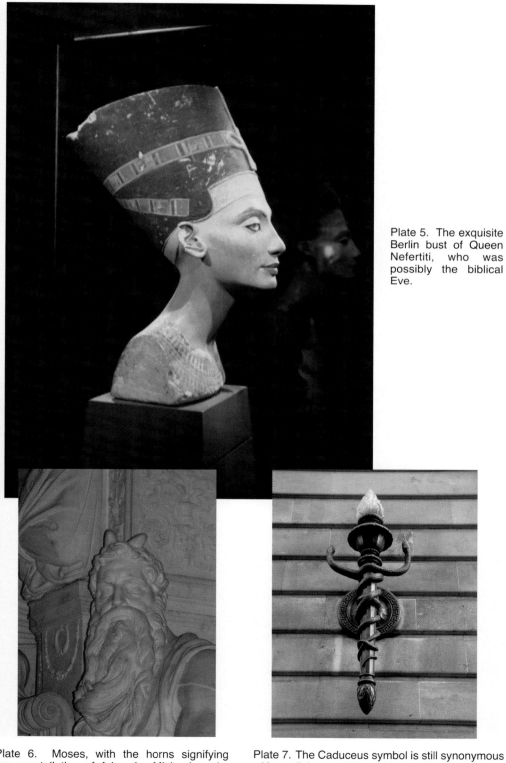

Plate 5. The exquisite Berlin bust of Queen Nefertiti, who was possibly the biblical Eve.

Plate 6. Moses, with the horns signifying the constellation of Aries, by Michaelangelo. Basilica San Pietro in Vincoli, Rome.

Plate 7. The Caduceus symbol is still synonymous with medicine and life to this day. Wellcome Trust medical library, Euston, London.

Plate 8. The god Thoth, writing the name of the pharaoh Seti I onto the fruits of the Tree of Life (Tree of Remembrance). Temple of Karnak, Luxor.

Plate 9. Two Babylonian winged sphinxes, British Museum, London. Note that one has the legs of a lion, while the other has the legs of a bull.

Plate 10. Two images of one of the only Jewish synagogues in the world to utilize an overtly Egyptian theme, in recognition of the Egyptian origins of Judaism. This is the Peitavas Iela synagogue in Riga, and it is the only synagogue in Latvia to have survived the holocaust of the Second World War.

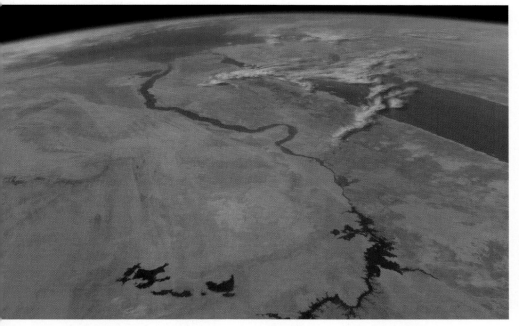

Plate 11. Satellite image of the sinuous course of the River Nile, looking like a snake (cobra) or perhaps even a palm tree.

Plate 12. Statue of Ramesses II from the Temple of Luxor. Note how the cartouche cuts across the image of the dagger, indicating that this statue was originally uninscribed and therefore usurped by Ramesses II.

Plate 13. The torso of Nefertiti [Eve?] showin how the sculptors exaggerated her figure an portrayed the queen as being virtually nake save for a barely perceptible, diaphanou gown.

Plate 14. The reassembled remains of the basalt pavement on the eastern side of the Great Pyramid, which may have originally been a black-and-white chequerboard pattern.

Plates 15-18.   Masonic tracing boards. The upper two images are from the First Degree, while the lower two are from the Second Degree.

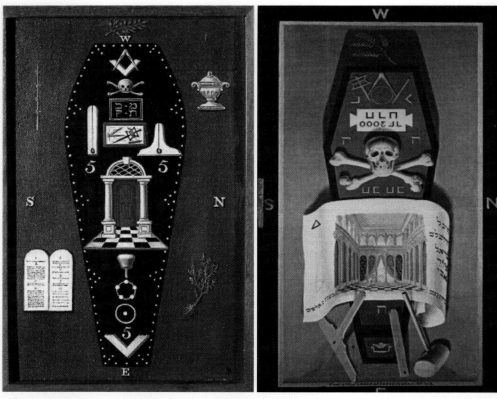

Plate 19. Two tracing boards from the Third Degree.

Plate 20. The capital city of Pharaoh Akhenaton at Amarna, built for the worship of the Sun-god Aton (or Adon). Within this barren-looking plain once stood a garden dedicated to this god, and so the garden was known as the Garden of Eden (Garden of Adon).

Indeed, from this explanation we can perhaps now 'back-engineer' the name of Babylon. It is known that the city across the Nile from the Giza plateau was called Babylon of Egypt, and that this name possibly predated the Sumerian equivalent. If so, then the name 'Babylon' could have been derived from 'Balbel of On', with the term On being a Hebrewised version of An 𓉔, the Egyptian name for Heliopolis. So Babylon 𓂋◯𓂋◯△ 𓉔 may well have meant 'Pyramid of Heliopolis' and would have also referred to the 'Pyramid of the Sun'.

The term for 'city' that is sporadically used in these verses is another poor allusion to the same great edifice of the Great Pyramid. The true translation is an *aiyr* עיר or 'watchtower', which was derived from the Egyptian *aer* 𓁹𓏏, meaning 'watch'. The connection here is that the pyramids of Egypt were always surmounted by a pyramidion, and inscribed on that capstone were the two eyes of Ra, watching over the efforts of mankind. The pyramids were Sun-temples, and also watchtowers for Ra.

However, there is another possible reason for this 'watchtower' terminology. The biblical account indicates that the tower (pyramid) was never completed, because god got a little angry or jealous and scattered the people across the land. Thus the Tower of Balbel was presumably never completed and, in like fashion, the Great Pyramid was also supposed to have never been completed; which is why this pyramid is shown to be unfinished on the back of the American one-dollar bill. The possibility exists, therefore, that the top of the Great Pyramid has always had the small platform on its summit, as it does today. But, if there was a method of getting the priesthood up to the top of this pyramid, then this structure could well have been the prime astronomical observatory of Egypt, with an unrivalled view over the land and an equally unrivalled view of the rising and setting of the Sun, planets and stars. For the astronomer priests of Egypt, such a structure would have been so convenient it would almost have had to have been designed that way.

Ladder

However, there is a problem with the convenience of this observatory; under the traditional explanations for its design, the sides of the Great Pyramid would have originally been finished with perfectly smooth, pure-white Tura limestone, and thus utterly impossible to climb without some form of scaffolding or stepladders being put in place. But if you think that I, or any of the high priests from the distant past, would dare climb up 150 meters of wobbly wooden stepladders to gain access to the top of this pyramid, then you had better think again.

VI Tower of Babel

The alternative scenario is that the Great Pyramid once had a set of steps cut into its casing blocks that led right up to the very top of this pyramid, where the small 'unfinished' platform could then have served as a perfect location for worship and for the observation of the rising and setting Sun. Since all the cladding stones have been taken from the great Pyramid, it is impossible to verify or disprove this hypothesis, but the tradition of there being a ladder that reached up to heaven is long and enduring. In Egypt, this ladder was known either as the *Aqa-t-ter-pet* 𓀀𓊖𓏏𓏏 or the *Maqet* 𓐂𓀀𓊖 – which were said to be the 'Ladder of Heaven' and the 'Ladder of Osiris' respectively. Wallis Budge says of the latter of these ladders:

> From the Pyramid Texts we learn that at a time when man believed that it was necessary to have a ladder to ascend into heaven from the Earth, Horus was regarded as the god of the ladder ... Sometimes Ra held one side (of the ladder) whilst Horus held the other, and sometimes the supporters were Horus and Set, but even so the deceased seem sometimes to have had difficulty in ascending it, for we read that Horus had to give him a push upwards with his two fingers.[3]

Not surprisingly, given the Egyptian origins of the Old Testament, we can also see a similar imagery in the Book of Genesis. Here it is the patriarch Jacob who lays down to sleep and sees the Ladder to Heaven:

> And he dreamed, and behold a ladder set up on the Earth, and the top of it reached to heaven: and behold the angels of God ascending and descending on it.[B4]

From the traditions of the Egyptian mortuary rituals and the texts of the Old Testament, the concept of a ladder that ascended to the heavens found its way into Rome and to the followers of Mithras. Among the many references to the heavenly ladder in Mithras is a remarkable mosaic of a ladder emblazoned with pseudo-Egyptian hieroglyphs.

Through this route, and perhaps more directly through the Old Testament traditions, the concept of there being a heavenly ladder then found its way into Masonry, where it became the focus of the First and Second Degree rituals. The tracing board for the First Degree initiation into the Craft focuses strongly upon the story of Jacob's ladder, which is depicted as rising up from between two of the three columns or pillars depicted (see the colour section). Now the two pillars in the foreground of the tracing board are not necessarily the pillars of Jachin and Boaz, as these are the subject of the Second Degree initiation. So what were these three masonic pillars originally representative of?

VI Tower of Babel

Take a look at the tracing board in some detail. Here we have representations of three pillars, the Sun and Moon, a black and white pavement, a ladder, and an amount of building equipment – so what is the common denominator to all of these elements, and what does it all mean?

As is usual with spiritual secret societies, the imagery that is portrayed to masonic candidates is enigmatic and confusing. This is a deliberate policy to ensure that only the most enquiring of minds within masonry achieve any degree of enlightenment, and it also ensures that any core secrets cannot leak out through lower-ranking lodges. A candidate is unlikely to go to the press and declare that he has found out what a Doric capital on a pillar looks like, and even if a complete tracing board was discovered in the local refuse department, the entire composition is so peculiar and confusing as to be totally meaningless to the public. The classical explanations for the layout of these tracing boards, which are given to candidates, try to invoke moral arguments and spiritual awareness for the candidate to absorb and act upon. But the true explanation, which is obviously known within higher levels in the Craft, is that these tracing boards actually portray graphic images of physical locations.

When looked at from this alternative perspective, the imagery that the First Degree masonic tracing board provides us with is unmistakable. Before the exodus scattered the Hyksos-Israelites from Memphis to Tanis, Jerusalem and beyond, the three pillars of Israelite theology were originally the three pyramids at Giza, as I have already demonstrated in previous works. Unlikely as it may seem, this is where the masonic three-pillar symbology originated and this is what the First Degree tracing board is attempting to portray. The 'map' of the tracing board is nothing less than the layout of the Giza plateau, and the evidence for this bold assertion lies in the detail of the composition.

For instance, this is why the tracing board portrays the three pillars as all being of different heights, with two larger pillars in the foreground and a much smaller one behind. This is not simply a matter of perspective, as the two foreground pillars can sometimes be placed at exactly the same depth within the picture, but are still given slightly different heights; while a much smaller pillar lies behind. Yet this depiction exactly reflects the reality at Giza, where the two major pyramids are nearly but not quite of the same height, while the third is much smaller. Note also that the two foreground pillars on the tracing board are associated with or surmounted by the Sun and the Moon, while the eye of Ra is placed over the smaller pillar at the rear. In a similar manner, the three pyramids at Giza were originally Sun-temples dedicated to the observation of the various astronomical bodies, and so their direct association with the Sun, the Moon and Ra is guaranteed. Indeed, I have already demonstrated in *Tempest* that the two major pyramids at Giza

179

should be identified with the Sun and the Moon, and this is exactly what we see on the tracing board: the Great Pyramid represented the Sun, while the Second Pyramid represented the Moon.

This imagery is probably the origin of the biblical story about the pillars of cloud and fire that guided Moses during the exodus. The fire represented the Sun and the cloud often represented the Moon, and so the pillars of cloud and fire were actually representations of the Giza pyramids once more (as will be explained in Appendix 1). The reason for these pyramids being physically visible during the first exodus is given in the book *Tempest*, where it was explained that some of this exodus story, especially the wanderings in the wilderness, represented rituals at Giza. The 'wanderings' were actually the origins of the processional rituals that are still performed at Mecca during the Hajj. Some of these Islamic rituals involve walking to hills, and these rituals were derived from the stories of walking towards pillars of fire and cloud, which in turn were based upon much older traditions that involved walking around the Giza and Dahshur pyramids.* These are the first pieces of evidence that demonstrate that when looking at the First Degree tracing board, we are really looking at a stylised image of Giza rather than a metaphysical depiction of the human soul or psyche.

The First Degree tracing board has many other items of interest upon it, and the next of these to be considered is the stone block with an iron ring in the top. This stone, together with its lifting tripod (which is not shown here) is known as a Lewis. This item is again connected to Giza, and it represents the movable entrance block that once plugged the entrance passageways to the Great and Second Pyramids, as was explained in the book *Solomon*. Then there is the key hanging from the ladder, which is representative of the keys to the Kingdom of Heaven. The link between the stone block and this key is made reasonably clear in the gospel of Matthew, verse 16:18-19, where Jesus is reported as telling Simon that he will be known as Peter, which means 'rock', and that he will become both the rock and the keeper of the keys to the Kingdom of Heaven. In reality, the keeper of the keys was probably the keeper of the seals by which all important and sacred Egyptian doors were sealed, and so in this case the reference to a key is actually a reference to the sealing of the stone entrance blocks that sealed off the many Giza passageways.

---

* The tradition of throwing small stones at the pillars in Mina during the Hajj also began during these Egyptian rituals. The pillars were originally pyramids, and if readers care to take a walk around Dahshur today, they will see that the Vega (Bent) Pyramid is surrounded by millions of small stones. No other pyramid displays this feature, and the stones certainly do not look like they are native to this area. Thus it is entirely possible that these stones were thrown at the Vega pyramid by the faithful of antiquity, just as Muslims throw stones at the pillars in Mina.

VI Tower of Babel

The floor plan for this tracing board composition is the black and white masonic chequerboard, and even this may be of Egyptian origins. I had previously presumed that the eastern base of the Great Pyramid was composed of massive slabs of black basalt, which formed a smooth glassy surface over which the priesthood trod barefoot, so that it did not get scratched or marked. However, upon looking again at the remains of this great basalt pavement, it would appear that what we see today has all been reassembled from the broken pieces that had been scattered across the plateau by the Arabs who destroyed the entire Giza complex.

Now Petrie, in his nineteenth century survey of the site, stated that he had found chippings of polished basalt and marble around the site, so the possibility exists that the original pavement was actually comprised of black and white stone. Therefore, this large pavement area to the east of the Great Pyramid could easily have taken on a black and white chequerboard pattern of marble and basalt squares. There is no particular sacred number or size associated with the equivalent squares that make up a masonic floor, and so this would be difficult to prove one way or the other, but it is worth noting that Petrie thought that the Giza pavement was formed from two squares, while an ideal masonic temple is formed from a double square. This similarity in design may indicate that the typical chequerboard layout to be seen in masonic lodges and tracing boards was derived from the floor plan at Giza.

The masonic explanation for this chequerboard pattern is that it represents the 'diversity of objects that decorate and adorn the creation', which I take to be a description of the stars and galaxies that dot the Universe: the spots of white that punctuate the blackness of the void. In addition to this, I also suspect that these black and white squares are based upon the standard Egyptian duality of the Sun and the Moon, with the white squares representing the brightness of the Sun and the black squares representing the contrasting darkness of the Moon. The dark eye of Ra or Horus was always said to represent the Moon, and so the Moon was said to be black even though it looks white.

According to the same masonic explanations, the tessellated border around the chequerboard floor represents the planets. Strangely enough, these masonic cosmological explanations begin to mirror the biblical description of the pavement that surrounded Mt Sinai:

> And they saw the God of Israel: and there was under his feet as it were a paved work of a sapphire stone, and as it were the body of heaven in his clearness. [B5]

The term 'clearness' is taken from the Hebrew *tehar* טהר, which can mean 'clearness' but also means 'lustre'. This was derived from the Egyptian *tehen* [hieroglyphs] meaning 'sparkle' or 'scintillate'. The traditional explanation for this 'body of heaven' that sparkles is that it was a polished mosaic of stones that looked like the night sky; and this is confirmed by the original Egyptian term, which can be expanded into *Tehentiu* [hieroglyphs] meaning 'the sparkling gods', which is a reference to the stars. This is, of course, exactly the same explanation that masonic tradition confers upon its own mosaic floor – that it represented the universe. But these two supposedly independent traditions start to converge upon each other when it is remembered that the biblical Mt Sinai was actually a pseudonym for the Great Pyramid, and so it is entirely possible that these separate traditions of sacred temples with sparkling pavements were all based upon observations of the same monument.

Since masonic tradition links the chequerboard pavement with the Temple of Solomon, this does mean that in some fashion or other the sacred mountain of Mt Sinai [the Great Pyramid] should be regarded as having the same attributes as the Temple of Solomon. In fact, it is always possible that the 'Temple of Solomon' story was originally based upon the construction of the Great Pyramid! Even masonic tradition tentatively suggests this possibility, as a venerable booklet called *The Free Mason Examined* from the year of 1754 indicates that the rituals of Freemasonry were actually derived from the building of the Tower of Babel, not the Temple of Solomon. [6]

As has just been explained, the Tower of Babel may have rather less to do with the ziggurats of Babylon, and a great deal more in common with the pyramids on the Giza plateau. In which case, the rituals of Freemasonry may have been originally based upon the construction of the Giza pyramids [the Tower of Babel] and not the Temple of Solomon. One piece of evidence in favour of this assertion is the fact that an ideal masonic temple is made from a room that represents a double square – or a rectangular room with one dimension twice the length of the other – that is aligned east-west. This happens to be the exact same layout as the King's chamber in the Great Pyramid, which measures 10 x 20 royal cubits (tc) and is similarly aligned with the longer dimension orientated due east-west. While the presence of the King's chamber in the Great Pyramid was a secret, and its entrance was concealed by massive granite plugs until about the fourteenth century AD, the concept of a double square chamber or temple could easily have been transmitted down the millennia as a tradition. The similar design and orientation of the central chamber in the Temple of Solomon, which predates the opening of the Great Pyramid by more than two thousand years, would again suggest that this was an ancient tradition that had endured the ages.

Another link between Masonry and Giza, one that will be unknown to the majority of secular Masons, is contained in the 'address to the first chair' lectures of a Holy Royal Arch Chapter. During the meeting there is another of these amateur-dramatic scenes to be acted out by the new candidate and the assembled brothers, where a chamber is 'discovered' and the candidate is (symbolically) lowered into this chamber to see what he can find. He eventually discovers a block of marble in the form of a double cube, the same shape as a masonic temple, on top of which is a gold plate. On this plate are inscribed a circle and a triangle, and in all the examples I have seen, this triangle is placed inside the circle with its apexes touching the rim of the circle.

Various banal explanations are given for these inscriptions, but none come even close to the truth of the matter. The simple answer is that the triangle that represents a circle can only be a reference to the Great Pyramid. Of all the pyramids in Egypt, only one has been designed around the fundamental Pi fractional approximation of 22:7, and that is the Great Pyramid of Giza. The height of this pyramid mathematically represents the radius of a circle, while its perimeter length mathematically represents the circumference of a circle; and so to all intents and purposes the 'triangular' Great Pyramid is a representation of a circle. The placing of this unique triangle-and-circle symbol (which can only represent the Great Pyramid) upon a block of stone that is representative of the dimensions of the King's chamber, which lies inside this same pyramid, just has to be significant.

Fig 6.3   Circle and triangle symbol.

These links between Masonry and the pyramids may well be true, but they do not necessarily mean that Mt Sinai [the Great Pyramid] *was* the Temple of Solomon. It is entirely possible that this similarity has come about because the later Temple was constructed as a replacement for the pyramid that had been taken from the Israelites when the two major Theban uprisings overran the Memphis and Giza area. If the Tanis [or Jerusalem] Temple was designed as a symbolic replacement for the original Temple at Giza, then it would naturally attempt to mimic the pattern of the chequerboard pavement that graced the eastern side of the Great Pyramid and the two great pillars. (The two 'pillars' at Giza may have been real pillars standing near the chequerboard pavement, or they may have simply been an allusion to the two largest pyramids on that site; whatever the case, it is relatively certain that two bronze pillars were manufactured for the Temple of Solomon.)

This link between pyramids and pillars can also be found in the Egyptian word *tu* 🏔 which primarily means 'two mountains' and is a word that has already been linked to the two pyramids at Dahshur. But this same word *tu* also means 'pillar', and this version refers to the four pillars that held aloft the heavens, which is a role that I have already assigned to the four largest of the pyramids at Giza and Dahshur. As I mentioned in *Tempest*, this 'four poster' symbolism was the basis of the layout of the Aya Sophia cathedral (now a mosque), and it is also duplicated in the design of altar canopies in many cathedrals and the Grand Master's chair in Freemason's Hall in London. Although the Temple of Solomon may have been a different physical monument to the pyramids of Giza, this does not preclude the traditions of the temple site and its associated ritual construction being far older, and so the venerable pamphlet's assertion that Masonry was descended from the rituals performed at the Tower of Babel [the Great Pyramid of Giza] may be correct. We know that the Great Pyramid was built at some point in time, whether this was in the fourth dynasty or in a much earlier period, and so it is entirely possible that during this construction process a brotherhood was established among the workers, and a series of rituals formulated.

In fact, there would have been an overwhelming imperative for establishing this kind of brotherhood bond among the designers and workers, because the Great Pyramid is known to have contained secrets. Whether the reader believes that the Great Pyramid was the tomb of a pharaoh, or whether the reader subscribes to the more esoteric explanations in the book *Thoth*, it is an established fact that the Great Pyramid contained secret chambers that were deliberately blocked off and rendered both inaccessible and invisible. There would be absolutely no point in making all these secret rooms and passages if the workers would then go back to their villages, have a drink at the equivalent of the local pub or bar and relate the story of the 'secret' chambers to all their friends. By necessity, all the people involved in the construction of these secret chambers would either have to be kept quiet, or they would have to be exterminated.

It is entirely possible that the strong fraternal bonds between Masons were devised and derived from this secretive construction project. This fraternal union of architects then maintained itself as a functioning entity, one of many self-perpetuating societies that have existed throughout man's history, and they subsequently invented yet more projects to give the brotherhood of masons (Masons) a sense of purpose. Since I strongly believe that the Giza pyramids were actually pre-dynastic, then these later projects would have included all the dynastic mud-brick and rubble pyramids that litter the west bank of Lower Egypt. These construction projects lasted right up until the beginning of the eighteenth dynasty, as Pharaoh Ahmose I was the last of the pyramid builders and was attempting to construct a small sand and rubble pyramid with a stone cladding.

This construction project takes us up to the first great exodus era, when the Hyksos were chased from Memphis up into the Delta region and even into what eventually became Israel; and at this point in time the great tradition of pyramid building in Egypt suddenly ceases. Why? Because the pyramid builders were the fraternal company of masons (Masons) who were allied to or a part of the Hyksos clans. Since the Hyksos were now in the northeastern Nile Delta, licking their wounds and refusing to divulge all their stone-working and architectural knowledge, all pyramid building ceased and the bulk of the eighteenth dynasty pharaohs who followed Ahmose I had to make do with simple burials in the rock-cut tombs in the Valley of the Kings.

It wasn't until the twenty-first dynasty and the rise of the ex-Hyksos pharaoh Psusennes II [the biblical King David] that the pyramid builders were at last given an opportunity to show their skills once more. But since Psusennes did not have full control over the Giza-Memphis region, this new temple was to be constructed in the northern stronghold of Tanis. Building materials were brought from Bubastis and perhaps Heliopolis, and a new and magnificent temple slowly arose out of the alluvial sands of the Delta. This was King Solomon's Temple [King Sheshonq I's temple] and since it was being constructed by the fraternal company of masons (Masons) who had already constructed the Great Pyramid (and another 90 or so smaller pyramids), the rituals and arrangements of this new temple strongly reflected those that had been used so many generations before at Giza. This is why the Temple of Solomon can be confused on occasions with the Great Pyramid, for the ancient traditions had survived the centuries and the millennia and had been revived once more in a flurry of grand construction projects in the Delta region. See Appendix 1 for further information on masonic terminology and symbolism.

Beehive

One other piece of pyramidal symbolism is missing from the masonic First Degree tracing board in the colour section, and that is the beehive. Many aspects of masonic imagery focus on the traditional beehive, which is conical in form and is known as a skip, and in these depictions bees are shown flitting to and fro from a small hole in the side of the skip. The true symbolism that is being generated by this imagery can be deduced once more through the Egyptian epigraphic evidence, where there is a convenient pun on the name for a bee, which can be shortened to *bat* ⟨glyph⟩ . As it happens, the Egyptian *bat* ⟨glyph⟩ can also refer to a 'cavern', and when this is taken into context with the conical (pyramidal) beehive, the cave in question may well refer to a chamber in one of the Giza pyramids.

Since the skip-type beehive is made of a spiral of straw, and since it is also generally shown as being comprised of seven coiled tiers, the humble beehive is actually a copy of the spiral masonic temple, a subject that will be discussed shortly. But the term *bat* ⟨glyph⟩ also has one other meaning, and that is 'king', or more correctly the king of Lower Egypt, the Hyksos pharaoh. Thus the humble bee entering a hole in the side of its seven-tiered conical (pyramidal) beehive was the perfect pictorial and epigraphic allegory for the sacred rituals at Giza – during which the king and his princes entered the doorway that was located in the side of the seven-tiered Great Pyramid. This is one small piece of evidence that shows that the Great Pyramid may once have had a strong association with seven spiral tiers.

This pyramid symbology was the reason for the humble beehive being adopted by the Merovingian line of French monarchs. The Merovingian dynasty first came to power in the fifth century AD, and they are said by many researchers to have been directly descended from Jesus. Since I have previously linked Jesus with the Hyksos line of pharaohs, the use of the bee symbology by the Merovingians would be entirely logical. But why include the humble straw hive in the royal heraldry too? The image of the hive would seem to be totally irrelevant to a monarch, until the symbolic linkage to the all-important Hyksos temple complex at Giza can be seen.

One other interesting aspect of masonic art is contained within Mozart's opera, the *Magic Flute*. Mozart was, of course, a Mason and this particular opera is said to have been infused with masonic ritual and the principles of the Third Degree of initiation. The artist, Friedrich Schinkel, designed and painted some stage sets as a backdrop for the opera, and yet the imagery he invoked is curiously familiar in places. The overall theme of Schinkel's work is undoubtedly Egyptian, as is the opera itself, but one piece of scenery incorporates a temple above a triangular stone archway that is the exact image of the entrance to the Great Pyramid. The link he is promoting, between the masonry of the *Magic Flute* and the imagery of the Great Pyramid, is inescapable.

Incidentally, the three women on the steps of the ladder in the First Degree tracing board in the colour section represent the concepts of Faith, Hope and Charity; while the letters W, B, S on the three pillars represent the masonic watchwords of Wisdom, Beauty and Strength. Other examples of masonic watchwords include: Brotherly Love, Relief, and Truth; the French favourite of Liberty, Egality and Fraternity; the moralistic-sounding Temperance, Fortitude and Prudence; and finally a rather familiar refrain from London which is See, Hear and Speak. The latter is actually the motto taken from the coat of arms of United Grand Lodge, and it is a trio of watchwords that have been lampooned in popular literature as the three wise monkeys exclaiming, 'Hear no evil, See no evil, Speak no evil'. This trio of expressions rather gives the impression that if one keeps away from evil it is possible to lead a pure life, but that is not the original intention of the phrase. It is actually an order to the brothers of the Lodge regarding the 'secret' material that they are to be shown and taught, and the phrase actually implores them to 'Hear it, See it, but don't Speak about it to anyone'.

These groups of watchwords may well have been based upon the 14 (or 15) characteristics or dispositions of Ra. The original watchwords of Ra were said to be composed of the following attributes: commands; strength; dominion; vigour; abundance; majesty; burial; preparedness; stability; sight; hearing; perception; taste; and life.

Tracing board

Looking again at the pictorial elements on the First Degree tracing board, if all of the speculations and comparisons I have outlined were indeed based upon an original masonic intention, then the First Degree tracing board actually represents the entire Giza complex. It portrays the chequerboard pavement to the east of the Great Pyramid; the three pyramids themselves; the overall astronomical symbolism of the site; the fact that the Great and Second Pyramids were associated with the Sun and Moon respectively; the rough ashlar that was supposed to finish off the top of the 'unfinished' Great Pyramid; the finely cut entrance block that once graced the northern entrance to the Great Pyramid; the seals (keys) that were used to seal this door; the architect's equipment that made the entire complex in the first place; the architect's plans for the site; and finally the tracing board also portrays a ladder. Clearly, all of these elements are to be found on the Giza plateau, but what of that final element? Was this simply a rickety wooden ladder that went up to the entrance block on the north face of the Great Pyramid? Or was this instead a vast flight of stairs that were carved into the limestone casing blocks and originally provided access to the very top of the pyramid, so that the vital astronomical observations could be made?

This simple, straight flight of stairs and the small platform on its summit would make the Great Pyramid look more like the pyramids of Central America, which also have steps leading up to the summit. This type of design was created so that the Mayan priesthood could get closer to their Sun-god to perform their daily ritual, and no doubt the daily itinerary of the priesthood included solar observations across the top of the jungle canopy as well as sacrificial rituals to appease the gods. Although there is no direct equivalent to the Central American pyramids among those to be found in Egypt, the fact that pyramids with stairways were built somewhere in the world demonstrates that the ancient megalithic societies did have this idea in mind. With there being so many similarities between the Central American and Egyptian cultures, and so many myths about contacts in the ancient past, would the Egyptian pyramids not have incorporated this architectural element too? Would a solar cult really have performed their rituals at ground level, as is suggested for Egypt, and never considered raising their perspective a little?

There is no direct archaeological evidence for a flight of steps up one of the faces of the Great Pyramid, but the myths, legends and texts that have been transmitted down through the millennia do point in that direction. Furthermore, since the Great Pyramid was positively referred to as the 'watchtower', and since it may have had an astronomical observation platform on its summit, this speculation is even more likely. I have previously positively associated the Great Pyramid with Mt Sinai, and yet the Torah claims that Moses climbed up the mountain (the pyramid) before entering inside and conversing with god. As I have already mentioned, with the original cladding stones in position this would have been a very difficult task indeed, and I initially had visions of a great buttress of scaffolding lying against the side of the pyramid to allow Moses and his priesthood to ascend up to the entrance on the northern flank of the pyramid, which leads into the internal subterranean chamber. However, this latticework of scaffolding would have been an eyesore on an otherwise perfect architectural design and construction – an 'unsightly carbuncle', as Prince Charles put it, in a comparable context regarding a modern extension to a classical art gallery in London. If this pyramid was supposed to have been designed from the outset as a 'watchtower' (an astronomical observatory), then it is certain that the great architect would not have allowed such a rickety monstrosity to ruin his smooth, perfect, solid and symmetrical monument.

By necessity, the architect must have included a flight of steps in the design that led up the north face of the pyramid to the entrance. But why stop there? These same steps could easily have gone beyond this point, onwards and upwards to the very top of this pyramid, nearly 150 meters above the level of the plateau. Here, above the habitual low-lying smog from the cooking fires of Memphis, resided the most perfect solar and astronomical viewing platform in the whole of the ancient world. It would have been a great and unforgivable omission for any solar cult not to have designed such an observatory. The workers building the Great Pyramid (in whatever era) would have related tales to the priesthood of the wonderful view they got from the top of the pyramid, of Aton-Ra peeping over the horizon; and they may even have boasted that they saw Aton-Ra several minutes before the priests down below ever did. Would the assembled religious hierarchy of Egypt have been content to allow humble artisans to see what they could not? Personally, I think that the compulsion to have constructed an observatory like the Great Pyramid would have been overwhelming.

However, there are a number of problems with this suggestion. Firstly, the north side of the Great Pyramid is pretty barren, and there is no indication that there were any ritual structures on this side of the pyramid. One would have thought that the base of the stairway would have been an important location and gathering point, and the Giza site to the north of the Great Pyramid does not reflect this function at all. Secondly, masonic tradition also does not dwell on the north or even a journey from north to south, which is the direction of this hypothetical flight of steps. On the contrary, Masonry actually underscores the importance of a journey from west to east. This direction of travel is based upon the Egyptian astronomer-priests' observation of the passage of the Sun-god Ra through the night skies of the Djuat.

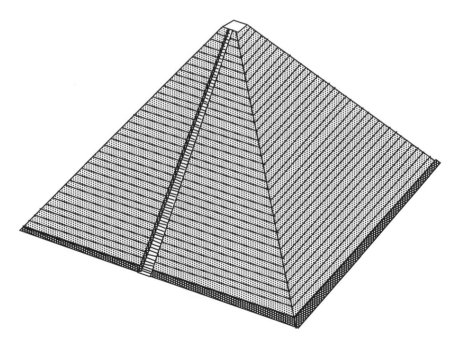

Fig 6.4   Straight flight of steps ascending the Great Pyramid.

The line of the ladder on the tracing board is also said to be in the east-west direction, although it does not look like this on the board itself. If there had ever been an equivalent flight of steps leading up the east side of the Great Pyramid, this orientation would make a great deal more sense, as the chequerboard pavement, the causeway, and all the 'mortuary' temple structures were located on the eastern side of the Great Pyramid. In this case, the conclave of Egyptian priests could have assembled in the valley temple on the eastern rim of the Giza plateau, walked up the eastern causeway to the 'mortuary' temple and the chequerboard pavement, and then ascended the flight of stairs directly in front of them. However, while all of this would have made complete sense for a ritual procession to the top of the pyramid, it would not have allowed the priests anywhere near the entrance to the pyramid, which lies on the northern flank. So in what way can this particular circle be squared? How can the entrance and the observatory both be served with the one flight of steps?

Masonic tradition may also come to our aid in this respect, for the Second Degree tracing board depicts a second flight of steps. Now this is not the same flight of steps at all, for they rise up from between the pillars of Jachin and Boaz, curve around a 90-degree corner and arrive at a doorway that is surmounted by an arch and a dormer window. Now this design could simply have been a piece of imagery that was taken from the great temples of Karnak or Heliopolis, which also had large obelisks placed at their entrance, but it is also possible that this design was taken from the original design of the Great Pyramid. One possible solution to the problem of access to the northern entrance of the pyramid is for there having once been a pathway that curved from the eastern flank of the pyramid, around the northeastern corner and onwards to the entrance on the northern face. The doorway and dormer window on the tracing board would then represent the entrance passageway and arched corbel of the Great Pyramid. If necessary, however, this same spiral pathway or ramp could continue its course all the way to the top of the pyramid.

What this produces, of course, is a design that is not unlike the standard interpretation of how the pyramids were constructed in the first place. Since a straight access ramp to the top of the pyramid would be excessively long, and as great a construction project as the pyramid itself, it has been logically argued that the access ramp for the construction workers must have spiralled up the sides of the pyramid itself. In essence, the spiral design depicted in fig 65 is exactly the same concept, except that the spiral walkway was never dismantled, and was subsequently used as a procession-way for the priesthood to reach the 'unfinished' platform at the top of the pyramid.

Fig 6.5   Spiral pathway or ramp on the Great Pyramid.

While this suggestion is still somewhat speculative, it would nevertheless explain the form of the ideal masonic temple. The accepted design of the ideal masonic temple is supposed to have been based upon the design of the Temple of Solomon in Jerusalem, a temple that may have actually been located in Tanis, as I have already shown in the book *Solomon*. There are many interpretations of the form that this temple took, but the masonic concept is taken from the biblical book of Kings, where it says:

> The door for the middle chamber was in the right side of the house: and they went up with winding stairs into the middle chamber, and out of the middle into the third. [B7]

But, as ever, this is not the only translation that can be given to this verse. Translations are a tricky thing as each word can have a variety of meanings, and so one needs to know the subject matter very well in order to achieve the correct context and meaning. An equally valid translation might be:

> The entrance to the middle chamber was on the right shoulder of the tomb (pyramid?), with winding stairs ascending beside the middle (level); and from the middle towards the third (level).

The changes that have been made are slight, but they nevertheless alter the entire context of the verse. Note that the term 'house' was derived from the Hebrew *bath* בּית, which was taken from the Egyptian *bat* 𓃀𓏏𓉐 meaning 'tomb'. Note also that this is a term that I have already linked to the *bat* 𓃀𓏏 'beehive' of the Great Pyramid. The phrase 'right side of the house' sounds like a description of a temple, whereas the 'right shoulder of the tomb' sounds much more like someone looking at the Great Pyramid from the eastern side. Note also that the stairs wind around the structure *beside* the middle, rather than *into* it, and then up to the third (level). Finally, note that the word 'chamber' does not actually appear twice in this verse, as it does in the English translation, and so it is more clear now that the third level does not necessarily refer to a chamber.

The inference from this verse is that there were three levels to this temple, just as masonic tradition suggests, and that a flight of winding stairs led up to these levels. If this was so, then the tradition of a 'circumperambulation' of Mt Sinai (the Great Pyramid) by the Israelites may not have been a ritual of walking around the base of the pyramid, as I have previously suggested, but instead it may have been a ritual of spiralling up the pyramid. Surprisingly enough, this ritual of walking up a spiral monument is a ceremony that is still acted out today at the ninth century mosque of Abu Dulaf in Samara. Here, the minaret to the mosque is a spiral tower, which can be perilously ascended by the faithful. Since the majority of Islamic ritual was derived from Israelite origins, the foundations of the many Islamic 'circling rituals' are likely to have been based in Israelite ritual. But what, in that case, were the Israelites perambulating around? Were they circling the base of a cube, as the faithful do today in Mecca? Or were they ascending a spiral tower (or pyramid), as they do today in Abu Dulaf? (See figure 66.)

Whatever the case, this tradition may also be the origin of the masonic ritual of 'circumperambulating the lodge'. Most of masonic ritual was derived from the Templars, and since the majority of Templar churches were circular in design, it is fairly certain that they also had a tradition of ritually walking around their temples. It was from these Templar origins that the masonic perambulation was derived, but since the Templars derived most of their traditions from Jerusalem and beyond into ancient Egypt, it is likely that the original custom was Islamic, which was in turn derived from earlier Israelite and Egyptian customs. Since there seems to have been an apparent confusion between the Temple of Solomon and the Great Pyramid, and since that same pyramid may now be connected with a spiral staircase design, it is entirely possible that this spiral Giza staircase was the fundamental origin of this masonic and Islamic circling tradition. *

While there seems to be an element of confusion between the Temple of Solomon and the Great Pyramid, it might be worthwhile exploring further the reasons why this confusion may have arisen. Although I think that these were quite definitely two separate constructions from two different eras, that looked quite different to each other, for some reason masonic tradition seems to blur the dividing lines between these two monuments.

In masonic tradition, the Temple of Solomon was reputedly never finished because the grand master and architect of the construction site, Hiram Abif, was supposed to have been murdered. But therein lies a problem, for however incongruous it may seem, the common masonic symbol for this unfinished 'Temple of Solomon' is actually the image of an unfinished pyramid – which is why this symbol has found its way onto the back of the US one dollar note. This version of the masonic unfinished pyramid is, of course, a representation of the Great Pyramid with its seemingly 'unfinished' platform on the summit. Because this concept of finishing the Temple is an important component of Masonry, a certain party of individuals tried to finish the Great Pyramid off during the millennium celebrations with a golden top lowered by a helicopter. The plan was proceeding smoothly until

---

*   **Ashura**

There are many of these ancient Egyptian rituals that have survived through the ages, and have been inherited by the daughter religions of the original Egyptian creed. For instance, Herodotus, who visited Egypt in the fifth century BC and wrote a comprehensive account of his travels, recounts a festival where the men flagellated themselves:

> In the city of Busiris (place of Osiris) ... the whole multitude, both of men and women many thousands in number, beat themselves at the close of the sacrifice, in honour of a god (the god in question was Osiris).

> The Carian dwellers in Egypt proceed on this occasion to still greater lengths, even cutting their faces with their knives. [1]

Both of these rituals are, of course, still practised by the Shia sect of Islam to this day. The Shia celebrate the martyrdom of the imam Ali and his son Hussain, who were murdered by the Sunni sect, in much the same way as Christians worship the martyrdom of Jesus. However, in the case of Shia ritual, the zealots of the faith still beat themselves rhythmically, flagellate themselves with sharpened chains, or even cut themselves on the head with large knives or swords. This self-flagellation is one of the climaxes of the festival of Ashura that is held each year in Karbala, Iraq.

Shia Muslims will claim that this self-abasement demonstrates their grief to the martyred Ali and Hussain, in the name of Allah the merciful. But it is quite obvious to more rational people that this is simply a continuation of the same Egyptian festival, which was originally held in honour of Osiris.

continued...

the Egyptian public got wind of the masonic undertones of the event, and such was the outcry that eventually the masonic Egyptian leadership were forced to bow to the will of the indignant, fundamentalist Muslim masses.

This link between Giza and the Temple may also explain why some Masons refuse to link their hero and architect of the Temple, Hiram Abif, with the biblical architect of King Solomon's Temple who was also called Hiram. This refusal is due to the claim that Hiram Abif was murdered, and so the Temple was never finished, whereas the biblical Hiram is thought to have completed the Temple and presumably went back to Tyre. But the masonic argument is rather fatuous, as both parties are speaking of the same Temple of Solomon. Whether the Temple was finished or not, its architect was called Hiram in both accounts and so one might suspect that they were indeed the same individual. Just to add to the intrigue, I demonstrated in the book *Solomon* that the biblical architect was actually called Hiram Abi, a name

Hanukkah

In a similar fashion, the Egyptians once held a Festival of Lights. Herodotus says of this event:

> At Sais (and the rest of Egypt) ... there is one night on which the inhabitants all burn a multitude of lights in the open air round their houses. They use lamps in the shape of saucers filled with a mixture of oil and salt ... these burn the whole night and give to the festival the name of the Feast of Lamps.[2]

Modern Judaism has a very similar festival known as Hanukkah, which is supposed to celebrate the victory of Judas Maccabeus over the Syrians in 164 BC. Over eight days the lamps of the menorah, the Judaic candlestick, are lit one by one until each home is ablaze with lamps, and so this festival is likewise known as the Festival of Lights.

So is this the same festival? Well, a simple festival of lights could be a coincidence; however, Herodotus goes on to explain that the Egyptian festival commemorates a night when the god Ares (Ari, the worker god who is often linked to Ptah) went to the temple to see his mother. But Ari was stopped by the guards at the temple, so he went back to the town to organise a mob armed with clubs. A battle ensued and Ari (Ptah) eventually forced his way into the temple. The Egyptian festival re-enacted this battle with sticks, in something akin to a large Morris-dance ritual, and Herodotus mentions that a few bruised heads were received by the more enthusiastic participants in the festival.

In a similar fashion, the Judaic festival of Hanukkah is also supposed to celebrate a battle, and it so happens that the nickname given to Judas, Maccabeus (Maqqabah מקבה), means 'hammer'. This was obviously in recognition of his military success, but this term could also give a clue to the true intent of the former Egyptian festival. Judas Maccabeus employed an armed militia that used an assortment of clubs and weapons to defeat the Syrian opposition and enter the Temple of Jerusalem, and the festival of Hanukkah celebrates the rededication of the Temple as a Judaic place of worship. However, in the light of the previous Egyptian festival, it would seem likely that Judas was nicknamed Maccabeus because his armed militia's entry into the temple was effectively re-enacting the events in the Egyptian Festival of Lights, and so the celebration of Judas' similar victory was also called the Festival of Lights.

1. Herodotus, Euterpe, 61.   2. Herodotus, Euterpe, 62.

which was based upon the Egyptian original of Heru-m-Atif. Both of these names are extremely similar to the masonic Hiram Abif – again suggesting that they were the same individual.

Fig 6.6 The spiral minaret at Abu Dulaf.

So how could the biblical Hiram have completed the Temple when masonic tradition insists that he was murdered halfway through the construction? The answer to this is that the Bible does not necessarily claim that Hiram completed the Temple, as is alleged. In fact, if anything, biblical tradition appears to agree with the masonic version remarkably well. The two verses that demonstrate this read as follows:

> And Hiram made the lavers, and the shovels, and the basins. So Hiram made an end of doing all the work that he made King Solomon for the house of the Lord. [B8]

When this verse says 'Hiram made an end of doing all the work', this initially sounds as though Hiram had finished the entire project and was ready to pack up his tools and go home. However, an alternative translation of the sentence might be 'Hiram ceased work', which merely indicates that he had stopped work for some reason. But why did Hiram stop work? Was this due to his murder? The Bible does not answer this question, but the following verse gives a different perspective to the masonic arguments:

> And Solomon made all the vessels that pertained unto the house of the Lord: the altar of gold, and the table of gold, whereupon the shewbread was, and the candlesticks of pure gold, five on the right side, and five on the left, before the oracle, with the flowers, and the lamps, and the tongs of gold ... So was ended all the work that King Solomon made for the house of the Lord. [B9]

Now this verse is indicating that King Solomon himself made the rest of the artifacts for the Temple, which certainly leaves the possibility open that Hiram Abif (or Hiram Abi) was no longer there on site to finish off the project. The reason why this possibility has been discounted is the improbability of a king being an architect and casting metal implements, but this view ignores the ritual use of the masonic title of 'Architect'. A speculative A̲rchitect is not necessarily an operative a̲rchitect, and so it is likely that neither Hiram nor King Solomon actually made the artifacts themselves; they merely planned and directed the whole project as Architects. Indeed the Kebra Nagast, the Ethiopian Bible, deliberately alludes to the fact that Solomon was an Architect by detailing all the masonic implements that he taught the artisans on the site to use. As was explained in the book *Solomon*, it is entirely possible that Hiram and King Solomon were brothers; and upon the untimely death of the elder brother, who was also known as Absalom, it was Solomon who became the chief Architect and eventually king.

Thus the Bible seems to indicate that the Temple *was* finished, and it was actually finished off under the direction of King Solomon. The reason for the masonic assertion that the Temple was not finished is due to this perennial confusion with the Great Pyramid. The pyramid was the primary temple of the Hyksos-Israelites, during eras when the site was available to them, and it is fairly certain that this 'temple' was never finished – and deliberately so.

While these explanations are rather speculative, there are still a number of hints that may point towards the correct scenario. Firstly, there are usually seven steps on this spiral stairway up to the door of the masonic temple. The height of the Great Pyramid is, of course, representative of the number seven, as is explained in the book *Thoth* – the Great Pyramid is a copy of the Pi fractional of $^7/_{22}$, with the height of the pyramid being represented by the number seven. In addition, some of the masonic imagery of the biblical Stairway to Heaven portrays a similar concept to the masonic spiral stairway, as these have a spiral staircase with seven tiers – as does the fifteenth century painting *Turris Sapientiae,* and William Blake's *Jacob's Ladder.* This imagery may again suggest that the circling rituals of the Hajj were once performed not simply around the base of the Great Pyramid, but around its very fabric, with seven tiers of steps being needed to reach the top. As mentioned previously, the resulting structure and ritual at Giza would then have been very similar to those to be found at the Abu Dulaf minaret in Samara, where the spiral tower so closely mimics the masonic concept of Jacob's 'Stairway to Heaven' (and similarly spirals in an anti-clockwise fashion).

Fig 6.7   Blake's spiral stairway to heaven.

This spiral concept would also make more sense of the seven masonic steps on the stairway to the middle temple, as the seven tiers or spirals around the Great Pyramid would now reach the very top, rather than just the entrance passageway. Thus the seven tiers would equate precisely to the number seven in the Pi fraction, which represents the height of this pyramid. Each tier, or rotation of the spiral stairway around the Great Pyramid, could then be divided into 40 steps of one cubit in height, to reflect the fact that the pyramid is a 40-times multiple of Pi. But if all this speculation were true, then Jacob's ladder – the famous Stairway to Heaven – was nothing more than a reference to the Great Pyramid itself.

Traditionalists would never contemplate these suggestions, as the Egyptian pyramids are still classically regarded as tombs – despite the fact that no burial has ever been found in a pyramid chamber. But the Giza pyramids never were tombs! It is also asserted that the Great Pyramid was built by a pharaoh called Khufu, but even the very name of this pharaoh is in doubt. The translators of this name would like us to believe that the cartouche contained the 'kh' ⊘ glyph, which invariably resides in the unclassified section of the dictionary and is variously described as either a 'sieve' or a 'placenta'. However, the only circular glyph that was used in the cartouches of the kings of this era were those of the Sun-god Ra ☉ .

The formal names of the kings were normally devised to demonstrate their allegiance to or dependence on the Sun-god Ra, which is why the other pharaohs from the fourth and fifth dynasties are called Djedef-Ra, Khaf-Ra, Menkau-Ra, Sahu-Ra, Neferirka-Ra, Shepseska-Ra, Neferef-Ra, Niue-Ra and Djedka-Ra. Without exception, the circular glyph in each case is correctly translated as being a Sun-glyph ☉ representing the Sun-god Ra; and yet when we arrive at the cartouche of Khufu this glyph is suddenly translated as being a 'kh' ⊘ sieve. The question is, therefore, which of these is the correct translation?

Fig 6.8   Cartouche of Khufu (top) and Ufu-Ra (bottom).

The difference between these two glyphs is that the Ra glyph either has a spot in the center or is left smooth, while the 'kh' glyph has horizontal stripes running across it. So which of these glyphs graced the cartouche of Pharaoh Khufu? Classical Egyptology would suggest the latter, but when the cartouche of Khufu is inscribed in the king-list upon the walls of the tomb of Seti I at Abydos, it is clearly using the smooth disc glyph of Ra. Now this would render a name for this king of Ufu-Ra.* However, the spelling is not quite the same as the traditional rendering, as the initial chick glyph is missing in this version, thus in the tomb of Seti I the name for this king is given as Fu-Ra. Likewise, when we come to the inscription of Neferseshem-Khufu,[10] a royal scribe of the fifth dynasty whose plaque was discovered at Giza. This plaque includes two cartouches of Khufu, but the spelling used on the plaque varies, with one cartouche giving Khufu and the other clearly using the Ra glyph and therefore spelling Ufu-Ra.

---

* The beginning of Seti's king-list is nothing like the classical interpretation of the first to fourth dynasties, but has distinct similarities with Manetho's list. Seti's list is given below, with Manetho's and the historical versions for comparison:

Seti's list	Manetho's list	Historical list
		0
		Narmer
I?	I	I
Meni	Menes	Hor-Aha
Teti (Atetis?)	Athothis	Aneddjib
Iuatch	Kenkenes	Djer
I......	Uanephes	Semerkhet
Spatu (Spatos?)	Usaphaidos	Djet
Mer-henemet....	Miebidos (Niebais)	Qa'a
....	Semempses (Mempses)	Den
....	Bieneches (Ubienthes)	
II?	II	II
Kebeh	Kaiechos	Hotepsekhemwy
Beti...u	Binothris (Biophis) (Bochus)	Raneb
Ka-kau	Tlas	Nynetjer
Ban-neter or Khnumen-neter	Sethenes	Seth-Peribsen
Uatchen....	Chaires	Khasekhemy
Sen...i	Nephercheres	
Tchaii-Ra	Sesochris	
III?	III	III
Nebka...	Necherophes	Sanakhte
Tchesar	Tosorthros	Djoser
Teti	Tyreis	Sekhemkhet
Setches	Mesochris	khaba
Neferka-Ra	Suphis	huni
	Tosertasis	
	Sephuris	
	Kerpheres	
IV?	IV	IV
	Soris	Snoferu
S-neferu	Suphis	Khufu
Fu-Ra (Khufu)	Suphis	Djedefre
Djedef-Ra	Mencheres	Khafre
	Ratoises	Menkaure
	Bicheris	Shepseskaf
	Sebercheres	
	Thamphthis	

Fig 6.9 Cartouche of Khufu being spelt as UfuRa.

The difference in spelling may actually give us a clue to the true meaning of this name. Rather than being a king's name, it may have originally referred to a temple, and in this case the spelling from the tomb of Seti I may be important. Here the initial 'u' glyph is omitted and so the name is given as Fu-Ra, which could be read as being a shortening of Fua-Ra ⟨glyphs⟩ , which can in turn be translated as 'Mountain of Ra'. So it is possible that, at some point in time, a king picked up and used the name of a temple which was known as the 'Mountain of Ra'. Since the only 'mountain' at Giza that had a viewing platform to study the movements of Ra was the Great Pyramid, it is likely that the name originally referred to that pyramid.

Burning Bush

Having trawled through many elements in the Book of Genesis, it has perhaps become clear that the majority of this biblical account was derived from Egyptian sources. While a complete translation of Genesis and Exodus from the Egyptian original would represent a massive undertaking, which will have to wait until further resources are made available, I would like to dwell briefly here upon a few peculiar verses in Exodus that detail the meeting between Moses and the infamous burning bush. I have covered some of this interesting topic already in the book *Tempest*, where I suggested that the event was based upon a ritual involving a tree that looked like a Christmas tree, complete with burning candles. I also suggested that the event took place upon the Giza plateau, as the accounts say that the 'bush' was located at Mt Horeb, which is another name for Mt Sinai. Since there were also several comments within the biblical and koranic accounts that similarly suggested a Giza location, the association with the Great Pyramid seemed justified.

All of this might sound a little peculiar, but there is a great deal of evidence to suggest that the Egyptians had several sacred trees that were essential to the rituals at the Temple of Heliopolis, which was located near Giza. Having deduced all this, however, the precise meaning of this ritual was still a total mystery. However, while I was investigating the Egyptian dictionary in the Appendix, I came across some words that shed new light on this subject, and these will eventually demonstrate exactly what this ritual once signified.

Little did I realise, when I first started this particular piece of research for a previous book, that this biblical story was actually an Egyptian account that appears to have been written in the original Egyptian. The biblical verses of this esoteric meeting are as follows:

VII Burning Bush

3:2 And the angel of the Lord appeared# unto him in a flame# of fire out of the midst of a bush#: and he looked#, and, behold, the bush# burned# with fire#, and the bush# was not consumed#.

3:3 And Moses said, I will now turn aside#, and see this great sight#, why the bush# is not burnt#.

3:4 And when the Lord saw that he turned aside# to see#, God# called# unto him out of the midst of the bush#, and said, Moses, Moses. And he said, Here am I.

3:5 And he said, Draw not nigh# hither: put off thy shoes from off thy feet, for the place whereon thou standest is holy ground.

3:2 And the king, the messenger of the gods, appeared in the evening in the middle of the base of the sloping face of the Great Pyramid: and he (the king) looked, and, behold, the Great Pyramid was illuminated with evening light. But (the north side of?) the Great Pyramid was not illuminated.

3:3 And Moses said, I will now go to the back, and see the pyramids of the Sun and Moon, and why the Great Pyramid was not illuminated.

3:4 And when Thoth saw that Moses had gone to the back to see, Thoth called out of the middle of the Great Pyramid, and said, Moses. Moses said, behold!

3:5 And Moses said, Do not give offerings here: and put off thy shoes from off thy feet, for the place whereon thou standest is holy ground.

The first thing to note is that the angel was no such thing. The term for angel here is *malak* מלאך, which laterally means 'messenger'; and yet it is more than likely that this word was actually referring to a *malak* מלך meaning 'king'. But perhaps we are only witnessing a half-truth here for, like the angels from the Torah, the pharaohs of Egypt were also said to have been the messengers of the gods. This was particularly true of Pharaoh Akhenaton, who claimed that he was god's sole representative on Earth, much as the Pope does to this day. Since I have previously identified Moses with Tuthmoses, the brother of Akhenaton, it is likely that these verses were once more referring to accounts that were written during or at the end of the Amarna era.

The explanation for this strange 'burning bush' is to be found in its name. The 'burning' was taken from the Hebrew *baar* בער, a word which definitely suggests burning. The Egyptian equivalent of *barga* 𓂝𓏭𓈖𓏏𓊖𓅓𓂋, however, is more equivocal and can also suggest 'illumination'. The really odd feature with this story, however, is the 'bush' itself, which was called a *sinah* סנה and was said to be 'thorny'. But compare this word with the equivalent spelling for Mt Sinai סיני, a name which was also said to mean 'thorny'. There is clearly a link between these two artifacts that needs investigating further, especially as this whole event took place at Mt Sinai,

202

and Mt Sinai has itself already been identified as the Great Pyramid. Was this enigmatic illuminated 'bush' simply another pseudonym for the Great Pyramid?

Further evidence for this suggestion can be found in the first half of this same verse, where the expression 'flame of fire' looks a bit odd, and so there is a good possibility that there has been a mistranslation here.

The term being used for 'flame' is *labbah* or *lehabah* לבה, which can mean either 'fire', 'spear' or 'point of a weapon'. The first of these was taken from *rehabu (lehabu)* 𓏏𓂋𓊃𓅱𓏤 meaning 'fire' or 'evening'. Meanwhile, the word being used for 'fire' is *esh* אש. However, when taken in the apparent context of mountains and pyramids, it is more than likely that the intended meaning here was actually *esh* אש which is the short form of *eshedah* אשרה and refers to a 'slope' or 'buttress'. Note, however, that the interpretation of *esh* can be even more specific than this, because it can also refer to the 'foundations' or the 'base of the slope', and this point may be significant later in this chapter. The reason for this suggestion is that the word *esh (ush)* actually forms the suffix to the short Egyptian phrase *per-em-us* 𓉐𓂝𓅓𓅱𓊃 meaning 'slope or edge of a pyramid', the full derivation of which is given in the dictionary in the Appendix. The *us* or *ush* suffix refers to the Hall of Osiris, which is sometimes regarded as a pseudonym for the Great Pyramid; hence, the word *per-em-us* may well have been the origin of the Greek word *pyramis* πυραμισ, which has been translated into the English as pyramid.

When putting all of these words together, a rather different picture of this 'burning bush' emerges, and this phrase would have to change from 'flame of fire' to something more like 'evening at the base of the pyramid'. Since this entire verse is to be associated with the 'bush' – which appears to have been a pseudonym for Mt Sinai, and which was in turn associated with the Great Pyramid – the choice of the *us* suffix from *peremus* (pyramid) seems quite appropriate. The final comment about the 'bush' (pyramid) not being 'consumed' (illuminated) may be an oblique reference to the north face of the pyramid being in shadow, as the next verse suggests.

Verse 3:3 continues the same theme, and the word for 'turn aside' or 'depart', *sor* סור, was derived from *sa* 𓋴�𓂻 meaning 'depart', a word which also tends to suggest the 'back' or 'backside'. Meanwhile the word *mareh* מראה for 'sight', was taken from *mer-t* which not only means 'to see', but also refers to the two 'divine eyes' of Horus, which is a coded reference to the Sun and the Moon. But since it has already been demonstrated that the Sun and the Moon can be equated with the two largest pyramids on the Giza plateau, it is not surprising to find that the word *mer (merab)* 𓌻𓂋𓏤𓉴 can also denote a pyramid. The reason for Moses going 'to the back' of the pyramid, rather than just 'turning around', is that the back (the north) of the pyramid may have been used to observe the position of the Sun – as checking to see if any sunlight struck the north face of the pyramid would determine the equinoxes. Accordingly, the 'back' of the pyramid was said to have been 'not illuminated', which would have been correct except during the summer months.

In the next verse, the term for 'call' is *qara* קרא, which could have been taken from either *kher* 🝆 or *qara* 🝆 . The former means 'sound', 'voice' or 'thunder' and the latter means 'thunder'. The latter interpretation is linked to *qarti*, the Twin Caverns that have already been linked on many occasions to the Giza plateau. However, on balance I think that the former of these possibilities is the correct root, as the Hebrew word *qara* is then counterpointed in the next verse by the rhyming word *qareb* קרב meaning 'approach', 'bring' or 'present'. This was derived from *kherep* 🝆 meaning 'present tribute' or 'give offerings', which suggests that the 'q' to 'kh' transliteration is correct in this case.

Lastly, the translation of 'here I am' from *hinneh* הנה is also problematical, as a more usual rendering would be 'behold!' This is based upon the exclamation of *hana* 🝆 , that is said to mean something like 'oh that!' It is not clear who was making this reply here, and I rather think that it was Moses who was saying 'behold!' or 'oh that!'

Reinterpretation

So what are we to make of the Bible's strange tale of the burning bush? The picture that I have just painted appears to be relating a solar observation at the Giza pyramids, rather than anything to do with a burning bush, so all of this fabulous story about a burning bush was probably a biblical smokescreen to cover up the truth of what was happening here. But it would appear that someone retained a core knowledge about the original story, and the evidence for this lies is our modern version of this ritual.

The *aser-t* tree has already been associated with the Christian Christmas tree in the book *Tempest*, but note now how the *aser-t* tree appears to have a similar pronunciation to that of Asar or Usar (Osiris). So the Hall, the Tree and the burning bush all have links with Osiris and the pyramids. In other words, this new interpretation of these verses does not entirely rule out the role played by the sacred *aser-t* tree, because if this tree was a similar species to the familiar, modern Christmas tree, then it would possess a triangular silhouette that was rather reminiscent of the pyramids themselves. If this same tree then had candles attached to it, it too could be viewed as being a 'burning' or 'illuminated' pyramid, just like the original was during these morning or evening rituals at Giza. This was the origin of the legend of the sacred tree that was burning (with candles) but not 'consumed'.

The advantage of the simple arboreal symbolism of this ritual would be that each temple or stately home, whether in Egypt or in exile, could have had a symbolic illuminated pyramid during the holy season that this event represented. The most logical season for this ritual would have been the five epagomenal days, the five 'fill-in' days that padded out the 360-day Egyptian calendar to a more acceptable 365-day calendar. These five extra days became a five-day celebration period, which represented the birthdays of the five influential gods: Osiris, Isis, Horus, Seth and Nepthys. Traditionally, the Egyptian New Year began on the 19th July, and was signalled by the heliacal rising of the star Sirius (Sothis). The five epagomenal days are thought to have been tagged onto the end of the previous year, representing the 14th to the 18th of July.*

However, as we saw earlier, the Hebrew version of these verses could well have been referring to the 'base of the slope', or the 'base of the pyramid'. The reason why this may be significant is that the base of the northern side of the Great Pyramid first begins to be illuminated at certain dates in the year and at certain times during those days. This process starts with the illumination of the base of the pyramid at noon on the 1st March. On subsequent days, the illumination of the base of the pyramid gets earlier and earlier during the day, until on the 21st March (and for the remainder of the summer) it is illuminated at dawn. Thus the tracking of the illumination of the base of this pyramid provides a countdown from March 1st all the way to the vernal or spring equinox on the 21st March. Since the vernal equinox was perhaps the most important astronomical event of the year – the date against which the precessional movements of the constellations were observed and judged – this countdown to the equinox would have been a highly significant

---

*   This dating of the Egyptian New Year is ignoring the possibility that the Egyptians did allow their civil calendar to drift through the seasons. Since there was a six-hour deficiency in the Egyptian calendar, and no leap year to make up the difference, it is likely that the rising of Sothis and therefore the start of their administrative year (immediately following the five epagomenal days) would drift apart. After 730 years, the solar year (the summer season) and the start of the administrative new year would be six months out of synchrony, but after another 730 years the new year would once again start in the summer.

This would mean that the five epagomenal days would not necessarily have been perfectly aligned with the start of the seasonal (solar) year. However, whatever the civil calendar was doing, the priesthood at Giza must have held a different calendar to this, as the position of the Sun relative to the pyramids (and their shadows) would have precisely informed them of the current season, month and day. This was the prime reason for the design of the Giza plateau, and to have ignored this astronomical data would have been inconceivable. But, of course, this information was not being ignored, and it is a component of these observations that the Bible was trying to describe here.

event. It was this event that the Bible was trying to initially explain, and it was this same event that the Bible was subsequently trying to cover up.

As already mentioned, it is entirely possible that these traditions of the illuminated pyramid, and therefore the illuminated pyramidal tree, have survived the millennia and thus they still take place in nearly every Christian home to this day. Without even knowing why, each Christmas millions of households will dutifully erect a pyramidal tree in their house and dress it with decorations and lights. These households may even claim this to be a 'Christian tradition', even though the only references to trees in the Bible were made to highlight the 'pagan' aspects of arboreal rituals.

In truth, the Christmas tree's lights and profile represent the slow but steady illumination of the Great Pyramid, as the days progress towards the equinox, and so an ancient celebration of the Egyptian calendar is being maintained to this day by vast swathes of the human population. It is no wonder that the holders of the core traditions from these Egyptian rituals supported the spread of Christianity around the world. This 'new' religion may well have been a gross distortion of the original Egyptian rites and beliefs, but it was frighteningly successful in covertly embedding large elements of these rituals into diverse cultures spread across the world.

Helen of Sparta

What the preceding chapters have amply demonstrated is that the core texts for the Torah were derived from Egyptian sources, and that they detailed events that occurred in Egypt. More specifically, most of these texts seem to have been associated with the failed Amarna regime of Akhenaton. What is now needed is an explanation of how these texts then came to be assembled and presented in the manner in which we see them today – how and why the material became so distorted that it is not readily recognisable as having anything to do with Egypt, let alone the maverick monarch: Pharaoh Akhenaton.

One of the principal events that prompted the production of the Torah was the perceived injustice of the exodus from Amarna. It has already been demonstrated that there were actually two of these exodus events, a fact which can further confuse this already complicated history. As I narrate in the book *Jesus*, Manetho gives an account of the great Hyksos exodus from Avaris to Jerusalem in about 1620 BC and then the later and smaller exodus of Akhenaton and his followers from Amarna to Avaris in around 1330 BC. The final action of the faithful, who had endured two expulsions in three centuries, was the writing of the great scroll that recorded these tragic episodes. But when it came to putting these events onto papyrus, there were two very dominant individuals who dictated the outline of the text: Akhenaton and his brother Tuthmoses, and like many dictatorial leaders they wanted to have a center-stage role in all these events. It was probably this fact that led to the conjoining of these two exodus stories.

Akhenaton and Tuthmoses [Aaron and Moses] had fled from Amarna to Avaris with their 80,000 followers, and there they prepared to defend the city from their Theban adversaries – who were probably under the military and political command of Horemheb. Thus Akhenaton and

Tuthmoses already had an epic tale to tell about their exodus from Amarna to Avaris, and so the scribes could start scribbling. But to reinforce his military position in Avaris, Akhenaton requested assistance from their fellow Hyksos refugees, who had fled to Jerusalem at the time of the first exodus nearly 300 years before. Since the Atonists in Avaris and the Hyksos in Jerusalem were roughly of the same blood and creed, they willingly sent a large force of some 200,000 soldiers. The numbers of combatants in Manetho's works are probably an exaggeration, as most of the ancient records are; and this apparent willingness to assist the people in Avaris may also have been due to a Hittite invasion of Palestine, which no doubt displaced a large number of people from this region.

The followers of Akhenaton and the new allies flooding in from the northeast now had two halves of an exodus to write about: there was the very recent forced expulsion from Amarna to Avaris, plus there was also the long-established tradition of the much earlier and much greater Hyksos exodus out of Avaris, which had been precipitated by a feud with the early eighteenth dynasty pharaoh, Ahmose I. It would appear that many of the descendants of the refugees from that earlier Hyksos event wanted their story telling too, and the resulting biblical exodus epic was therefore a compendium of all the tragedies that had befallen the Hyksos-Israelite-Atonist people during their centuries-long battle with the Theban pharaohs of Upper Egypt. Thus, the resulting biblical exodus is a combination of the original Hyksos exodus and the later Akhenaton exodus. To this epic tale, the scribes then added some of the creation myths of Egypt, much of Akhenaton's Hymn to the Aten, a mix of assorted genealogies, and an outline of the history of the royal family who had ruled the Hyksos nation for many centuries. The accounts of Genesis and Exodus would now have been substantially complete in their original Egyptian format.

Trojan wars

But it is entirely possible that the ever-industrious scribes of the Amarna family created another epic story that has survived the millennia, and so this influential family may have influenced Western culture more than any other family in the history of mankind. It was explained in the book *Solomon* that the pharaoh who Manetho calls Dannus may well have been Pharaoh Aye, who was probably the uncle of Akhenaton. I floated this suggestion because it would seem that Dannus was also called Armais, while Aye was also known as Armait, and so the names match rather well. In addition, Dannus is said to have reigned for just four years, and that this reign commenced shortly after the pharaoh called Akhencheres. Since Akhencheres has already been positively identified in Chapter V as Pharaoh Akhenaton, the chronology and reign-length of this Dannus character corresponds precisely with that of Pharaoh Aye.

Manetho then relates that due to a dispute with his brother Egyptus [Ramesses], Pharaoh Dannus [Aye] went into exile in Argos (Greece) and set up a new colony there (apparently taking fifty princesses with him). Again, this account seems to equate very well with the historical evidence for a forced exodus from Amarna. It is known that Aye was the last of the Amarna pharaohs, and although his fate is not historically known, the possibility does exist that he fled into exile somewhere. Manetho simply provides us with evidence that points towards Aye [Dannus] going into exile in Argos (Greece). The slight discrepancy of a pharaoh called Ramesses having a conflict with Aye is explained by Manetho's chronology having Ramesses I's reign immediately following Aye's.

However, the recorded history of Dannus does not end there, for it would appear that the descendants of Aye [Dannus] were then to play a leading role in one of the most famous stories of the ancient world. Homeric legend relates that long ago there was a great battle between the ancient Greeks and the citizens of Troy, an epic tale that was eventually recorded in the *Iliad*. But it is interesting to note that the Greeks are constantly mentioned in the *Iliad* as being either the Akhaoi or the Danaoi. Joachim Latacz, professor of Greek philology at Basle University, suggests that the Danaoi were connected to the Danya who were recorded in Egyptian documents – in other words the Greek Danaoi were the Egyptian Dannaoi from Manetho's account.[1] Likewise, the title for the Akhaoi bears a certain resemblance to the first syllable of Akhenaton's title, Aakhu. The Greek writers Apollodorus and Hyginus also relate that Dannus came to rule Argos (Greece) from Chemmis (Egypt).[2]

In addition to this, it would appear that the chronology of the Trojan wars also fits in well with this scenario. Although the identification is by no means entirely certain, the city of Troy is thought by many to have been located on the northwest Turkish coast at Hisarlik. A great deal of archaeology has been completed at Hisarlik over the years, and it has been decided, through the usual method of stratigraphy and pottery comparison, that one of the primary destructions of this ancient site occurred in about 1180 BC. It is this destruction stratum that has been strongly associated with the Troy of the *Iliad*; although it has to be stressed that this date is by no means certain, and an error of plus or minus one hundred years for this destruction level would not be exceptional.

In comparison, Pharaoh Aye's [Dannus'] four-year reign is thought to have ended in about 1320 BC. His tomb was prepared in the Valley of the Kings, but since the mummy is missing and the tomb has been thoroughly trashed by his successor, Horemheb, the fate of Aye is not known. Significantly, no *ushabti* figures, which are normally produced upon a person's death, have been found for Aye; and so all of this leaves open the prospect that Aye [Dannus] did indeed flee into exile, as Manetho relates. So the intriguing question remains: was this Dannus [Aye] connected in any way with the Danaoi people who laid siege to Troy? Well, under the current chronology, the destruction of Troy was only 140 years after the exile of Aye. Thus, at the very best the Danaoi of the *Iliad* would have been referring to the descendants of Aye [Dannus] – the new Greeks.

However, if these two characters were connected, as is appearing increasingly likely, then the scenario for the events that lead to the Trojan wars would have to be modified. This alternative history suggests that a small party of refugees from Amarna fled to Argos (Greece). Rather than being forced into the lower echelons of their new host society as surfs and slaves, which is often the fate of refugees, Aye's small band of supporters were able to slip into the privileged ranks of leaders and monarchs, and were soon able to control the population. This may have been due to these emigrants holding key areas of knowledge and expertise, such as metal and stone working, that would have been very useful to the host population. Alternatively, it may have been simply due to the projected authority of the individuals involved, and their ability to organise and lead others. (Apollodorus suggests it was through subterfuge, but this would still not work without an air of authority.) Gaining the respect of people and being able to organise a governmental system that crosses family and tribal boundaries is a prized skill in itself, and if the followers of Aye were able to confidently and rapidly organise the local families and then tribes into ever larger social units, they may have been able to acquire and hold the balance of power in their new homeland.

This scenario would tend to imply that only the leadership of the Danaoi were of Egyptian origin, and so the customs and language of the host nation may well have been retained. Like the monarchs from Holland and Germany who took over the monarchy of Britain in the seventeenth and eighteenth centuries, the new immigrant leadership are invariably forced to adopt the ways of the host nation rather than the other way around. Thus, the fact that the Danaoi Greeks of Troy did not conform to Egyptian customs and language is not an insurmountable problem here, and perhaps only a few important names and titles would have reflected the Egyptian heritage of the Danaoi Greek leadership.

The name given to Helen of Sparta may be an example of this process in action. In the Egyptian, there are not too many words beginning with *her* (*hel*), and the primary of these is *her* ☻ meaning 'face'. As usual, this word may have been transliterated into *hel*, and the full title of Hel-en would then have meant something like Hel-en ☻ 〰 meaning 'the face'. Since Helen was famed for her great beauty, and since this great beauty was said to have precipitated the entire Trojan War, she was subsequently known as 'the face that launched a thousand ships'. Thus the connection between Helen and the Egyptian word *her* are quite strong, for both are directly associated with the face.

Even if this association between Helen and the Egyptian Hel-an were true, it would still not get us any closer to identifying who this Helen may have been in the historical record. However, the answer to this problem may just about be visible from a lateral look at the legends pertaining to Helen, for she was reputed to have been semi-divine. This gloriously graphic and suggestive mythology claims that Helen's mother, Leda, the beautiful

Fig 8.1 Classical bust of Helen of Troy (Helen of Sparta).

queen of Sparta, was raped by Zeus in the form of a swan. Looking at this claim from the Egyptian perspective, it is not to hard to deduce what was being implied here. Zeus was the king of the gods, and he was therefore said to have been a Greek rendering of Ra. So when Zeus arrives in the image of a swan, he is just imitating the winged Sun-disk imagery of Ra or Aton. However, this was reputed to have been a dual union, within Leda, of the essence of Zeus and also of her husband, Tyndarecus. Thus it was both Aton-Ra and Tyndarecus who had impregnated Leda, and so princess Helen would have been fathered both by her father and by the gods, just as every self-respecting prince and princess of Egypt would have claimed.

This union then, rather surprisingly, produced two eggs, which hatched into Polydeuces and Helen, and Castor and Clytemnestra. The former of each pair of twins are rather better known as the two stars of Castor and Pollux in the constellation of Gemini, and so here we can again see that the story of Helen involved a cosmic tale of the gods as much as it did a real history of Greece – for Leda's two sets of twins are representative of Gemini (the twins). These cosmological aspects to Helen's ancestry bear all the hallmarks of an Egyptian religious mythology, and could be compared very favourably with the Heliopolian creation epic.

The Greek version of this tale is indicating that the winged form of Ra (Zeus) bore four children, two girls and two boys. In a similar fashion, the Egyptian version is indicating that Atum-Ra eventually gave birth to four children, which again formed the standard dualism of two girls and two boys. But the Egyptian foursome were rather famous, and they were popularly known as Osiris and Isis, and Seth and Nephthys. The Greek link between these gods and Gemini is interesting. Since much of Egyptian religion appears to have been based upon the precessional movement of the Sun through the constellations, this link with Gemini could provide a date during which the Heliopolian myths were originally formulated. The eras of the constellations are given in the following table: [3]

Constellation	Date entering	Date exiting	Duration
Aquarius	2860 AD	4860 AD	2000
Pisces	00 AD	2860 AD	2860
Aries	1740 BC	00 AD	1740
Taurus	4300 BC	1740 BC	2560
Gemini	6300 BC	4300 BC	2000
Cancer	7730 BC	6300 BC	1430
Leo	10450 BC	7730 BC	2720

Thus, if the Heliopolian theology of Osiris and Seth were devised to reflect the new era of Gemini, it would have been formulated in about 6500 BC. Likewise, the emphasis in the Noah story of the animals being in pairs could also have been based upon the symbolism of Gemini.

If the Heliopolian epic was the intended symbolism for the nativity of Helen and her siblings, then the radiantly beautiful Helen would have been a pseudonym for Isis and, of course, the title Her-ti (Hel-ti) 𓂋𓏏𓃀𓃀 is another name for Isis and Nephthys, so this would make a great deal of sense. But, as has already been discussed in some detail, the goddess Isis was modified and refashioned by the Egyptian priesthood into the ritual position of Virgin or God's Wife, and this role eventually, in its turn, became the basis for the Christian New Testament's Virgin, or Mary. It was from this ritual title, I believe, that the descriptions for Helen were originally derived. Just as the New Testament Mary was supposed to have possessed a transcendental beauty that surpassed all mortal equivalents, so too did Isis and Helen. This is why Nefertiti, who was in some respects a personification of Isis, was likewise said to be so beautiful – although it has to be said that if her Berlin bust is a true likeness, then this claim was not solely a literary or spiritual device.

So, if the cult of Isis had been introduced to Argos (Greece) by Aye [Dannus] and his descendants, and if Helen (the face) had become a nickname for this perennially beautiful goddess, then this would explain much of the Trojan story. It had always amazed me that Homer could have believed that Princess Helen could have had so many suitors (32), and that all of these suitors and the city states that they controlled would have gone to her rescue. It seemed obvious to me at the time that this element of the story was simply based upon an exaggeration or a myth. However, if the Helen that had been abducted were actually a goddess, rather than a princess, then perhaps the 'nationwide' reaction to this abduction is rather more believable. Just as the pillaging of the bones of Mary in Medieval Europe, had they been available, would have provoked a continent-wide crusade; so the pilfering of a statue of Isis, in a land of revered icons, would have likewise provoked a nationwide military response.

So my best-guess explanation for the siege of Troy, at this stage, was that the Trojans had launched a raiding party to the lands of Argos, which was probably an annual event. However, on this occasion they took back with them a statue of Isis from a major Isis cult center in Sparta. Since Aye's administration were promoting the cult of Isis in these new lands, they would have seen this abduction as a golden opportunity to unite an otherwise fragmented nation around a common cause – and so the mighty fleet, assembled from the city states all over Greece and beyond, sailed off to engage the common enemy at Troy. As the Americans have demonstrated at Pearl Harbour and the Twin Towers, sometimes it is better to wait patiently, and perhaps nervously, for an unprovoked attack, so that the overwhelming military response can be made from an indignant, united nation. (Note the symmetry between the Twin Towers and the Twin Peaks at Giza.)

If any of this argument is true then, when looking at the names involved at the siege of Troy, we may be able to find some additional snippets of Egyptian history. The next name I looked at was the city itself, which was called Ilios. Unfortunately, the texts from the Hittite empire suggest that the lands of western Anatolia (Turkey) were known as the kingdom of Arzawa; and one of the city states governed by Arzawa was Wilusa. Professor Joachim Latacz has further suggested that the name Wilusa would have been known as Wilios by the Greeks, and this name was eventually trimmed into the more widely known name of Ilios. If this name for Troy really was an Anatolian title, then it will not be found in the Egyptian record.

However, Ilios did have an alternative name, and that was 'Troy', and since the name Troy does not appear in the Hittite record it is possible this name may have been donated to the city by Aye's Hyksos-Greek victors, and it may therefore have been derived from Egyptian sources. But what sort of name would the victors of the Trojan War have given to a city that had withstood such a long siege? It was unlikely to have been a favourable appellation that described the beautiful geographical setting for the city or the great wealth of its former citizens. No, the name would be more likely to reflect the unimaginable obstacles that the Hyksos-Greek campaign faced, and the strength of the city that withstood and repelled their many assaults. The sort of name a victor might choose is *thrai (tray)* 🏹⛪ meaning 'fortress'. The lower ranks of the Hyksos-Greek army may have thought this name was highly appropriate, and the Helenised version of this word became Troy.

There are also vague echoes of Egypt contained within the names of the various heroes of the battle. The first syllable of Paris mimics the first syllable of Per-aa ⬭⚊⬍ meaning Great House, a title which is the basis of our word 'pharaoh'. The first syllable of Hector is reminiscent of the title Heq ⎰ meaning 'king' or more specifically 'Hyksos king'. More interesting still is the name Achilles, which may have originally been rendered as Ach-cherres, with the usual 'l' to 'r' transliteration. This is, of course, exactly the same name that Manetho gave to Pharaoh Akhenaton, as was explained earlier. So all three of these heroes from the *Iliad* have similarities with Egyptian names for royalty.

Sea People

The exile of Dannus to Argos is already placing an Egyptian spin on this ancient tale, but can this line of enquiry be taken any further? Actually, there is a rather compelling alternative to the standard historical interpretation of the *Iliad*. Despite all the exhaustive archaeology at Hisarlik in Turkey, there is still no concrete evidence to link this ancient city with the city of Troy from the *Iliad*. So let's throw caution to the wind once more, and speculate on an alternative destination for Achilleus (Achilles) and the rest of the Greek army. What we are looking for, therefore, is a motive for the Trojan War, an era during which many tribes formed a large naval and martial confederation, and an historical account involving the Danaoi people from Argos (Greece). What we are also looking for is an event that has escaped the eyes of countless historians through the ages, and one might speculate that the greatest area of historical blindness lies in the history of Egypt.

True enough, there was an event in the annals of historical Egypt that involved the Danaoi, and that is the peculiar invasion of the Sea People into Egypt, a subject I have already tackled in the books *Jesus* and *Solomon*. The Sea People were a diverse coalition of Mediterranean states that decided, for no apparent reason, to attack Egypt. I have never seen a convincing historical rationale for this bold assault on the most advanced nation in this entire region, but nevertheless it is an established fact that the Shardana, Teresh, Lukka, Shekelesh, Ekwesh, Danyen, Tjeker, Weshesh and Peleset tribes did form a naval and martial confederation that did indeed manage to make substantial inroads into the Egyptian empire and nation. But who exactly were these people? A typical commentary on this invasion explains that:

> Study of the 'tribal' names (of the Sea People) recorded by the Egyptians and Hittites has shown that various groups of the Sea People can be linked with particular homelands ... thus the Ekwesh and the Danen may possibly be correlated with the Achaean and Danaean Greeks of the *Iliad*.[4]

So the Ekwash and the Danyen may have been the Greeks. But this association would mean that during the same era in which the battles of the *Iliad* were being fought, the Greeks were also engaged in attacking Egypt. But another reference source goes one stage further:

> ... some have associated the Danyen with the Danaoi of the Iliad ... Little is known about the Weshesh, though even here there is a tenuous link to Troy. As you may know, the Greeks sometimes referred to the city of Troy as Ilios, but this may have evolved from the Hittite name for the region, Wilusa, via the intermediate form Wilios. If the people called Weshesh by the Egyptians were indeed the Wilusans, as has been speculated, then they may have included some genuine Trojans, though this is an extremely tenuous association.[5]

The evidence may be tenuous, but if it is true then both the Trojans and the Greeks can be seen to be in an alliance involved in attacking Egypt during the same era as the Trojan wars were said to have occurred. This may seem bizarre at this stage, but there is a possible explanation for this. The fact that the Greeks and the Trojans may have been closely related allies, rather than enemies, is further reinforced by their names. The Greeks were known as the Danen (or Danaoi), while the Trojans were called the Dardanai (Dar-Danaoi) – hence the term 'Dardanells', referring to the sliver of sea between Greece and Turkey and adjacent to what is historically considered to be Troy. Since the name for the Danaoi was derived from the pharaoh Dannus, this name probably has an Egyptian origin, and a likely derivation might be from *dan* or *dandan* 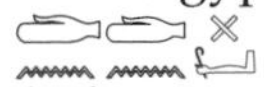 meaning 'attack' or 'invade'. I have already linked Dannus with the Amarna pharaoh Aye, and so this meaning may imply that the title of 'Dannus' was conferred upon Aye in recognition of his invasion of Greece.

The Egyptian spellings for the Danaoi (the Greeks) and the Dardanai (the Trojans) are fairly certain, as these names have been recorded as the Daanau  and Dardanai , and both are described as being 'Mediterranean nations'. Note that the Daanau (Danaoi) title uses the Hyksos-Israelite throw-stick and three-hills glyphs, as well as the Red Crown of the Lower Egyptian royalty. In the circumstances, the link between the Danaoi tribe and the exiled pharaoh Dannus [Aye] seems inescapable. The prefix of *dar* for the Dardanai tribe may have been taken from *dar* ⌒🗙 which again has strong connotation of destruction and conquering, and so the Dardanai may have been even more warlike than the Danaoi. Once more, this is an appellation that would be eminently sensible for a contingent of the Sea People alliance.

However, since the Greeks were said to have attacked and wiped out the Trojans, this would all seem to be highly unlikely – unless, of course, the city of Ilios from the *Iliad* was not the city of Ilios on the northwest tip of modern Turkey. Perhaps we should be looking for a city called Ilios or Troy in another part of the Mediterranean altogether; perhaps we should look instead towards the known destination for the attacks by the Ekwesh (Achaen), Danen (Danaean) and Weshesh (Wilusan) tribes – Egypt.

When trying to decipher the true import of the *Iliad*, what we are looking for is a location in the Mediterranean where the Achaeans and Danaeans (the Greeks) went to war, and inscribed upon the walls of the temple of Ramesses III at Medinet Habu there is just such a historical account. Apart from an acute historical blindness by modern academics, there is absolutely nothing to prevent the story of the *Iliad* being a historical account of the attacks by the Sea People on the Egyptians.

However, this rather novel suggestion would also provide a compelling rationale for these attacks by the Sea People, an important element which conventional history simply fails to explain. The many tribes of the Sea People came from all over the northern and western Mediterranean, and for no apparent reason they all suddenly decided to join forces in a pan-national alliance and attack Egypt. Thus, on the face of it, the Sea People invasion appears to be fairly inexplicable, for why did these people hate Egypt so much? Why did all these relatively backward nations think that they could possibly defeat the technologically superior massed armies of the Ramesside pharaohs of Egypt? As I have speculated previously, one possible explanation for all of this is that the Sea People confederation was organised and led by elements of the exiled Hyksos-Israelite nation, who were now spread across large areas of the Mediterranean; and two of those elements were the Achaean and Danaoi tribes from Greece, led by the descendants of Pharaoh Dannus [Pharaoh Aye].

The Sea People could have gained a great deal of new technological expertise from these exiles from Egypt, and there would also be a very compelling motive for their attack on Egypt – revenge. The Hyksos-Israelites had been unceremoniously thrown out of Egypt by both Ahmose I and

Horemheb, and they wanted their homeland back, even if it took local mercenary soldiers from all over the Mediterranean to achieve this goal. In this strategic quest, the Danaoi became the original Hyksos-Israelite Zionists, but at least the Danaoi were fighting for a homeland in the right region.

Furthermore, as I mention in the book *Solomon*, the attacks by the Sea People actually form a central component in the biblical Book of Judges. In the story of the attack by Gideon on the Ammonites [the Egyptian worshippers of Amun], the attack was preceded by a line of soldiers holding fire in pots, and this exactly mimics the accounts of the Sea People's advance into battle, as is written on the walls of Ramesses III's temple at Medinet Habu.

We were looking for a number of things in this investigation into the account of the *Iliad*, and these included: a military campaign in which many tribes came together to defeat a common enemy; an invasion that utilised hundreds of ships; an historical account that involved the Danaoi tribe; and also a rationale for the Trojan War. Strange as it may seem, in the Sea People campaigns against Egypt during the reign of Ramesses III, we can see convincing explanations for all of these requirements. In addition, the writings of the Greek historian Herodotus seem to support this proposal, for he tells a tale about Helen being taken to Egypt instead of Troy. This version of the Trojan War suggests that Alexander (Paris) and Helen were blown off course as they fled from Greece and landed in Egypt. The Greeks thought the couple had landed in Teucria (Troy) and so the great armada set off to the Troas, laid siege to and eventually destroyed the city of Troy. However, on not finding Helen in the ruins, the victors were then informed that she was safe and well in Egypt, and so they set sail to investigate:

> So Menelaus travelled to Egypt, and on his arrival sailed up the river as far as Memphis, and related all that had happened (to pharaoh). He was met with the utmost hospitality, received Helen back unharmed, and recovered all his treasures. [6]

Thus even in this very early era, it is apparent that there were strong traditions of Helen being closely connected with and living in Egypt, rather than Turkey. However, Herodotus' tale does not ring entirely true, for it would seem unlikely that any ship could be blown all the way from northwestern Turkey and end up in Egypt. One suggestion that might make more sense of this story is that Troy was not in Turkey at all, but was instead a city rather closer to Egypt. Evidence will be given shortly that confirms this notion, and so in this case the attack by Menelaus and his men was probably an attack on and destruction of a city in the Nile Delta. If this was the case, then Menelaus was probably received so warmly by the Egyptians in Memphis because he was a conquering hero who had already destroyed one city and was threatening to invade the rest of Egypt. The treasures that Herodotus mentions, together with the return of Helen, may represent the tribute that was extracted by Menelaus' promise not to attack deeper into Egyptian territory. As was explained in the book *Solomon*, this continual extraction of tribute from Upper Egypt by the Sea People alliance was the root cause of the collapse of the Ramesside twentieth dynasty, so the details in Herodotus' account do have a familiar ring to them.

The dates of these two events – the invasion of Troy and the Sea People invasion of Egypt – seem to dovetail fairly well too. The Trojan War is said to have taken place somewhere around 1180 BC, whereas the most penetrating of the Sea People invasions into Egypt is said to have taken place early in the reign of Ramesses III, which is from about 1184 to 1153 BC. There is also commonality in the duration of these wars, for the Sea People invasions carried on for almost thirty years, whereas in similar fashion the *Iliad* is simply an account of the final events in a war that had already lasted ten years.

Thus, all of this speculation is pointing towards a rather startling conclusion. The *Iliad's* massed navy and army, the thousand ships of the pan-Hellenic confederation that sailed for Troy, were actually one and the same as the massed navy and army of the pan-Mediterranean Sea People alliance. Far from sailing to Hisarlik in Turkey, this great armada of ships sailed instead to the Nile Delta and began a campaign against the increasingly unstable rule of the nineteenth dynasty pharaohs; a campaign that eventually retook most of Lower Egypt and threatened and caused great hardships even in the Upper Egyptian capital city of Thebes. It was these attacks that allowed the later United Monarchy of Israel to rebuild their nation in both Palestine and Lower Egypt, which is why I am certain that Kings David and Solomon were Egypto-Israelite monarchs whose primary capital city was actually Tanis in the Nile Delta. Thus the biblical United Monarchy is known in modern history as the Lower Egyptian twenty-first dynasty.

What, then, of the cause of this long and bitter war? One compelling motive has already been suggested – the Hyksos-Israelites had been displaced from Lower Egypt and they wanted their homeland back. But the *Iliad* itself gives another reason for the start of this war: the abduction of Helen. I have already speculated that Helen was perhaps a statue of Isis, and it was the loss of this statue that united the Sea People confederation. But there does exist another possibility. Helen was the face that launched a thousand ships, and so her name may have been based upon the Egyptian *her (hel)* 𓁷 , meaning 'face'. But who in Egyptian history would have been known as the 'face'? With countless generations of Egyptian art reproducing largely representational artwork, the one true individual and beautiful face that stands out in all of Egyptian history is the bust of Nefertiti.

As the Danaoi tribe were directly linked to the Amarna regime through Pharaoh Aye [Dannus], it is entirely possible that Aye would have taken drawings and busts of his immediate family with him to Greece; thus it is possible that the Danaoi had an image of Nefertiti or one of her many daughters (or, indeed, Queen Kiyah). Both Aye and Nefertiti would have been long dead by the time the Sea People invasions began, but as another unifying force to galvanise the disparate confederation of Mediterranean tribes, the rallying cry of 'Save Nefertiti from the Infidel' would have been very potent. It is also possible that the mortal remains of Nefertiti or Kiyah still resided somewhere in Egypt, and so the campaign to bring back those remains would have been similar to the Medieval Crusader's aim of bringing back remains from Jesus' supposed crucifixion.

Evidence

Considering the fact that thousands of scholars have been poring over the texts of the *Iliad* and *Odyssey* for countless generations, it might seem surprising that so many strands of evidence can be seen to be pointing at a completely different interpretation to the classical explanation. I think that this is again down to the rigid orthodoxy of the historical establishment, who have set up a chronological and geographical creed of facts and events that is every bit as rigid as a theological orthodoxy. Thus each and every researcher is constrained firmly within the established historical framework and does not dare look outside for alternatives. However, it is a great shame that historians and linguists do not have more lateral minds, for they would otherwise have quickly spotted a final couple of connections and similarities that prove that the Trojan War did indeed take place upon Egyptian soil.

Firstly, we need to look again at the location of Troy. I have been arguing here for the *Iliad* to have been an account of the Sea People invasion, an event that was probably instigated by Hyksos-Israelite exiles, and this invasion eventually resulted in the setting up of the (Hyksos-Israelite) Egyptian twenty-first dynasty in the Nile Delta region. Thus it would have taken a full century of intermittent warfare and receipt of tributes from Thebes before the Ramesside twentieth dynasty effectively ceded control of the kingship to the Lower Egyptian twenty-first dynasty pharaoh, Smendes I. The city that the Hyksos-Israelites captured and expanded into their capital city was Tanis in the northeastern Delta, and it is this city that I have already identified as being the biblical Jerusalem. As it happens, Jerusalem was called Jebus and Zion, while Tanis was called Tchebet and Zoan. While it is possible that the Hyksos-Israelites used the same city-names in two completely different locations, a body of evidence is remorselessly pointing towards

Tanis being the original biblical Jerusalem, up until the Babylonian exile. After this exile, the Hyksos-Israelites appear to have been exiled once more, this time to the modern Jerusalem in Israel, and so they were at this time permanently exiled from Egypt.

But the city of Tanis had one more ancient name that is rather more pertinent to Greek mythology, and that is Therayu (Thray) 𓄿𓏏𓇋𓂋𓃭𓈖𓊖 , which was based upon the word *theray (thray)* 𓄿𓏏𓇋𓏥 meaning 'fortress'. So once again, the very city that the Danaean Greek seaborne alliance were attacking during the Trojan War appears to be precisely the same as the location that the Sea People alliance were attacking in Egypt. Both of these cities were described as being great fortresses, and both were called Thray (Throy or Troy). The 'u' on the end of the Egyptian version of this name simply indicates a plural, and so there may have been multiple fortresses or multiple defensive systems in this location.

Secondly, the most conclusive piece of evidence for a link between Troy and Thray (Tanis), in my mind, involves the most famous element in the Trojan War – the Trojan horse. There has been much debate in academic circles as to whether this story was based upon an actual event, but the mere fact that it is such a central element of the story means that for the Egyptian interpretation of the *Iliad* to be in any way valid and true, this central facet of the story must also be translatable in Egyptian terms. Whilst most readers will be familiar with the Trojan horse myth, perhaps I should quickly explain that the battle against Troy had reached a stalemate, and so the Greek forces outside the city decided that some subterfuge should be employed. To gain access to the city, the Greeks constructed a large wooden horse as a gift to the Trojans, and then withdrew from the battlefield to make it appear as if they were leaving. Flattered and jubilant, the Trojans took the horse into their city; but unfortunately there were Greek soldiers hiding inside the horse who crept out at night and opened the gates for the invading Greek army. The result was the complete destruction of Troy. (It is from this 'myth' that the adage 'beware of Greeks bearing gifts' is taken.)

It should be noted, however, that if the Greeks were being led by exiled Hyksos-Israelite royalty, then they already had a history of this kind of subterfuge, for the Bible explains that the siege of Jericho was ended in a similar fashion. The prostitute Rahab had been bribed into housing Israelite spies; and the blowing of the horns outside the city walls by the Israelites was merely a diversion, in order that the spies could open the gates of the city. Similarly, during the siege of Shechem, a complex scenario developed where a marriage alliance was proposed to the royalty of this city. The princes agreed to be circumcised before the betrothal took place, but while all this was going on the Israelites stormed the open gates of the city and killed all the inhabitants. So, the possibility that the exiled Hyksos-Israelite royalty used a cunning ruse to open the gates of Thray (Troy) would not be unusual.

But the one thing that always puzzled me about the horse myth was the very nature of the offering given to the Trojans. While horses were a very valuable and prized possession in this era, they were not exactly venerated as gods. Thus if the Trojans were presented with a model horse they might think it very charming and beautiful, but would they really pull it back into the safety of their city? Surely, for this ruse to work effectively, the statue would have to be of one of the Trojans' gods. The Trojans would then be quite flattered that an enemy had made an image of their god, a god that the Greeks did not worship, and they would also feel compelled to take this icon of their god into the safety of their city. For the gods would certainly be displeased if their statue or icon was left out in the open; vulnerable to the predations of men and wild animals alike. But if this revised scenario were true, then what kind of god would the Trojans have worshipped, and so what kind of statue did the Greeks really build?

The answer to this lies in the noun being used for a horse, and while the modern Greek word for a horse is *alogo* αλογο, the ancient name was *ippos* ιππος. Here, then, is the answer to all of these conundrums, and the very proof that the city of Thray (Troy) actually lay in the Nile Delta and is today called Tanis. However, if readers have not spotted the connection yet, they should bear in mind the possibility that the *Iliad* epic was an oral history for a few centuries before it was eventually transcribed into written form by Homer in the seventh or eight century BC, and also the fact that the Egyptians did not use vowels. So let us assume that there has been a very slight change in the pronunciation of the vowels for the Greek word *ippos* ιππος, and one possible variation might then be *appos* αππος or even *appis* αππις. Perhaps now the link with an invasion of Egypt can be more clearly seen – for the Egyptians called their sacred bulls Hep 𓇳𓎡𓂋 , but when the Greeks came across this word they changed it to Appis αππις. It is from this poor Greek transliteration of Hep that the sacred bulls of Egypt are known today by the tautological term 'Apis bull'.

So it is more than likely that the Greek statue of an *ippos*, the horse that was presented to the Trojans, was actually an Egyptian Appis, the sacred bull of Upper Egypt – and thus the Trojan story would only make sense within an Egyptian context. Indeed, when it is placed within an Egyptian framework, the entire story of the Trojan War now makes complete sense.

The Hyksos-Israelites were ejected from Egypt by Ahmose I in about 1600 BC and again by Horemheb in about 1300 BC. But over the years and centuries the exiles had grown strong in their new homelands of Greece, Turkey, Sardinia and the Balearic islands. With the aid of local mercenary soldiers, or indeed with new subjects who followed their leaders willingly, the exiles gathered together the great Sea People alliance, who are recorded both in Egyptian history and the Greek *Iliad,* and sailed off to Egypt to retake their homeland and home city. This is why there is some confusion with Trojans possibly fighting alongside the Greeks against Troy, for some of the exiles originally came from Thray (Troy) and would indeed have been known as Trojans. But the campaign against Egypt nearly failed at the first fortress they encountered, as the siege of Thray (Troy or Tanis) had lasted for a decade or more. In desperation, the Hyksos-Israelites hatched a ruse and constructed an enormous statue of a god that was central to Egyptian Ramesside theology – the Apis bull. Because it was a sacred icon, the besieged (Upper) Egyptian citizens of Thray (Troy) pulled the Apis bull into their fortress, and so their fate was sealed.

The evidence would appear to be overwhelming – the Trojan *ippos* (horse) was actually an Egyptian Apis (bull), and therefore the siege of Troy was actually the siege of Thray (or Tanis). Thus the *Iliad* is actually a documentary about the invasion of Egypt by the exiled Hyksos-Israelites, and thus Homer's epic story is also inscribed upon the walls of Ramesses III's temple at Medinet Habu. However, since the Bible also documents the Sea People invasions in the Book of Judges, this would mean that the *Iliad* and *Odyssey* epics are simply alternative versions of the great body of literature that was recorded in the Torah. Indeed, I personally think that most of the biblical narrative would have originally been presented in this fashion, as a secular historical documentary, but the books that were selected to form the Tanakh (Old Testament) have received a Judaic theological gloss in more recent eras.

This new interpretation of the *Iliad* not only represents a fundamental shift in our historical perspective, it also demonstrates the addiction that the Hyksos-Israelite people had with their history. Countless cultures have evolved, thrived and been extinguished all around the Mediterranean basin, but time and again the written and oral records that have survived the millennia seem to revolve around the royalty of the Hyksos-Israelites.

Delta Judaea

The novel but compelling suggestion just explored again points towards a Hyksos-Israelite re-occupation of the Nile Delta during the Ramesside twentieth dynasty, because the largely successful attacks of the Sea People form a significant part of the Book of Judges, which details the military campaigns of the exiled Israelites. The Judges era was a period of instability, during which time the Israelites gained greater and greater control over the Delta region by employing mercenary fighters.

But, as has already been pointed out, the exodus events from Egypt may not have involved a complete evacuation to Palestine and other Mediterranean coastal districts. Many of the Hyksos-Israelite refugees may have clung on to the remoter areas of the northern Delta region, and these people would have been actively assisting in this retaking of the Delta. But this suggestion appears to contradict the biblical account, and also contradict the first exodus account of Manetho, who clearly states that the Hyksos [Israelites] emigrated instead from Egypt to Jerusalem in Syria. But what, exactly, did Manetho mean by the terms Egypt Αιγυπτου and Syria Συριαυ?

As it happens, the term 'Egypt' has already been identified with Upper Egypt, rather than Lower Egypt, while the term 'Syria' may actually have been a corruption of Seriad Σηριαδ, which refers to Egypt. The historian Josephus used this same term when discussing the two pillars that were built by the biblical Seth (Set), and these pillars are sometimes taken to be the great obelisks erected at Heliopolis by the twelfth dynasty pharaoh Sesostris (Senusret I). Likewise, Syncellus says of Manetho that he translated some of his works directly from the inscriptions in the temples of Egypt, which were said to be written in the Seriadic language.

So, was the Hyksos-Israelite exodus from Egypt to Syria, as Manetho initially seems to indicate, or was it instead from Upper Egypt to Seriad (the Nile Delta)? If the latter were the intended meaning, then the first (and greatest) exodus could easily have been a mass migration from Memphis, Giza and Avaris, which may have been viewed as being in Egypt proper, to Tanis in the distant northeastern reaches of the Nile Delta. While Manetho clearly states that the second exodus of Akhencheres [Akhenaton] initially went to Avaris, it is now entirely possible that the first of these exoduses from Egypt proper may have ended up in the Delta region at Avaris or Tanis, with only a small contingent continuing on to Israel and across the Mediterranean. Whatever the case, it would now seem to be clear that the campaigns of the Greeks, and the rest of the Sea People alliance involved in the Trojan War, firmly established the Hyksos-Israelites back in the Delta region during the twentieth dynasty (c. 1180 - 1070 BC). Thus the subsequent history and identities of Kings David and Solomon are highly likely to be one and the same as the twenty-first dynasty pharaohs of Tanis – as I relate in some detail in the book *Solomon*.

Further support for this hypothesis is to be found in another account of Josephus regarding a later invasion of Egypt. The traditional chronology of this region is confident that King Nebuchadnezzar of Babylon defeated the Egyptian army at the battle of Carchemish on the Euphrates in 605 BC and subsequently began to annexe all of Judaeo-Israel under his control. There were further skirmishes along the Egyptian borders in 602 BC, and Jerusalem finally fell to the Babylonians in 597 BC. This event is known in the

Bible as the Babylonian exile, where a great number of the ruling and artisan classes of Israel were transported to Babylon to be slaves for the expanding Babylonian empire. The next stage in this history is that the Persian king, Cyrus II, defeated the Babylonians in 539 BC and his son Cambyses II went on to conquer Egypt in 525 BC. In other words, there were two campaigns that emanated from the Arabias, one was directed against the Israelites and a city called Jerusalem in Israel, and a later expedition marched into Egypt. However, Josephus quotes the account of Berosus, the Babylonian historian, as saying:

> His father Nabopalassar, hearing of the defection of the satrap (governor) in charge of Egypt ... sent his son Nabuchodonosor (sic) ... against the rebel. Nabuchodonosor engaged and defeated the (saratap in charge of Egypt) in a pitched battle and replaced the district under Babylonian rule ... Nabuchodonosor settled the affairs of Egypt and the other countries. The prisoners – Jews, Phoenicians, Syrians, and those of Egyptian nationality – were consigned to some of his friends, with orders to conduct them to Babylonia.[17]

Josephus' own interpretation of this passage is that:

> In his narrative of the actions ... (Berosus) relates how Nabopalassar sent his son Nabuchodonosor with a large army to Egypt and to our country ... he adds that the Babylonian monarch conquered Egypt, Syria, Phonecia and Arabia, his exploits surpassing those of all previous kings of Chaldea.[18]

In other words, the Babylonians themselves considered that they had conquered Egypt as well as Israel during the first series of campaigns during the era of 600 BC and the reign of Nebuchadnezzar. But, of course, Egyptian history does not record a Babylonian king ruling Egypt at this time. The first of the new line of pharaohs from the Arabias appears to have been the Persian king Cambyses II (c. 525 BC), and so it has long been considered that Josephus was mistaken on this point. So what are we to make of this, and how can these two divergent accounts be amalgamated?

The answer may lie in this familiar division between the Delta lands and Egypt proper, or the lands that lie to the south of Memphis. Berosus may be indicating that Nebuchadnezzar had conquered the lands of the Delta and, if my interpretation is correct and Jerusalem was another name for Tanis, then the captives from this campaign would indeed have comprised 'Jews, Phoenicians, Syrians, and those of Egyptian nationality'. However, the Jews were the Hyksos-Israelites and the Syrians were likely to have been the Seriads, the other natives of Lower Egypt.

Thus, when both Josephus and the Bible confidently state that

Jerusalem was besieged and taken by the Babylonian king Nebuchadnezzar, it does not necessarily follow that this city was located in Israel. Jerusalem could just as easily have been a Lower Egyptian city located in the Delta lands that Nebuchadnezzar had taken control of – a city like Tanis in the northeastern Delta.

The reason that this defeat of the Delta lands does not show up in the historical record, and is therefore largely ignored, is that the Lower Egyptian record is scanty in the extreme. It is also possible that some evidence does exist, but it may not have been recognised for what it is because the belief that Jerusalem was located in Palestine at this time is absolute. But if Jerusalem really was located in the Delta, then how on Earth did Judaic history become so strongly associated with the Jerusalem in Judaea?

The answer to this lies in the multitude of migrations that the Israelites and Jews have suffered over the millennia. In this particular case, the critical migration was the Babylonian exile. Under this new theory, the Hyksos-Israelite hierarchy were abducted from the Jerusalem of the Delta (Tanis), after Nebuchadnezzar had overrun the majority of Lower Egypt in 597 BC. These Israelite exiles then lived and worked in Babylon for three generations and had begun to settle into the region very well, and it was here on the banks of the Euphrates that they began to assemble their texts into the modern Torah. But since Egypt was fast becoming a distant memory, and since many of the more settled Jews of Babylon had no intention of returning to Lower Egypt, this new scroll began to lose much of its Egyptian influence and content. But any plans for a future in Babylon were then dramatically upset when the Persian king Cyrus II suddenly invaded Babylon in 539 BC.

An unexpected by-product of this campaign was that the exiled Israelites (now the Jews) were allowed to go 'home' if they wanted. While many Jews had become quite successful in Babylon and had no intention of going anywhere, the regime change brought new uncertainties for them, and many of the less successful and the more pious Jews did want to return anyway. Thus a large queue of Jewish emigrants from Babylon eventually formed. But since Cyrus II already had designs on taking control of all Egypt, which was still the richest land in this region in this era, he would hardly have allowed the Jews to take up residence in the Delta once more, where they could have fomented resistance to his intended military campaigns against Egypt. It is far more likely that Cyrus' benevolence towards the Jews would only have extended as far as giving them a relatively barren patch of real estate that nobody else really wanted – Palestine. Thus modern Judaean Jerusalem, and its associated temple, would only have been founded in about 530 BC. As was tentatively explained in the book *Solomon*, the more famous Temple of Solomon was actually located in Tanis in the Nile Delta – in Zoan rather than Zion.

Faith

Having come so far down the road of rational explanations for the Old Testament accounts, and seen the true evidence that is available within the texts, it is perhaps not surprising that the adherents to the Judaeo religions, including Christianity and Islam, have had to shore up the foundations of their belief system with the simplistic tenet of faith. Telling the faithful to trust their faith has been a useful confidence trick by the religious authorities to ensure that the inconsistencies in the accounts and the lack of historical confirmation were overlooked. However, with three hundred years having elapsed since the Enlightenment, and having entered the twenty-first century, using faith as a comfort-dummy to ward off the curse of uncomfortable facts, and adopting an ostrich-like response to the evils of difficult questions, is simply not good enough.

The fact of the matter is that it has long been accepted, in the rarefied circles of academic theology, that there are innumerable Egyptian influences within Judaism and its daughter sects of Christianity and Islam. However, for whatever reason it has been collectively decided that little or none of this knowledge should ever trickle down to the faithful or the general public. The religious instruction that I received at school was highly sceptical of biblical claims for miracles, and sought to rationalise many of the less believable aspects of the story, but not once did they point out the similarities with Egyptian mythology and ritual. They could have mentioned, for instance, the similarity between Isis and Horus and Mary and Jesus. Wallis Budge was writing about this topic back in the nineteenth century, and yet the subject was still taboo in the relative freedom of a twentieth century Protestant school curriculum. Likewise, the biblical exodus epic was taught as a subject that was completely divorced from history, and yet the Hyksos exodus is almost identical to this event in all except its date. How could the school curriculum have missed out this obvious historical correlation, even if only as a discussion topic, if it were not due to a wish to deliberately deceive the public?

Another failing of academia has been their own reaction to the knowledge that the Bible contains elements of Egyptian history and theology. One would have thought that a truly enquiring mind would have taken this information as a spur to further investigations, and yet none were done. Instead, the likes of Donald Redford merely sought to belittle the biblical scribes for handing down to us reams of unreliable tittle-tattle and scores of deliberate fabrications. But the Torah is nothing of the sort; instead, it represents a reasonably accurate account of the ideology and subsequent history of the people of Amarna. What Redford and others fail to do is understand what the scribes originally wrote before the distortions crept in. For instance, as god's sole representative on Earth, Akhenaton and his wife were indeed the 'first couple' on Earth, but the phrase referred to their position in society, not their chronological position in history. Just as the American president's wife is known as the 'first lady', so Akhenaton and Nefertiti (or Akhenaton and Kiyah) were called the 'first couple'.

Akhenaton and Nefertiti (or Kiyah) have already come down to us through history as being an enigmatic, idealistic couple whose naturalistic ideology and monotheistic theology have had a measurable impact on contemporary society. However, in the guise of Adam and Eve (and also as Aaron and Helen of Troy), this same couple have actually been the most influential personalities in the history of mankind. The Torah or Tanakh has been reissued and revised under the guise of the Old Testament and the Koran, and these ancient texts have gone on to provide the foundations for three of the world's great religions. Thus the lives and philosophies of Akhenaton and Nefertiti (or Kiyah) have profoundly influenced more than half of the world's population, spread across more than three quarters of the world's habitable land. And while these three books held the faithful enthralled, Akhenaton had one more trick up his sleeve. A significant proportion of people began to reject the standard theological history as being unreliable, but the parallel history in the *Iliad*, which had been maintained by the Greeks, was viewed as being a secular history that was somehow more acceptable or reliable. Thus the whole of the Western hemisphere, whether religious or secular, has been influenced in one way or another by this epic history of the Hyksos-Israelites. While Akhenaton obviously hoped his theological revolution would change the world, I doubt that even he would have believed how stunningly successful his reforms would eventually be.

I suppose the final question to address is the ramifications of this new theological perspective, and I think the public's reaction will largely depend on their level of indoctrination. The Islamic world, which is still locked in a Medieval time-warp, has no capacity for logical or rational thought and will dismiss such ideas in their usual intolerant and aggressive manner. However, I have a sneaking suspicion that many in the Judaic and Christian West have been longing to put a real face to the mythical apparitions of Adam and Eve for centuries. Now we can do just that, and the picture we can create is of these two semi-naked lovebirds, Akhenaton and Nefertiti (or Akhenaton and Kiyah), gliding through the idyll of their palaces at Amarna in Middle Egypt.

Perhaps an equally poignant image is the subsequent downfall of the royal couple, and their astonishment and horror at having to cover their naked bodies and mix with the common people. This was the primary moral that was being woven into the first chapters of the Genesis story. It was not supposed to be a warning for us to obey god's commands or face the consequences; instead it was intended as a reminder that even the most powerful of leaders and monarchs can fall from grace if they isolate themselves too completely from the lives of the ordinary people. But, of course, this is a lesson that is rarely learned or heeded. Even in our recent history both Nicholas II and Pu Yi, of the Romanov and Manchu dynasties respectively, have fallen from grace and been deposed. It is all too easy to become the last link in the royal chain – the Last Emperor.

❀❀❀   End   ❀❀❀

Appendices

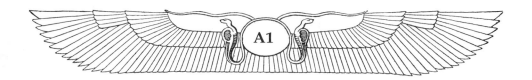

Masonic lexicon and symbolism

This is going to be a highly controversial chapter that explores a wide range of terms and recognition words that are to be found within the initiation rituals of Masonry. Apart from the one or two words and phrases that are taken from the Bible, these terms are unique to Masonry and are not to be found within the English language; which begs the question of their true origins. While this area of research may seem to be a diversion from the arguments being outlined in this book, it is not, for the roots of Masonry also lie within the fertile borders of Egypt. As I have tried to demonstrate on many occasions, the biblical story is infused with masonic hints, rituals and personalities, and so the history of the Craft lies at the core of this investigation into Egyptian history, theology and mythology.

While masonic history, myths and teachings are valuable in divining the true history of the Craft, so too are the signs, grips, knocks and recognition words that form masonic initiations and entrance to Lodge. Since these words and phrases have been largely handed down by rote, and often without any knowledge of their true meanings, their original pronunciation may have survived the centuries. The distortions of the Chinese-whisper syndrome only apply to words that are thought to have a real meaning, and so the receiver tries to derive this meaning out of the odd-sounding syllables that they have heard. But if the word is known to be a nonsense word, like *hocus pocus* or *abracadabra*, it is likely that the syllables will be simply learned and transmitted phonetically without interpretation or distortion.

But while Masonry uses and preserves these ancient words and phrases, the list of presumed meanings given for them are so bland and contrived, it is almost certain that the true meanings have been lost. Since Masonry appears to have lost the original meanings, and since the Templar origins of Masonry would tend to suggest that this unique selection of terms were formulated during the era in which the Templars were primarily based in France, many authors have sought to discover the meanings of these terms within the French language. But again, I think that many of the derivations that have been 'discovered' through this technique appear forced and contrived, and so they are unlikely to be the true fundamental root for these strange words.

However, bearing in mind the investigations that have been made in this book so far, and the strong inference that masonic ritual was derived from Egyptian originals, I would suggest that these words and phrases are more likely to have been descended from Egyptian origins, and there is every possibility that the original pronunciation has been preserved. It is also possible that the original meanings have been preserved in some fashion, and that they can be inferred and derived from the context in which the word or phrase is used. If this is so, it may be useful to explore more thoroughly the possibilities of an Egyptian origin for Masonry.

Perhaps the first point to note is that the history of Masonry is reputed to be far older than the public proclamations of Grand Lodge would suggest. The Grand Lodge website will only admit to a possible heritage for the Craft that is derived from Medieval guilds of Masons, while in contrast the Third Degree initiation states that:

> ... by the Worshipful Master's command, I invest you with the distinguishing badge of a (Master) Mason. It is more ancient than the Golden Fleece or Roman Eagle, more honorable than the Garter or any other Order in existence... [1]

The era of the Golden Fleece would place the Craft back to about AD 1430, when the Order of the Golden Fleece was created by Philip, Duke of Burgundy; while the Roman Eagle would place the Craft back to AD 200 or so. But it is likely that Masonry has a deeper history than this and, surprisingly, it is the First Degree initiation into the Craft which places masonic history directly into the domain of ancient Egypt. One of the word formats used in the working of the First Degree ritual is:

> The usages and customs among Freemasons have always borne a close affinity to those of the ancient Egyptians. Their philosophers, unwilling to expose their mysteries to vulgar eyes, couched their systems of learning under signs and symbols which were communicated to their chief priests alone, who were bound by solemn oath to conceal them. [2]

Despite Grand Lodge's carefully crafted public image, which suggests a masonic history that only stretches back to 1717 and may or may not have been based upon older guilds of Medieval craft masons, it is obvious that according to its own initiations the Craft has potentially much deeper roots. The general thrust of all my books has demonstrated that Masonry was based upon the original religious system of the ancient Egyptians, and it has evolved into its current format over thousands of years. But, as I explained in Chapter V, it is also possible that rather than being descended from the Egyptian priesthood and their belief systems, the true core of Masonry may have been based upon the close-knit architectural guilds of craftsmen who designed and constructed the many pyramids of Egypt.

This is perhaps the reason for the close association not only between Masonry and all things Egyptian, but between Masonry and the Egyptian obelisk and pyramid in particular. In the nineteenth century, Victorian masonic adventurers went out to Egypt looking for artifacts and evidence, and no doubt simultaneously researching the heritage and history of the Craft. While these Victorian descendants of the pyramid builder's 'guilds' could not hope to bring back a pyramid to their adoptive nations, they could reasonably easily transport an obelisk. It was this Egyptian heritage that prompted Masons from France, America and Britain to go to the expense of requesting ancient obelisks from the Egyptians, transporting them to their respective countries and placing them in prominent locations in their capital cities. These obelisks were installed and dedicated utilizing masonic ritual and, at the London obelisk which is commonly known as Cleopatra's Needle, a masonic 24-inch rule was placed under its foundations. The Americans then went one stage further and built an enormous Egyptian obelisk of their own, which is known as the Washington Monument; although this is not a true obelisk as it is built from individual blocks.

This artisan heritage for Masonry may also explain its republican nature. Although the Egyptian monarchy were intimately associated with the religious workings of the great temples, and it was the priesthood who fundamentally ran these temples, it was the fraternity of architects and masons who constructed these great edifices. Although the Egyptian monarchy and priesthood held deep theological secrets at the heart of their initiatory-based religion, the temple's architects and masons would have had equal access to those secrets: as these were the people who designed the temples, tombs and pyramids and carved the sacred inscriptions onto their walls. So in many respects these humble artisans and their architect masters were as important as the ruling elite, if not more so, and this is one of the reasons why the monarchy and priesthood were all included within the ranks of the masonic artisans. Thus, while the monarchy and the priesthood were leaders of their own respective organisations, they were also the members of a separate organisation with its own independent structure and power base – the operative masons had become the Speculative Masons.

Although there would have undoubtedly been a great deal of

nepotism within the ranks of the masonic fraternity, and many a favoured son may have become the next chief priest or the next grand master, the history of the Craft suggests that it is likely that the masonic hierarchy were also elected in some manner. In this fashion, the two or three power bases of the monarchy, priesthood and the fraternal Craft were kept apart as power rivals, and this competition between the three organisations has filtered down through the ages. It was probably for this reason that the Israelites alternately opted for republican rule by judges and then monarchal rule by kings, as each of these organisations fought for national supremacy. This separation between Masonry and royalty, with the former often appearing superior to the latter, is maintained today by the regulation that the ruling monarch cannot simultaneously become the grand master of the United Grand Lodge – which is why the current grand master is HRH The Duke of Kent and not the Queen.

This concept of a society governed by a meritocracy is contained in the common masonic adage that 'we meet on the square and part on the level', which implies that all Masons are equal when at Lodge. This republican ethos is also enshrined in the fourth of the Ancient Charges of Masonry, which states that:

> All preferment among Masons is grounded upon real worth and personal merit only ... therefore no Master or Warden is chosen by seniority, but for his merit.[3]

While this is an eminently sensible and laudable ruling, it is slightly tempered by other aspects of Masonry. Firstly, there is the problem that this republican meritocracy only spreads down the ranks of fellow Masons, and so the *muggles** of this world are invariably not considered suitable for prestigious public roles. Thus the masonic republican image is almost as hollow as the communist aspirations of the former USSR – all men are equal, but Communist Party members are more equal than others. Secondly, despite the intent of these Ancient Charges, there is still an inevitable pecking order and presumed class structure even within the ranks of Masonry, as the etiquette of the Craft explains:

> Don't presume upon your masonic association with those in a higher social station than yourself.[4]

---

* Masons sometimes use the word *infidel* for non-Masons, which can be a confusing term bearing in mind its more usual usage by Muslims for non-Muslims. As an alternative, the term 'muggles' serves the same purpose admirably, even though it has been lifted from a children's book. (With apologies to J K Rowling.)

While things have changed within Masonry since this code of etiquette was written in the 1930s, alongside many of the rules of our modern society, this code of etiquette is still in print today and no doubt influences the great differences that exist between, say, Trade Union Lodges and City of London Lodges. Despite the hypocrisy, this republican ethos has survived within Masonry to this day, and it has been the prime motivator behind the establishing of the American and French models of government; indeed, Masonry is also the leading organisation pressing for a federal United States of Europe.

But if Masonry was originally based upon Egyptian traditions and terminology, and if those signs and tokens (words and phrases) have survived largely intact, is it possible to derive the original meanings of these ancient rituals? The following paragraphs try to explore this problem in some detail.

Due guard

This term refers to the hand signals that are used for identification of fellow members of the Craft. It is said that this term may have been derived from the French phrase *geste du gard* which refers to a protective gesture. However, while the result of invoking a particular hand signal may 'protect' a Mason, the *due guard* itself is more of a symbolic, inquisitorial gesture – it is fundamentally used as a form of identification.

In Egyptian terms, this kind of personal identification was often conducted through the use of signet rings. The signet is a personal seal, often embossed into the form of a finger ring, which represented an individual's signature and was historically used for sealing letters and doors etc. Indeed, the term 'signet' comes from the Latin *signum*, meaning your personal sign or signature. These rings are still used today in masonic circles and, for the more covert members of the Craft, the face of these signet rings is designed to flip over in order to alternately reveal and conceal the square-and-compass insignia. In other words, the prime method of identification for members of the Craft in Egypt would have been the showing of signet rings. As it happens, the Egyptian term *dju garti* 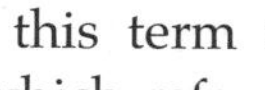 means to 'give a signet ring', and this, I believe, is the true origin of this term.

The reason why this long-established procedure of displaying rings changed is that the Templars were arrested, tortured and persecuted by Philip IV of France on October 13th 1307. Under these new and challenging circumstances, having a ring that identified you as a member of an heretical, banned organisation would have been foolhardy in the extreme. By necessity, the system had to change and the new form of *due guard* became a complex system of covert hand signals and phrases.

Tyler

This term refers to the doorman who guards the door of the temple during Lodge meetings. It is said that this may have been derived from the French word *tailleur* meaning 'one who cuts', which is presumably a reference to the sword that the *tyler* would have worn in the past. But when considering the nature of the *tyler's* post, and the fact that the Templars derived much of their knowledge from Jerusalem, I think that a much better derivation for the word *tyler* is the Hebrew term *tara (tala)* תרע which means 'door'. (The 'r' and the 'l' being transposed in the normal manner.)

But, as has already been demonstrated, most of the Hebrew language can be derived from Egyptian sources and the word *tyler (tyrer)* is no exception to this rule. Thus the Hebrew word *tara (tala)* has been derived from the Egyptian *taraa (talaa)* 𓏏𓂝𓏤𓈙𓉐 which also means 'door'. Bearing in mind that the masonic term *tyle* is used as a verb to close the door, as well as a noun for the doorman himself, a meaning of 'door' for this term would be far superior to one of 'cut'. Thus, both the pronunciation and meaning of this original Egyptian word fits the masonic usage very well indeed. It would seem likely that in the multitude of intervening generations since the early Egyptian dynasties, the word *tara* has become *tala* – in line with all the other 'l' to 'r' transliterations from this region – and thence to the pronunciation of *tyler*, and so this masonic term was probably taken from the Egyptian.

There is only one possible objection to this derivation, which is that in masonic terms the tyler secures the door against *'cowans* and eavesdroppers' who might listen in to the masonic ritual and discover the masonic secrets. However, while this might have been an absolute necessity for renegade Templars after the persecutions of 1307, this may not have been such a priority for the Egyptian priesthood in the security of their temples, or the Egyptian Masons forming a Lodge in a chamber deep inside one of their pyramids. Having said that, the Egyptian religion is likely to have been initiatory, with candidates progressing through the various degrees of initiation; as did the Masons building King Solomon's Temple and all modern Masons. Thus, although the Egyptian priesthood would have felt physically secure, they would still have required protection from eavesdroppers who wanted to learn their secrets.

Cowans

Cowan refers to an outsider who might wish to gain entrance to or listen in on a Lodge meeting. Again this word does not get a mention within the Oxford English Dictionary, which I find surprising considering the overt masonic influences within the Oxford University system. I would not have thought that a short entry in the dictionary saying 'cowan: term for an eavesdropper, origins unknown', would have been too contentious.

Anyway, there appear to be no French, Latin or Hebrew origins for this word, but there may be an Egyptian foundation. The Egyptian *ku* means 'other people, or 'strangers', while *unu* refers to people who open doors. The combination in the singular would be *ku-un*, and refer to a stranger trying to open a door. Since the *tyler's* responsibility was to prevent *cowans* from opening the temple door while the Lodge was meeting, a term like *ku-un (cowan)* would be highly appropriate.

Cable tow

The masonic *cable tow* is a rope that is tied either around the new candidate's neck or his waist, depending on the initiation. This ritual is likely to have been derived from the chord that Templars used to wear next to their skin at all times, but exactly what did this rope signify? The French derivation is supposed to be from the word *cable* which refers to a horse's halter, and the connection is supposed to be linked to the candidate being restrained by the *cable tow* around his neck. But the primary image of the *cable tow* is not as simply a halter (the loop around a horse's neck) but as a rope that can be tied in various locations around the body, including the waist and the wrist, and so this French derivation is probably invalid.

I suspect myself that the primary source of this word is firstly the Hebrew word *cabal* חבל meaning 'rope'. The reason why this rope was so important, however, is that the word also means 'pledge' or 'oath'. So the *cable* portion of the *cable tow* is a symbol of the Templar's or Mason's oath to the organisation, and the reason for this link between a rope and oath is that the rope symbolically *binds* the candidate to the organisation. It was through this process that the simple rope became a symbol of the Hebrew Cabbalah (Kabbalah), the ancient Jewish mystical sect. This usage has, in turn, spawned the English word cabal, which refers to a political clique. So the Jewish Cabbalah and European Masonry are likely to have once been brother organisations that shared a common heritage, which was presumably derived through the activities of the Medieval Templars in Jerusalem.

If the Cabbalah was based upon the Hebrew word *cabal*, or the masonic word *cable*, an equivalent symbolism should be visible in both of these sects, and so we ought to be able to find a similar ritual use of a rope in the Cabbalah. As predicted, the rope or thread is central to Cabalism, and in the modern cabalistic ritual the initiated still wear a simple red thread around the wrist. The red thread is actually a symbol of the redness that weaves its way through the Old Testament:

And afterward came out his brother, that had the scarlet thread upon his hand: and his name was called Zarah. [B5]

As mentioned before, the redness that is associated with so many of the Israelite leaders is an allusion to the Red Crown of Lower Egypt, for all of these individuals were actually Hyksos leaders and pharaohs of Lower Egypt.

So much for the redness, but what was the purpose or symbolism of this chord? Was it originally used as a symbol of binding an organisation together, as it appears in modern Judaism? That is certainly a possibility for when we look at Egyptian traditions and ritual, the similarity with the custom of the Semai Taui 𓎛𓏌 – the tying of the knot that bound together the Two Lands of Egypt, as discussed in Chapter V – is undeniable. But what exactly did the Semai Taui knot represent? In Chapter V, I suggested the symbolism was of speech, because the Semai Taui knot was tied around a trachea and the strands of the rope may have represented the vocal chords, but was that the entire story? An alternative, or even complementary, explanation is as follows.

The Hebrew word *cabal (cabbalah)* may well have been derived from *qab* meaning 'snake' or 'intestine', and through the imagery of these two meanings we can easily see how the word *qab (cab)* 𓈎𓃀𓎟 eventually became linked to a cable or rope. But how did a snake or a piece of intestine become linked with the concept of brotherhood?

There are two possible answers to this, and in the first the word *qab (qeb)* 𓈎𓃀𓈗 may give us a clue; for one of the other primary meanings of this word is the river Nile and there is an obvious parallel to be drawn here between the winding sinusoid nature of a snake and the aimless meandering of the river Nile, with the Delta lands perhaps representing the image of a cobra's flared head. So the mystical *cabal* may be nothing more than a reference to the Nile and the *uraeus* snake symbolism of the northern Hyksos-Israelites. But the fact that the Israelites were Egyptians became a deep secret in later Judaic traditions, and so the *cabal* became the Judaic Cabbalah, or an English cabal – the secret of the true history of the Egypto-Israelites.

The second possibility is perhaps the more simple and mundane of the two explanations. The word *qab* 𓈎𓃀𓎟 can mean 'snake' or 'intestine', as we have seen, and bearing in mind the imagery of the masonic *cable tow,* this may also refer to a rope. However, an alternative rendition of the word *tu (tow)* 𓈋 refers to two hills, or two pyramids. The connection between two pyramids and a coil of rope is that it is impossible to descend into the Great Pyramid's subterranean chamber without the aid of a rope. In the book *Tempest,* a quote from the Koran implied that initiates into the Israelite priesthood were lowered into a subterranean chamber, as indeed some masonic candidates are to this day. The Medieval masonic crypt at Royston in Bedfordshire is a good example of this type of initiation chamber, where the only opening into the crypt was through a 'chimney' from above.

In which case, the coil of rope that is arrayed around various parts of the masonic and cabalistic initiate may be a reminder that all candidates in the Egyptian mystery schools were originally lowered into the initiation chamber on a rope. Indeed, the candidate may have been able to keep a portion of the rope as a memento of the occasion, from which the cabalistic tradition of wearing a rope was derived. If this were the case, then the rope would obviously have become a symbol of brotherhood, as only initiates who had descended into the Great Pyramid's lower chamber would have been permitted to wear this device.

Mount Heredom

This is a not a recognition phrase as such, but something that is unique to Scottish Masonry and is supposed to represent a sacred hill somewhere near Kilwinning, which is linked to the 18th Degree title of 'Rose Cross of Heredom'. The rose-cross can refer to a four- or five-leafed wild rose, which is why this symbol became the emblem of the houses of Lancaster and York during the Wars of the Roses; but it can also refer to a rose- or red-coloured cross or, in other words, the insignia of the Knights Templar. The link here between a red rose and the Templars is not so much due to an error in translation, as to the politics of the era. The Wars of the Roses took place in England between 1455 and 1485, which was just 150 years after the Templars had been eradicated and excommunicated by the Catholic Church. To have indicated that this was a war between two factions with Templar-Masonic affiliations would have been problematic, but a war between two factions with rose emblems was more obscure and acceptable.

It is likely, therefore, that the term 'Heredom' may have been something to do with the Templars, but if this was so then it is likely that this word may well be a transplanted tradition and not native to Scotland. It is possible, therefore, that the original Mount Heredom was located where these masonic traditions originated – that is, either in Palestine or perhaps in Egypt.

The first thing to note is that *har* הר means 'mountain' in Hebrew, and that this was taken from the word *har* which also means 'mountain', and so we appear to be on the right track with this translation. This leaves the syllable 'edom', which was taken from the word *edom* אדם and means 'red'. But, as has been explained earlier in this book, the term *edom* also refers to Adam, the 'first' man of the Bible, and it was further linked to Adjom , the god of the setting Sun, the dualist counterpart of Akhenaton's Aton.

237

This constant reference to redness is also mirrored within the initiation rituals of the 18th Degree. This degree prominently uses a number of red roses, a red room of initiation, and vivid 'rose-red flames' to consume the four cards that are inscribed with the letters I, N, R and I. Indeed, such is the concentration on redness that elements of this degree have been likened to the redness associated with the devil and hell. This imagery gives the ceremony distinctly satanistic undertones, especially as the name of Jesus is being burned in a (chemically enhanced) red flame. However, this redness is simply another oblique reference to the monarchy of Lower Egypt, who wore the Red Crown, and Jesus' association with that monarchy.

In summary, what we have in the name Heredom is a reference to a 'mountain' that is somehow linked to redness; to the Edomites; to Adam; to the setting Sun; and perhaps even to the Aton. In other words, Heredom could be translated as the 'Mount of Adam' or even the 'Red Mountain'. But, as ever, the biblical sacred mountains were invariably sacred pyramids, and so we could also deduce from this reasoning the phrase 'Red Pyramid' or the 'Adam Pyramid'. This is probably the answer to this mystery, for it would directly link Mount Heredom with the Hyksos-Israelite traditions from the Torah and Lower Egypt.

The fact that a red mountain was also important in ancient Egypt is well known, as many ancient texts refer to the Mistress of the Red Mountain. This is taken nowadays to be Gebel el-Ahmar, a hill to the east of Cairo, but it is unlikely in the extreme that the ancient Egyptians revered a rugged mountain in preference to one of their own magnificent, perfectly formed, man-made mountains. Why go to all that bother of creating the perfect pure white mountain that turned blood red in the rays of the setting Sun, if the Mistress of the Mountain sat on a rugged natural crag?

So which of the pyramids was the original Red Pyramid? There is a 'Red Pyramid' (Draco Pyramid) at Dahshur, but I rather suspect that any link between Mount Heredom and the pyramid currently known as the Red Pyramid is tenuous. This pyramid is known nowadays as the Red Pyramid because of its red granite interior and its rusty-orange core blocks. While I have speculated previously that the two pyramids at Dahshur, which are megalithic and therefore probably original, may once have represented the Red and the White emblems of Lower and Upper Egypt respectively, the evidence for this is not overwhelming. Alternatives may be the Great and Second Pyramids, which turned red in the evening light, or the Third Pyramid, which has a substantial red-granite lower section.

In summary, however, I have no doubt that Mount Heredom was originally a reference to one of the pyramids, at either Giza or Dahshur, but the fact that Scottish Masons are still looking for Mount Heredom near Kilwinning in Scotland demonstrates how much of this history has been lost.

Tubal Cain

This is a Second Degree password that is simply taken from the name of the biblical Tubal Cain, the son of Lamech who was supposedly about six generations down from Adam. On the face of it, there was not a lot one could say about this, other than it was an ancient name; that is until it was noticed that this name is always written in close proximity to that of Hiram Abif. Since both of these people were metalworkers, and since Hiram in particular was known for the making of bronze pillars, there may indeed be an Egyptian translation for Tu-Bal. There are two possibilities here: this name may have been taken from *tu* 𓏏𓏺 meaning 'pillar' and *bal (bar)* 𓃀 meaning lord or, more tantalisingly, the latter word may have been derived from *baa* 𓅡 meaning 'copper' or 'bronze'.

The second component in this name is Cain (Qan) קַיִן, which means 'smith' or 'metalworker', and is likely to have been derived from *qan* 𓈎 which refers to the refining of metal and hammering. The likely origin of the name Tu-Bal Cain is therefore Tu-Bar Qan or Tu-Baa Qan, which mean 'Lord Smith of the Pillars' and 'Bronze Pillar Smith' respectively (where 'smith' means a metalworker).

But this seems to be placing a great emphasis on the similarities between the characters Hiram Abif and Tubal Cain. Is this correct? Could the identities of these two individuals be intertwined? Initially, this may seem unlikely, as Tubal Cain was one of the first heroes of the Bible and Hiram does not appear on the scene unto the era of King Solomon; but nevertheless Masonry does indeed closely link these two individuals. The Master Mason's Book says:

> The word Tubal Cain in Hebrew means only a blacksmith ... hence ... an allegorical title has ... been mistaken for the name of an actual person, for the name itself means 'A worker in metals'. Therefore, the connection with Hiram Abif is obvious.

> The word (Tubal Cain) as it stands ... clearly refers to Hiram Abif, who made the two pillars, and whom the candidate is to represent. [6]

Traditionally, the chronology of the Bible placed several thousand years between these individuals, but clearly Masonry has a separate tradition that claims that Tubal Cain and Hiram Abif were actually the same person. So how can this be? Why should Masonry equate the Book of Genesis with the much later United Monarchy of King Solomon?

Here again we see evidence that Masonry has indeed lost its

true history, for nobody can explain this dichotomy. However, the new interpretation of Genesis that has been forged in this book can explain everything. In this new version of Genesis, Adam becomes Pharaoh Akhenaton, and since there are only a few generations between the Amarna regime and the United Monarchy of Solomon, Tubal Cain and Hiram Abif could easily have been of the same era or generation.

So is there any biblical evidence that indicates Tubal Cain was Hiram Abif? Well, the evidence in not overwhelming, but there are certainly a few similarities between these characters:

Generations of Tubal Cain	Generations of Hiram Abif
Sister was called Naamah נעמה	Sister is likely to have been called Naamah נעמה. (Naamah was the wife of King Solomon)
Step-brother called Joabel יובל	Step-brother called Joab יואב.
Joabel's aunt called Zillah (Zerrah)	Joab's mother called Zeruiah צרויה.

The evidence is sketchy, but then so are the genealogies and information that are contained in the early part of Genesis. But I think that this, together with the confident assertions from masonic sources, indicate that Tubal Cain was indeed Hiram Abif.

Machaben (Machabenach)

There are two similar recognition words used during the Third Degree initiation, and these are Machaben and Machabenach, which are sometimes pronounced as Machabone and Machbonach. However, it is highly likely that these are actually different renditions of the same word, so in reality there is only one recognition word to this degree and candidates are only given both so that they can recognise brothers from other Lodges who use other variants.

As a complete alternative to this pronunciation, the masonic authors Lomas and Knight seem to understand these words as Maatba'aa and Maatbinnaa, which are not renditions that I have ever come across before. They then proceeded to break the former of these words into a series of syllables and so derived Maat-ba-aa, which they then argued may mean 'The spirit of Maat is great' in Egyptian; but there again this pronunciation conflicts greatly with masonic tradition and so it is probably entirely spurious.

In truth, there has been a great deal of variation in this recognition word over the centuries. The *Sloane Manuscript* of 1700 gives Mahbyn; *Trinity College* of 1711 gives Matchpin; *A Mason's Examination* in 1723 understands it as Maughbin; whereas *L'Ordre Des Francs-Macon* suggests Makbenak or

Machbenac.[7] But UGL Masonry has finally settled upon the terms Machaben or Machbenach, and one presumes that these represent the most accurate renditions of this word that we are likely to get. This word was purportedly first spoken as Hiram Abif was being raised from his grave, and so it is said that this recognition word represents the death of Hiram Abif. What we are looking for, therefore, is a strong epigraphic association between Machaben and Hiram Abif.

The first syllable is now likely to be Macha, rather than Lomas and Knight's Maat, and yet the conjunction of these two terms should be rather familiar to readers of these books. As has been demonstrated previously, one of the primary uses of the word Maat was in the titles of the Maakare (Maat-kare) 𓏞𓃾𓇳 queens. However, in the biblical tradition the Egyptian name Maakare was Hebrewised into Maakhah מעכה, and it was used for many of the famous Israelite queens including the two chief wives of King David and the mother of King Solomon. In the book *Solomon*, I identified Maakhah Tamar I as possibly being the mother of Hiram Abif, and I also showed how she would have been known as a 'widow', after her position as chief queen was usurped by the younger Maakhah Tamar II. Thus Hiram Abif would have become the 'Son of a Widow', which is exactly what masonic tradition maintains.

It is entirely possible, therefore, that the recognition word Machaben has been primarily derived from the title of the Maakhah queens – it may well be a Hebrewised version, where the syllables 'Maat-ka' have been reduced to 'Maacha' (Maakhah). Since the masonic pronunciation of this word uses the Scottish 'ch', as in 'lo<u>ch</u>', the pronunciation of <u>Macha</u>ben is exactly the same as the Hebrewised biblical version of the <u>Maakh</u>ah queens. But if this secret term was somehow based upon the name of an Egypto-Judaic queen, then what could the suffix of 'ben' or 'benach' possibly mean?

The initial thing to note here is that the last syllable of 'ach' (akh) appears to be optional, and so there is a clear division between the two words, 'ben' and 'ach'. When looking at the first of these, it can be seen that the word *ben* בן means 'son' in the Hebrew. But this is not strictly a term that could have been derived from Egypt, as the normal word for 'son' in the Egyptian was *mos* 𓀀𓏤𓈝 , from which the name Moses was derived. However, a translation from the Egyptian may still be possible because the word *ben* or *benu* 𓃀𓈖𓅢 refers to the Phoenix; a bird that was so intimately associated with new birth that its symbology is still used in the modern era – where it takes the form of a stork carrying a baby in a cloth draped around its beak, flying off to deliver its precious cargo to expectant parents. This imagery is such a familiar part of our modern culture that we tend to forget the fact that it is actually an Egyptian icon that was conceived back at the very dawn of man's recorded history. Given this close and well-known association between the Phoenix and a baby, it is likely that it was from the *benu* Phoenix that the Israelites derived their word *ben* בֶן, meaning 'son'.*

When applying this suffix to the word Machaben (Makha-ben) we can then derive the phrase 'Son of Maakhah'; or, when following the logic regarding the Maakhah queens that I have already touched upon, we can also derive 'Son of the Widow'. It would also seem that this phrase translates equally well from both the Egyptian (Maakhare-benu 𓈖𓏏𓎼𓊹) and the Hebrew (Makhah-ben מעכה בן), and so it is likely that this is the true foundation from which this recognition term was derived.

Through this series of translations, we can now see the rationale behind the formulation of this recognition word. The phrase 'Son of the Widow' (in the English) refers to the masonic hero Hiram Abif, and it is the most potent recognition phrase within Masonry. So the use of this phrase during the key Third Degree 'raising' initiation – which happens to represent the raising from the dead of Hiram Abif – would be highly appropriate. Hiram Abif was the chief architect of King Solomon and he is the prime hero of Masonry and, as I have already explained, he is also likely to have been the son of Queen Maakhah Tamar I. But there is a degree of circular logic to be derived from all this, for if the phrase Macha-ben literally means the 'Son of Maakha', then Hiram Abif must have indeed been the son of Maakhah Tamar I, as I have already predicted.

A possible confirmation of these arguments is to be found on the Third Degree tracing board. The most prominent feature of this important diagram is the skull and crossbones on the lid of the coffin, but exactly whose bones were they? The obvious answer would be that the skull is that of Hiram Abif; but the skull that is used as a theatrical prop in masonic ritual is supposed to be female, so were the bones depicted on the tracing board supposed to be of a woman instead? Despite many Masons presuming that they know this tracing board's entire meaning, the answer to this is not entirely clear cut.

However, there are some additional clues that may unravel, or perhaps deepen, this mystery, and the first of these is a series of letters of the alphabet that appear above the skull. These presumably denote the owner of the coffin, and the first line of characters is usually given as HAB,

---

* Since the 'ben' in the term Macha-ben refers primarily to the 'son', this may be the source of a very famous Scottish title. The Hebrew and Egyptian words for 'son' are actually the 'ben' portion from this recognition word, but in a society that had long been detached from its Middle Eastern roots, the Scots may have decided that it was the Mach portion of this name instead. Having made this slight error, the tradition of calling the next generation 'Mac', or 'Son of', has persisted in Scotland to this day.

which stands for Hiram Abif. Sometimes these letters are written in Hebrew, and sometimes they are implied through a simple noughts-and-crosses code, where the letters of the alphabet are represented by the shape of the noughts-and-crosses 'cell' that they sit in. See the following diagram for an explanation of this code.

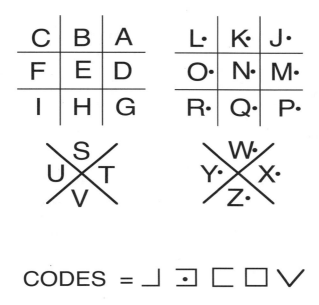

Fig 9.1   Crossword code for deciphering the Third Degree tracing board.

To the side of the skull and crossbones are the letters T and C, which stand for Tubal Cain, and these represent the biblical patriarch who was reputedly the first smith, or metalworker. Since Hiram Abif was also a metalworker (mostly in bronze), Tubal Cain has become a masonic nickname for Hiram; indeed, they are generally regarded as being the same person, as has just been explained. (The letters on the coffin are often given in reverse order to agree with the Hebrew method of writing.)

Thus, from the evidence already given, most Masons might reasonably imply from these explanations that the skull and crossbones that are drawn on the coffin – and also on the Templar naval battle flag, the Jolly Roger – represent the bones of the primary masonic hero Hiram Abif. But is this assertion correct? The two letters that appear underneath the skull and crossbones are M and B. These letters are sometimes repeated twice, and they stand for the recognition words Machaben and Machabenach. Note that the word Machaben is being split here into the two components Macha and Ben or Benach. Dividing the word at this particular location most certainly concurs with the arguments that have just been given in favour of this word meaning 'Son of Maakhah' (Son of the Widow).

Further confirmation of these explanations is to be seen in the examples of tracing boards that use the Hebrew lettering instead of the noughts-and-crosses code. One such board has two pairs of letters in a simple box – TQ and MB (ק ת and מ ב). (Cain is being spelt with a 'q' ק in the Hebrew.) Tubal Cain is most definitely a pseudonym for Hiram Abif, and thus the two letters, T and C, represent the initials of someone's name. But since the other two letters, M and B, are treated in exactly the same fashion, then surely these two letters must also represent the initials of a name or title? As has just been explained, Macha-Ben is indeed a title, one that is related to an influential lady who is most certainly closely associated with Hiram Abif.

Thus, on this coffin we have the initials of Hiram Abif and also those pertaining to his mother, or rather to Hiram's title as the 'Son of Maakhah Tamar' (Macha-Ben). And thus the initials HB and MB must indeed both refer to the same person – Hiram Abif. However, since I have not previously come across any association between the word Machaben and the mother of Hiram, let alone an association with Hiram himself, I do wonder if anyone has before deciphered the true meaning of the initials MB.

While this explanation is probably more comprehensive than is ever given in any Lodge or in any degree, this would still not explain the use of a female skull in the ritual, and so we may need to take these arguments a stage further. These explanations have demonstrated that the initials MB refer to Hiram Abif being the son of one of the Maakhah Tamar queens, possibly Maakhah Tamar I. But there was another Maakhah Tamar who was also closely associated with Hiram Abif [as Absalom], according to my identification in the book *Solomon*, and that was Maakhah Tamar II. The reason why I think that the skull of the Third Degree is more likely to have been associated with this particular lady is that she was rather more famous than her mother. In fact, this particular Maakhah Tamar (II) was, according to my deductions, the daughter of Maakhah Tamar I, and she was more popularly known in the Bible as the Queen of Sheba. It is likely that the Queen of Sheba and Hiram Abif would have been associated in the same ritual because it is highly likely that they were brother and sister, and for a short period they were also man and wife.

This explanation may in some respects identify Masonry with the refugees who fled from Jerusalem at the time of the Babylonian invasion in about 590 BC, who also appear to have associated themselves with, and venerated, a deified form of the Queen of Sheba. Most of these refugees ended up in Saba, in modern Yemen, which was well known for its veneration of the Queen of Sheba. But these refugees were to further enrich the global extent of these traditions, for the Marib Dam that maintained the economy of the Sabaean nation burst in AD 610, causing yet another exodus that had a significant historical repercussion. As it happens, the rise of Islam in Arabia is dated to about AD 620, and this similar era is probably of no coincidence. Thus Islam and the Koran, which contains many references to the Queen of Sheba, may have been greatly influenced by the traditions that were flowing out of Southern Arabia from the disintegrating Sabaean Empire. But, of course, it was from their Arabic-Islamic contacts that the Templars gained, or regained, much of their esoteric knowledge, and so much of this eastern esoterica may have had Judaeo-Sabaean origins.

We can also find, in all these explanations, a possible confirmation that Hiram Abif was related to King Solomon, as I have already predicted. A common inscription on the lid of this coffin is 555, which is sometimes denoted by the Hebrew equivalent of ההה, and yet I have not been able to find a rational explanation for this important-looking set of numbers or letters. Using the traditional Hebrew number-code gives the words *tknh* תכנה or *srnh* שׂרנה, neither of which seem to mean anything significant. But in the book *Solomon* I have already demonstrated that the biblical sign of the devil, the infamous number 666, referred to King Solomon – the association between this sign and the devil being promoted by Solomon's later detractors because of their dislike of Solomon's enormous wealth. But Hiram Abif has 555 inscribed on his coffin, so does this imply that he lived (or died) just before King Solomon? As I have already identified Hiram Abif as being the elder brother of King Solomon, this would certainly make sense.

In fact, the method through which these number associations were derived looks remarkably similar. The primary reason for calling King Solomon '666' was the fact that the number six in Egyptian was *sas* ﾉﾟﾉﾟ ﾟ , or *shesha* שׁשׁה in the Hebrew, and the Egyptian name for Solomon was Sheshak (Shishak). Thus the designation 666 that was given to Solomon could be translated as 'shesha(k), shesha(k), shesha(k)', which would be quite appropriate. In a very similar fashion, Hiram Abif was nicknamed T̲ubal Cain, because both of these individuals were metalworkers, and Hiram was known in particular for his great bronze pillars. As it happens, the Egyptian word for pillar was *djua (tu)* ﾟﾟﾟ , and the Egyptian word for five was also *dju* ﾟﾟﾟﾟ . Thus the designation 555 that is being given to Hiram could easily be translated as 'pillar, pillar, pillar', which would again be quite appropriate.

Masonry admits to an association with King Solomon, his temple, Jerusalem, and someone called Macha, and it also covertly admits to a possible Egyptian heritage. The explanations that have been explored, both in this work and the book *Solomon*, explain all of those diverse associations. If the truth were known, King Solomon and his mother Maakhah Tamar II were actually the historical characters called Pharaoh Sheshonq I and his mother Maakhare MuTamhat II, and they presided over an Egypto-Judaic empire that stretched from Thebes to the Euphrates. But, in the guise of the Queen of Sheba, King Solomon's mother was so famous that she became deified after her death, and the memory of this magical queen and her equally talented brother-husband Hiram Abif [Absalom] has lived on through the centuries and through the continents. All I can say is that she must have been an extraordinary woman.

Shibboleth

Although the Hebrew word *shibboleth* שבלת is sometimes taken nowadays as a masonic recognition word, it was not originally formed with that intention. It was simply a word that the Ephrameites of the Bible could not pronounce properly, and thereby betrayed their racial origins to the questioner. The word *shibboleth (shabboreth)* שבלת was derived from the Egyptian *shabareth* , and this simply means 'river' or 'stream' in both languages. For the reasons just described it is unlikely that this word has any deeper meanings.

Since this word is spelt using the same type of hieroglyphs that became popular with the twenty-second dynasty Lower Egyptian pharaohs, including Sheshonq I, who I have shown to have been King Solomon, it would seem that the Ephrameites were enemies of the Hyksos United Monarchy.

Jahbulon

This is said to be the secret masonic name of god, and it has come in for a great deal of criticism recently by non-Masons as it is said to have been derived from three god-names. The word is supposed to be divisible into the syllables Jah יה Baal בעל and On אן, which are said to be representative of the three deities of Yahweh, Baal and Osiris. It is this presumed presence of the 'pagan' gods Baal and Osiris in a Judaeo-Christian masonic context that tends to get some commentators in a bit of a lather. However, the link between the syllable On and Osiris is tentative in the extreme; Osiris' Egyptian name was Asar , and to transliterate this pronunciation into 'On' is somewhat cavalier. Even the Greeks, whose translations are often suspect, managed to derive Osiris, which is a reasonable attempt at pronouncing Asar.

Martin Short, who wrote *Inside The Brotherhood*, came as close as I have seen to deciphering this word. He noted the claim by Reverend Heydon, another masonic researcher, that the syllable 'On' most likely referred to the biblical On, or Heliopolis, a name that was derived from the Egyptian An or On 🏛. In its turn, the syllable Baal could refer as much to a 'lord' or 'king' as the god Baal. This new interpretation would then derive a phrase something like 'Yahweh is Lord of Heliopolis', which is probably not much more acceptable to fundamentalist Judaeo-Christian sensitivities and so Grand Lodge predictably stays silent on this topic.

This translation by Martin Short is very nearly correct, and the only adjustment that needs to be made here is to the god-name and the title. The term Yah was originally derived from Yah 𓇳, the Moon-god; but of course Yah is only another name for Djehuti or Thoth. The only other amendment is the translation of 'bul' or 'bal'. The obvious connection to make is with Baal, as we have seen, but an alternative is the link to Babel that was made in Chapter V. Here it was shown that the Tower of Babel actually referred to the Great Pyramid, since the Egyptian term *belbel* referred to pyramids.

Thus, the final translation of the masonic god-name Jahbulon or Yahbulon could well be 'Thoth, Lord of Heliopolis', or perhaps even the 'Thoth Pyramid of Heliopolis'. Both of these phrases again display the true Egyptian origins of Masonry, but the latter once more demonstrates the possible links with Giza. As was explained in the book *Tempest* and again in this book, the two largest pyramids of Giza may well have been associated with the Sun and the Moon, or in terms of the equivalent Egyptian deities, Ra and Thoth. Since Heliopolis was the temple and city that was adjacent to Giza, the Second Pyramid may well have been known as the 'Thoth Pyramid of Heliopolis'.

One objection that has been raised to dispute the assertion that On refers to the city of Heliopolis, is the strong inference in masonic lore that the 'On' syllable in Jahbul<u>on</u> was supposed to have been associated with Hiram Abif. But this masonic hero has traditionally been associated with the city of Tyre in Lebanon, and so an apparent link between Hiram Abif and Heliopolis looked highly unlikely. However, in the book *Solomon*, I positively identified Hiram Abif as being Heru-m Atif, the chief architect of the pharaoh Psusennes II [King David], and equally demonstrated that the name 'Tyre' did not refer to a city in Lebanon but to a 'stone' (a Mason). Since Heru-m Atif was resident in both Thebes and Tanis in the Nile Delta, under this new interpretation, the close association between Hiram Abif and the city of Heliopolis is not so surprising.

Geblum

This secret recognition word is said to mean 'Excellent Mason'. It was probably taken from a spelling that was more like *geberem*, with the 'l' being changed into an 'r', as is the normal practice in many of these conversions.

The Hebrew version of *geberum* is *geber* רבג, which refers to a strong man or even a warrior. The latter version could possibly project this term back into the Knights Templar era, especially as it means much the same in Arabic. However, looking further back into the past and into ancient Egypt once more, the equivalent term is the surprisingly similar *gebier* 🔲⫴⫴⛿ meaning 'great man', or perhaps *gebier-m* 🔲⫴⫴⛿ 🦅 meaning something like 'among great men', 'like great men' or perhaps 'in the capacity of great men'. Note that this word used the lion glyph for the 'r' consonant, and it was this lion glyph that became used much later as an Egyptian 'l' consonant. The latter interpretation would produce a pronunciation like *gebiel-m*.

Abroeth

Taken from the address to the third chair in Holy Chapter Masonry, the term Abroeth refers to a triangle. More specifically, the triangle is said to represent the 'sacred name of god'. The masonic lecture says:

> In times of antiquity, names of god and symbols of divinity were always enclosed in triangular figures. In the days of Pythagorus, the triangle was considered the most sacred of emblems, and when any obligation ... was to be administered, it was invariably given on the triangle. [8]

> The Egyptians termed it the sacred number, or the number of perfection, and so highly prized was it by the ancients that it became an object of worship. [9]

What they are talking about, of course, is not a triangle as such but a pyramid. The pyramid was considered to be a sacred number because all of the major pyramids, at both Giza and Dahshur, encoded within their external designs fundamental mathematical functions. The Great Pyramid represents Pi (π), the Second Pyramid represents the Pythagorean 3:4:5 triangle, whereas the Draco (Red) Pyramid at Dahshur represents the Pythagorean 20:21:29 triangle.

Thus the triangles (pyramids) that were being venerated represented, at the very least, items of very useful mathematical wisdom; and so the conventional 'translation' of Abroeth as meaning the 'Soul of Nature' leaves one feeling rather deflated. Surely such a fundamental piece of iconography should have a more profound meaning. However, from the Egyptian, we can derive Ab-Roeth 𓂝𓏤𓆓 𓏏𓏤𓀭𓁹 which translates as 'Wisdom of Mankind'. All in all, I think that the latter is far more suitable, even if the evidence is lacking.

Abaddon
This is given during the 17th Degree of Ancient Rite, and is possibly derived from the syllables Ab-Addon 〔hieroglyphs〕, which in the Egyptian would refer to the 'Wisdom of Adhon' or the 'Wisdom of Aton'.

Apron
Another demonstration that masonry was originally a Hyksos Egyptian organisation is the ritual regalia of the masonic apron. The Egyptian royalty invariably wore an apron, which was often pyramidal in design. But the original masonic apron differed significantly from this in being formed from a simple lambskin, a symbol which is said to be 'older than the Golden Fleece and the Roman Eagle'. In some respects this statement is true, and the reason for the ancient Egyptian apron evolving into this lambskin design is because the origins of masonry were derived from the Hyksos pharaohs and people, who were known as 'Shepherds' – the astrological reasoning for this title having been fully explained already in the book *Jesus*. However, the fact that this lambskin tradition survived the transition of the constellations from Aries (sheep) to Pisces (fish) at the turn of the first century, indicates that the reasoning for its design and usage had been lost even in this early era. Modern First Degree Masons should have an apron made from fish-scales!

Juwes
The three Juwes who were supposed to have murdered Hiram Abif were named as Jubela, Jubelo and Jubelum, and it is entirely possible that they were originally known as the three Jubes. This name was derived from the Egyptian *tchoab* 〔hieroglyphs〕, meaning 10,000, and it was a reference to the number of men that an army general was in command of. The biblical equivalent of this name was Joab, the army commander of King David who was the commander of 'thousands' of men. Indeed, a reference in 2 Sam 18:3 suggests that Joab was actually the commander of 10,000 men, just as the Egyptian translation suggests. See the book *Solomon* for further details.

Abracadabra
Firstly, perhaps I should discuss the possibility of this term being masonic. This is, of course, the word that has been uttered by magicians since the dawn of time while they perform their tricks, and yet masonry and magicry have always been close compatriots. It has been claimed that the 'magic circle' contains more Freemasons than any other profession, and that even Houdini was a Freemason, having been initiated at St Cecile Lodge Nº 568 in New York.[10]

One of the more famous practitioners who regularly used the magic word *abracadabra* was Tommy Cooper, who used equal portions of humour and magic in his stage act. In fact, Tommy became such a legendary comic that he only had to come on stage and say 'not like that, like that' and everyone would fall about laughing. But why was that? Just what was so funny about this peculiar routine?

In fact, the joke was on us, for Tommy was simply pulling a masonic stunt. He came on stage wearing a black suit with a white shirt, white gloves, and a red fez placed precariously on his head. In effect, he was dressed as one of the Ancient Arabic Order of the Nobles of the Mystic Shrine, or the Shriners for short; a masonic order that is more widespread in America. In fact, Tommy Cooper was initiated into the Westminster Lodge N° 4518 in London in 1952. When Tommy said 'not like that, like that', he also placed his hands in the *due guard* for the initiation of a Master Mason. All the Masons in the audience would fall about laughing, as they knew what the symbolism really meant, while the rest of the audience joined in with the general merriment because they were sure there must have been something funny, otherwise why were all these other people laughing. Tommy's act was simply to lampoon Masonry, but the Masons loved it because only the 'in crowd' knew the joke, while the *muggles* just wondered (secretly) what all the fuss was about.

Having demonstrated a link between Masonry and this magical term, it should be noted that the staccato pronunciation of *Ab-Ra-Ca-Dab-Ra* sounds remarkably Egyptian. As ever, the best method of finding an Egyptian word begins with a perusal of possible Hebrew equivalents, and in this case we find a distinct possibility. This incantation most probably came from the Hebrew phrase *abrek(a) dabbarah* אברך דברה, meaning 'Command the Word'. The reason why this could be the true origin of this Hebrew phrase is that it appears to be a direct and meaningful translation out of the Egyptian, which has some very royal and very Israelite connotations. In the Egyptian, this phrase would have been pronounced as *Abreka-Tepre* 𓀀𓏤𓂝𓄿 𓊨𓏤 , which again means 'Command the Word'.

But let's look at the two elements of this phrase in more detail, for the Hebrew term *abrek(a)* אברך is actually much more specific than a simple 'command'. It was actually used in the Bible to instruct the people of Egypt to go down on their left knee before the patriarch Joseph, and it is based upon the Egyptian word *abrek(a)* 𓀀𓏤𓂝𓄿 which has exactly the same meaning. Meanwhile, the Hebrew word *dabbarah* דברה meaning 'word', was derived from the Egyptian *tep-ra* 𓊨𓏤 meaning 'mouth' or 'speech' (words). It can also mean something rather more commanding, like Tep Ra 𓊨𓏤 ⊙ meaning 'Word of Ra' or 'Word of God'.

Once more, we have a situation where a Hebrew phrase has come directly from the original Egyptian, in both pronunciation and meaning. Furthermore, this ancient phrase has also managed to find its way directly into the modern world virtually unchanged. In this case, the complete incantation of *Abreka-Tep-Ra* ✝⅃◠◠ ◈◯ ◉ would originally have been a command that meant 'Go Down on your Left Knee before the Word of Ra'. Although not uttered today in Lodge, *abraca-dabra (abraca-tepra)* may well have been part of an ancient Egyptian ritual, just as the Bible suggests.

Since the biblical Joseph is acknowledged as having become vizier to pharaoh, it is extremely likely that he would also have been elevated to the position of Grand Master of the original Heliopolian Lodge. But the biblical wording of this masonic-style initiation is misleading, as it says:

> And he (pharaoh) made him to ride in the second chariot which he had; and they cried before him, "Bow the knee *(abreka)*" , and pharaoh made him ruler over all the land of Egypt. [B11]

This makes it appear as if the people said 'bow to the knee' to Joseph, which is highly unlikely; and so some Bibles have amended this to indicate that footmen on the chariot were calling to the crowd to kneel before Joseph, which does sound a little better. However, there may be yet another version of this verse, and a more literal translation without embellishment might read as:

ו:ירכב את:ו ב:מרכבת ה:משנה אשר-ל:ו ו:יקראו ל:פני:ו אברך
ו:נתון את:ו על כל-ארץ מצרים

> He (Joseph) did ride in the second chariot. (Pharaoh) proclaimed directly (joyfully) to his face, 'Bow down on the left knee'; and he appointed him over the whole land of Egypt.

This new translation seems to indicate that it was the pharaoh who said 'kneel' to Joseph. Therefore, it would appear that Joseph was undertaking an initiation ceremony, presided over by the pharaoh, which was not unlike a modern knighthood ceremony in Britain. But this initiation probably conferred masonic as well as secular authority to Joseph, who is acknowledged in the Torah as becoming the vizier or prime minister, the most important individual in Egypt under the pharaoh.

Monty Python

Having briefly looked at the usage of masonic symbology in contemporary art and media, no discussion on this topic would be complete without a look at the Monty Python team. In the 1970s the BBC commissioned a new, offbeat comedy series entitled Monty Python's Flying Circus – staring John Cleese, Michael Palin, Graham Chapman, Eric Idle and Terry Jones – which became a comedy classic in many countries. But, like the Tommy Cooper routine, many viewers were left in the dark in regard to the nature of the humour being employed. (This is in itself a masonic phrase which refers to those who have not seen the light – hence the eighteenth century philosophical movement known as the Enlightenment.)

In truth, many of the stunts and gags in this television series were based upon masonic symbolism, and so only Masons could fully understand the humour. This is why the later Python films concentrated on topics like the Holy Grail and the Life of Brian (Jesus). In the latter film, the character called Brian was actually a coded reference to John the Baptist, the primary hero of Templars and Masons, which is why the film portrayed Brian as the true (if reluctant) Judaic saviour. Brian even starts his 'ministry' by losing a sandal, which is a reference to the masonic 'slipshod' dress-code and was also the identifying feature of Jason in the Argonaut saga.

It would take too long to go through all of the masonic symbology in the Python series, but what of that strange title – Monty Python's Flying Circus? Were the Python team just choosing an offbeat title to amuse us, or was there a deeper symbolism to this? As ever, there is symbolism in every aspect of both Egyptian ritual and Masonry, and the clue to the real meaning for this title is contained, curiously enough, in the magazine 'Flight International'. This rather serious aviation magazine contains a humour page at the back and one of the enduring heroes of this section is one Monty Orangeball. This is yet another strange title and once more it is designed to display 'to those with eyes that can see and ears that can hear' (Math 11:15, Mk 4:9), the allegiances of the magazine's editor or proprietor. The answer to this first conundrum is that since Egyptian religion and Masonry are both based upon solar 'worship', this strange name is, of course, a reference to the Sun.

The title of Monty, which is being used for the Sun, was derived from the Egyptian Mandjii (Mondjii, Monty) which refers to the barque of the Rising Sun. So Monty is simply another name for Adon (Aton), the dawn solar-deity of Akhenaton. (Note the 'd' for 't' mis-transliteration in both names.) Having realised the solar significance of the name, the 'Orangeball' part of this strange name becomes a clear reference to the Sun.

The evidence that this term for the rising Sun is still being used in contemporary Masonry can be seen in the full title for the Python comedy show – Monty Python's Flying Circus. Here we have a series of seemingly unconnected words that appear to be humourous more through their disjointed juxtaposition, rather than any hidden meaning. However, if the full title is now perceived in terms of the Egyptian solar deity, Ra, all will be revealed. Take a look at the flying Sun-disk of Ra that adorns the beginning of each chapter in this book. Here you will find that Monty (the Sun) is portrayed as a python (cobra) with wings which bear aloft the image of a circle (the Sun). This is Monty Python's Flying Circle (Circus).

Fig 9.2 Monty Python's Flying Circle, above a shop in Leicester Square.

Open sesame

The origin of the word *sesame* is probably the Egyptian *sesen* 𓏴, meaning 'open' or 'breathe'. The inference here is probably to the opening of the mouth ceremony, where the mouth is opened and the divine breath can fill the body with life.

Mason

The term 'Mason' may or may not be ancient Egyptian, but if it was an ancient term it does not appear to have had an architectural meaning at this time. The primary, indeed the only, translation available for an equivalent pronunciation is *masen* 𓏴, which refers to 'being born'. Although this is far from certain, it is possible that this could have been derived from the Third Degree resurrection ritual, where the candidate is literally 'born again'.

British Empire

It was said that the 'Sun never sets on the British Empire', which was a reference to the fact that the Sun was always high in the sky over one of the Empire's far-flung lands. This was taken from the Second Degree ritual which states that the 'Sun is always at its meridian with respect to Freemasonry', a phrase that means exactly the same as was used with respect to the British Empire. Since it is highly likely that this Second Degree ritual predates the Empire by several centuries, this phrase must have been derived from Masonry.

Golgotha

Although Golgotha γολγοθα is a well-known name from the Bible, this is still sometimes used as a masonic recognition word. This was the 'place of the skull', where Jesus was crucified in the New Testament accounts. This gives a slight problem in translation as these texts were written in Greek, but the origins of this location were certainly Hebrew, as it was originally called Gulgoleth גלגלת. So did even this location have Egyptian overtones? Well, this is possible because if the 'l' is replaced with 'r' we derive Gurgorth and this is not a million miles away from the Egyptian *gorgut* meaning 'brethren'. Since *gorgut* ⟨glyph⟩ uses the bones glyph, Golgotha was known as the 'place of the skull', and as the Egyptian version of this word referred to the 'brethren', it rather sounds as if Jesus was being taken to a Lodge emblazoned with a skull and crossbones insignia.

Perhaps the reader does not need to be reminded that the skull and crossbones was a traditional component of masonic symbolism and that it was taken up by the seafaring contingent of Masonry, where it gained worldwide renown. In addition, it would seem that many American presidents were once members of the Skull and Bones Club, a pseudo-masonic society based at Yale University that takes fifteen selected students from each year, who often rise to positions of power and influence.

Rough to smooth ashlar

The traditional interpretation of the rough ashlar (a rudely cut block of stone) being shaped into the smooth ashlar is that of the raw masonic candidate being shaped and smoothed into the upright, upstanding, masonic citizen. The perfect model citizen can then 'steer the barque of this life over the seas of passion, without quitting the helm of rectitude, (which is) the highest perfection to which human nature can attain', as the ritual states. This explanation for the ashlar has, of course, been taken from the Torah. In the Book of Psalms it says:

> The stone which the builders rejected is become the head stone of the corner. [B12]

This is an adage that has been repeated in the New Testament, where Jesus prophesied that the 'Kingdom of God' would be taken from orthodox Jews and given to a new sect. However, as with all of these social and humanistic interpretations of masonic signs and symbols, there may once have been a more fundamental meaning to this ashlar adage. If masonic ritual were once based upon the rituals that were employed at the Giza temple site, as I strongly suspect, then there is one obvious instance of a piece of rough stonework that has to be turned into an exemplary piece of smooth stonework. I refer, of course, to the rough cavern at the foot of the Great Pyramid.

The bulk of the chambers in this pyramid were originally concealed and were therefore unknown to the priesthood and to later travellers and explorers. But, as has been explained in the books *K2* and *Tempest*, it is fairly certain that the descending passage to the rough cavern at the base of this pyramid had been accessible throughout history. But why was this lower cavern so roughly cut? Egyptologists will argue that the pyramid builders made a mistake or changed their plans, and decided to take the unusual step of placing chambers higher up in the pyramid. Having constructed what is known as the Queen's Chamber, they then changed their plans again and constructed another chamber even higher up in the body of the pyramid. But these arguments are not only suppositional and speculative, the events they describe are also highly unlikely.

The impression is often given that the entrances to these pyramids were highly concealed and their whereabouts unknown. But, as the clearly marked entrance to the Third Pyramid demonstrates, some of these entrances must have been known about in ancient times. The truth of the matter is that the entrance to the Great Pyramid was always known about and open to the priesthood, and these pyramids functioned more like cathedrals or masonic initiation chambers than tombs. The reason for the rough chamber at the bottom of the Great Pyramid was to fool the priesthood and later tomb-robbers and thus preserve the important chambers that lay above. A tomb-robber or even a priest who could not find the entrance to a pyramid may be tempted to destroy the pyramid in search of imagined treasures. However, a pyramid that is open and obviously empty is not such a target, and the reason for a rough chamber rather than a perfectly cut chamber is that this lower chamber takes no part in the symbology that this pyramid provides.

The rough to smooth ashlar adage may well have been a prompt to later generations that there was more to this pyramid than met the eye. In order to understand its symbolism, one needs to look past the rough chamber and discover the perfectly smooth hidden chambers that lie almost directly above it.

The Big Secret

Masonry has long stated that it is not a secret society but a society with secrets. This understated sense of mystery has intrigued people down through the ages, and doubtless one or two have been tempted to join the fraternity because they thought it could provide them with some kind of esoteric understanding; something that may even explain the meaning of life, the Universe and everything. So what is this secret that the Masons keep so close to their chests? What kind of secret could be so important that it needs hiding even in the enlightened, liberal twenty-first century? What kind of secret could be so fundamental and so important that, of the millions of Masons who have existed throughout the ages, not one appears to have been tempted to write publicly about this secret or give interviews to the press?

One possibility is that all of this 'secrets' business could simply be a massive fraud. In this scenario, the fraternity convinces the world that it harbours a fundamental secret regarding the history of mankind, which inevitably attracts members to its organisation, and then it simply leaves them hanging. These new members would be loath to simply leave the fraternity, because that would make them look foolish; and besides, the fraternity could always indicate that the next initiation would eventually divulge the secret, then the next and the next and so on. Meanwhile, the fraternity can fleece the unwitting new member of substantial amounts of cash through its fees and dues, which can be quite onerous.

In effect, this is largely what happens, because many of those in the lower degrees never do discover the core secrets of Masonry. For even if one has become a Mason and risen through the ranks to the Third Degree, there is no guarantee that any secrets will be divulged. As the Mason's handbook points out:

> I am now permitted to inform you that there are several degrees in Masonry, and peculiar secrets restricted to each; these, however, are not communicated indiscriminately, but are conferred on candidates according to merit and abilities. [13]

In other words, it matters not how high you climb through the ranks of Masonry; if you are not deemed to be fit and worthy, you will be told nothing more than your local Christian priest divulges in his or her Sunday School lessons for seven-year-olds. In addition, many of the higher degrees represent nothing more than masonic 'degree inflation'. Many an initiate has struggled through the inane and banal rituals and initiations to finally emerge as a Master Mason, only to find that there is nothing of interest to be found bar the odd business contact. At this point, disappointment sets in and the member drifts into disillusionment and discontentment. The answer to this endemic problem was the formulation of further degrees, which always promise something extra; a real secret or two may be just beyond your reach. As it says in a recruitment pamphlet for the Royal Arch (the Third-and-a-half Degree):

> The reason (for taking this extra degree) was that this was how they could learn the true secrets which were lost at Hiram's death. [14]

Having previously been told that the secrets of Masonry were lost, suddenly the search is back on for these lost secrets of Masonry – the 'lost word', an arcane secret that may explain the basis of our religious systems. Although the brighter candidate, looking towards Royal Arch, might simply save their time and money and inquire of the Worshipful Master why nobody in King Solomon's Temple thought to ask the other two Master Masons (Grand Masters) what the true secrets of Masonry were.

> Our Master, true to his obligation, answered that those secrets were <u>known to but three in the world,</u> and that without consent of the other two he neither could nor would divulge them. [15]

As the Third Degree lecture clearly states, there were supposed to be three Master Masons (Grand Masters?) in the world who held the secrets of Masonry and one of them, Hiram Abif, had been murdered. Now in my view that leaves two Masters that still hold the true secrets of Masonry, who can between them raise another candidate to fill the vacant post. In this manner the true secrets can never be lost, and no doubt this is why this system was devised in the first place. However, masonic lore appears to be trying to convince us that every time a Master Mason dies, all the secrets of Masonry are lost with him.

In short, the prospective candidate is led by the nose through a mishmash of mystical and metaphysical biblical nonsense that purports to be a deep and secret mystery; whereas the facts would tend to suggest that some enterprising Masons went through the Old Testament texts during the eighteenth century, picking out odd words and sentences at random, which then became the masonic 'hidden words'. Had the prospective modern candidate been given these obscure biblical passages to learn and study in any other context, in a Sunday School environment for example, he would have told the person to take a running jump. But since there is the lure of a 'secret', candidates will endure endless rituals and come back for more on a regular basis.

Degree by degree the initiate rises through the system to find that the 'lost word' may be Jahbulon, a term that has already been explored in this chapter. But then, as he reaches the Ancient Rite's 19th Degree and becomes a Knight of the Pelican and Eagle, the Puissant Prince of the Rose Cross of Heredom, he discovers the four mysterious Latin letters that eventually spell out the secret name that lies behind this great mystery:

> Worthy Knights, by the aid of Faith, Hope and Charity, you have indeed succeeded in finding the Lost Word ... taking the initials of the last four steps

of your journey, and putting them together, you have found the Name of him who is the Word...[20]

The four letters on the steps are I, N, R and I, and so the lost 'Word' is INRI,* or Jesus!

So the mysterious 'lost word' of Masonry, that monumental, ineffable secret of the entire Universe that has been sought by millions of devout Masons for millennia was .... Jesus! It's a wonder that candidates don't storm out of the temple in disgust, knocking the tyler off his stool *en route*.

The fact of the matter is that the higher degrees of Masonry, in other words those degrees of Ancient Rite that are above the three Craft degrees, differ considerably from each other across regional and national boundaries. The fact that Craft Masonry is reasonably consistent and Ancient Rite is highly variable, would tend to suggest that the latter is a recent invention that has been devised on separate continents by separate sects during the eighteenth and nineteenth centuries, when international communication was poor and sporadic. On the other hand, the three degrees of Craft Masonry are quite old and consistent, and so must have spread out from a single source. Since the Templars had been largely dispersed in France, with many fleeing to Scotland, that prime source became England and Scotland. All of this tends to debase the value of the higher degrees, and frankly, those interested in discovering the secrets of the Universe would do better purchasing the entire compendium of Harry Potter books than aspiring to the higher degrees of Masonry.

Another telling aspect that devalues these higher degrees is their overt Christian content. It is absolutely clear from the general content of masonic ritual that Masonry has been derived from Old Testament events concerning King Solomon and his construction of the Temple of Solomon; an event that lies at least nine hundred years prior to the birth of Jesus. Yet the 19th Degree in Masonry would have us believe that the lost word of Hiram Abif, who was supposed to have lived in about 950 BC, was the Greek title for Jesus, who lived at the turn of the first century AD. Common sense would dictate that any Christian content within Masonry is a later addition to the Craft, and thus the Royal Arch 'secret word' of INRI is not worth a dime in terms of enlightenment.

---

* The four letters spell out INRI, which are the four initials for the Latin phrase *Iesus Nazarenus Rex Iudaeorum*, meaning 'Jesus of Nazareth, King of the Jews'. The link between the Word and Jesus is derived from the opening verse of the Gospel of John which states that:

And the Word was made flesh, and dwelt among us, full of grace and truth. John 1:14

So, if the overt 'secrets' of Masonry – as given during initiations and published in code in pamphlets – are not representative of the true secrets of masonry, then what are those deeper and more fundamental secrets? The main historical claim for Masonry involves the Temple of Solomon and the death of its Architect, Hiram Abif [Herum Atif]. But the circumstances of this death, even if they are based on a real event, are simultaneously allegorical. In other words, the death of Hiram has been used to tell an allegorical story, and so it would appear that there is an initiation within an initiation, and only the brighter and more worthy candidates will see the inner truths.

At the surface level, Hiram Abif is said to have been attacked by three assailants, who struck him in the south, north and east of the Temple, resulting in his death. Twelve of the other conspirators then recant and go in search of Hiram's body. In fact, the tale of this 'brightest light' of Masonry being killed and searched for by the twelve conspirators betrays the cult's original solar origins. Hiram Abif is taking on the mantle of the Sun-god, and the tale actually represents the diurnal death of Ra, where the Sun has been 'killed' as Amen by setting in the west. Then, according to the Book of the Dead, the Sun begins its perilous journey through the Djuat – from the west, through the north and onwards to the east – and passes through the twelve hours of the night in order to reach the eastern sunrise. Continuing with the story, the twelve conspirators are eventually successful and Hiram's body is found in a grave (in a coffin according to the ritual), upon which is a small acacia tree. This section of the story is undoubtedly a retelling of the Osirian myth, where Osiris is cast adrift in a coffin on the Nile, eventually coming to rest in an acacia tree.

The apparent confusion that is being made here between Osiris and Ra is easily explained by Osiris being considered within Egyptian beliefs to be the *ba* of Ra. So, Osiris was the night Sun, the aspect of Ra as he travelled through the night hours of the underworld. But Ra was considered to be dead during this period, exactly the same as Hiram Abif was. Thus the twelve searchers for the body of Hiram were the twelve night hours through which the deceased Ra (Osiris) travelled, before being resurrected into the dawn of a new day; and so the raising of Hiram Abif (and Lazarus and Jesus and all Master Masons) is a re-enactment of the rising of Ra (Adhon-Aton) during the dawn of a new day.

This equivalence between the Hiram story and the solar cults of Egypt gives us yet another yardstick to measure Masonry by. It would now appear that even the Temple of Solomon myth, which is perhaps the most central aspect within the Craft, is simply another addition that has been grafted onto the rituals in later years. Alternatively, as has been argued previously, the original myths of the building of the Temple may have been based upon the construction of the original Temple of Masonry – the Great

Pyramid. The later myths about the Temple of Solomon were amendments to the original story that were made during an era in which access to the Great Pyramid had been lost.

Either of these scenarios would tend to suggest that if we were to part the obfuscating veils of the millennia, the core of Masonry and masonic ritual would be seen to be based in the solar cults of Egypt. But if this is so, then what kind of secret could lie at the heart of such an ancient cult that would still have any relevance in today's world? What kind of secret could a high priest of Ra from five or more millennia ago know, which would make people go to Lodge in the twenty-first century? The answer must, perforce, be nothing; and if this is so then it would seem that we have hit the well-concealed buffers of Masonry, and the Craft must therefore be a house of cards that is based upon the bluff that it contains hidden secrets.

Actually, that is not so, for there *is* a 'big' secret at the center of Craft Masonry, and the first clue may come from Canon Demant, Professor of Theology at Oxford University. In answer to a question from a non-Mason investigator, as to whether the rituals of Masonry are compatible with Christianity, he stated:

> If (the masonic oaths of initiation) are taken seriously then it must be put down as rash swearing, for there is no certainty that the Christian initiate will not find afterwards that he has joined <u>an alien cult</u>. [21]

As far as the questioner was concerned, Canon Demant's answer was supposed to be implying that Masonry and Christianity were incompatible, but the answer may also be taken to be a literal explanation of Masonry itself, as we shall see. It is entirely possible that the canon was actually a Master Mason himself and was issuing a carefully crafted reply to his non-masonic questioner in order to play a small joke upon the *muggles* of this world. The second clue is perhaps contained in the Master Mason's manual, which states that:

> The lost secrets are the nature and attributes of god, which must be realised by each man himself. [22]

If Bro Ward is correct, then we are possibly looking for a secret that will tell us something profound about who or what god was, or is. But, as has already been established, that secret would also have to be somehow relevant to the Western world in the twenty-first century as much as it was to the Old Testament patriarchs and the priesthood of Heliopolis. So what could this secret be? And what kind of secret could have perpetuated a secret society for five or more thousand years?

A1 - Masons

The teaching of this 'big secret' tends to be centered on the Holy Royal Arch (HRA), which is comprised of a conclave of selected Master Masons who are cordially invited to join another, separate club. Holy Royal Arch is sometimes said to be another degree, although many would dispute that, but nevertheless the organisation of HRA is slightly different from Craft Masonry with members meeting in Chapters instead of Lodges – although the same temple is normally used for meetings to save on expense. This is why many Masons have no idea what their organisation is really all about; for unlike the introductions to Craft Masonry, in which a candidate can apply for membership, Chapter Masonry is by invitation only. There is also the problem that there are some Chapters that are so overtly religious that this particular lecture would be unacceptable, and so the brothers of that Chapter will be none the wiser. Indeed, one American Christian Mason I spoke to about this subject banged the table and declared that this was impossible, as Masonry would not allow such a suggestion. There are none so blind as those who will not see, as they say.

The reason for this 'big secret' never reaching the public domain is twofold. Firstly, in the not too distant past anyone airing this secret in public would have been burned at the stake – not by angry Masons I might add, but by the Catholic priesthood. Secondly, in the more liberal modern era, this same public airing of the 'big' masonic secret may well result in public ridicule and possibly a floundering career – and again, this persecution would not necessarily be orchestrated by fellow Masons, but by the media in general. Both of these perceived 'punishments' have been, and still are, very effective ways of ensuring that the masonic secret remains hidden, even to this day.

So what kind of secret can be so diabolical to the ancient ear, and yet so humorous and possibly embarrassing to the modern ear? What kind of secret could be so important and so potentially devastating that it has been held back from the public arena for five or perhaps even twelve thousand years? Furthermore, if this secret is such a thorny issue that it has taxed the minds of monarchs, theologians and leaders for millennia, should anyone be so cavalier as to unilaterally divulge it to the world? What of the social ramifications? What if there were to be rioting on the streets?

Well, fundamental as this secret may be, I don't think that its public airing will cause any social disruption. For a start, this explanation is not coming from a 'reputable' source, and so it can and will be dismissed as complete nonsense by all and sundry. It will especially be dismissed by the Craft as being nonsense, as they have a vested interest in maintaining their secret – even after it has been divulged. In effect it will still be secret, because nobody will believe that the secret has actually been given already and so the allusion of a secret will still be maintained. This is the problem when dealing with secret organisations, for an intelligent, logical individual starts to distrust everything that is said and done in the name of that organisation. But not everyone is quite so rational and one esoteric researcher stated on a discussion site that, soon after joining the Masons, he was told all of their secrets – which did cause some general amusement that anyone could be quite so naive. Secret societies, especially those designed around three or thirty-three levels of initiation, are purposely designed to maintain secrets and divulge them on a strict need-to-know basis.

So, in regard to the masonic 'big secret', although this secret information would definitely cause an amount of social upheaval if it was announced on the six o'clock news by the president of the United States, its publication in the back of a relatively obscure esoteric book will certainly not set the world on fire. So it is a justifiable and socially responsible act to disclose this secret to readers, and personally I believe that a lot of the world's religious infighting may be curbed by this knowledge – although there is an outside possibility that some religious groups would actively resist this knowledge and thus cause further disruption.

'So stop blabbing and tell us what the secret is,' I hear readers cry. 'What is the big secret of Masonry?' Well, simply put, the big secret of the last few millennia is that god was an astronaut – or more precisely they were astronauts in the plural, and they arrived here complete with a suitable spaceship. In essence, this revelation does not change the world one iota. God is still god, and all we have done here is to dress him (or her) up in a spacesuit of some description. I suppose this may mean that god is not as all-powerful as some people would like to imagine – and so they may have to re-adjust themselves to a world in which god does not look over their shoulder every minute of the day and they therefore have to take the responsibility of making their own judgements and decisions – but in theory nothing should change.* But of course, theory and reality are two different worlds.

Try walking into Mecca and declaring to the faithful there that Allah was a spaceman! I can guarantee that any such foolhardy individual would be torn literally limb from limb by the practitioners of the 'Religion of Peace'. Of course this foolhardy proposal will never happen, primarily

---

* This is a logical truth anyway. If there were an all-powerful deity constantly looking after mankind, then it is guilty of failing to prevent wars, volcanos, hurricanes, pestilence, earthquakes and tsunamis, and thus guilty of failing to save millions of lives. Either such an ever-present deity is relatively powerless, or it is a scheming, malevolent being reminiscent of the gods of both the Torah and Greek mythology. This would be a deity who enjoys stirring up mayhem in the world of man, fascinated with the panic and destruction it can create; a petulant child who likes poking holes in an ant's nest to see the ants scurry around.

because the Religion of Peace is such an open and welcoming faith that it bans all non-Muslims from entering Mecca in the first place, and the penalties for transgressing this law are severe. So although Atheists, Agnostics and the majority of Protestants would not have a problem with this 'alien' suggestion, there are still many sects and societies around the world that would. It is these backward elements in theology that give the masonic hierarchy a problem in dealing with this knowledge, for the reactions of these unstable, fundamentalist religions are unpredictable. The obvious solution to this problem would be to have an army and police force in the Arab states during the unsettling period when the information is being divulged, to cool the irrational Muslim hotheads, which may be one of the reasons why America has invaded Iraq.

What then of these aliens? What was the purpose of their visit and their effects on man's history? Well, it would appear that there was more than one astronaut on this interstellar vessel, and it would seem that they were flesh-and-blood beings that looked remarkably similar to the modern science-fiction depiction of the Grey alien.** Their primary task was one of exploration and research, and each individual 'alien' was given the task of educating and imparting one aspect of a functioning civilisation to the ignorant hominids who inhabited the Earth at that time. It was through this process that the myriad of Egyptian deities were formed, with each god

** As mentioned in the book *Jesus*, this knowledge is very ancient and it is the explanation for Pharaoh Akhenaton's distorted physique. Like all Grand Masters, Akhenaton was aware of the bodily form of the gods that landed on Earth, an event that is said to have occurred some 12,500 years ago, as this was the original foundation upon which the Egyptian religion was conceived. Akhenaton therefore instructed his artists to draw the Amarna family in this same likeness, and it was this requirement that prompted the gross distortions in the representations of the Amarna family – with the fat hips, slight bust, no genitalia and elongated heads with narrow jaws and almond-shaped eyes.

It has been suggested by some Egyptologists that Akhenaton suffered from a disease, and Cyril Aldred in particular cites Frohlich's syndrome as a possibility. But clearly this was not the real shape of these people as the whole family all degenerate by degrees into these profoundly distorted figures, and then they seem to become more human again at the end of the Amarna period. More importantly, perhaps, are the busts of Nefertiti, Akhenaton and the princesses, which were found in the art studios of Djhutmose at Amarna. It is an undeniable fact that all these busts are anatomically precise and correct; indeed, the Berlin bust of Nefertiti could not be more perfect if it tried. Undoubtedly, the distorted representations of the Amarna royal family were deliberate artistic representations of something very special to the king in particular, and that something was the true shape of the gods. It was a shape that was not to be represented again until the rise of the 'grey' alien in popular science-fiction literature and, like their Amarna predecessors, the 'greys' have a slight bust, no genitalia and elongated heads with narrow jaws and almond-shaped eyes.

(alien) having their individual functions and responsibilities. These were not anthropocentric social divisions, with each trade and social sector in Egyptian society devising their own patron god; quite the reverse, the deification was a direct response to individual gods (aliens) creating those trades and social sectors in the first place. If a 'female' alien called Maat presided over justice, then justice was linked to the goddess Maat, and so on and so forth.

One of the most fundamental sectors of knowledge given to mankind by these aliens was the secrets of secular (that is operative) masonry and architecture – how to build in stone – and so it is not surprising that this section of the emerging society saw their 'god' in architectural terms. It was through this process that the masonic 'god' became the Great Architect, who taught the functions and usage of the level, the compass, the plumb and the square. He was the all-powerful being who always spoke in terms of length and breadth, and who could cut granite like butter with his infinitely superior technology. This was the masonic 'god' who conceived and designed the Great Pyramid, a structure that was designed to indelibly encode mathematical and other esoteric secrets into a structure that would endure the millennia, and so it is not so surprising that the fraternity who inherited these traditions in later generations should revere the Giza site and couch their every ritual and function in architectural terms. The smiths (metalworkers), farmers and arkwrights (boat-builders) would have said the same about the aliens (gods) who taught them their trades, but unfortunately these alternative legends were scattered to the four winds in later generations and their traditions are lost to us. Thus, of all the trade guilds that were established at this pivotal starting point in man's history, only the masonic (Judaic) history of this era survives, which is why the Torah is so littered with construction details and sacred measurements.

That is the masonic secret in a nutshell, and it goes some way towards explaining an enduring facet of Masonry. It has long been accepted by adherents of masonic mythology that there are various pseudo-masonic cults scattered across the globe. It is because of these scattered sister-societies that the phrase 'the Sun is always at the meridian in respect to Freemasonry' was derived. As mentioned previously, this phrase is probably the foundation for the Victorian boast that 'the Sun never sets on the British Empire', and both simply refer to the global extent of these institutions and the fact that it will always be midday (local time) over one Lodge or another on some part of the globe.

However, this worldwide spread of Masonry was not thought to have been a recent globalisation that rode upon the back of the British Empire, for these alternative masonic societies are thought to be thousands of years old. The general understanding here is that the 'gods' (aliens) spread their educational message to all of the various primitive hominid groups that were already spread across the globe. This enforced diversity was a sensible precaution, to guard against mother nature or social incompetence from snuffing out one particular culture and thus ending the entire educational project. It is also likely that there was an element of social experimentation involved, with various differences in these proto-cultures being deliberately introduced to see which would prosper and which would fail. Whatever the reasoning for this global diversity, each of these manufactured human cultures also had a masonic-type cult embedded at its core, which was charged with keeping and propagating this secret history. It is the remnants of these masonic cults that are the source of these myths of a global masonic presence.

Having disclosed this rather controversial and contentious information, perhaps the next biggest secret that should be considered is where these aliens came from, what they looked like, when this all happened and when they expect to return. Unfortunately, I am not privy to most of this information and I am not even sure that anyone in the world is, but I can make some calculated guesses.

The ancient astronauts are thought by many to have arrived on Earth some 12,000 years ago, when Leo was the dominant precessional constellation. They looked something like the image that Akhenaton tried to portray with his distorted head and body, as has been explained in the notes to this chapter. They preferred to operate in hot climates, which may reflect their own physiological preference. Their point of origin could well have been Sirius, as this is one of the predominant stars in Egyptian theology; although this is likely to have been a staging post rather than this civilisation's home star. Finally, one of the most important questions is: are these aliens still visiting us, as people like to make out with all these 'abduction' stories?

The answer to this is a resounding 'no', and for three reasons. Firstly, one of the prime beliefs in Judaeo-Christianity concerns the 'second coming'. The implication of this fundamental belief is that the second visitation, if it ever happens, will be a well-known stage-managed event in the distant future, and not something that could be covered up by the authorities. Besides, the idea that an intelligent, technologically superior race of beings would wish to travel hundreds of light years across the galaxy in order to cut some fancy shapes in a field of corn is utterly laughable. One newspaper cartoon recently summed up this theory rather succinctly by portraying a forlorn-looking alien standing in a muddy field saying: 'Damn, it's winter, we'll have to go home again!' But the fact that such a bizarre explanation is acceptable to so many people demonstrates the desire that large sections of the population have to 'believe' in something. Indeed, that is the prime function of the nocturnal groups who traverse the fields of Wiltshire in England with grass-rollers, balls of string and GPS sets – they seek to encourage people to believe in the possibility of alien life.

Secondly, one of the basic tenets of the Emerald Tablets – the supposed writings of Thoth that were assembled by esoteric groups with a similar interest to the 'corn-rollers' – was that mankind is alone in making his deliberations and the 'gods' are not necessarily looking over our shoulder, guiding us along some predestined path. The pre-Christian traditions maintain that we are alone in the world and have to make our own judgements and future.

Thirdly, the recent alien abduction craze, and all its associated reporting, is yet more masonic propaganda that is deliberately designed and executed to keep the subject of alien life in the public eye. From films like *Star Wars* and *Men in Black*, to television series like *Dark Skies* and *The X-Files*, it has been a masonic priority to keep the possibility of intelligent alien life in the public arena so that the acceptance of these views becomes commonplace. This propaganda, although very crude in some respects, is nevertheless highly effective. Only three hundred years ago the reader would have been burned at the stake for suggesting that alien life from another star had visited this Earth; a hundred years ago, you might have been placed in a lunatic asylum; nowadays, you might be laughed at; tomorrow, it might be accepted as an absolute truth – just look at how far we have come in the tolerance of these beliefs in such a short space of time.

Whether the disclosure of the masonic secret in this book will ever be acceptable to society in general, as a historical truth, will ultimately depend on there being similar disclosures from more authoritative sources. However, even if there were an open admission by presidents and prime ministers that god was an alien, there would still be a significant percentage of doubters, and the absolute proof will perhaps depend upon whether these same masonic sources have any real evidence that they can demonstrate to the world. There are elements of proof that are already visible, of course, and these comprise the impossible constructions that are dotted around the world; constructions like Giza, Cuzco and Baalbek. At Giza they were struggling with 300-tonne blocks of stone, whereas at Baalbek they incomprehensibly decided to use 1,200-tonne blocks of stone. These huge masses are utterly impossible for a Bronze Age society to have worked and manipulated, and yet they did. So there *is* evidence out there, if readers will allow their minds the freedom of movement to digest it. But in all probability this will not be enough, and so eventually the demand will arise for further proof. And what form will that evidence take?

The answer to this lies in the nature of the Holy Grail. The Grail, as I explained in the book *Thoth*, was a composite image of a cup or chalice that represented the womb of Mary Magdalene and thus the bloodline of Jesus. This truth was explained very well recently in the entertaining novel *The Da Vinci Code*, but what this book failed to highlight was that Mary Magdalene was Jesus' sister-wife and that the bloodline of Jesus was the bloodline of the pharaohs of Egypt. [Jesus followed the normal pharaonic tradition and married his sister.] But there is one large snag with this bloodline theory, and that is the enduring wealth and influence of the Grail family.

It is said that this wealth and influence was based upon documentary evidence that Jesus was married and had children, evidence that was rediscovered by the Templars in the twelfth century AD. That may be so, but in that case, how did the Grail family manoeuvre themselves into the Merovingian dynasty of French kings in the fifth century? Simply stating that your family was descended from Jesus would, in that era, have resulted in a slow grilling over a fire rather than a marriage alliance with a king. Somehow, throughout the millennia, the pharaonic and Grail family have maintained, lost and then regained power and influence across Europe and the Western world. So how was this done?

Well, the Grail was always envisioned as being a multifaceted concept and so it may have had both a material and a metaphorical nature. The masonic hierarchy like to hint at there being a really foolproof alien artifact of some nature, hidden away in the vaults of some secret U.S. government facility, something that will convince the greatest of ancient kings and modern sceptics alike. If so, then this could be the material Holy Grail that has been guarded so carefully through the ages. But for the foreseeable future, that possibility remains a well-controlled rumour – one of the many strands of information and disinformation that are liberally spread around the world in order to further fuel and confuse both the common man and the common Mason alike.

DNA

Because of this tradition of an other-worldly origin for Freemasonry, the Craft has always contained elements of knowledge about the arts and sciences that were supposed to have been derived from these alien sources. It is for this reason that Masonry has long venerated the sciences, even during eras when that kind of freethinking activity was banned. The activities of Sir Isaac Newton and his fellow scientists would have been considered heretical by the Catholic Church, and he could only have carried out his work under the guidance of masonic influences. Although it has been said that there is no evidence that Newton himself was a Mason, he is sometimes claimed to have been a Grand Master of the Priory of Sion, reputedly one of the most important of the many branches of Masonry.

It was due to this desire for rational scientific discovery that one of the first institutions set up by the Masons, after their emergence into the public arena in 1717, was the Royal Society. The Royal Society is still, of course, one of Britain's premier scientific institutions, which demonstrates the level of support for scientific understanding within early Masonry.*

Part of this early masonic gnosticism is what we would understand as being pure science to this day. The tradition, for instance, that there were accurate spheres (representations) of the Earth and of the Cosmos perched on top of the pillars of King Solomon's temple is regarded as being true in masonic circles. If so, however, this represents a level of knowledge about the world and the Universe, dating from 1000 BC, that was not regained until the voyages of Christopher Columbus in the Middle Ages.

However, much of the additional scientific knowledge within Masonry would be regarded as being metaphysical to modern scientists, as it lies outside the realms of modern understanding. Having said that, it is true that this metaphysical knowledge has turned out to be correct on occasions. Newton's concept of 'action at a distance' was pure metaphysics to the 'scientists' of the era, perhaps akin to modern scientists factoring psychokinesis into their equations. Yet we quite happily accept Newton's improbable proposal today, and call it gravity.

One of the pieces of ancient knowledge that was passed down to mankind through the conduit of Masonry, was a knowledge of the fundamental components of biology and life – DNA. It is of no coincidence that the symbol of medicine and life in Egypt was the double intertwined snake of the Caduceus, a symbol that invokes a clear image of the double intertwined molecules of DNA. What are the chances that the Egyptians just happened to pick out the same double-helix imagery for their version of the symbol of life and medicine? One would have thought it to be an infinitesimal chance, but nevertheless the Greeks adopted the same symbol and so, eventually, did the English. Shakespeare says of Life:

> For in that sleep of death what dreams may come, when we have shuffled off this mortal coil.[23]

From exactly where did Shakespeare get the image of life being a coil? The answer seems to be obvious, as he was following in the established Egypto-Greek concept of the Caduceus, the double-coiled snake imagery of the DNA molecule. So here we have the odd notion that the ancients knew of the exact molecular structure of DNA thousands of years before the technology was available to investigate the subject. There are only two ways of dealing

---

* The early Gnostics could also perhaps be termed 'scientists'. The Greek word *gnosis* means 'knowledge', as does the Latin *scientia*. It is from the latter that the English term 'science' was derived.

with this conundrum; either you close your eyes to the obvious and blindly shout 'coincidence', or instead you look at the situation more rationally and wonder if the ancients were assisted in some manner. The truth is, of course, that the precise structure of DNA was given to the ancients by the aliens. Indeed, the ancients probably did not fully understand the information they were being given, but simply knew that the double snake imagery was closely linked to life and the medical profession.

Fig 9.3   The double snakes of the Caduceus.

Having preserved that information into the modern era through masonic channels, twentieth century scientists were then in a better position to study the subject, because they already had an inkling of what they might find. I can imagine that there were some very satisfied people around the world when Watson and Crick announced in 1953 that life was created and composed of tiny double helixes. It was scientific confirmation that the history of Masonry really was based upon a previous technical knowledge that was far in advance of our own.

Hollow Earth

One other enduring component of masonic mythology is the hollow Earth. This enduring concept has spawned many a tale including the famous *Journey to the Center of the Earth*, by Jules Verne in 1864. But the suggestion that the Earth might be hollow is regarded as laughable today, and so the topic is regarded as being on the fringes of fringe science. However, it is a fact that gravity results from the attraction of matter to matter, and so for any particle that lies at the very center of the Earth, its local gravity attraction will be away from the center of the Earth. This attraction away from the center would be the same in all directions, and so the particle at the center of the Earth would be essentially weightless.

But what if the gravitational field were not symmetrical, or what if a small bubble formed in these weightless conditions at the very center of the Earth? In the bubble scenario, logic would dictate that for a particle at the edge of the bubble, the gravity field would be very slightly stronger on the particle's side of the bubble than the opposite side of the bubble. In other words, there would be an infinitesimal gravitational component that would tend to perpetuate the bubble's growth, or at least ensure that the bubble was a stable entity. Furthermore, the larger the bubble, the greater this differential gravitational attraction across the bubble, and so the dimensions of the void would tend to increase and accelerate. In addition, the centripetal reaction (centripetal force) resulting from the bubble rotating with the Earth would further increase the forces expanding the dimensions of this central void.

No doubt an equilibrium would be achieved at some point in time, but the result of all these forces would be an Earth with an elliptical hollow core. This would not be the habitable environment of popular lore, of course, just an incredibly hot void of whatever dimensions at the center of the Earth. Since contemporary science is unable to detect what lies at the very core of the Earth, the explanations currently given for the Earth's composition are wholly based upon guesswork. The main plank of contemporary arguments are based upon the mass and magnetism of the Earth, which strongly suggests a solid or liquid (depending on local temperature and pressure) iron core. However, it is also true that a small void a few hundred miles across at the center of the Earth would not significantly affect any of these arguments and calculations.

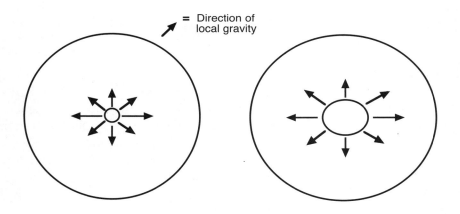

Fig 9.4   A growing, slightly elliptical (oblate) void at the center of the Earth.

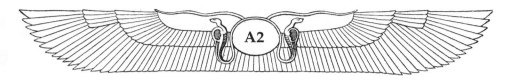

St George and the Dragon

The small snippet of information that led me to write this sub-thesis was a very simple connection between Aapop (Apophis) ⟨hieroglyphs⟩, the evil serpent of the Underworld (the Duat or Djuat), and fire. It would seem that Aapop was described as having fiery attributes in the original Egyptian mythology. Furthermore, from the convoluted tales in the *Shat am Djuat* ⟨hieroglyphs⟩ – which is more commonly known as the *Book of the Dead* – it would appear that Aapop was also supposed to have been capable of producing thunder, lightning, clouds and fog, in addition to fire. Since Aapop was being described as a fiery serpent, I began to wonder if this imagery was connected in any way to the typical Medieval dragon. Further research led me onto a possible connection with the Hebrew word *saraph* שרף which also refers to a fiery serpent. In fact, these creatures were the other-worldly *seraphim* from the Book of Isaiah, which could fly and breathe fire just like a Medieval dragon. Was it possible that these Hebrew and Egyptian terms could be linked in any way? Was Aapop the archetypal dragon from western mythology?

By its very nature, this research then led me onto Medieval legends and dragon mythology. Like the *seraphim* of the Old Testament, these Medieval creatures were often depicted as being akin to long scaly snakes with wings, claws and the ability to breathe fire. Apart from the wings and claws, this was a description that was very similar to depictions of the Egyptian Aapop. But although Aapop is not depicted as a flying snake, it must have had flying attributes as the word *aap* ⟨hieroglyphs⟩ means 'fly' while *aapi* ⟨hieroglyphs⟩ or ⟨hieroglyphs⟩ refers to the winged Sun-disk. Note that the Sun-disk of Ra can be flanked with either the wing motif, the snake motif or both.

So it would seem that Aapop and the Medieval dragon had many similarities. Both of these creatures were also said to be evil creatures that fought with people or gods on many occasions. In Medieval tradition it was

St George who fought the fiery dragon, but in Egyptian mythology it was Seth who fought with Aapop. So what were these legendary battles with dragons all about, and are there any similarities and common traditions that might link these two stories together?

Seth ∏ 🐾 was visualised as a doglike creature, which is why he is sometimes confused with Anubis, the jackal god of the mortuary, and why his attributes and title have occasionally been confused with those of the *sab* 🐾 meaning 'wolf' or 'jackal'. The main differences between these two gods is that Anubis is recognisably a jackal, while Seth has long floppy ears, an upright tail, and a resemblance that is difficult to pin down to any one particular canine. It has been suggested that Seth may be an abstract animal, or perhaps even a donkey, but the latter is unlikely because of the tail position. The tail was definitely a representation of an animal marking its territory through spraying, which is not a trait of the equine family. That this tail imagery was linked to the marking of territories is fairly certain, as wherever the name Seth can be found in the Egyptian dictionary, with its many varied spellings, there is sure to be a reference to smells. Sometimes the smell is described as a perfume, but it can equally be a stench, which may be considered to be an accurate description of the marking of a fox or jackal, but may also be propaganda designed to demonise Seth.

The apparent dichotomy between a perfume and a stench is easily explainable, as there are numerous instances in the Egyptian lexicon where the same word has acquired diametrically opposed meanings – an oddity which is most probably due to the long-standing differences between the two major religious factions in the country. This opposition in meaning has also occurred in English on occasions, and one example is the name given to a wallflower. This particular sweet-smelling flower was supposedly named after William, the Duke of Cumberland, who defeated the Scottish army of Charles Stuart on the fields of Culloden Moor in 1746. As this was an English victory the flower was known in that country as the 'sweet william', whereas the defeated Scots had their own opinion about this army commander and so called the same flower 'stinkin billy'.[1]

Although Seth is often regarded as being a personification of evil, in addition to being the god of chaos and confusion, his violent nature was put to good use in the protection of the Sun-god Ra from Aapop (the snake-dragon or sea serpent), as the night-barque sailed through the underworld of the Duat. During this perilous night journey, Aapop barred the way of the solar-barque and in the ensuing fight between Seth and Aapop the latter was wounded each evening and morning, and it was the serpent's blood that turned the sky red. (Note the dualism here, with this story contrasting greatly with the feminine story of Nut giving birth to the Sun each morning, and the redness being the blood associated with this birth.) Seth was also sometimes considered to be one of the eyes of Ra, and since Seth was considered to be evil, the notion of the 'evil eye' developed. To 'give the evil eye' implied that there was a possibility of impending conflict, the very attribute that was associated with Seth.

In comparison with this ancient Egyptian mythology, the legends regarding St George only go back to the 4th century AD, where he is sometimes associated with a tribune in the Roman army who was martyred at Lydda in Syria. However, the fact that this soldier may have been associated with St George in some manner does not mean that he was the original St George, and so it is highly likely that the traditions attributed to St George go back much further than the late Roman era. Indeed, the main problem with these assertions about a real soldier from the third century AD called St George, is the fact that this same character also seems to appear in the Bible:

> And there was war in heaven: Michael and his angels fought against the dragon; and the dragon fought and his angels. And prevailed not; neither was their place found any more in heaven. And the great dragon was cast out, that old serpent, <u>called</u> the Devil, and Satan, which deceiveth the whole world: he was cast out into the earth, and his angels were cast out with him. [B2]

Here we have a story about an 'archangel' called Michael, who was considered to be the patron saint of the Israelites, and his battle with a serpent or dragon that was the personification of evil. If this tale sounds a little familiar then it should do, as this is exactly the same story as the St George legend, but this story goes all the way back into the Old Testament and the history of the Israelite's exile in Babylon – or about 580 BC. As well as slaying the dragon, St Michael was also the heroic archangel who fought for Israel in its time of need, and so he represents both the power of good over evil and the protector of the people, just as does St George. In the book of Daniel, for instance, we read that:

> ...at that time shall Michael stand up, the great prince which standeth for the children (of Israel) and there shall be a time of trouble. [B3]

This event demonstrates that St Michael was known for assisting the whole Israelite nation in times of need, and it was reputed to have occurred in the third year of the reign of Cyrus, king of Persia; which again places St Michael at a much earlier date than is traditionally attributed to St George. St Michael was therefore the heroic champion of the Israelite people, but when significant elements of the Israelite nation emigrated to Europe during the many exiles and emigrations from their troubled homeland, they naturally took their traditions with them.

In which case, it should not be so surprising that the same story should be repeated in a European context, and that is exactly what we find when William of Malmesbury informs us that St George was seen to be assisting the Franks at the battle of Antioch in 1098 during the Crusades. It was these legends and attributes that made St George the patron saint of armies as well as nations, and it was for this reason that Shakespeare had Henry V powerfully invoke the memory of St George, as the respective armies of the English and French squared up to each other on the fateful field of Agincourt:

> I see you stand like greyhounds in the slips,
> Straining upon the start. The game's afoot:
> Follow your spirit; and, upon this charge
> Cry God for Harry, England and St George! [4]

Certainly it would seem that the characters of St Michael and St George share some very similar characteristics, which may indicate that they were once considered to be the same person. But if this is so, then this represents yet more evidence to demonstrate that the European royalty and elite were descended from Hyksos-Israelite ancestors. St Michael was an Israelite hero, and yet he had been metamorphosed into a distinctly European champion.

So is there any further evidence that might demonstrate that these two mythical heroes were one and the same? Well, perhaps the best evidence comes from an event that occurred back in 1818, when the Prince Regent created a new chivalrous order that was curiously called 'The Most Distinguished Order of St Michael and St George'. Rightly or wrongly, it would appear that many people did consider St George and St Michael to be closely linked at the very least.

At a later date this chivalrous order was divided into three elements by William IV: these were the Knight Grand Cross of St Michael and St George; Knight Commander of St Michael and St George; and Companion of St Michael and St George. I would imply from this constant dual emphasis, contained as it is within one of the most prestigious royal orders, that someone wants us to know that St Michael and St George were actually the same character. But if this is so, then the true era for the life of St George must be pushed at least back into the early Israelite era, a thousand years or more before the Roman period that is currently assigned to him.

Another famous order that is directly associated with St George is the Order of the Garter. Legend has it that the Order was begun by Edward III in 1348, when he was supposedly rather taken by the beauty of Joan, the Countess of Salisbury. While dancing, her garter is said to have slipped from her leg and so Edward picked it up and placed it on his own left knee. Noting the peculiar glances from his companions, he apparently exclaimed "*Honi soit qui mal y pense*" or "Shame on he who thinks evil of this", and this quotation became the motto of the order. [5]

But this is simply another sugary tale to hide a deeper meaning, for does anyone really think that the most prestigious royal order would be based upon an event so trivial as an eye for a pretty woman and a lost garter? What possible chivalrous duties could its members be charged with; checking ladies for loose hosiery perhaps? It sounds more like a recipe for an assault charge than the basis for a respectable royal order. And why should this wayward garter be so closely associated with the heroic deeds of St George?

Instead, one rather suspects that the imagery of placing a garter on a leg has more to do with Masons rolling up their trouser legs for an initiation than an undergarment of the Countess of Salisbury. A more rational explanation, which is sometimes given, is that the imagery of the garter was actually derived from the design of the ribbon and pendant badge that was often shown in depictions of St George; and so the badges of the Order of the Garter are still known as 'the George'. The blue ribbon of the garter may equally reflect the blue ribbon that bears the jewel of a Master Mason. But these may still not be the full explanation, and an alternative can be derived by employing the usual Hyksos delight in wordplay: Edward III's exclamation was most probably "*Honni soit qui mal y pense*", rather than "*Honi soit qui mal y pense*" and the alternative version would mean "Honour on he who thinks evil of this". Or, in other words, this new interpretation implies that only the honoured, that is the members of the Order, would know that the garter was an icon of 'evil', or more accurately an icon of Seth.

But perhaps this association between St George and Seth needs further explanation. The epigraphic evidence seems to indicate that the Egyptian words *shet* and *seshet* refer to 'Seth', a 'secret' and a 'garter'. More precisely, this Egyptian garment was supposed to have been a hidden, blue-coloured garter. Surprisingly enough, this is also what the garter of St George is – a hidden, blue-coloured garter. If this explanation is in any way true, then the Order of the Garter would seem to be honouring the memory of Seth, and therefore intimately linking the legends of Seth with the legend of St George. In support of this Egyptian connection, perhaps it is worth pointing out that Pharaoh Akhenaton was often portrayed as wearing a garter (and not much else). Thus it is entirely possible that the Order of the Garter goes back at least as far as the Egyptian New Kingdom era.

The precise function and form of this hidden blue garter is difficult to fathom. Presumably Seth was linked in some way to a blue ribbon, but Egyptian evidence for this is lacking. The only evidence that I could find does, however, give an explanation for how the Torah has managed

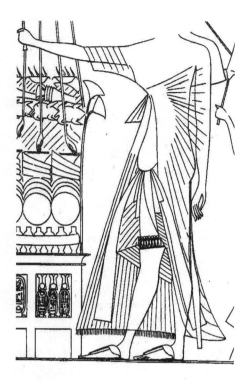

Fig 10.1   Akhenaton wearing a garter.

to derive the name Michael for its equivalent hero. This alternative name for St George has been created simply because the word *maker (makel)* ⬛⬛ means 'blue', and so the name used for St Michael in the Old Testament was derived from the colour of St George's garter. These references to a blue ribbon may also be related to the fact that Craft Masonry is known as Blue Lodge Masonry; although whether this title was derived from the blue ribbon symbology, or from a more fundamental source that eventually led to the blue ribbon symbology, is uncertain. Whatever the case, the jewel of a Master Mason is usually hung on a blue ribbon and so the wearing of that same ribbon in a concealed location on the leg, and thus concealing the allegiances of the wearer, may have been part of the reasoning for this custom.

Some of the other names and phrases which were used in the biblical verses from the Book of Revelations – as quoted at the beginning of this chapter and which were originally written in Greek – may also have been taken from Egyptian originals. The serpent that St Michael [St George] fought was called Ophis Οφις in these New Testament verses, which just has to be a shortening of the name Ap<u>ophis</u>, which is the Greek form of the Egyptian serpent Aapop. So St Michael was fighting the Egyptian Aapop, just as Seth and St George were. Then we see that Satan – the Devil – was called Satanus Σατανας, and this term was derived from the Hebrew Seten (Satan) שטן, which was in turn derived from the Egyptian Set (Seth) ⬛⬛ .

Finally, the devil is also known as Diablos Διαβολος in the Greek, the slanderer, which could have come from the name Djebha ⬛⬛ . It is said that this alternative name for Set was derived from his association with the *djeb* hippopotamus, but I think it more likely that it was primarily derived from the number 10,000, which was *djeba* ⬛⬛ . As I demonstrated in the book *Solomon*, the word *djeba* was also a title as it referred to an army commander (and was spelt with a 𓉔 glyph) who presided over 10,000 men – and a link between the warrior-god Seth and an army commander would be eminently suitable.

Fig 10.2   Horus as St George.

But if this were the case, then this verse from Revelations seems to mix all of these characters together at various points in its narrative. If this is so, then it would seem that the Bible has sometimes confused and amalgamated Seth with Aapop, as does Egyptian mythology on a few occasions. This is entirely possible, as the later traditions of Ptolemaic Egypt elevated the role of the more honourable and heroic Horus over the dubious credentials of his uncle Seth. This is why we can sometimes see St George depicted as Horus fighting the crocodile figure of Seth. Thus, in this revised montage, we see the heroic Horus taking the place of Seth, and a pseudo, dragon-like Seth taking the place of the serpent Aapop. With this mythology being so malleable, it is no wonder that confusions have arisen so frequently.

These arguments and translations, if they are accepted, firmly equate St Michael and St George with the Egyptian mythology surrounding Seth (and Horus), and so this may well take this Medieval legend right back into the dimmest regions of history that existed at the very birth of Egyptian culture. This is why St George would appear to have been a lot more influential than a simple Roman soldier, and why he was able to become the patron saint of the Templars, helping them to victory in the first battle of the first crusade, at Dorylaeum in 1097. It was through these Templar military traditions that St George became the patron saint of the scouting movement in Britain, a quasi-military organisation for young boys. Likewise, it was also from the Templar's famous red and white insignia that the English flag was derived, and it is through the Templar veneration of St George that this flag is still called the cross of St George.[6]

In addition to this level of recognition, this rather 'insignificant Roman soldier' also managed to become the patron saint of Moscow, of Aragon, of Catelonia, of Portugal and last but not least, the patron saint of all England. It was in England that his veneration rose to the greatest of heights within the upper echelons of society, and he became associated with (and a patron of) chivalry, English soldiery, and the distinguished Order of the Garter. The humble St George even managed to have a country named after him – Georgia. It is through this shared association with St George that this remote little state on the shores of the Black Sea shares a common national flag with England; with both nations proudly flying the Templar flag of a red cross (sometimes splayed) on a white background.

So where does this leave the investigation? Well, apart from the slaying of the fire-breathing dragon (Aapop), there now appears to have been a number of close connections between the Egyptian god Seth and St George. These include:

The fact that the story of St George was brought back from Palestine during the Crusades, a location where many of these Egyptian legends then resided.

The legend that St George was hacked to pieces and the many parts of his body buried, but that god brought him back to life. This is, of course, a later rendition of the Osirian myth, and since Osiris was the brother of Seth it places the story in the correct Egyptian era and context.

The fact that both Seth and St George were associated with redness. Seth was the god of deserts and considered to be the 'red god', while the emblem of St George is the red cross on a white background. It was through this stylised imagery that St George was also associated with the red, five-petalled rose, which became the emblem of the victorious Lancastrian Tudor royal dynasty in England.

That Seth wounded Aapop with a spear, whereas St George used a lance.

That St George's magic sword, Ascalon, may have been associated with the word *asq* ⟨𓏲𓂝𓂡⟩ , meaning to 'cut up', 'hack to pieces' or 'behead' – the latter being the fate of the serpent-dragon, Aapop.

Both Seth and St George were associated with masculinity, conflict and protection.

And finally, and perhaps most importantly, is the fact that both Seth and St George appear to have had the same name. One of the titles for Seth was Djudju (Djeudje) ⟨𓇥𓅱⟩ , and this is not a million miles away from the Anglicised name, George.

The latter point is rather important, and so is worth exploring further. The Egyptian Dju were actually the mountains of Bakha and Manu, the two mountains of the sunrise and sunset, mountains which I have previously identified with either the Dahshur or Giza pyramids. That the name Djeudje [George] may have been associated with these two pyramids is perhaps confirmed both by the similar hieroglyphic spelling and by the duality of the name. The name for St George is comprised of the two pyramids Djeu and Djeu (Djeu-dje), the pyramids of the sunrise and sunset, and thus the imagery that is being invoked by St George's red cross (or red rose) was originally taken from the imagery of the rising and setting Sun. In reality, the red rose and the red cross invoked the rising and setting of Ra, or perhaps more accurately they portray the blood of the slain Aapop that was splashed across the horizon as Ra emerged triumphant from the perils of the Djuat.

But if St George was red, Seth was red, and the blood of their opponent (Aapop) was red, then how did St Michael become *makerr*, or blue? For the answer to this little conundrum we need to step back into Egyptian mythology once more, and test the waters of some of Seth's other achievements. The other great event in the life of Seth was his epic battle with Horus, the son of Osiris. With Seth having killed his own brother Osiris, Horus decided to avenge his father's death, and during this long conflict with Seth, Horus lost an eye while Seth lost his testicles. This is the well-known Osirian myth, but the important piece of imagery lies in the detail, for Horus was sometimes known as the *khesbetch* ⌀⏀ ⌡⏋ ⏢ , the blue-eyed god. Here, then, is a possible origin of the garter myth; for the ring of blue that represents the garter was probably the blue ring of Horus' iris.

But Horus lost this eye in his epic battle with Seth, and now Seth was the possessor of the blue ring, the 'garter'; and presumably in a piece of mythology that has been lost to us, Seth once wore this ring on his leg. Furthermore, this lost eye of Horus was considered to be a representation of the Moon, which is why we now have in modern mythology the strange notion of there being a 'Blue Moon'. Thus the title for St Michael may have represented a token of Seth's wounding of Horus, the blue eye of Horus.

In conclusion, it was Seth who was the protector of Ra as he journeyed each night through the underworld (the Djuat). It was Seth who, despite, or perhaps because of, his evil nature, completed the Egyptians' love of the duality of life; and yet also performed the heroic deeds that allowed Ra to rise triumphant each morning and illuminate all of creation.

In later generations and traditions, Seth retained this schizophrenic duality of good and evil, but because the concept of theological duality was no longer in vogue, the scribes were forced to separate Seth's various characteristics and names. So as the evil one of the underworld, Seth (Set) retained his original name, and the Torah called him Satan (Setan) שׂטן, the devil who was somehow supposed to be the equal of god in an outwardly monotheistic religion. The peculiar assertion that there was an alternative god of evil, in addition to the usual god of goodness, was a strange Judaeo-Christian dichotomy that appears to demonstrate that the Church was as schizophrenic as Seth's character. But in reality, the Church authorities were simply trying to grapple with these old Egyptian legends and desperately trying to make them fit the contemporary theological environment. Having started with a polytheistic religion of great antiquity, which had a multitude of traditions and gods, it was never going to be an easy task to squeeze it all into a monotheistic, Judaic straightjacket. Undoubtedly there were going to be some bulges and contortions in this unforgivingly rigid bodice, and the invention of two (or more) gods in a monotheistic religion was just one of those contortions.

Another problem for the scribes was the alternative heroic character of Seth as the saviour of Ra (god); for in the rigid, single-minded Judaic world, how could Satan be seen to be a hero and a saviour of god? The answer, as ever, was a name change, and so Seth (Satan) also became the Old Testament's heroic archangel called St Michael (Makerr or Makell), and then the heroic St George (Djeudj) of Medieval mythology.

Here, then, is St George, the patron saint of England. He was nothing less than Seth, the son of Geb and Nut and the brother of Osiris. Seth, the heroic masculine figure who typified the phallic masculinity of Lower Egypt and contrasted himself with the virginal femininity of Upper Egypt. It was the masculine Seth who took on the mighty dragon called Aapop each night and arrived each morning victorious with Aapop slain. It was also Seth [as St George] who likewise slayed the mighty dragon and saved the virginal damsel in distress, who in turn represented the femininity of Upper Egypt. So it was Seth [St George] who became the patron saint of armies throughout the ages, the patron saint of the cavalry in particular, and – since the one word was derived from the other – Seth [St George] naturally became the patron saint of romantic chivalry.

Lucifer

This explanation is also the reason for the masonic veneration of Lucifer – a topic that has long been a problematical aspect of Masonry that the Craft has a great deal of trouble justifying. Like St Michael, Lucifer was an Archangel, but Lucifer was supposed to have been a bit of a rebel and 'fell' from heaven.

> How art thou fallen from heaven, O Lucifer, son of the (dawn)! How art thou
> cut down to the ground, which did weaken the nations! [B7]

As is usual, this translation is not entirely certain, and perhaps the prime
conundrum is the identity of Lucifer. The English translation mentions
'Lucifer', and this was taken from the Hebrew *heylel* הירכב, which can be
taken to mean 'shining one'. This was supposed to be a reference to the
Morning Star, or Venus, which the Greeks called *phosphorus* φωσφωρος and
the Romans called *lucifer*, with both of these names denoting the 'shining
one' or Venus. But the Syriac Torah appears to break the word into two
components and produce *h-eylel* ה-ירכב, which rather changes the meaning
as we can now derive 'the howling one'.

So which interpretation was right: the 'shining one', the 'son of the
morning', or the 'howling one'? The correct version is probably the 'shining
one', although the astronomical body in question may not have been Venus
at all, because *herar (helal)* refers more to the Sun. Venus is said to
be the morning star as it is the only 'star' that is visible in the predawn glow,
but the Sun itself is also a morning star; only a little larger. The 'shining one'
was said to be the 'son of the morning', and yet the Sun is also a son of the
morning, as it was sometimes said to be ritually born from the vagina of the
goddess Nut each morning in the never-ending cycle of death and rebirth.

But there are other deficiencies in the established translation, and
sorting out these problems may assist in clarifying who Lucifer really was.
The keywords in this verse, in their original order, are:

איך נפלת מ:שמים הילל בן-שחר נגדעת ל:ארץ חולש על-גוים

How, fallen, heaven, shining-one, son of dawn, cut down, Earth, weak,
people.

Now this is a strange and varied smattering of words that does not make
any immediate sense. Disturbed by this randomness and senselessness, the
Brenton's Septuagint Bible has managed to contort these words and derive:

> How has Lucifer, that rose in the morning, fallen from heaven! He that sent
> orders to all the nations is crushed to the earth.

All of which goes to show how some Bibles take liberties with the text.
Readers may again see why I tend to stick to the King James translation, as
at least it tries to present a literal translation – even if it does pad out the
keywords somewhat, and the results of the translator's efforts do not always
make sense. The reason for the King James version not always making sense,
however, is that its translators were unaware of the text's true meaning and

they were translating from the wrong language.

In actual fact, the term for 'fallen' is *nefel (nefer)* נפל, and this is more accurately translated as 'miscarried', or 'born'; and the Egyptian *nefer* 𓏏𓊵𓀔 for 'child' seems to confirm this. The word for 'morning' is *shakher* שחר which is more likely to mean 'dawn'. This is likely to have been taken from the Egyptian *sakhera* 𓏏𓏏𓏏𓇌𓋴𓊖 , which refers to the 'Field of Reeds', a well-used pseudonym for the Djuat, the Underworld or Abode of the Dead. The phrase 'cut down' was taken from *gada* נרע, which in this context is more likely to have been *qadja* 𓏲𓏏𓂻 meaning 'turn back' or 'revolve'. The word for 'weaken' was taken from *khalash (kheresh)* חלש and is better translated as meaning 'prostrate', and was taken from the Egyptian *kher* 𓂝𓂋𓏲𓏛 meaning 'destroy', 'throw down' or even 'prostrate'. And finally we have *gouy* גוי which actually means 'heathen' and was taken from *kaiu* 𓏤𓄿𓂝𓀀 meaning 'strangers' or 'foreigner'.

Taking all of these amendments into account, the sentence now seems to make a great deal more sense, if one views it in an Egyptian context, of course:

> How the Child of Heaven, Lucifer, son of the Djuat, revolves around the Earth and prostrates the Heathens.

Note how the word *nefel (nefer)* is also similar to the Egyptian *nefer* 𓋴𓊹 meaning 'breath', a word that has already been used to define the Holy Spirit. If this were the intention of this word, then the verse would become:

> How the Spirit of Heaven, Lucifer, son of the Djuat, revolves around the Earth and prostrates the Heathens.

Now the word order of the original Hebrew makes a great deal more sense and there is no need to bastardise the text as some Bibles tend to do. Here we have a clear and unmistakable story of a celestial body going about its daily cycles and forcing even the Heathens in foreign countries to bow before its majesty. In Egyptian terms, the meaning is unmistakable.

So was Lucifer the planet Venus, or the Sun? Personally I think that this has got to be a reference to Ra, but in terms of the masonic interest in this verse perhaps the exact astronomical identity of Lucifer is not so important. Another interesting aspect of this verse, which may point towards an identification with the Sun, is the fact that Lucifer has somehow become identified with Satan. In strict biblical terms, this association was simply due to the subsequent verses that said Lucifer went back down into the underworld, which the biblical scribes identified with their image of Hell. But in Egyptian mythology, Ra went back into the underworld each evening, and so there was nothing peculiar or evil about this event at all. It may be that Lucifer's identification with Satan was also influenced by the fact that the 'pagan' worship of the Sun was deemed to be evil by the later Judaic priesthood, and so any reference to the Sun-god, Lucifer, was deemed to be a reference to the Devil, or Satan.

But Christians walk a very fine line with this identification of the 'morning star' with Satan. Because if the 'morning star' was evil, then what about Jesus? Was he evil too? The Book of Revelations says:

> I Jesus have sent mine angel to testify unto you these things in the churches. I am the root and the offspring of David, and the <u>bright and morning star</u>. [B8]

Those who insist that Lucifer is Satan risk sending their precious Jesus to Hell at the same time, for both Lucifer and Jesus were identified with the 'morning star'. The reason for Jesus identifying himself with both King David and a morning star is given in the book *Solomon*. The true identity of King David was Psusennes II, whose original Egyptian name was Pa-seba-kha-en-nuit (⟨hieroglyphs⟩). This name included the elements *seba* ⟨hieroglyph⟩ and *kha* ⟨hieroglyph⟩, which can be translated as 'dawn star' or perhaps even 'morning star'. So the true name of this pharaoh may not have been 'My Star Rises (shines) in His City', but instead it was probably 'I am the Morning Star of Our City' or even 'I am Lucifer of Our City'. It is likely that Jesus was simply following in the ancient family tradition, which demanded a close association with Aton-Ra, Phosphorous or Lucifer – the morning aspects of the Sun-god. The pharaohs of previous dynasties simply identified themselves with Ra, but the events of the Thera eruption and the two exoduses irrevocably divided the nation, and now the parties were either identified with Amen-Ra (the evening star) or Aton-Ra (the morning star).

So it would seem that the masonic veneration of Lucifer is nothing quite so dramatic after all, to have created all this fuss from the Christian detractors. If Lucifer was simply a manifestation of Ra, as I suspect, then he is yet another manifestation of the Judaic Adhon (Aton), who was also the Sun-god of the sunrise. In this case, the Masons are simply venerating an alternative rendering of the same Judaic god – Lucifer was not the 'fallen one', he was actually the 'revolving one'. The confusion with the 'falling one' is that Amen, the evening manifestation of Ra, 'fell' towards the horizon whereas the Aton, the morning manifestation of Ra, 'arose' into the morning sky. That the later Judaic scribes mistook the winged Sun-disk of Amen-Ra for an 'angelic being' falling from the heavens is perhaps understandable.

However, by the time the later masonic scribes looked at the verse, the damage had already been done, and Lucifer was already identified with Satan in some fashion. But the masonic scribes obviously knew a great deal more about Satan than did the Christians and they understood, as has already been demonstrated, that this Satan was only a representation of the Egyptian god Set. But Set was not simply evil, he was just misunderstood; he was probably abused as a child or deprived of love and attention, which was always being directed towards his brother Osiris, and so we should really be blaming his parents, Geb and Nut, and not the poor wayward child. But Seth eventually became the wild-child made good, and so the testosterone-charged, masculine god Set eventually became Ra's knight in shining armour, his Sir Galahad who protected the Sun-god during the perilous night hours. Since modern Masons are undoubtedly descended from the Knights Templar, it is highly likely that this chivalrous order of warrior monks would have delighted in portraying themselves as the champions of their god; the knightly (and nightly) protectors of Aton or Ra.

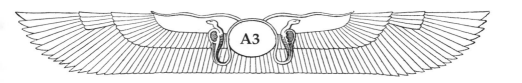

Great Hymn to the Aten
by
Akhenaton

Splendid you rise in heaven's light-land,
O living Aten (Aton), creator of life!
When you have dawned in the eastern light-land,
You fill every land with your beauty,
You are beauteous, great, radiant,
High over every land,
Your rays embrace the lands,
To the limit of all that you made.
Being Ra, you reach their limits,
You bend them for the son you love,
Though you are far, your rays are on the Earth,
Though one sees you, your strides are unseen.

When you set in western light-land,
Earth is in darkness, as if in death;
One sleeps in chambers, heads covered,
One eye does not see another,
Were they robbed of their goods,
That are under their heads,
People would not remark it.
Every lion comes from its den,
All the serpents bite,
Darkness hovers, earth is silent,
As their maker rests in light-land.

Earth brightness when you dawn in light-land,
When you shine as Aten of daytime,
As you dispel the dark,
As you cast your rays,
The two lands are in festivity,
Awake they stand on their feet,
You have roused them,
Bodies cleansed, clothed,
Their arms adore your appearance,
The entire land sets out to work,
All beasts browse the herbs,
Trees are sprouting,
Birds fly from their nests,
Their wings greet you ka,
All flocks frisk on their feet,
All that fly up and alight,
They live when you dawn for them,
Ships fare north, fare south as well,
Roads lie open when you rise,
The fish in the river dart before you,
Your rays are in the midst of the sea.

Who makes seed grow in women,
Who creates people from sperm,
Who feeds the son in his mother's womb,
Who soothes him to still his tears,
Nurse in the womb, giver of breath,
To nourish all that he made.
When he comes from the womb to breathe,
On the day of his birth,
You open his mouth wide,
You supply his needs.
When the chick in the egg speaks in the shell,
You give him breath within to sustain him,
When you have made him complete,
To break out from the egg,
He comes out from the egg,
To announce his completion,
Walking on his legs he comes from it.

How many are your deeds,
Though hidden from sight,

O sole god beside whom there are none,
You made the Earth as you wished, you alone,
All peoples, herds and flocks,
All upon Earth that walk on legs,
All on high that fly on wings,
The lands of Khor and Kush,
The lands of Egypt,
You set every man in his place,
You supply their needs
Everyone has his food,
His lifetime is counted,
Their tongues differ in speech,
Their characters likewise,
Their skins are distinct,
For you distinguished the peoples.

You made Hapy in Duat (rain in heaven),
You bring him when you will,
To nourish the people,
For you made them yourself,
Lord of all who toils for them,
Lord of all lands who shines for them,
Aten of daytime, great in glory,
All distant lands, you make them live,
You made a heavenly Hapy (rain) descend for them.
He makes waves on the mountains like the sea,
To drench their fields and their towns,
How excellent are your ways, O lord of eternity!
A Hapy from heaven for foreign peoples,
All lands' creatures that walk on legs,
For Egypt the Hapy (rain) who comes from Duat (heaven).

Your rays nurse all fields,
When you shine they live, they grow for you.
You made the seasons to foster all you made,
Winter to cool them, heat that they taste you,
You made the far sky to shine therein,
To behold all that you made,
You alone shining in your form of living Aten,
Risen, radiant, distant, near,
You made millions of forms from yourself alone,
Towns, villages, fields, the river's course,

All eyes observe you upon them,
For you are the Aten of daytime on high.

You are in my heart,
There is no other who knows you,
Only your son, *Neferkheprure, Sole one of Ra,*
Whom you have taught your ways and might.
Those on Earth come from your hand as you made them,
When you have dawned they live,
When you set they die,
You yourself are lifetime, one lives by you.
All eyes are on your beauty until you set,
All labour ceases when you rest in the west,
When you rise you stir everyone for the king,
Every leg on the move since you founded the Earth.
You rouse them for your son who came from your body,
The king who lives by Maat, the Lord of the Two Lands,
    Neferkheprure, Sole one of *Ra.*
The son of Ra who lives by Maat, the lord of crowns,
Akhenaton, great in his lifetime,
And the queen whom he loves, the Lady of the Two Lands,
    Neferneferu-Aten Nefertiti, living forever.

Psalm 104

The following is a comparison between Psalm 104 and the Hymn to the Aten. Numbers are biblical verse numbers, whereas HA denotes a verse from the Hymn to the Aten.

Psalm 104:

2   Who coverest thyself with light as with a garment: who stretchest out the heavens like a curtain:
HA   You are beauteous, great radiant. Your rays embrace the lands.
HA   Bodies cleansed, clothed. Their arms adore your appearance,

3   Who layeth the beams of his chambers in the waters: who maketh the clouds his chariot: who walketh upon the wings of the wind:
HA   Though you are far, your rays are on the Earth. Though one sees you, your strides are unseen.

4   Who maketh his angels spirits; his ministers a flaming fire:
HA   Your rays light up all faces.

5   Who laid the foundations of the earth, that it should not be removed for ever.
HA   Who made every land, created what is in it.

6   Thou coverest it with the deep as with a garment: the waters stood above the mountains.
HA   He makes waves on the mountains like the sea,

8   They go up by the mountains; they go down by the valleys unto the place which thou hast founded for them.
HA   The lands of Khor and Kush. The lands of Egypt. You set every man in his place.

11   They give drink to every beast of the field: the wild asses quench their thirst.
HA   A Hapy (rain) from heaven for foreign peoples. And for all creatures that walk on legs.

12   By them shall the fowls of the heaven have their habitation, which sing among the branches.
HA   Birds fly from their nests. Their wings greeting your *ka*.

13   He watereth the hills from his chambers: the earth is satisfied with the fruit of thy works.

HA   He makes waves on the mountains like the sea, to drench the fields. How excellent are your ways.

14   He causeth the grass to grow for the cattle, and herb for the service of man: that he may bring forth food out of the earth.

HA   Your rays nurse all fields. When you shine they live, they grow for you.

15   And wine that maketh glad the heart of man, and oil to make his face to shine, and bread which strengthen man's heart.

HA   You supply their needs, Everyone has his food.

16   The trees of the Lord are full of sap; the cedars of Lebanon, which he hath planted;

HA   Trees, herbs are sprouting.

17   Where the birds make their nests: as for the stork, the fir trees are her house.

HA   Birds fly from their nests.

18   The high hills are a refuge for the wild goats, and the rocks for the hyrax.

HA   All flocks frisk on their feet.

19   He appointed the moon for seasons: the sun knoweth his going down.

HA   You made the seasons to foster all that you made. When you set in the western light-land.

20   Thou makest darkness, and it is night: wherein all the beasts of the forest do creep forth.

HA   Earth is in darkness, as if in death. All the serpents bite,

21   The young lions roar after their prey, and seek their meat from God.

HA   Every lion comes from its den.

22   The sun ariseth, they gather themselves together, and lay them down in their dens.

HA   Earth brightens when you dawn in light-land. As you dispel the dark,

23   Man goeth forth unto his work and to his labour until the evening.

HA   Awake they stand on their feet. You have roused them, the entire land sets out to work.

24   O Lord, how manifold are thy works! In wisdom hast thou made them all: the earth is full of thy riches.

HA   Aten, how manifold are your deeds. You made the Earth as you wished. All people, herds and flocks.

25   So is this great and wide sea, wherein are things creeping innumerable, both small and great beasts.

HA   A Hapy (sea, rain) from heaven for foreign peoples, All lands' creatures that walk on legs. You made millions of forms from yourself alone.

26   There go the ships: there is that leviathan, whom thou hast made to play therein.

HA   Ships fare north, and fare south as well.

27   These wait all upon thee; that thou mayest give them their meat in due season.

HA   You made the seasons ... Winter to cool them, heat that they taste you.

28   That thou givest them they gather: thou openest thine hand, they are filled with good.

HA   You supply their needs. Everyone has his food.

29   Thou hidest thy face, they are troubled: thou takest away their breath, they die, and return to their dust.

HA   When you set in the sky's western light-land. They lie down as if to die, Their heads covered, their noses stopped.

30   Thou sendest forth thy spirit, they are created: and thou renewest the face of the earth.

HA   When you have dawned they live, By the sight of your rays all flowers exist, What lives and sprouts from the soil grows when you shine.

31   The glory of the Lord shall endure for ever: the Lord shall rejoice in his works.

HA   O lord of eternity, How excellent are your ways. You are the living Aten whose image endures.

32   He looketh on the earth, and it trembleth: he toucheth the hills, and they smoke.

HA   High over every land, your rays embrace the lands.

33   I will sing unto the Lord as long as I live: I will sing praise to my God while I have my being.

HA   Singers and musicians shout with joy, In the court of the Benben shrine.

34   My meditation of him shall be sweet: I will be glad in the Lord.

HA   Your holy son performs your praises.

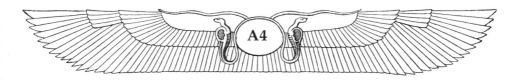

Hebrew - Egyptian
Dictionary

The overriding agenda in many academic quarters, both historical and theological, is to attempt a complete cultural separation between Israel and Egypt. Due to this erroneous strategy a significant point in this area of research has never been properly highlighted previously, and this is the close similarity between the original Egyptian language and the later Hebrew. Since the biblical patriarchs spent – even at the admission of the biblical texts – many generations in Egypt, this should not be unexpected; but more often than not the reader is simply not informed about these similarities and is therefore unable to make a reasoned judgement.

However, the undeniable truth that is emerging from this series of books is that the Israelites were the Hyksos pharaohs of Egypt, and so one might expect very close links indeed between these two languages. The Hebrew-Egyptian dictionary that follows, demonstrates some of the many similarities that I have uncovered so far. Approximately half of these words have been derived from the works of Wallis Budge, and the other half have been derived through my own endeavours. Considering that my knowledge of Hebrew is fairly limited, and the ease with which equivalent Egyptian words can be discovered, I would estimate that a competent native-speaker could easily double this tally of equivalent words.

Indeed, for readers who wish to take this subject further I would direct them towards a book entitled *Semitic Words in Egyptian Texts of the New Kingdom and Third Intermediate Period*, by James Hoch. Although this is an impenetrable book written for the specialist, it does appear to contain another 500 or so Hebrew words that have been discovered in the Egyptian language, and at least half of these words seem to be in addition to those in the following dictionary. But note here the unwarranted preconception that is immediately placed on these similarities between Hebrew and Egyptian – the title of the book is 'Semitic Words in Egyptian'. Who said these were Semitic words? Which is the more ancient language here, Hebrew or Egyptian? Why are these not 'Egyptian Words in Hebrew'? The modern Judaic cultural slant is also taken up by the commentators to this book. Orval Wintermute, for instance, says:

> This is the definitive study of Semitic loan-words in Egyptian.

Semitic loan-words? It was the Jews who spent hundreds of years in Egypt, even by the admission of the standard biblical texts, so surely these must be 'Egyptian loan-words in Hebrew'. The cultural blindness to the obvious is astounding, and so Judaeo-Christianity is still doing all in its power to separate itself from its Egyptian heritage. Why this should be so I do not know, for in historical terms an ancient Egyptian heritage should be regarded as highly prestigious. I presume the reasoning is based upon a desire to separate Judaic monotheism from Egyptian polytheism, a desire motivated by the theological assumption that the Old Testament is the 'word of god', and so by inference we might presume that Judaism has never evolved in its entire history. But this reasoning is infantile: people evolve; our culture evolves; society evolves; our understanding evolves; and our theology evolves alongside these essential elements.

How can a slow transition from Egyptian polytheism to Judaic monotheism be an embarrassment? Indeed, Christianity has regressed to polytheism, by including Jesus, the Holy Spirit and the Devil in its pantheon of gods, and it seems perfectly happy with the prospect. Muslims and Jews likewise insist that their singular god should be described in the plural; are they embarrassed by this?

Format

Since this book will be predominantly read by readers who are unacquainted with the Hebrew language, I have chosen to reference all the entries by their English equivalents. Thus referencing the English word for 'breath' will derive the Hebrew *hauh* and the Egyptian *hah*. I hope that this is a satisfactory arrangement that allows for an easy cross-reference of words.

There is one important amendment that has been made to many of these Hebrew pronunciations and that is the conversion of the 'r' consonant to an 'l'. The Egyptian language did not have an 'l' consonant, and so in the translations the Egyptian 'r' has often mutated into a Hebrew 'l' ל. In the following dictionary, the bracketed Hebrew word gives the original pronunciation, with an 'r' instead of an 'l', to match the Egyptian equivalent.

Readers will also note a number of other common transliteration conversions between letter pairs. A typical example is the Egyptian 'tch' becoming a Hebrew 'ts' צ. Additionally, there appears to be a general confusion between the 'b' and the 'p', which is not surprising as they are very similar consonants.

The 's' and 'sh' are also exchanged frequently. Finally, while the Egyptian 'k', 'q' and 'kh' generally became the Hebrew 'k' כ, 'q' ק, and 'kh' ח respectively, there is an amount of overlap between these consonants. To preclude words in this dictionary from being unnaturally forced to fit their Hebrew equivalents, through selective interpretations, I have allowed a maximum of only one transliteration error per word.

Egyptian-Hebrew Dictionary

abyss

    tehom תהום   abyss, the deep, sea

    tehamu   abyss, the deep

    Derived from the Egyptian *tah* and *mu* meaning 'submerge' and 'water' respectively, a logical division which clearly shows that this was originally an Egyptian word.

adultery

    naph נאף   adultery

    nahp   copulate

    Possibly from the Egyptian *nehp* meaning 'morning's work' (or should that be chore?).

ahah!

    ahah! אההה   an exclamation

    ahai!   an exclamation, joy

altar

    harel (harar) הראל   altar

    harara   mountain of god (Ra)

    In the Hebrew, the term for 'altar' was derived from *har* הר meaning 'mountain'. In the Egyptian, the 'mountain of god (Ra)' was also derived from *har* meaning 'mountain'. As I have explained in the book *Tempest*, it is likely that the primary altar of the Israelites was once the Great Pyramid at Giza; which is another reason for speculating that this pyramid has always sported a flat (unfinished) top, and that this platform was once used for ritual sacrifice and celestial observations.

    This is perhaps the origin of the Israelite rule that an altar should be unhewn (unfinished), just as the top of the Great Pyramid was similarly 'unfinished'.

Amen – see 'dark'.

anger

> qana קנא   anger, jealousy, envy
>
> qanedj   anger, rage

ape

> kuph (quf) קוף   ape
>
> kufi   ape
>
> gufi   ape

The Hebrew dictionary simply says 'of foreign origin'. Conversely, the Egyptian version was most probably derived from the terms *kefa* meaning 'naked' and *kefa* meaning 'bottom'; the ape being a humanoid with a naked bottom, that swells alarmingly in the female of the species. Bearing in mind that 'naked' and 'swollen' were the two attributes associated with Nefertiti (Eve), the term Khavah (Eve) may therefore have also been a derogatory reference to an ape. But it is also worth noting that Akhenaton's second wife was called Kiyah ⌐◁|| 𓃟 meaning 'monkey', and thus the link between Eve and an ape may well involve a reference to Kiyah.

apple

> tappuach תפוח   apple, apple tree
>
> taephu   apple
>
> djephu   apple

Probably linked in some way to a similar Egyptian word meaning 'cavern', perhaps through a method of storage.

archer

> rab רב   archer
>
> tcheb   spear, harpoon, stab

Archer may actually be a better translation here, as I think the derivation is from *tcheba* meaning 'iron finger'. This may have been a reference to the finger-guards worn by the archers. Another possibility is that an army of foot soldiers arrayed for battle looked like row after row of iron fingers, to the commanders who remained at a safe distance. See also 'ten thousand'.

armour – see 'clothing'.

armour

> khagor חגור   armour, apron
>
> khakhet   armour

army

> tsaba צבא   army, soldiers, warfare
>
> tchaba   army, soldiers

Taken from *tcheba* meaning 'thousands' or even 'ten thousand'. The word Tchoeb also became the title for a commander of 10,000 troops, rather like a Roman centurion was a commander of 100 troops. In the Bible this title was called Joab, which was the name of King David's army commander. See *Solomon, Pharaoh of Egypt* for details.

ash – see 'dust'.

Aten – see 'ground'.

attic

    aliyah (ariyah) עלייה   attic, roof chamber

    aarata   upper chamber

awake – see 'watch'.

axe

    garzen גרזן   axe

    qardem קרדם   axe

    qartchan   axe

    qarthan   axe

        Similar to the Egyptian *qarta*, meaning 'seal'. Was this type of axe used for breaking the seals?

Baal

    Baal (Baar) בעל   the god Baal

    Bar   the god Baal

        Originally used in the Hebrew as a term for a mortal lord or master, and the Hebrew and Egyptian sub-meanings of *baraka* and *bareka*, meaning 'pay homage' and 'present tribute' bear this out. Baal was later identified with storms and mountains, especially Zaphon north of Ugarit. See the entries 'bless', 'bow' and 'pyramid' for further information.

babble – see 'breath'.

backbone

    atseh עצה   backbone, spine

    at-t   backbone

        This was often imagined as the backbone of Osiris, and was an allusion to the shape of the Nile river, which Osiris helped in flooding each year.

bagpipe

    nebel נבל   skin bag, skin bottle, jar

    nefer   heart (lung) and wind pipe

        Since the Hebrew *nebel* was also a musical instrument, and the *nefer* referred to winds, it is possible that this was also a musical instrument and the origin of the bagpipe.

barley

    sarah שערה   barley

    saru   barley

bark

    nabach נבח   to bark

    nabehenu   to bark

basket

    tene טנא   basket, weave

    tene   basket, metal basket

battle

    qerab קרב   battle, war

qerai-t   victory, conquest

Since Qera was a storm-god related to Seth, perhaps this battle was the enduring saga of the battle between Osiris and Seth.

bean

puwl (puwr) פול   bean

pur   bean

beginning

reshiyth ראשית   Beginning, first, best

res   wake up, watch (for dawn)

This is the basis for Rosthau, a name that was used to describe the Giza plateau. This demonstrates that the primary usage for the pyramids was as part of an astronomical observatory.

bitumen

khemer חמר   bitumen, slime

kem-t   black

black

khum חום   brown or black

kemen   black

This term also refers to the Egyptian people, but it was not derived from their skin colour, rather it was due to the colour of the soil. Egypt was known as the 'black lands', as opposed to the 'red lands' of the surrounding desert. It also means 'garden', from whence the title 'Garden of Eden' was coined.

bless

barak ברך   bless, kneel

baraka   bless, kneel

Based upon the name of the god Baar or Baal. Note the more consistent use of the letter 'r' in comparison to the Hebrew Baal (Baar). Note also the consistency with *abrek* in the entry for 'bow'.

bow

abrek (aberek?) אברך   bow to the knee

abrek   go to the left!

The Hebrew version was the command given to the people as Joseph's chariot approached. This word was of unknown origin, until the Egyptian equivalent was discovered. More accurately pronounced *aberek*.

    The Egyptian version is also interpreted as a command to go down onto the left knee, as recipients of a knighthood do to this day before the monarch. This demonstrates the power that Joseph held in Egypt. See the entry for 'bless' for further information. In the Egyptian, the term is used in connection with the east and the Moon. Refer also to the entry for *abracadabra* in the index.

bind

itsar יצר   bind

issu   bind

bird – see 'fly'

bird

oph עוֹף   bird, fowl

apa 𓇋𓊪𓄿𓅽   to fly

boat

kaliy (kariy) כְּלִי reed boat, vessel, armour

kariy 𓎡𓇌𓊃   boat,

boat

tebah תֵּבָה   ark of Noah

keben-t 𓎡𓃀𓈖𓊛 large boat

  See also 'coffin'. The basket of Moses was also called a *tebah*, and this was nothing like a large boat.

body

besar בָּשָׂר   body, mankind, euphemism for penis

bes 𓃀𓋴𓅭   body, statue, image of a god

  Presumably the euphemism for 'penis' comes from the fact that the Egyptian *bah* means penis. The penis on a statue would therefore be a *besbah*, or perhaps *besah*.

box

rebiy רְבִיעִי   four, fourth, four sides, square

tcheb 𓍿𓃀𓏏𓋩   box, coffin

  There are a few words that demonstrate a link between the Egyptian 'tch' and the Hebrew 'r'. See also 'stretch'.

bread

chametz חָמֵץ   bread

kamutt 𓂝𓅢𓅢𓊪𓏤𓏤𓏤 bread

  Since the word *kam* means black, this was presumably a dark brown loaf.

bread

kikar כִּכָּר   bread (round?)

akikat 𓎡𓎡   bread cake

  Could this be related to the famous KitKat brand, first created in London in 1937? The Rowntree brothers who started the factory were Quakers, and it is not beyond the realms of possibility that they would have known that the Old Testament sacrificial bread was known as a *kikar* – which would make this brand name some 4,000 years old. The Egyptian description suggests a black bread, as *kik* means 'dark'; although since the biblical description is of a burnt offering, the bread could have become black during the course of the offering.

breath

khuah (Khavah) חַוָּה breath, tell, Eve (wife of Adam)

kaui 𓂝𓃀𓈖𓁶   speak, sing

  The association with Eve may be due to the name for Nefertiti being associated with speaking or babbling. In addition, Nefertiti was also associated with necks, for the *nefer* glyph was formed from the trachea glyph. The 'babbling' may refer to the trilling ululation that Arabic women still make with their tongues when lamenting, and it may also be associated with the Breath of Life. The Egyptian *kaui* is also very similar in spelling to Kiya, the second wife of Akhenaton and another possible candidate for the biblical Eve.

breath

nephakh נפח   breath, blow

anaph אנף   hard breath

nefu 〰〰🔲   breath, wind, breeze

Note the two different words denoting 'breath'. Above we have *khuah (Khavah)*, the name of Eve, and then we have *nephakh*, which may have been derived from the name for Nefertiti. Clearly there was a link between these two individuals. Did these two words denote Kiya and Nefertiti?

bright – see 'light'.

bronze

khashmal חשמל   bronze, shining metals, amber

hasmen 🔲   bronze, amber

Taken from the tanning effects that natron *(hesmen)* has on mummies; it produces bronzed skin.

bull

abiyr אביר   bull, mighty

abiar 🔲   bull, stallion, horse

bundle

kiniah כנעה   bundle, bag, pack

kinanu 🔲   bundle

burn

baur בער   burn, kindle

barga 🔲   make light, illuminate

burn

lehet (rehet) להט   burn, blaze

rehiyt 🔲   sunset

As usual, a reference to burning invokes the Sun.

burn

saraph שרף   burn, fiery serpent (dragon)

seref 🔲   hot, flame, warmth, Aapop

seraf 🔲   hot, flame, warmth, Aapop

See Appendix 2 for the connection between Aapop, the dragon and St George.

bush

shibol (shibor) שבל   branches, corn

sabori 🔲   bush, thicket, berries, vine

The change between the 'sh' and the 's' is given in the Bible, where the word *shibboleth* was used to test the pronunciation, and thus identify, of certain tribes. It is also possible that the word *shab-t* was the alternative 'sh' pronunciation that the Israelites were testing for, as this word means 'corn' and 'stick'.

cage

supar סוגר   cage, prison

shagar   cage

In both cases this is taken from the idea of a ring (a fence) around something. The Egyptian equivalent is *shagar*, meaning 'ring' or 'ditch'.

cake

tsapiychith צפיחת   cake, wafer

tchapurti   round cake

The answer to the origin of this word lies in its preservation in the Urdu language, where it is known as a *chapati*. The *chapati* is a flat pancake of bread which is made by twirling and throwing the dough in the air, and so its derivation must be from the Egyptian term *tchapeqa* meaning 'dancer'. No doubt the Whirling Dervish dance, in which the dancer's skirt is spun out like a pancake, is an ancient custom. It is known that dancing and acrobatics were an important part of Egyptian ritual, and the *muu*-dancers were always portrayed as wearing kilts or skirts. Note also how the Urdu pronunciation has better preserved the Egyptian original.

call

qara קרא   call, preach, proclaim

keruai   call, cry

May be related to *kara-t* meaning 'prison', but see also the entry for 'voice'.

camel

gamel (gamar) גמל   camel

kamaar   camel

The word *kam-aar* was derived from 'Egypt' and 'stone', and it represented the obvious and slightly humorous allusion that can be drawn between a camel's two humps and the two greatest pyramids at Giza.

castor oil

qiqa-one קיקיון   castor oil

kika   plant with bitter taste

chamber

dabir דביר   chamber, holy of holies

djebar   inner chamber, shrine

Similar to *djeba-t* meaning 'tomb' or 'sarcophagus'.

chamber

tsela (tsera) צלע   chamber, side

tcheres   chamber, room

Judging by the spelling, this is possibly referring to a granary.

chariot

agalah (agarah) עגלה   chariot

A4 - Dictionary

aagarta 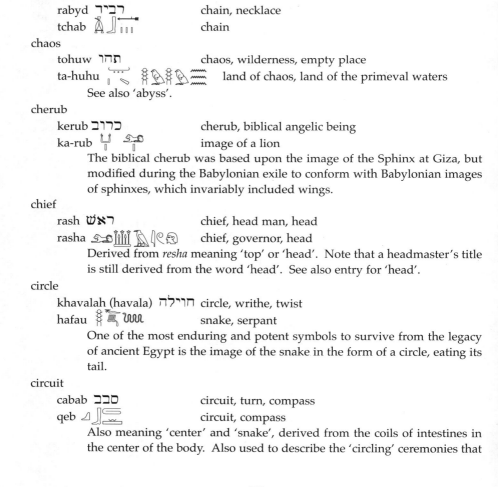 chariot
chariot
    markab מרכב   chariot, saddle
    markabtat   chariot
chariot
    tsab צב   covered waggon, litter
    tchebu   chariot

cave
    meharah מערה   cave, den, hole
    magarta   cave

Associated with *magadjar* meaning 'tower', and probably derived from the form of the pyramids. The pyramids were often labelled with the euphemism of 'tower', and each and every pyramid contained a 'cave' deep inside its structure.

chain
    rabyd רביד   chain, necklace
    tchab   chain

chaos
    tohuw תהו   chaos, wilderness, empty place
    ta-huhu   land of chaos, land of the primeval waters
    See also 'abyss'.

cherub
    kerub כרוב   cherub, biblical angelic being
    ka-rub   image of a lion

The biblical cherub was based upon the image of the Sphinx at Giza, but modified during the Babylonian exile to conform with Babylonian images of sphinxes, which invariably included wings.

chief
    rash ראש   chief, head man, head
    rasha   chief, governor, head

Derived from *resha* meaning 'top' or 'head'. Note that a headmaster's title is still derived from the word 'head'. See also entry for 'head'.

circle
    khavalah (havala) חוילה circle, writhe, twist
    hafau   snake, serpant

One of the most enduring and potent symbols to survive from the legacy of ancient Egypt is the image of the snake in the form of a circle, eating its tail.

circuit
    cabab סבב   circuit, turn, compass
    qeb   circuit, compass

Also meaning 'center' and 'snake', derived from the coils of intestines in the center of the body. Also used to describe the 'circling' ceremonies that

I have argued used to take place at Giza, and now take place at Mecca.

clothe

khabash חבש wrap up, clothe

hebes ⸮⸮⸮ dress, cover up

Possibly from the Egyptian *heb* meaning 'festival'. In both the Judaic and Muslim traditions, the great festivals were marked by dressing the shrines or monuments in expensive draperies. In Mecca, the entire Ka'ba is covered with new draperies each year, with the previous covering being divided up and sold on as souvenirs.

clothing

lebush (rebush) לבוש clothing, armour, garments

rebashaiu ⸮⸮⸮ leather jerkin, armour, cuirasses

Since a lion was called *rabu*, no doubt this clothing did indeed refer more to armour than normal clothing.

coffin

tebah תבה Ark of Noah, basket of Moses

tchebe-t ⸮⸮⸮ coffin, sarcophagus, wicker basket

Also related to *keben-t* meaning 'boat'.

column – see 'pillar'.

companion

khabar חבר companion

khaber ⸮⸮⸮ companion

From the equivalent Egyptian word *khab-t*, meaning 'neck' or 'shoulder', with the inference of grasping a friend on the shoulder.

corn, measure of

ephah אפה grain measure

apt ⸮⸮⸮ grain measure

Derived from the Egyptian *ap* meaning 'count' or 'reckon'.

count

sephar ספר count, write, scribe

sep ⸮⸮ multiply

covenant

bariyth ברית covenant, alliance, treaty

bartha ⸮⸮⸮ covenant, contract

Bearing in mind the explanations for 'bless', 'gift' and 'bow', this was a covenant with god. More specifically, it was a covenant with the Moon-god Thoth. As the Moon rose on the eastern horizon the assembled congregation bowed onto their left knees and chanted their covenant with god, much as Christians do each Sunday to this day.

covering

kacuwth כסות covering, clothing

kathuti ⸮⸮⸮ covering, garment

cry out

    tsaq צעק   cry out, call

    tchaqati   cry out

cumin

    kammon כמן   cumin

    gemnen   cumin

cunning

    amem עמם   cunning, sly

    Amen   secretive

    A similar meaning to that given for 'dark'. It demonstrates how secretive the Amen priesthood and religion really were, and so it is not so surprising that we know so little about them and it.

cut down

    khatab חטב   cut down, carve

    khatab   kill, slay

cylinder – see 'roll'.

dark

    amem עמם   darken, eclipse

    Amen   hidden one

    The term can also mean 'eclipse' in terms of the Sun setting over the horizon.

dark

    arab ערב   dark, night, evening, sunset, Arabs

    Ar(t)aab(t) (Ar-aab)   Dark eye of Horus, or the Moon

    A good illustration of how words can be confused over time. The Egyptian word is from the term 'eye of the east', which referred to the 'dark eye' of Horus, or the Moon. But since the Moon was associated with night, the Hebrew has translated this as 'sunset', or 'west'. So east has become west. It is possible, therefore that the Hebrew term for the Arabs was originally due to their eastern homeland and their veneration of the Moon, rather than their dusky complexion.

darkness

    khowshak חשך   become dark, be hidden

    khau   darkness, evening, altar

    sek   finish, make an end

    Once again the darkness refers to the sunset. The allusion to being hidden is taken from the god Amen, the evening Sun-god who was called the 'hidden one'.

dawn

    beqer בקר   dawn, morning, first light

    beka   morning, light, radiance

    baka   morning

    Since the Sun was born each morning from the vagina of Nut, this word is closely connected with the word *beka-t*, meaning 'pregnancy'. But it is uncertain which word came first, the sunrise or the pregnancy. See 'empty' for further details.

dawn (double)

sha-kharayim שחרים   the double dawn

sa-Heru 🔲🦅   the dawn of Horus (the Sun)

The literal meaning is the 'knowledge of Horus'. The double dawn refers to the two eyes of Horus, which were the Sun and the Moon. A double dawn of these two bodies would actually create what we call today the New Moon, the period when the Moon cannot be seen in the night sky.

deer – see 'stag'.

delicate

qalel (qerer) קאלאל   delicate, light, slight

qerer ⌐𝆑🜊𝆑𝅘   delicate, light, weak

depart

sur רור   depart, turn aside

sa 𝈓𝆑   depart, turn back

Possibly related to *sa*, which refers to a walled enclosure or castle.

desire

ab or abah אב אבה   desire, longing (father)

abor 𝈓𝆑   desire, wisdom, understanding

Perhaps the term refers to the innate desire for divine wisdom? The sub-meaning of *ab* 𝈓 meaning 'thirst' would suggest so, as we still 'thirst' for knowledge.

destroy

shadad שדד   destroy, spoil, rob

shadj 𝈓   destroy, kill

dew – see 'mist'.

die – see 'pain'.

die

muth מות   die, dead, kill

mut 𝈓   die, dead, death

A variation on *mer-t*, meaning 'death', which was probably derived from the vulture hieroglyph, and was sometimes pronounced *mut*; the vulture obviously being a symbol of death. Why *mut* meaning 'death' does not use the vulture glyph is a bit of a mystery, but it is possibly due to the scribes not wanting to link the concept of death with the mother goddess Mut, who mimicked Isis and so represented the ideals of 'birth' and 'motherhood' and whose title did use the vulture glyph. This word was possibly the root of the Latin *mortalitas*, the French *mort* and the English 'mortal', meaning 'death'. See also reference for 'pain'.

dirt

tiyt טיט   dirt, mud, clay

tiit ⌐⟨⟨⌐ 〰   dirt, pus, excrement

It would be nice to see when this word was first coined, as it may be a derogatory response to the despised name of Nefertiti. A similar case may be made for the word *nefer*, which refers to a strong negative. Since most of the meanings to *nefer* refer to something good, beautiful or prosperous, the meaning of 'negative' jars somewhat, and this may again be a later derivation invented by the Theban Amun priesthood who deposed Nefertiti and the Amarna regime.

divide – see 'spread'.

divide

     parad פָּרַד   divide, separate, scatter
     paratcha ⌐◡⌐   divide, split
        Connected with the splitting of stones.

divide

     palag (purag) פֶּלֶג   divide, split
     penega ⌐◡⌐   divide, separate
        See also 'open'.

divide

     parash פָּרַשׁ   separate, scatter
     puresh ⌐◡⌐   separate, divide
        Associated with the shelling (opening) of beans from a pod. See 'bean'.

divide

     pasac פָּסַק   divide, cut off
     pasekh ⌐◡⌐   divide, split

dominion

     radah רָדָה   dominion, dominate, rule
     redjah ⌐◡⌐   imprison, catch, snare

door

     tara תְּרַע   door, gate
     tsela (tsara) צֶלַע   the leaves of a door, plank of wood
     taraa ⌐◡⌐   door

This was not any old door but an allusion to the door of the Great Pyramid. An alternative meaning is 'bread oven', and the traditional bread oven of the region looks exactly like the skip beehive that was discussed earlier in the book. The door to the bread oven would therefore be the equivalent of the door to the beehive and thus the door to the Great Pyramid.

       This word may also have influenced the title for the doorkeeper at Masonic lodges, who is known as a 'tyler'. It is said that this title may have been derived from the French *tailleur* meaning 'cutter', but I think a more sensible derivation is from the Egyptian *taraa*, with the usual Hebrew 'l' consonant replacement, giving *talaa* – a doorkeeper.

dress up

     rabad רָבַד   dress up, deck

tcheb 𓀀𓈖𓂋𓏏 dress up, deck
Refers to providing linen for, or the actual wrapping of, a mummy.

dry land

tsimman צִמָּאוֹן dry land, drought
tchamau 𓈖𓃀𓄿𓅱 dry land, parched
Related to *tchamma* meaning a roll of parchment. Notice how we still have a similar link between dryness and parchment (parched) in the modern English.

dust, ashes

aphar (afar) עָפָר dust, powder, ashes
afu 𓆓𓏤𓏤𓏤 corpse of Ra, which was turned to ashes every night.

ear

azan אֹזֶן hear, listen, give ear
adjen 𓇋𓂝𓏤𓂋 ear
Note that this is the same spelling as one form of the Aten-god. Again it demonstrates that the Aten made sounds as well as light.

earth – see 'ground'.

east

qedem קֶדֶם east, ancient, old
qedjem 𓊃𓃀𓈖 the country of the east
Since the 'three-hills' glyph actually refers to the three pyramids at Giza, this may well refer to the 'pyramid of the east'.

eat

akal (akar) אָכַל eat, feed
aqa 𓂝𓃀𓈖𓏤 feed, give
Taken from a name of the god Geb, who was closely associated with food.

ebony

heben הֶבֶן ebony
hebeni 𓈖𓏤 ebony
yiban 𓏏𓏏𓃀𓏤 ebony
Possibly taken from Yiban, one of the titles of the snake-god Aapop. Since Aapop was the personification of evil and the eternal opponent of Ra, he would naturally have been linked with darkness. Ebony is, of course, a black wood and its branches may well be reminiscent of black snakes. The alternative pronunciation of *heban* was probably derived from *heb*, meaning 'plough', and no doubt the freshly turned furrows of black earth again reminded someone of black snakes. Note how the English word 'ebony' still reflects the original Egyptian pronunciation.

Egypt – see 'fortress'.

eight

shemenee שְׁמִינִי eight
khemeneh 𓈖𓏤 eight
Note the change from 'kh' to 'sh'. There has been a confusion within the

Egyptian numbering system, as *khemet* refers to the ordinal number three. Perhaps the Israelites wanted to get away from the confusion between *khemeneh* (8) and *khemet* (3). If so, however, they did themselves no favours by then choosing the word *khameshee* חמשי for the ordinal number five.

The prefix of 'kh' on each of these ordinal numbers actually means 'thing' in the Egyptian. Thus *khemeneh* (8) means 'eight things' and *khemet* (3) means 'three things'.

embrace

khabaq חבק   embrace, link arms, fellowship

habaq 🔲📐🔶   embrace, clasp

Linked with the word *hebener* meaning 'neckband', or 'collar', which were the gold torqs that were presented to worthy individuals in Egypt, Celtic Ireland and Britain. Not only did the torq embrace the individual, but no doubt the presenter of the torq did likewise.

empty

beohu בהו   empty, void

begsu 〗⬚🐦   weak, miserable, empty

Since the English word 'beg' is of uncertain origins, this may be the root for this term.

empty

bakaq בקק   empty, make void, fail

baqbaq 〗△〗△   pour out, empty, flow

The derivation of this word is not clear. It can also mean 'olive oil' and 'sunshine', so did the golden oil pour out of the presses like the Sun poured out its rays?

In the book *Tempest*, I compared *beq* with its reversal, *qeb*, which refers to cool waters and to the Nile itself. The Hebrew emphasis on 'void' and 'empty' may well come from its reference to Nu, the cosmic void of the primeval waters. See 'dawn' for further details.

enchantment

nachash נחש   enchantment, divinity

nehes 〰️🔶〗   mutter incantations

enemy

aueb איב   enemy

ab 🔶〰️🔶   enemy, oppose, face to face

Has connotations of elephants locking horns together, hence the tusks.

end

khadal (khadar) חדל   end, cease, seal

khatam ⊘🔶   finish, end, seal

Derived from the term *khetem* for a finger ring. These rings were used for sealing documents with wax, a tradition that survived into the nineteenth century.

face

paneh (phaneh) פנה   face, presence, person

fenedj 〰️🐍   nose

The Bible often uses terms for 'nose' when referring to a face. A good example of this is *aph* אַף, which primarily means 'nose', but is also used for 'face'.

fall

havah הָוָה   fall, exist, happen

hai 𓉐🦅🦅🔺   fall, enter, embark on a boat

The falling being described here is the falling of the Sun into the 'sea' at the end of the day. This is why the same word can be linked to boats, which is a reference to Ra embarking on his solar-boat that took him through the Djuat each night. The word can also refer to flames, burning, a day, time, rejoicing and praises, words which again suitably describe the scene of the Sun setting at Giza or Thebes and the priesthood conducting the evening ceremony. Christian and Muslim worshippers still follow this ancient ritual, with services being held in the morning and evening. See also 'rise'.

feast

mishteh מִשְׁתֶּה   feast

masatah ⬜🔲🪶🧍〰️⬭   feast, revel

field

shadeh שָׂדֶה   field, land

shadj 🔺🦅🌿   field, cultivated land

Derived from *shedj*, which refers to the digging of ditches or irrigations canals. This was an annual chore in Egypt, after the season's floods had deposited silt in all the ditches.

fig

tan תְּאֵן   fig

tun ⌒🦆🌿   fig

finger

atseba אֶצְבַּע   finger, toe

atcheba 𓏏🔲🔺🪶𓏤𓏤   finger

finish – see 'end'.

finish

tamam תָּמַם   finish, accomplish, spent, consume

tamam ⬌🦅🦅   finish, complete, entire, whole

gamar גָּמַר   complete, end

kam 🦆🪶⬭   end, finish

Now the first of these examples is most definitely an Egyptian concept, as it is based upon the great god Tem. Tem was the dualist counterpart of Akhenaton's Aten, and became known as Adjem. The Aten represented the dawning Sun, while Adjem represented the setting Sun – the latter's name was eventually superceded by Amen, meaning 'west'.

fire

ashah אֵשׁ   fire (for cooking)

asher 🐦〰️ fire

Has connotations of the setting Sun and also of the roasting of meat for a sacrificial offering.

fire

laqach לָקַח fire

rakeh (lakeh) 〰️ fire

firmament

raqiya רָקִיעַ firmament, surface, expanse

rekh-t well-known woman, wise woman

The firmament described the mythical vault or surface that encircled the Earth and held the stars in place, which was later called the crystal sphere. However, in Egypt that same vault of the heavens was formed by the body of the goddess Nut – hence the link between the firmament and a woman.

first

ekhad אָחָד first, one

hatt or first, finest, forepart

flame

lehab (rehab) לַהַב flame, tip of weapon

rehabu flame, heat

Again the context of this 'flame' is the evening Sun.

flame

shabib שָׁבִיב flame, spark

shaubu flame, fire,

flee

nood נוּד flee

nodja flee, escape

flood

mabuah מַבּוּעַ flood, spring

mu-bah flood of water

flour

qemach קֶמַח flour, meal flour

qemehu flour

Also spelt in the Egyptian as *kamahu-t*, which can be broken down into *kam* and *hu-t*. The word *kam* is taken from Kam meaning 'Egypt', while *hu* can mean either 'thresh' or 'food'. My favourite interpretation is therefore 'food of Egypt', or perhaps in the more modern parlance of international trade, 'produce of Egypt'.

flour

soleth (soreth) סֹלֶת flour

thoreti bread from fine flour

Since *thar (thor)* meant 'enclosure' and 'shield', the bread may well have been circular.

flower

> perach פרח   flower, bud, blossom
>
> perekh   flower
>
> Again taken from *per* meaning 'sprout'. See 'grain' and 'swift'.

flower

> tsiyts צץ   flower, bloom
>
> tchitch   flower

fly

> ouph עוּף   to fly, bird
>
> ap   to fly, pertaining to the winged disk of the Sun
>
> apa   to fly, pertaining to birds

food

> maakal (maakar) מאכל   food, meat, fruit
>
> makeru   food, sustenance, tribute
>
> From the Egyptian *makher* meaning 'grain store'. This probably explains the Greek story that the pyramids were grain stores. See also 'tower'.

foot

> regel (reger) רגל   foot, journey
>
> redj   leg, foot
>
> Also spelt as *ret*. Related to *redj*, meaning 'stairway' and possibly to *resh* meaning 'top' or 'elevation'. For the latter, see also 'head'.

footstool

> hadem הרם   footstool, stool, leg
>
> hadjem-t   footstool,
>
> From the Egyptian *ha-t*, which refers to the limbs of the body.

footstool

> kebesh כבש   footstool
>
> kabusa   footstool
>
> The Hebrew word *kebes* כבש also means 'lamb', and so the derivation of 'footstool' is obvious. Even in the era of the Templars, effigies of knights were portrayed with their feet resting on lambs. The imagery is supposed to be of Jesus, but this displays an ignorance of the astrological connotations that lay behind this symbolism. Precession had moved the constellations backwards in the dawn sky and it was now Pisces that was dominant, not Aries. The fallen Knights Templar should have been resting their feet on a fish. That the word was originally Egyptian is perhaps demonstrated by its similar meaning in that language, where *kapu* simply meant 'foot'.

fortress

> matsur מצור   fortress, defence, a name for Egypt
>
> metchur   fortress, walled town

frankincense

> lebonah לבנה   frankincense

nibun frankincense
There are a couple of transitions between 'l' and 'n', see also tongue.

fruits

perah פרי   fruits, rewards

per-t or kheru   'offerings by voice'
Symbolic offerings that appeared in a tomb when the deceased commanded
them to do so. The images of these offerings show fruits, vegetables and
various meats, and they are similar to the offerings that are proffered to the
gods during a Christian harvest festival.

full

mala (mara) מלא   full, accomplish, satisfy
mara-t   full, satisfy
The word *mer* referred to the pyramids, and since the Giza pyramids were
the prime symbol of Egypt, the word Mera became a name of Egypt. But
because Egypt was the land of plenty, populated with well-fed citizens, the
word *mera-t* also became synonymous with fullness.

garden

gan גן   garden, enclosure, defend
qan   land, earth, dust
kam (kan)   garden
The latter version, *kam,* can be spelt with a water glyph ('n') as well as the
owl glyph ('m'). There is an obvious link here between the word 'garden'
and Kam meaning Egypt, which is a good indication that the Garden of
Eden may have been in Egypt.

garden

karmel כרמל   garden, orchard, plantation
kam (kan)   garden
See previous description.

garment – see 'covering'.

gather

qavah קוה   gather, collect
khefkhef   gather, collect
Probably related to the detritus that is left in heaps after a flood.

gift

barakah ברכה   gift, tribute
baraka   gift, tribute
Refer also to the entries for 'bow' and 'bless'.

goat

tsaphiyr צפיר   goat
tchapurema   goat

god

El (Er) אל   god
Ar (Er)   watchers, pass time

One of the most significant attributes of the Egyptian gods was their eyes, which represented the various heavenly bodies. In a more human context, the priesthood also watched the movement of the heavens, noting the rise and fall of each heavenly body.

good

    kethem כתם   fine gold

    katem ＵＭ𓅓 í í í   fine gold

good

    towb טוב   good, good things

    tep (top) 𓁶   best, first, head, top

    Somehow the English word 'top' has managed to preserve the original meaning of the Egyptian word.

gorge

    baqa בקע   cleave, valley, cleft, split open

    baka 𓃀𓏏𓅓   gorge, cleft in rock, tree

    Taken from *baka*, the sunrise. In the hieroglyphic lexicon, the Sun always rose in a valley between two hills, and so the sunrise became associated with any valley or cleft-type structure.

grain

    peruda (perada) פרודא grain

    peratu   grain

    Perhaps derived from *per* meaning 'sprout', which was in turn derived from *per* which referred to the rising or appearance of the dawn Sun. The imagery was of the growing seedling, from which similar words for 'fruit' and 'offering' were derived. See also 'swift' and 'flower'.

Greece

    Yavan (Yuan) יון   Greece

    Uinn   Greece

    Since the alternative meanings for *uinn* are 'light', 'window' and 'see', one might interpret this as referring to the enlightened citizens of Ionia (Greek Asia Minor). However, an alternative and more compelling derivation for Ionia is most probably from the Egyptian An (Iunu), the city of Heliopolis. Since traditions derived from Manetho say that a pharaoh called Dannus fled to Argos (Greece) during the late eighteenth dynasty, it is likely that the 'enlightened ones of Ionia (Iunu)' were something to do with his fellow exiles. There is also a tradition that the name of the sacred Scottish island of Iona was derived from the same sources. Following on in this manner, one might also speculate that the city of Athens was named after the Aten. Since I have previously linked Pharaoh Dannus with the Amarna pharaoh Aye, the original primary deity of Athens is likely to have been the Aten (Athens was later associated with the goddess Athena).

ground – see 'land'.

ground

    adama אדמה   ground, earth, land

aten (adjen) ⟨glyphs⟩   ground, dust, earth

The Egyptian version is taken from *adam*, meaning 'red land', or the land of the Hyksos. The redness in the Hebrew interpretation comes from the redness of the setting Sun, the Aten.

guard

   shamar שָׁמַר   guard, keeper, watchman

   shemes ⟨glyphs⟩   bodyguard, follower

guitar

   nebel (neber) נבר   stringed instrument, skin bag

   nefer , ⟨glyphs⟩   stringed instrument, guitar

Also called a *psaltery*. The word *psaltery* was derived from 'psalm', which demonstrates that the Psalms were originally sung and accompanied by instruments. The Egyptian word *nefer* is also comprised of the heart (lung) and trachea glyph, hence the Hebrew meaning of 'skin bag'.

guard

   netar נטר   guard, keep

   nu or nuit ⟨glyphs⟩   guard, shepherd

Probably from *nu* meaning 'time'. The action of guarding is inextricably linked with time, which is why soldiers still go 'on watch', a term which refers to both vision and a time period.

guide

   derek דֶּרֶךְ   guide

   ter or djer ⟨glyphs⟩   guide

hair

   saarah שַׂעֲרָה   hair

   saarta ⟨glyphs⟩   hair

hammer

   kilaph (kiraph) כִּילָף   hammer, axe

   garebu ⟨glyphs⟩   to hammer

Also spelt as *garepu* and related to *gara* meaning 'furnace'.

hand

   kaph כַּף   hand, hollow of hand, palm of hand

   kep, kapu ⟨glyphs⟩   hollow of hand, palm

To record a tally of the number of enemies slain, the Egyptians used to cut off a hand from each corpse. These hands of the dead were called *kaput*, which is probably where the German term for 'dead' came from; although the Latin precursor *caput* tends to invoke a decapitation rather than a severing of the hand.

harp

   kinowr כִּנּוֹר   harp, lyre

   keneniur ⟨glyphs⟩   harp

Obviously an Egyptian term, as it is taken from *qena* meaning 'embrace', a term that graphically describes the musician's movements as he or she plays a large harp. The reason for the change in glyphs is not immediately obvious.

hate

    setam שׂטם   hate, oppose, animosity

    shetam   revile, fight

        No doubt related to Set and Shet, the god of evil and conflict and the brother of Osiris.

head – see 'good'.

head

    resh ראשׁ   head, top, height

    resha   head, top, summit

        Again this is probably related to *res* meaning 'keep awake' or 'watch'. The scene is of the Watchers of Guardians, standing on a prominent peak (the Great Pyramid) and watching for the sunrise or sunset. See also entries for 'foot' and 'south'.

hear – see ear.

hear

    shemah שׁמע   hear, listen, obey

    stchem   hear

        Related to *tchem*, meaning a 'pair of wings'.

heart

    leb לב   heart, mind

    iab   heart, mind

hero

    arale (arare) אראל   hero, valliant

    aaraar   hero

        The Hebrew version suggests root words of *ar-el*, meaning 'lion-men'. This is also possible in the Egyptian, but since the word pointedly uses the canal or ditch glyphs I would suggest an alternative. The root words are probably *aar* and *arar*, meaning 'ditch' and 'go up stairs' respectively. The imagery this gives is of the army's vanguard who had to cross a moat and scale the glacis slope that defended the fortified tells (towns) in Egypt. These would indeed have been heroes.

hew

    qatsats קצץ   hew, cut off

    qatchatcha   hew

        Derived from Qedju, the divine potter who created mankind, a name that spawned a few phonemes about construction.

hide – see 'dark'.

high place

    merom מרום   high place, elevation, noble

    mer (emer)   pyramid

        The possibility exists that ceremonies once took place on the top of the Great Pyramid, which would make it a high place for the nobles. The primary meaning for *mer* is 'lake', but there again the Great Pyramid was also known as the Tchau, or the lake that measured 440 x 440 cubits – which are the exact dimensions of this pyramid. It is from the close association between Egypt and the pyramids that the name Mera, for Egypt, was derived.

horn – see 'trumpet'.

horse

sus סוּס		horse
sus 𓏴𓏴𓃗		horse

horses

susem סוּסִים		horses
susem 𓏴𓏴𓈖𓅭𓃀		horses

hot

kham חם		hot
khams חמץ		hot
kham-t ⬤𓅭⬡𓏭		hot
khamam חמם		hot
khamam ⬤—𓅭𓅭𓏭		hot
shemam ▭𓅭𓅭𓏭		hot

Budge indicates that this referred to the '50 hot days', as *khamash* means 5 (50) in Hebrew. In the Egyptian this is more likely to have been the 3 (30) or 8 (80) hot days, as *khem-t* and *khemen* mean '3' and '8' respectively.

The Egyptian *shemem* is similar to the word *shem*, meaning 'summer'. This word is similar to the Hebrew words *shemaneem* and *shemaneh*, which refer to the numbers '4' and '8' respectively. This mix-up of similar sounding names for the ordinal numbers, in both of these languages, indicates that there may have been a degree of confusion and a lack of standardisation between the various temples that held the Egyptians' mathematical knowledge.

house

baith בית		house
bait 𓃀𓅭𓉐		house

Probably derived from a combination of *baba* meaning 'cave' and *ba-t* meaning 'bushes'. A house would then be a cave covered in bushes.

illuminate – see 'lightning'.

image

kah כה or kakah כה		like, in this manner
ka 𓂓		image, likeness

The ka 'soul' was viewed as a separate entity to the body, and could thus be regarded as its image or likeness.

image

tselem צלם		image, likeness
sem 𓏲—𓏏𓀠		image,

incense

qatoreth קטרת		incense

qatoreta ⌐𓅭⌐𓅭𓋴𓊪𓏏𓏥 incense

insect

> sherets שֶׁרֶץ creeping things, swarming things, insects
> sheret 𓂝𓅬 small things
>
>> By derivation, also means 'son' or 'youth'.

intestine – see 'middle'.

iron

> barzel (parzar) בַּרְזֶל iron, iron ore, strength
> parthar 𓃵𓂝𓃭𓋴𓏏𓏥 iron
>
>> The 'b' and 'p', and the duck glyph in particular, are often interchanged, even within the Egyptian. I would estimate that the Egyptian translation is correct, and so the derivation would be *pa-thar*, with the Egyptian *pa* referring to 'matter' and 'material', and *thar* meaning 'protection', 'fortress' or 'shield'. Thus, iron was derived from the phase 'material for protection'. Incidentally, in the book *Solomon* I have identified Thar with Tanis, the capital of Solomon and David's United Monarchy, and so Tanis may have been associated with iron production as well as being a fortress city. Bearing in mind the name of the king of Tanis, Pa-sebakhaennuit II (David) *pa-r-thar* may also be translated as 'this is my protection'.

irrigate

> shaqah שָׁקָה irrigate, drink, water
> seckhet 𓊪𓈒𓏤𓏤𓏤𓏤𓈖 reeds, meadow, also water meadow

Israel

> Ishrale (Ishrar) יִשְׂרָאֵל Israel
> Yisraar 𓏭𓏤𓅭𓏏𓏏𓁷 Israel
>
>> Just for fun I looked at a possible derivation of this Egyptian word for the Israelites and found just one possible option, which was Yiser-Aar 𓏭𓏤𓅭 𓅭𓏤𓅡 meaning 'Papyrus Lions'. However, since the papyrus was the popular emblem of the Lower Egyptians, we might also derive from this same spelling 'Lower Egyptian Lions'. Such a title would be eminently suitable for a faction such as the Israelites, who I maintain were Lower Egyptians and actively engaged in conflict with their Upper Egyptian cousins.

jackal

> sab זְאֵב wolf
> sab ⌐𓃀𓃭𓃥 jackal
>
>> And from the Hebrew version, the Russians no doubt derived *sabaka* meaning 'dog'.

judgement

> shaphat שָׁפַט judge, plead, defend
> sepa 𓊪𓏤𓁿 judge

kill

> damah רָמָה kill, destroy
> tam 𓏏𓏤𓃀𓁿 kill, destroy

know

    yada יָדַע   to know

    yiadja   to know

knowledge

    dea דֵע   knowledge, opinion of god

    tcheas   wisdom, knowledge, speech of wisdom

    Derived from the seven wise gods that advised Thoth.

lamentation

    qiynah קִינָה   lamentation, dirge

    qineh   lament, bewail

    Related to the Egyptian *qena* meaning 'hug' or 'embrace', but which of these meanings came first is difficult to ascertain.

lamb

    kar כַּר   lamb

    karkar-ti   lamb

    Taken from *ka* meaning 'bull'. The sacred *ka* bulls were representations of the constellation of Taurus, but precession had made Aries the dominant constellation of the eighteenth dynasty, and so *karkar-ti* may have been an attempt to supersede the bull imagery.

land – see 'ground'.

land, estate, world

    ehrets (arits) אֶרֶץ   land, world

    arit   land, estate – also: fruit, produce

leather

    tachosh תַחַשׁ   hide, leather

    thehas   hide, leather

    Taken from the name of one of the four bulls of the god Atum.

leaves

    ophiy עֳפִי   leaves, foliage

    aufti-t   leaves

leg

    shebel שָׁבֵל   leg, skirt

    sebeq   leg

left hand

    shemale (shemar) שְׂמֹאל left, left hand, left side

    semer   left hand

    Possibly derived from *semer (semel)*, meaning 'leader', 'nobility' or 'priest' – a title that could easily be broken down into *sa* and *mer* and therefore mean 'Man of the Pyramids'. Since the left side also referred to the east, this might imply that the Giza priesthood observed the sunrise from the eastern side of the pyramids. Since the eastern causeways at Giza were aligned with the various seasonal sunrises, this is highly likely.

lentil

adash עֲדָשׁ   lentil

aadjna ▭   lentil

life

kha חַי   live, life, living things

ka   life

The *ka* was the life-force, which differentiated the living from the dead. Since the *ka* came into existence at birth and was regarded as a slightly separate entity to the physical body, the *ka* was also used to describe an 'image', or 'double'.

life

nefesh נֶפֶשׁ   life, things that breathe

nef   breath of life

Taken from the *nefer* glyph, which comprised a heart and trachea. While *nefer* predominantly referred to 'beauty', its link with breathing is inescapable. This is the basis of the name for Nefertiti.

light – see Sun.

light

ore (auere) אוֹר   light, day, bright, morning sun

auu (aur)   light, brilliance

Has connotations of travelling, suggesting that this was the light of the Sun as it crossed the sky

light

maure מָאוֹר   light, bright

mau-ti   light, brilliance

lightning

baraq בָּרָק   lightning

bureqa   sparkle, shine

barega   illuminate, give light

lightning

reshep רֶשֶׁף   lightning, spark, coals

reshepu   lightning

Related to *resha*, meaning 'top'. No doubt it was noticed that the high points in the land, like the Giza pyramids, were the first to be struck by lightning.

lily

shushan שׁוּשָׁן   lily

seshen   lily

sesshen   lily

linen

shesh שֵׁשׁ   linen, silk, marble

ses-t   garment

lion

ary אֲרִי   lion

lion

ar	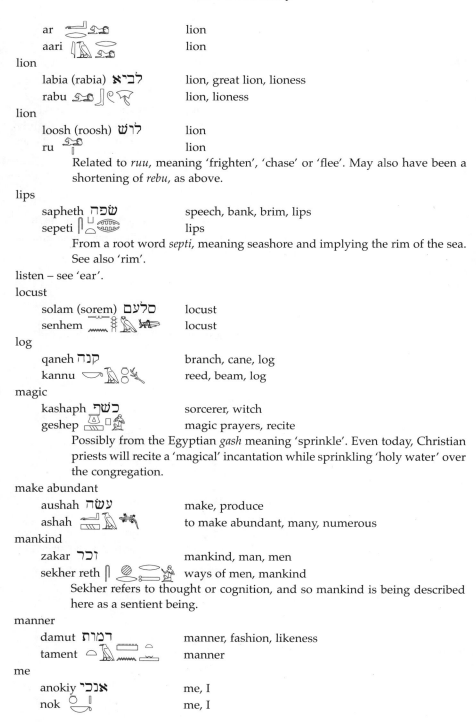	lion
aari		lion

lion

labia (rabia) לְבִיא		lion, great lion, lioness
rabu		lion, lioness

lion

loosh (roosh) לוּשׁ		lion
ru		lion

Related to *ruu*, meaning 'frighten', 'chase' or 'flee'. May also have been a shortening of *rebu*, as above.

lips

sapheth שָׂפָה		speech, bank, brim, lips
sepeti		lips

From a root word *septi*, meaning seashore and implying the rim of the sea. See also 'rim'.

listen – see 'ear'.

locust

solam (sorem) סֶלַעַם		locust
senhem		locust

log

qaneh קָנֶה		branch, cane, log
kannu		reed, beam, log

magic

kashaph כָּשַׁף		sorcerer, witch
geshep		magic prayers, recite

Possibly from the Egyptian *gash* meaning 'sprinkle'. Even today, Christian priests will recite a 'magical' incantation while sprinkling 'holy water' over the congregation.

make abundant

aushah עָשָׂה		make, produce
ashah		to make abundant, many, numerous

mankind

zakar זָכָר		mankind, man, men
sekher reth		ways of men, mankind

Sekher refers to thought or cognition, and so mankind is being described here as a sentient being.

manner

damut דְּמוּת		manner, fashion, likeness
tament		manner

me

anokiy אָנֹכִי		me, I
nok		me, I

measures

hiyn הִין   liquid measure, said to be about 5 liters

hanu ▢◭◦℮○   liquid measure, said to be about 0.5 liters

From the Egyptian *hanu* meaning 'wave' or 'stream'. This demonstrates the problem of converting measures, a problem that dogs the study of measurements of gold and income in the ancient world.

memorial

shem שׁם   memorial, monument, name

semen-t 𓂝𓈖𓏏   memorial, statue, establish

Related to the *smer* nobility. See also 'image'.

middle

qebah קבה   belly, stomach   (qereb קרב middle)

qab ◿𓄿𓆑𓏭   middle, intestine

The intestines were an important component of Egyptian theology, and I have no doubt that divining the future through looking at the intestine was originally an Egyptian custom. The word *qab* also refers to the coils of a snake, and so divination of the future may have been related to the eternal battle between Ra and Aapop, the serpent of evil and possessor of the 'evil eye'. It is worth noting that the Hebrew word *qereb* קרב also means 'war', and so this may well be an oblique reference to this eternal conflict between Ra and Aapop, between good and evil.

migrate

tsen צֹאן   migrate, sheep, flocks

tchen 𓂻𓆑𓂻   advance

mist, dew

ad אֵד   mist, dew

adj 𓇋𓂧𓏏𓏭   dew, mist

The spelling shows the moisture coming out of the hand, and so the hand must be that of Atum, who masturbated Shu (air) and Tefnut (moisture) into existence.

mole

kholed (khored) חלד   mole, weasel

kheret 𓐍𓂋𓏏   mole-god

Taken from the Egyptian *kheri* meaning 'below' and also *kheriu*, which refers to those in the underworld, or perhaps under the ground.

money

kikar ככר   talent (money)

kerker 𓎡𓂋𓎡𓂋𓏤𓏤𓏤   talent (money)

From the Egyptian *kerker* or *karkar*, meaning 'round'.

money

qasitah קְשִׂיטה   money, a weight

qesitet 𓂝𓈖𓏏𓏭   market

For much of Egypt's history, goods were traded by barter, thus a market would mean much the same as money.

Moon

    Yarech יָרֵחַ   Moon

    Aah (Yah)   Moon

    Aach (Yach)   Moon

        As noted previously, Yah is the root for the god-name Yehovah יְהוָה.

money

    mene מְנָא   a weight of 60 *shekels*, but also used as a unit of money

    menana   a weight

        Weights were only required for expensive items, like gold, and so in time these weights became units of money. Thus the word *menana (mene)* is probably the basis of the English word 'money', just as the weight of a *shekel* has become the Israeli unit of money.

morning – see 'dawn'.

mortar

    khemar חֹמֶר   mortar

    qemai   resin

        The change in spelling here from *kemen*, meaning 'bitumen', to *qemai* is supported by the term *qemait (kemet)* for flour, which makes the same transition.

mound

    selelah (sererah) סֹלְלָה   mound, bank

    thererit   mound, rampart

        There are a few of these transitions between 's' and 'th', see also 'trumpet' and 'shield'.

mountain

    har הַר   mountain, hill

    har   mountain

        Derived from the Egyptian *heru*, meaning 'day'. The connection here is that the length of the day was observed by watching the shadows of the pyramids and obelisks as they tracked across the ground. Thus the term 'day' became linked with 'pyramids', and in their turn the mighty pyramids were often referred to as 'mountains'. See also 'altar'.

mountain of god – see 'altar'.

nation – see 'people'.

natron

    nether נֶתֶר   natro, soda

    netera   natron, soda, cleanse, purify

        Derived from the Egyptian *neter*, meaning 'god'. No doubt the link here is something to do with the ritual use of natron during the embalming process; it was the natron that dried out the corpse and preserved it.

nettle

    sarpad סַרְפַּד   nettle, brier

    serpet   nettle

night

layil (rair) לִיל   night

rui   evening, drive away, depart, door

Once again the entity that was being 'driven away' through the 'doors' was Ra as it sank beneath the horizon and entered the great doors of the Djuat, the underworld.

nine

teshi תֵּשַׁע   nine

pestch   nine

A name for the 'nine' – the nine great gods. This may have been originally taken from *pauti*, which is a little-known name of a very ancient god of Egypt. The change from *pestch* to *tesh* may be due to a misreading of the first hieroglyph, as a poorly drawn square can look like a rounded bun.

oak tree

eloun (eroun) אַלּוֹן   oak tree

anrana   oak tree

The word used the glyph for Heliopolis, which may indicate that the oak was the sacred tree. But there appears to have been a number of different sacred trees associated with Lower Egypt in general and Heliopolis in particular, and this spelling is rather similar to *anraham* which refers to the pomegranate.

offering

hebheb חֶבְהֶב   offering, gift

heb   offering, festival

oil

mashach מָשַׁח   oil

masakh   oil

oh!

hah הַהּ   oh!

hah or hai   oh!

one – see 'first'.

open

paqach פָּקַח   to open (eyes), perception

pathah פָּתַה   be open, wide, deceive

pega   open, open arms, divide

peteh   to open

peteh   look, see, glance

Osiris – see 'backbone'.

oven

tannur תַּנּוּר   oven

tarer   oven

pain

merar מָרַר   pain, bitter, poison

mer-t 𓏏𓏤   pain, suffer, sick, die

In the Egyptian the term *mer* also refer to a tomb or a pyramid. See the explanation for the word *mort* in the reference 'die'.

papyrus

gomeh גמא   papyrus, reed

qomet 𓏲𓄿𓎡   papyrus

peace

shalom (sharom) שלום   peace, health, a greeting

sharem 𓉘𓃀𓏏𓄿𓀀   peace, salutations, a greeting

Related to *shar* and *sharem* meaning 'prayer', idle weapons' and 'tribute'; all of which represent peaceful activities, but it is difficult to see which of these came first. Nevertheless, it is clear that the traditional Jewish form of greeting was once an Egyptian greeting.

people

am עם   people, nation

aam (Aamu) 𓏤𓄿𓏏𓀀   the Hyksos nation

people

lam (ram) לאם   people, nation

ramu 𓂋𓄿𓀀   people, mankind

pharaoh

parah פרע   pharaoh

per-aa 𓉐𓉻   Great House

Just as the British monarchy are known as the House of Windsor, the various dynasties of the pharaohs were known as the Great House of .... The term *per-aa* thus became synonymous with the monarch, and so subsequent monarchs were traditionally called *pharaa* (pharaoh).

pillars

saderah שדרה   rows, ranks, to do with buildings

sadjerta 𓏏𓊃𓈖𓉐   colonnade

The Hebrew dictionary states 'rows', 'ranks' and 'soldiers'; but then goes on to say 'technical term for a building, meaning unknown'. So what part of a building looks like ranks of soldiers? Well, the Egyptian dictionary would have assisted them with the answer, for it is summed up neatly in one word – a colonnade.

pilgrim – see 'stranger'.

pitchfork

qilashown
(qirashown) קלשון   three pronged fork, pitchfork

garetchana 𓏤𓃀𓏏𓈖𓄿𓏲   fork

place

meqomah מקומה   place, region

mekat 𓎡𓏤   place, station, protection

plank

    tsela (tsera) צֶלַע   plank, board, rib (of man)

    tchera-t 𓂝𓃀𓐩   planks, palings, wall

        Derived from *tcher* meaning 'boundary', and more specifically referring to the boundary or defensive wall around a town.

plants

    asheb עֵשֶׂב   plants, herbage

    ashed   trees, sacred trees

plants

    desha דֶּשֶׁא   plants, vegetation

    tchase   plants, vegetation

pleasant

    naiyim נְעִים   pleasant, nice, sweet

    netchem   pleasant, sweet, happy

        Derived from the seeds of a sweet-smelling plant, as the glyphs graphically demonstrate.

pole

    mowt מוֹט   pole, bar, staff

    maut   pole, pillar

        Probably related to the Egyptian *mau-t* meaning 'radiance', and referring to the shafts of light that stream down between clouds. See also 'rod'.

pool – see 'well'.

pool, pond

    barehah בְּרֵכָה   pool, pond

    barakata   pool, pond

    baregata   pool, pond

        Bearing in mind the explanations for 'bless', 'gift' and 'bow', these were obviously sacred pools, and perhaps even a reference to the watery void of Nu.

pot

    merqachah מִרְקָחָה   pot for ointment

    mantcheqeta   pot, flask

pot

    qalachat (qarachat) קַלַּחַת pot, cauldron, kettle

    qarehuta   metal pot

potter

    yatsar יֹצֵר   potter

    yitchar   potter

pregnant

    harah הָרָה   pregnant, conceive, bear a child

    aur   pregnant, conceive

        In the Egyptian *h-aur* would mean 'self-conceived', which may have been a reference to the traditional 'virgin birth' expected of God's Wife.

present

qareb קרב   bring, present

kherep [hieroglyphs]   present, give tribute

For a confirmation of the Hebrew transliteration of this word, see the spelling of *kher* in 'voice'.

price

mahar מהר   barter, obtain by payment, dowry

makher [hieroglyphs]   price, dowery, wages

Probably derived from *makher* meaning 'grain store'. Money was a late invention in the Egyptian world, and for much of this nation's existence, 'wages' were paid in grain and beer.

prison

kalua (karua) כליא   prison

kariu-t [hieroglyphs]   prison

produce – see 'make'.

procreate

benah בנה   have children, build

ben [hieroglyphs]   copulate,

Derived from Benben, the phallic tower of Heliopolis that was surmounted by the Benben stone and personified the fertility of the nation. This is still true today, as the *bennu* bird of fertility became the Greek *phoenix* of rebirth, which in turn became the Christian stork of new birth. See 'son' for further details.

pyramid

babel (baber) בבל   tower of Babel, pyramid

berber [hieroglyphs]   pyramid, pyramidion

Associated with the word *ber* and meaning 'eye' and 'gateway'. It is likely that the pyramids were symbolic gateways into the *djuat*, and the pyramidions were always inscribed with the two eyes of Ra. This is also the same spelling as the god Baal (Baar), and so the reason for Baal being associated with mountains and storms is obvious.

pyramid

puramis πυραμισ   Greek name for a pyramid   (There appears to be original Hebrew version of this word, as pyramids are never explicitly mentioned in the Torah.)

per-em-us [hieroglyphs]   literally meaning the 'slope of a pyramid'.

However, the component words used were probably *per-em-us* [hieroglyphs] which refer in turn to 'marching about', 'upon', and 'hall' or 'building (of Osiris)'. Thus the complete word *peremus* (pyramis) refers to 'walking around the Hall of Osiris'.

If this were the intended meaning of the word, then 'pyramid' would actually mean 'walking around the monument' and it would therefore be graphically describing the ritual in which the faithful marched around the pyramids. However, the references to the slope of the pyramid would seem to be confirming that this perambulation of the faithful spiralled up the sides of the pyramid, and therefore a spiral pathway is likely to have been in place around the sides of the pyramid in question.

quiver (arrows)

ashpah אשפה   quiver

aspat   quiver

raise

room רום   raise up, lift, exalt

rema   elevation, high place

Related to *remen* meaning 'shoulder', but more accurately refers to something being carried on the shoulders. No doubt famous individuals were carried aloft, as they are to this day. It is also related to *remi* meaning 'weep' or 'mourn', and I expect that it was the dead being held aloft while the mourners wept all round. The events that take place at a modern Arabic funeral will illustrate this scene perfectly.

ram

ail (air) איל   ram, deer.

air-t   ram, deer

ayir   stag

No doubt since Aries was the dominant constellation in this era, the Hebrew *air* איל was influenced by the word *El* אל meaning 'god'. It is presumably from the Egyptian *ayir*, meaning ram, that the constellation of Aries was named.

reeds

akhu אחו   reeds, rushes, meadow

aakh-t, aakhu-t   reeds, rushes

The word *akhu-t* would be the feminine plural.

reed

qaneh קנה   reed, cane, stalk, branch

qenneh   reed

Also spelt in the Egyptian as *kenn* and *gann*.

refuge – see 'shelter'.

regret

nekham נחם   regret, sorry

nekhi   lament, sorrow, sorry

rejoice

atsal (atsar) אצהל   rejoice, shout, cry out

atchanar   rejoice

return

shuwb שוב   return, turn back

saubaba   return, turn back

roast – see 'fire'.

right

imiyn יָמִין right, right-hand side (south)
amen (imiyn) right (western side)
Since Amen was the god of the setting Sun, the Egyptians denoted the Amen as 'west'. But for the west to be on the right-hand side, one must be facing south, and so the Hebrew has equated this word with south instead.

rim

sapheth שׂפה rim, bank, brim, lips
sepeti rim
Meaning the edge of a lake or sea, but also used for 'lips'. See also 'lips'.

ring – see 'end'.

ring

khathemeth חתמת ring, marriage
khetem ring
These rings were also used for sealing documents, hence the derived meanings of 'seal', 'end' and 'shut up'.

ring

tabath טבעת ring, signet ring
tchabait ring seal
Taken from the word *tcheba* meaning 'finger'. Note that a signet ring is for sealing purposes, since that is where we derive the term 'signature'.

rise

haia היה rise, become, to exist
hu-ia rise, flooding of Nile
In the Egyptian, *hai* also refers to the Sun and Moon and terms like 'rejoice' or 'praise'. Again, the rising was not simply of the Nile, but also of the Sun. See also 'fall'.

river

nehar נהר river, stream (nekhal נחל)
nekhar river
Associated with or derived from *nekhakha-t*, which refers to large breasts. Rivers were the 'milk' that nourished Egypt, just as a mother's milk nourished her offspring. The Nile itself was thought to spring metaphorically from between the twin pyramids at Giza, or the Twin Breasts, which only served to reinforce the 'milk' analogy.

The Hebrew word nekhal נחל may be the origin of the Greek word Neilos Νειλοσ, from which the name for the Nile was ultimately derived. Note the 'r' to 'l' conversion even within the Hebrew.

river

yam ים river (Nile), sea, lake
yima (yam) river, sea
A term used regularly in modern Israel, with the Sea of Galilee being called the Yam Kinneret.

328

river

    yehor יאֹר   river, stream, Nile

    yiaur   river, stream

river

    yubal (yubar) יוֹבֵל   river

    yibal (yibar) יְבַל   river

    yiber   river

    Also pronounceable as Eeber. This is my favourite origin for the word 'Hebrew', and thence 'Iberia' (Spain) and 'Hibernia' (Scotland). The great river of Egypt was the most sacred aspect of the country, and it is not so surprising that the people and their new colonies should be named after the Nile.

    The reason for the name 'Hebrew' spreading out towards Spain and Scotland is intimately linked with the journey of Princess Scota, the Egyptian daughter of Akhenaton who fled to these countries following the fall of the Amarna regime. A later book will explore this topic in much greater detail.

roast

    qalah (qarah) קלה   roast, dried, parched

    qarer   roast, offering

    Related to *qer*, which referred to the Twin Caverns at Giza and their associated thunderstorms and floods. Whatever the ritual that accompanied the annual flooding of the Nile, which was supposed to issue from these caverns, undoubtedly there was a lot of sacrifice and burned offerings that accompanied and celebrated this event.

robe

    shuwl (shuwr) שׂרל   robe, skirt, tunic

    suar   robe, tunic

    In the Hebrew version, we probably see the origins of the English word shawl.

rod

    maqel (maqer) מַקֵּל   rod, staff, stick

    maqer   stick, staff

    Related to the Egyptian *maq-t* which refers to a ship's mast or the ladder whereby Osiris ascended to heaven, the latter being rather similar to the account of Jacob's ladder.

rod

    shebet שֵׁבֶט   rod, staff, stick

    shabed   rod, staff

roll, cylinder

    karar כרר   roll, whirl, dance

    gelgel (gerger) גַּלְגַּל   roll, whirl, wheel

    karkar   roll, cylinder, staff

sack

shaq (saq) שַׂק   sack

saq ⟨hieroglyphs⟩   sack, bag

Like many others, *saq* has become an English word.

sailor

malech (Marech) מלח   sailor, mariner

marit ⟨hieroglyphs⟩   sea, coast, boats, shipping

The Egyptian word *mar* meaning 'lake' or 'sea' has been inherited as *mare* in the Latin and *mer* in the French. It also exists in the English in the guise of words like 'maritime'.

St George – see Appendix 2.

salt

khameets חמיץ   seasoned

hemai-t ⟨hieroglyphs⟩   salt

scatter

poots פרץ   scatter, break into pieces

putput ⟨hieroglyphs⟩   crush into pieces, trample, smite

Possibly describing the breaking of bread.

scales

mazan מאזן   scales, balances

Maat ⟨hieroglyphs⟩   Maat, the goddess of justice

The primary symbology for Maat was the feather, against whose weight on a pair of scales the heart of the deceased was measured. Thus, the secondary symbology for Maat became the scales of justice, which is why the goddess Maat still stands over the Old Bailey courts in London.

sea – see 'sailor'.

see – see 'watch'.

see – see 'Sun'.

see

ra-au (ra-ah) ראה   see, look, spy

iyr עיר   watch, watcher, angel

ar (ar-ti) ⟨hieroglyphs⟩   see, eye, two eyes

The predominant spelling is *ar*, but the two eyes become *ar-ti* and sometimes *arui* (plural). Associated words are *ar* meaning 'make', and *ari* meaning 'image'; but somehow I feel that the true basis of this word is Ra, the Sun-god. The Sun was the eye of Ra and the eye of Horus, and doubtless our eyes were considered to be the image (or mirror image) of Ra's eye. No doubt the pronunciation *ar* was chosen to reflect that close association between the eye and Ra.

seed

zera זרע   seed

tcherut ⟨hieroglyphs⟩   seed

servant – see 'slave'.

servant

obad עבד    servant, worker
abata   slave, servant

serpent

tanniym תנים   serpent, dragon, worm
djenem   serpent, worm, Aapop
See also 'snake'. See also Appendix 2 and the story of Aapop, the Egyptian dragon.

serve

shemesh שמש   serve, minister
shemes   follower, retinue, bodyguard
Since *shemm* (Egy) and *shemesh* (Heb) referred indirectly and directly to the Sun, the followers in question were obviously the followers and priests of the Sun-cult of Ra. This terminology obviously rubbed off onto anyone who was a servant, and hence the royal bodyguards also became *shemes*.

sew

tephar תפר   sew
teftefa   embroider, sew
The derivation is probably from the god Tefnut, who was produced from the ejaculation of Atum. In this manner, the word *tef* describes mostly penile things, and I suppose that the action of sewing with a needle is one of those.

scribe

tiphsar טפסר   scribe, official
thupar   scribe
The Egyptian version also refers to a trumpeter which corresponds to the Hebrew *shuphar* שופר meaning 'trumpet' or 'horn'. See also 'trumpet'.

shield

sheryn שרין   breastplate
thariyn   shield

side

gab גב   side
ges-ab   left side

six

shesh שש   six
sas (sis)   six
Note how the 's' has been turned into a 'sh'. The English number six was obviously derived from its Egyptian forerunner.

shake

noot נוט   shake, quake
nautha   shake, tremble, move quickly
Possibly from *nau-t*, meaning 'foliage' or 'leaf'. Hence the English phrase to 'shake like a leaf'; it is not only an apt observation, but in the Egyptian it also makes a very good rhyme.

shawl – see 'robe'.

sheep

sa שֶׂי   sheep, lamb

sa   sheep

sua   sheep

  In both cases identical words *als* refer to walking or travelling, and so I would suspect that these terms for sheep were derived from the nomadic lifestyle of shepherds.

shelter

khesah חסות   refuge, shelter, protection

khatha   refuge, protection

shibboleth – see 'stream'.

skin

aur עור   skin, hide

aur-t   skin, hide

 From the word *aur-t*, meaning 'goat', 'deer'.

slave

abad עבד   servant, slave

aabadj   slave, worker

slaughter

tabach טבח   slaughter, butcher, slay

djebakhu   slaughter, slay, kill

sleep

ishen ישֵׁן   sleep

akhen   sleep

small

qatan קטן   small, young

kat   small, tiny, helpless

snake – see 'serpent'.

snake

epheh (afeh) אפעה snake, viper

afu   snake

  Presumably the same as Aapop, the mythological serpent that fought with Ra in the Djuat. Aapop was the personification of evil, and was known by 77 accursed names.

snow

shalag (sharag) שלג snow

sarequ   snow

soldier – see also 'young'.

soldier

naray נערי   soldier of King David

naruna   soldiers

The Hebrew *naray* נערי is a corruption of *kary* כערי meaning 'soldier', or *vice versa*.

son

ben בן   son, man

benu   man,

In the Hebrew this is used in names to denote a family lineage, as in Ben Joseph, the son of Joseph. This tradition has survived in the Irish 'O' and Scottish 'Mac', which denote 'descendant of' and 'son of' respectively.

sorcerer – see 'magic'.

south

resh ראש   top, elevation, upper part, head

resi   south, southern

This may seem an odd comparison to make, but the Egyptians viewed the south as being 'up', or the top of the world.

snake – see 'circle'.

speech

midbar מדבר   speech, wilderness

midju   speech, command

speech

dabar דבר   speech, utterance

djabhu   to pray, to beg, to petition

spear

khanith חנית   spear

henit   spear

From this was derived *henn*, meaning 'penis'.

spread – see 'divide'.

spread

push פוש   spread, scatter

pussh   divide, split, cleave

sprout

tsamach צמח   sprout, grow

tcham   copulate, beget

square

pen פן   corner of square object

p   the glyph for 'p' is a square

stag – see 'ram'.

stag, deer

ahyal (ahyar) איל   stag

ayir   stag

stallion – see bull.

stars

tseba צבא   many stars, army

seba   star

Probably taken from *seba*, meaning 'door', or *vice versa*. The door in question was the great door of the Djuat, the underworld, a concept which was inextricably linked to the heavens above. The door to the Djuat was a doorway to the stars.

star
kowkab כוכב   star, stargazers
khakha ⌀🦅⌀🦅☆   star
Perhaps from the Egyptian *khakha*, which refers to grains of corn – the link being in the number of small grains.

stick
ats עץ   tree, stick, timber
at 🪶   branch, twig   (See also 'backbone'.)
The tree often had the same imagery as the backbone, and both were an allusion to the Nile.

stone
gelgel גלגל   wheel, rolling thing
karkar כרר   roll, cylinder
karkar ⌒🦅⌒🦅□   stone boulder
This circular imagery also influenced the name for money.

stone
eben (aben) אבן   stone
aba ⌒𓏲🦅□   stone
stone (precious)
behat בהט   stone (precious)
bahet 🌾□ ∘ ∘   stone (precious)
Possibly referring to a phallic symbol made of stone.

stranger
ger גר   strangers
geri 🖼️𓏏🚶   pilgrim
stream – see 'river'.

stream
nakhal (nakher) נחל   stream, brook, valley
nakher ⌀   stream, brook, river

stream
shibboleth שבלת   stream, flow, flood (pronounced shabboreth)
shabareth 𓏤□🦅   stream, flow
This was the famous word that the Ephramites could not pronounce correctly, which gave away their ethnic origins and led to their destruction by Jephthah and the Israelites:

"Then said they unto him, Say now Shibboleth: and he said Sibboleth: for he could not frame to pronounce it right." (Jud 12:6.)

stretch
raba רבע   lie, stretch out

tchab 𓀭 𓂡 𓋩   mummy, sarcophagus, coffin

There are a few words that demonstrate a link between the Egyptian 'tch' and the Hebrew 'r'. However, this one could also have been influenced by the word *rabia* meaning 'lion' – an animal that is known for its lazing around. See 'lion' for details.

strike

     naga נָגַע   strike, touch
     naga 𓊖 𓂡   strike, cut off, cut open

strong man

     geber גָּבַר   strong man, warrior
     gebir 𓊖 𓈖 𓂋   strong man, hero
     kebesh כָּבַשׁ   subdue, tie
     kebes 𓂝 𓈖   subdue, tie

It is likely that the Arabic *gafir* meaning 'foreman' is derived from this term, and from this we derive the English 'gaffer'.

subdue

     kaphah כָּפָה   subdue, pacify
     kapusa 𓂧 𓅓   suppress, oppress

Related to the cutting off of hands of the enemy. See 'hand'.

suckle

     yanaq יָנַק   suckle
     seneq 𓈖 𓏌   suckle

Sun

     mer ram or marah מַרְאָה   light, luminary or vision, sight, appearance
     mer-t 𓌻 𓂋 𓏏   see, look, eyes of Ra (Sun and Moon)

Ra, or Horus, had eyes representing the Sun and the Moon, and so vision and eyes were inextricably linked to light and to the Sun and Moon. The Sun was the bright eye, while the Moon was the dark or missing eye.

Sun

     shemesh שֶׁמֶשׁ   Sun, open, public
     shem 𓈞 𓇳   summer
     shem 𓈙 𓅓 𓅓   hot, flame

The *shemsu Ra* were the followers of the Sun-god Ra.

sunrise – see 'dawn'.

sweet

     niychech נִיחֹחַ   sweet, soothing
     netchem 𓇋 𓅓 𓊪   sweet, pleasant

See also 'nice'.

swift

     perper פִּרְפֵּר   swift (stream)
     perper 𓂋 𓂋 𓂻   run swiftly, leap about, gambol

An exaggeration of *per* meaning 'go out' or 'arise', which originally referred to the movement of the Sun. To emphasise a word, it was a common feature to double it, so *per* could mean 'walk' while *perper* means 'walk quickly'. See also 'grain'.

sword

khereb (hereb) חרב	sword
herepu	sword

take away

laqach (rekach) לקח	take away, fetch, bring
reqa	to fall away, to rebel

temple

heykal היכל	temple, palace
het-ka	temple of the spirit

The Temple of Jerusalem was called the Heykal Yahweh, whereas the Temple of Tanis was known as the Hetka Ptah. This temple is said to have been at Memphis, but since the reference was from the 21st dynasty, it could also refer to Tanis.

tent

ahal (ahar) אהל	tent
ahar	tent

ten thousand

rabab רבב	ten thousand, many, multitude
rabu רבו	ten thousand, many, myriad
tchaba	ten thousand, myriads

The spelling indicates that this number is connected with fingers. This could either be due to army commanders counting their archers by their fingers (see 'archer'), or perhaps through the tradition of accounting for enemy dead through the severing and counting of hands. Personally I feel the former of these is the more likely, as I demonstrated in the book *Solomon* that the army commander of Psusennes II (King David) was called Tchoab, and that this meant 'ommander of thousands'. Clearly his title referred to the number of soldiers under his command, rather than the number he had slain.

thread

pathel (pathar) פתיל	thread, lace, ribbon
peter	thread, cord, wick
pedjer	thread , plait, wick

An association with reeds and flat lands may indicate that this was flax.

thorn

qats קץ	thorn, thorn bush
qatcha	thorn, scrub, stubble, thorn bush

thorn bush

seneh סנה	thorn bush
senu	Two Brothers

The term *seneh* is related to *sinai* סיני, from which the name of Mt Sinai was derived. In the book *Tempest* I demonstrated that Mt Sinai was a pseudonym for the Great Pyramid, and also that the Two Brothers was a similar pseudonym for the same site.

throw

yadad יָדַד throw

djadj give

thunder

qel (qer) קֹל thunder, noise, voice

qeri thunder, tempest

See also the entry for 'voice'.

tower

magdal מִגְדָּל tower, castle, pulpit

maktar tower

The *maktar* has already been linked to the pyramids, but since the term *makher* refers to a 'grain store', no doubt it was through this route that the Giza pyramids became known as the grain stores of the pharaohs. The word *makhen* also means 'ferryboat', and there are two of these buried at the base of the Great Pyramid.

town

qiryath קִרְיַת town

qathiret town

travel, walk

asher אָשֵׁר travel, walk

asya walk quickly

trees, valley of

baka בָּכָא mulberry trees, valley of mulberry trees.

baka both a tree and a gorge.

The Egyptian tree is thought to be an olive. See *also* 'gorge' for further details.

tribe

shebat שֵׁבֶט tribe, clan

shabat tribe

tribute

shalumah שְׁלֻמָה reward, retribution (or sharumah)

sharemta tribute

tell

chay חַוָּה tell, declare

kai speak, cry out, repeat

The Hebrew form is the same as the name for Eve (Khava).

time

yume יוֹם time, day

unu time

tongue

    leshon לְשׁוֹן   tongue

    nesu   tongues

        For another transition between 'l' and 'n' see also 'frankincense'.

top – see 'good'.

trumpet

    shuphar שׁוֹפָר   trumpet, horn

    thuphar   trumpet

        There are a few of these transitions between 'sh' and 'th'. See also 'mound' and 'shield'. See also 'scribe'.

tunic

    tachara תַּחְרָא   corset

    takher   leather tunic

turn – see 'circuit'.

turn

    hephak הֶפֶךְ   turn, stopping

    hep   turn

        The Egyptian *hep* refers more specifically to the stopping and turning of the Sun at the solstice. At midsummer or midwinter, the Sun reaches its most northerly or southerly rising or setting location, and starts to turn back towards the due east or due west points.

turn

    paneah פָּנָה   turn, look back

    pena   turn over, capsize

two

    sheniy שֵׁנִי   two, second, another

    sennu   two, second, brother

        Derived from *senu*, the Two Brothers, a reference to the two largest pyramids at Giza.

understand

    sakal (sakar) שָׂכַל   understand, consider, wisdom

    sakha   remember, think

    sakau   memory, memorial

        Again possibly related to *sekh-t* meaning 'field', and referring to the annual re-laying out of the fields after the floods, the positions of which had to be remembered and re-plotted.

valley – see 'gorge'.

villiage

    kaphar כָּפָר   village

    kafar   village

violence

    khamas חָמָס   violence, cruelty

    khamatha   violence, evil, bitterness

voice

qera קרא   call, preach, proclaim

kher   voice, word, sound

qera   thunder

The latter term is based upon a storm-god Qera, who was related in some way to Seth. In turn this name was based upon *qer-t*, which referred to the two mythological caverns that caused the flooding of the Nile, and which I have identified as being located at Giza. Although the flooding of the Nile is not based upon local thunderstorms, no doubt a link was made between such storms and the water that eventually flooded the Nile. *Kheru* appears to be an important term in Egyptian and, bearing in mind the link with *qera*, this was probably considered to be the voice of the gods. See also 'call'.

vomit

qa-ah קיה   vomit, disgorge

qaa   vomit

The Egyptian is spelt with either a single or a double 'a'. Possibly derived from *qaqa* meaning 'boat', and the effects thereof.

walk – see 'travel'.

wash

rachats רחץ   wash, bathe

rakht   wash

rakht   wash

wasteland

malachah מלחה   waste and, salty, barren   (or marachah)

maritt   wilderness, desert

watch

ayr עיר   watcher, awake

aer (ayr)   see, watch

water

maim מים   water, urine

mai(mu)   water (the water glyph can also be read as 'mu')

mai(mu)   urine

This was the water from which Moses was 'drawn' in the Book of Exodus, and this Hebrew explanation of Moses' birth actually gives us a very good idea of what this common Egyptian royal name actually signified. The Hebrew name 'Moses' is said to mean 'drawn', which signified the drawing of the infant Moses out of the waters of the Nile. But in actual fact this word was taken from the Egyptian *mos* meaning 'produce', 'birth' or even 'child', and the name was a common feature of pharaonic titles where it signified the 'Son of' a particular god. The Hebrew reference to 'drawing' may have referred graphically to the drawing of a child out of its mother (as can be seen in the hieroglyph).

However, this explanation can be further refined by looking at the water out of which Moses was said to have been drawn. This water was the *maim* םימ or *maim* 𓈗𓈖𓈖 mentioned above. However, in the Egyptian the *maim* could also refer to male semen or even to the royal seed itself, and it is this aspect of the word that the birth-story of Moses was referring to.

Pharaoh's daughter is reputed to have said that she called the child (or her child?) Moses, 'because she had <u>drawn</u> the child out of the <u>water</u>'. In addition to the obvious Osirian mythology involved in this story, this phrase may also have referred to the princess '<u>drawing</u> a child out of the <u>royal seed</u>'; meaning that the child was sired by a close member of the royal family. (Exodus 2:10.)

There are two important reasons why this sentence could not be translated correctly by the ancient biblical scribes. Firstly, the true translation indicates that Moses was actually the son of a pharaoh. Secondly, the sentence further infers that the pharaoh's daughter may have had conjugal relations with her father, as was normal practice within the Egyptian royalty. This sentence was therefore deemed heretical on two fundamental counts, and thus we see the bland translation that has been placed into every Torah and Bible ever since.

However, with our new-found biblical knowledge, we can now say with some confidence that the pharaoh in question was Amenhotep III and the child was Tuth<u>moses</u>, the brother of Akhenaton. The identity of the princess is more problematical, bearing in mind the number of wives that Amenhotep III had and the biblical assertion that the child did not actually belong to the princess. However, on the latter point, although there may have been some political manoeuvering within the court regarding the royal succession, I rather think that this part of the story was actually a scribal device to distance Moses from a direct lineage to the royal family of Egypt. Thus it is likely that the child did belong to the royal princess.

watermelon

    abetyach אבטיח   watermelon (or a-bedech)

    beddeka 𓊪𓂝𓎡𓈖   watermelon

weak – see 'empty'.

well – see 'pool'.

well

    ayin עין   well, fountain, eye, sight

    ayin 𓂝𓈖𓈖   well

The Hebrew meaning of 'eye' for this word may seem incongruous, but in the Egyptian the word can be spelt with the eye glyph. The similar word *ain*, which is also spelt using the eye glyph, means 'beauty'.

well

    bar (bore) באר   well, cistern

    bar 𓃀𓄿𓈖   well, pool

We still use the word 'bore' to describe the tube for a well, or the action of making one.

wells

barowth בארות   place of wells

baarut   wells, pools   A plural of *bar*

       Taken from *bore* באר, a cistern or well.

well

mashab משאב   place for drawing water

mashaab   place for drawing water

       This is not a well as such, just a place of water associated with reeds. This may be the origin of the English word 'marsh', perhaps through the Latin *merso* meaning 'immerse'.

west

yam (im) ים   west

am-en (im-en)   west

       See the explanation for 'right', and note how the Egyptian is more consistent here. Amen should be 'west', because that is where the Sun sets.

wheat

khettah חטה   wheat, corn

khendj (khentch)   wheat

wet

tsaba ebu   wet, dip

tchabagi   wet, immerse

       Related to *tchabgatchaqa* meaning 'overturn' or 'upside down'. The initial thought is that this is related to a boat capsizing, but knowing the Egyptians' passion for religion, it may also be based upon the solar-boat sinking into the waters on the horizon at sunset. The great evening celebration was not only about the entry of Ra into the Djuat, but also the sinking of his boat.

whip

show שׁוֹט   whip, scourge

shadj   whip

       Related to *shadj* meaning 'quarry'. No doubt many of the quarry workers were slaves, and needed a little encouragement.

whirl around

karar כרר   whirl around, round

qarar-t   circle, grotto, cave

       In the Hebrew the word is related to *kares* כרש, meaning 'stomach'. In the Egyptian the word was related to the source of the Nile, which was supposed to spring metaphorically from two caverns that lay between the Twin Peaks. I have already identified the Twin Peaks with the two largest pyramids on the Giza plateau, and so the *karar (qarar)* must be associated with these pyramids. The similar word *harar* has already been identified with the Great Pyramid, which makes this association quite likely. See 'altar' for details.

       The link between circling and stomach was noted in the book *Tempest*, where it was proposed that the circling ceremony at Mecca originally took place at either Giza or Dahshur; and since Mecca is known today as being the 'navel of the universe' (the stomach), undoubtedly the original Egyptian site for this ritual was also known as the 'stomach'.

The Muslim ritual also involves the throwing of stones at a pillar, and so it was interesting to note that the Vega (Bent) Pyramid at Dahshur is surrounded by a deep carpet of small stones. These stones do not appear to be native to that area and so must have been brought there for some purpose. No doubt that purpose was identical to the Muslim practice of throwing pebbles, which is supposed to represent Abraham resisting the temptations of Satan, or the Egyptian god, Set. This observation once again supports the theory that the ritual circling ceremony once took place at Dahshur rather than Giza.

white

lebanah (rebanah) לבנה   white, white stones, pale Moon

repanan   bitumen

The change from black to white was due to a different perception about the Moon. In Egyptian terms the Moon was dark (black) in contrast to the brilliance of the Sun, and so it was called the dark eye of Horus. In reality, of course, the Moon looks white, so when separated from its original theology, the term transmuted into 'white'.

width

sakal שׂכל   lay crosswise

sakh   width, breadth

Possibly related to *sekh-t* meaning 'field', and referring to the annual re-laying out of the fields after the floods.

wife

shadah שׂדה   wife, concubine, nurse

shedj   nurse a child, suckle

Related to *shedj* meaning a 'water skin' and an 'irrigated field'.

wing

kanauf כנף   wing, border, end

ganush   wing

wisdom – see 'desire'.

wise

sakal (sakar) שׂכל   wise, understand

sekau   wise

wolf

zab זאב   wolf

sab   wolf, jackal

djab   wolf

The former spelling is related to *sab* meaning 'judge', as it was Anubis (Anapu) the jackal god who presided over the judgement of the dead. This word may have survived into the Russian, where a dog is called a *sabaka*.

The latter spelling is similar to words related to the funerary rituals, over which Anapu presided.

wood – see 'stick'.

wood

shittiym שׁטּים acacia wood

ssentchem sweet-smelling wood, costly wood

 This was the wood used to make the Ark of the Covenant.

woman

neqabach נקבה woman, female

nekheba-t mother goddess of Upper Egypt

 Obviously an Egyptian word, as *nekheb* refers to Upper Egypt itself.

world – see 'land'.

yea

shaneh שׁנה year

shenur the Great Circle of the Sun

 Derived from *shenn* meaning circle, which described the perceived orbit of the Sun around the Earth.

yoke

rekesh רכושׁ livestock, property, movable goods

rekeshu yoke

young man

nar נער young man, youth, servant

narana young soldier

List of diagrams

* Image courtesy of Dover Egyptian Designs.

Photo credits

Plate 1. Satellite image of the River Nile flowing into the fertile Delta region. (Earth Data Analysis Center).

Plate 2. The main door for the Wellcome Trust medical library near Euston, London.

Plate 3. Examples of *Cypress Sempervirens*.

Plate 4. The Abu Dulaf minaret in Samara: a Persian spiral pyramid.

Plate 5. The exquisite Berlin bust of Queen Nefertiti, the biblical Eve. (Corel Photolibrary).

Plate 6. Statue of Moses with the horns signifying the constellation of Aries.

Plate 7. The Caduceus symbol is still synonymous with medicine and life.

Plate 8. The god Thoth, writing the name of the pharaoh Seti I.

Plate 9. Two Babylonian sphinxes, British Museum, London.

Plate 10. Two images of the one of the only Jewish synagogues in the world to utilize an overtly Egyptian theme.

Plate 11. Satellite image of the sinuous course of the River Nile. (Earth Data Analysis Center).

Plate 12. Statue of Ramesses II from the Temple of Luxor.

Plate 13. The torso of Nefertiti.

Plate 14. The basalt pavement on the eastern side of the Great Pyramid

Plates 15-18. Masonic tracing boards.

Plate 19. Two tracing boards from the Third Degree.

Plate 20. The capital city of Pharaoh Akhenaton at Amarna.

Notes & references

Bible: All references taken from the King James edition, although the text is often modernised for clarity.

Josephus: AA = Against Apion, Ant = Antiquities, JW = Jewish War, L = Life.
Page references are to the Loeb Classical Library system.
Quotes taken from William Whiston's translation, which was first published in 1736; some references are from the Penguin Classics edition by G. William-son, first published 1959.

Manetho   All page numbers are taken from the LCL edition, editor G. Goold.

Within the referencing system in this book, some of the reference numbers are prefixed with letters. This is to give the reader an idea of the source of the reference, without having to look up that particular reference. This only applies to the more popular reference works, and the following have been prefixed:

B = Bible, M = Manetho, J = Josephus, H = Herodotus,
T = Talmud, KN = Kebra Nagast, K = Koran, S = Strabo.

All references to Egyptian words are taken from:

An Egyptian Hieroglyphic Dictionary, E A Wallis Budge, Dover Publications. The entries in the dictionary are substantially in alphabetical (glyph) order, and so the references are easy to find and have not been listed in the references by their page number.

Notes & References

Chapter I

1. Josephus Ant 1:29.
2. Josephus Life 418.
3. The Works of Josephus, William Whiston.
5. Biblical Concordance, Adam Clarke, Online Bible.
6. Arabia Felix, Alessandro de Maigret.
7. Ibid.
8. Bible John 1:1-2 and 14.
9. Koran sura 20:50.
10. Bible Genesis 3:8.
11. Adam Clarke, CD Online Bible ver 3.0 notes on Chap 1 of Genesis.
20. CD Online Bible and Concordance ver 3.0, by Ken Hamel.
21. Early Islam by Desmond Stewart. 1967.
22. Sunday Times Magazine, 8th June 2003.
23. Bible Rev 13:18.
24. Great Hymn to Osiris, Ancient Egyptian Literature, M Lichtheim, p82.
25. Hymn to the Sun-god by Harakhti, overseer of works of Amun. Ancient Egyptian Literature, M Lichtheim, p82.
26. Ancient Egyptian Literature, Miriam Lichtheim.
27. Ibid. Some quotes are from the Short Hymn to the Aton, some are from the Great Hymn to the Aton (the latter is given in Appendix 3). The last quote is from the Hymn to the Sun-god by Akhenaton's father, Amenhotep III.
30. Bible Genesis 1:1.
31. Ibid 2:7.
32. Ibid 1:4.
33. Ibid 1:30.
34. Ibid 1:20.
35. Ibid 7:22.
36. Ibid 11:7.
37. Ibid 11:8.
38. Ibid 7:12 & 19.
39. Ibid 1:14.
40. Ibid 1:2.

Chapter II

1. Josephus, William Whiston notes bk 1 ch 1.
2. Josephus Ant 1:38.
3. Josephus Ant 1:34.
4. Avaris, the Capital of the Hyksos, Manfred Bietak.
5. Ibid.
6. Bible Ex 34:13, Deu 7:5, 12:3, 16:21.
7. Bible Gen 21:33.
8. Bible 2Ki 23:7.
9. Bible Jere 10:2-9.
10. Bible Math 16:1-3.
11. Bible Math 16:4.
12. Bible Jonah 1:17-2:10.
13. Bible Same as in 11 above.
14. Freemasonry Today Magazine, Autumn 2004.
15. Exhibition in United Grand Lodge of England, March 2005.
20. Legends of the Egyptian Gods, Wallis Budge.
21. Josephus Ant 1:39.

Chapter III

1. Joyce Tyldesley, Nefertiti, p145.
2. Ancient Egyptian Literature, Miriam Lichtheim.
3. Ancient Egyptian Literature, M Lichtheim p120.
4. Bible John 20:22.
5. Daily Mail 8th August 1903.
6. Inscription on the KV55 coffin. Journal of Egyptian Archaeology 43:10-25, A Gardiner.
7. Bible 1Chr 15:16 - 22.
8. Aye's prayer to the King, Ancient Egyptian Literature, M Lichtheim, p95.
9. Koran 21:63.
10. Bible John 3:16.
20. Biblical concordance, Adam Clarke.
21. AROE, J Breasted para 995.
22. Bible Luke 8:2.
23. Bible Ex 3:13 - 15.

Chapter IV

1. Bible Gen 2:10.
2. Bible Jud 14:14.
3. Bible Jud 14:8.
4. Bible Gen 3: 6 - 7.
5. Josephus Ant 1:51.
6. Aegyptica, Manetho Fr 54 (p123).
7. Aegyptica, Manetho Fr54.
8. Aegyptica, Manetho Fr54.
9. Aegyptica, Manetho Fr54.
10. Aegyptica, Manetho Fr54.
15. Nefertiti, Joyce Tyldesley, p 101.
16. Adam Clarke's Commentary to the Bible, Online Bible software CD.
17. Adam Clarke's Commentary to the Bible, Online Bible software CD.
18. Bible Gen 2:10.
19. Aegyptica, Manetho, Fr 54.

Chapter V

1. Bible Genesis 6:2 - 4.
2. Bible Deu 2:20.
3. Josephus Ant 1:80.
4. Ancient Records of Egypt, H Breasted, para 213.
5. Michael C Carlos Museum, Emory University, USA. http://carlos.emory.edu/RAMESSES/

Chapter VI

1. Akhenaton, Cyril Aldred p136.
2. During the tours that can be made of Grand Lodge, it is stated that the Grand Temple is aligned due east-west, but the plans of the building contradict this. The alignment of the chamber is actually 15 degrees south of due west, and at a latitude of 51.5 degrees north this equates to 22 days after the autumn equinox – or October 13th.
3. Gods of the Egyptians, W Budge p 490.
4. Bible Genesis 28:12.

5. Bible Ex 24:10.
6. Mentioned in The Freemason's Pocket Reference Book, by Pick and Knight.
7. Bible 1Ki 6:8.
8. Bible 1Ki: 7:40.
9. Bible 1Ki: 7:48 - 51.
10. Plaque in the British Museum, London.

Chapter VIII

1. Evidence from Homer, Joachim Latacz, Archaeology Magazine May '04.
2. The Greek Myths, Robert Graves bk60.
3. Dates are derived from the IAU coordinates for the ecliptic latitudes of the constellations, and calculated manually. There are a variety of P.C. software planispheres which attempt to take this precessional cycle back through the millennia, but the resulting dates are highly inconsistent. See the book *Thoth* for a discussion on this topic.
4. Oxford History of Ancient Egypt, Ian Shaw.
5. About Ancient History Encyclopedia. www.ancienthistory.about.com
6. Herodotus, The Histories, 2:119.
7. Josephus AA I 133.
8. Ibid AA I 131.

Appendix 1 - Masons

1. Extracted from the various works listed a-d below.
2. Extracted from the various works listed a-d below.
3. Emulation Working Explained, H Inman.
4. Ibid.
5. Bible Gen 38:30.
6. The Master Mason's Book, Bro J S Ward.
7. Royal Arch Terms Examined, Bro Roy Wells.

Notes & References

8. Darkness Visible, Walton Hannah.
9. Ibid.
10. Freemasonry Today, Spring 2004.
11. Bible Gen 41:43.
12. Bible Psalms 118:22.
13. The Lecturess of the Three Degrees in Craft Masonry, Emulation Lodge of Improvement (no authorship quoted).
14. Why join the Royal Arch? PGC of Northhamptonshire, England.
15. Extracted from the various works listed a-d below.
20. Extracted from the various works listed a-d below.
21. Darkness Visible, Walton Hannah.
22. The Master Mason's Book, Bro J Ward,   Lewis Masonic Press.
23. Hamlet, Act III, Sc I,   Shakespeare.

a. Emulation Workings, a ceremonial guide.
b. Royal Arch Working Explained, Spencer & Co.
c. A Drill Book of Craft Masonry, Bro A Lewis.
d. The Royal Arch Work, A Lewis. Your Lodge Work, Masonic record, London.

Appendix 2 - George

1. Born in Blood, J Robinson p185.
2. Bible Rev 12:7-9.
3. Bible Daniel 12:1.
4. Henry V, Shakespeare Act 3, Scene 1, l. 31.
5. Britannia Magazine, Michael Collins MA MPhil.
6. Medieval History, Melissa Snell.
7. Bible Isaiah 14:12.
8. Bible Rev 22:16.

Index

351

Index

Index

Hyksos ~ 52, 56, 57, 86, 101, 105, 108, 126, 131, 164, 166, 185, 207, 236.
  Aamu ~ 164.
  Amarna ~ 52.
  exodus ~ 126.
  grove ~ 57.
  Masons ~ 185.
  Ramesses II ~ 131.
Hymn to Osiris ~ 42.
Hymn to the Aton ~ 42, 46, 47, 49, 51, 52, 65, 66, 88, 90, 94, 100, 101, 106, 107, 145, 208, 285, 289.

I

Iberia ~ 329.
ibis ~ 129.
Idle, E ~ 252.
Idumaeans ~ 37.
Iliad ~ 209, 214, 215, 216, 217, 218, 219, 220, 221, 222, 227.
Ilios ~ 213, 215, 216.
INRI ~ 258.
Iona ~ 313.
Ionia ~ 313.
Iraq ~ xiii, 263.
Ireland ~ 60.
Isaac ~ 36.
Isaiah ~ 271.
Isis ~ 68, 89, 90, 91, 147, 205, 212, 213, 218, 226.
  Eve ~ 89, 91.
Islam ~ 7, 8, 16, 137, 192.
Israel ~ 76, 131, 317.
Israelites ~ 317.
Issa ~ 89, 90, 91.
Italy ~ 78.

J

Jachin ~ 178, 190.
Jacob ~ 36, 198, 329.
  ladder ~ 197, 329.
Jahbulon ~ 246, 247, 257.
James ~ 39, 95.
Japheth ~ 167.
Jebus ~ 219.
Jehovah ~ 25, 51.
Jephthah ~ 334.
Jeremiah ~ 63, 64.
Jericho ~ 220.
Jeroboam ~ 59.
Jersey ~ 78.
Jerusalem ~ 39, 57, 68, 105, 145, 183, 191, 207, 219, 224.
Tanis ~ 219.
Jesus ~ 27, 39, 70, 71, 95, 102, 124, 180, 186, 219, 226, 238, 267, 283, 294, 311.
  Aton ~ 71.
  brother ~ 39.
  carpenter ~ 102.
  Heredom ~ 238.
  Lucifer ~ 283.
  opening mouth ~ 95.
  polytheism ~ 294.
  rock ~ 180.
  weather ~ 70.
Jewish Civil War ~ 75.
Joab ~ 240, 249, 296.
Joabel ~ 240.
Joan, Countess ~ 274.
John the Baptist ~ 252.
John the Divine ~ 39.
Jonah ~ 71, 73, 75, 160.
  Sun disk ~ 75.
Jonas ~ 71.
Jones, T ~ 252.
Jordan, M ~ 155.
Joseph ~ 67, 250, 251, 298.
  abracadabra ~ 251.
Josephus ~ 3, 4, 51, 89, 90, 91, 129, 151.
  Eve ~ 89.
  old texts ~ 3.
Jubela ~ 249.
Jubelo ~ 249.
Jubelum ~ 249.
Judaea ~ 63.
  grove ~ 63.
Judaism ~ 137.
Judas Iscariot ~ 39.
Judges ~ 217, 222.
Juwes ~ 249.

K

ka ~ 46, 80, 142.
Ka'ba ~ 303.
Kam ~ 53, 84, 120, 142, 310, 312.
Kamose ~ 55, 57, 63, 82.
Karab ~ 139.
Karabus ~ 139.
Karma Sutra ~ 155.
Karnak ~ 31, 45, 155, 170.
Kebra Nagast ~ 84, 196.
Khaf-Ra ~ 198.
Khavah ~ 87, 88, 89, 91, 92, 106, 107, 113,

357

Index

Menelaus ~ 217, 218.
Mengele, J ~ 79.
Menkau-Ra ~ 198.
Menmaatre ~ 122.
Mephrammuthosis ~ 128.
Mephres ~ 128.
Mera ~ 315.
Meritaten ~ 124, 132, 148.
Merovingian ~ 186.
Mesektet ~ 11.
Mexico ~ 171.
Michael ~ 273.
Michelangelo ~ 44.
milk ~ 117, 118, 119.
Milky Way ~ 72.
Minoans ~ 96.
Mistress of the Mountain ~ 238.
Mitannite ~ 126.
Mithras ~ 178.
monkey ~ 147, 148.
Monty Orangeball ~ 252.
Monty Python ~ 252.
Moon ~ 16, 19, 49, 111, 112, 159, 160, 161,
    168, 179, 181, 203, 303, 304, 305,
    328, 335, 342.
  Allah ~ 16.
  Boaz ~ 179.
  full ~ 16.
  Horus ~ 19.
Morning Star ~ 281.
Moscow ~ 277.
Moses ~ 3, 4, 35, 50, 52, 68, 110, 111, 114,
    117, 126, 127, 128, 130, 145, 146,
    172, 188, 201, 202, 207, 339.
  Achencheres ~ 130.
  Akhenaton ~ 68.
  Avaris ~ 117.
  exodus ~ 128.
  Giza ~ 188.
  name ~ 339.
  Nile ~ 145.
  Osiris ~ 126, 145.
  rod ~ 114.
  single day ~ 4.
  Yahweh ~ 110.
Mother Earth ~ 170.
Mount Heredom ~ 237, 238.
Mozart ~ 186.
Mt Heres ~ 129.
Mt Hermon ~ 164.
Mt Horeb ~ 201.
Mt Shinar ~ 164, 165, 166.

Mt Sinai ~ xiv, 85, 124, 128, 133, 165, 166,
    169, 181, 182, 183, 188, 192, 201,
    202, 336.
  Armageddon ~ 169.
  Giza ~ 181, 182, 183, 188.
  Great Pyramid ~ 165.
muggles ~ 250.
Muhammad ~ 44.
music ~ 98, 100.
Muslim ~ 15.
  Allah ~ 15.
  Ra ~ 14.
Mussolini ~ 78.
Mut ~ 305.
Mutnodjime ~ 153.

N

Naamah ~ 240.
Nabopalassar ~ 224.
nachash ~ 114.
Naharin ~ 126.
naked ~ 113, 115, 116, 121, 227, 296.
Nebetah ~ 91.
Nebuchadnezzar ~ 7, 8, 223, 224, 225.
Neferef-Ra ~ 198.
Neferirka-Ra ~ 198.
Neferkheprure ~ 288.
Neferkhepure ~ 102.
Neferneferu-Aten ~ 124, 288.
Nefertari ~ 90, 108, 172.
Nefertiti ~ 36, 90, 91, 92, 100, 101, 103,
    104, 106, 107, 108, 113, 114, 115,
    116, 117, 121, 123, 124, 125, 132,
    146, 147, 149, 151, 156, 212, 218,
    219, 227, 288, 296, 299, 300, 306,
    319.
  deposed ~ 123, 125.
  Eden ~ 121.
  Eve ~ 92, 104, 106, 113, 115, 151.
  exodus ~ 132.
  fruit ~ 124.
  Khiyah ~ 149.
  Kiyah ~ 147, 149.
  Mary ~ 107.
  mummy ~ 125.
  naked ~ 132.
  name ~ 92, 98.
  swollen ~ 106, 116.
  Troy ~ 219.
  uraeus ~ 114.
  virgin ~ 156.
  voice ~ 100, 101, 103, 104.

Index

Index